CONTEMPORARY RELIGIOUS THOUGHT
AN ANTHOLOGY

CONTEMPORARY RELIGIOUS THOUGHT

AN ANTHOLOGY

Compiled by
THOMAS S. KEPLER
S.T.B., Ph.D., D.D.
Professor of Religion, Lawrence College

ABINGDON PRESS
NEW YORK • NASHVILLE

CONTEMPORARY RELIGIOUS THOUGHT

Copyright MCMXLI by Whitmore & Stone

Library of Congress Catalog Card Number: 41-25071

F

SET UP, PRINTED, AND BOUND BY THE
PARTHENON PRESS, AT NASHVILLE,
TENNESSEE, UNITED STATES OF AMERICA

To
FLORENCE

PREFACE

THE LAST twenty years have brought before the American public a host of religious literature with many thoughtful writers attempting to answer the perennial religious problems with a contemporary tone. There are tides in religious thinking, not to say eddies and cross currents, and all this is reflected in the writings which men put forth to express the faith—or lack of it—which may be in them.

In general, it may be said that the American religious thinker of our era has been more concerned with the philosophy of religion than with theology. He has desired to read intelligently and widely for the purpose of deciding what he *might* believe, rather than have some ecclesiastical interpreter tell him what he *must* believe. Hence he has delved into various religious philosophers, so that his own mind might become stimulated. Out of such studies he has been able to create his own interpretations of religious ideas which man has always felt to be important.

The war of 1914-18 acted as a stimulant for the religious philosopher and the theologian. In Europe, crisis theology came to the fore and received increased interest and development on account of the hopeless portrait of humanity created by war-shattered countries. The writings of Barth, Brunner, and others found English translations introducing their viewpoints to British and American publics in the late twenties, and these were received with eager interest. In America, meanwhile, neosupernaturalism began to assume prominence in the works of such men as Reinhold and Richard Niebuhr, Homrighausen, Pauck, and G. W. Richards. Although the American thinkers were not very thoroughly captured by the vogue of neosupernaturalism, they were deeply corrected of many of their homocentric attitudes.

Scientific discoveries, ushered forth during and after the war, had made many an American, cuddled in his realm of modern comforts, deify the scientific method of observation and experimentation. Such a method he carried into the realm of religion, becoming especially enamored by antitheistic humanism. As a panacea of an individualistic, "arm-chair" theology which had allowed a world to war amidst its members, humanism seemed to offer an answer to the world's need of a social religion. And besides, it was intellectually respectable! Men like Dewey, Haydon, Ames, Lippmann, and M. C. Otto seemed for many to have the answer for an American philosophy of religion.

Theism in her various varieties gave a vivid answer for others. The books of men like Brightman, Wieman, Rufus Jones, Fosdick, and Lyman gave searching replies to perplexing religious problems. Theism took on a new dignity as scientists like Millikan, Whitehead, Arthur Compton, Eddington, and Jeans came to her support in their speaking of the universe as having mind-stuff, indeterminacy, and a part-whole organic relationship.

Some of the literature which has emerged from the ebb and flow of religious thinking in these twenty years has been so classic that it has naturally assumed a pinnacle place. This anthology is an endeavor to collect these definitive writings into one volume. The selections are thus primarily from the books and articles which have seemed to point the way and give direction to religious thought during these years. Other selections not quite so influential or so oft quoted have been included also, however, because they present points of view in a colorful or poignant manner. The anthology presents a group of religious philosophers—and a few theologians —of varying beliefs who reflect with excellence the modern religious temper as it particularly stimulates the American scene. They belong mainly to American schools of religious philosophy, but represented also are some British and Continental writers who have intellectual fellowship here among American thinkers and have exerted influence on the American religious temper.

Like any anthology, this reflects one person's sense of evaluation, and undoubtedly lacks a complete comprehension of various men and diverse schools of thought. The compiler is a teacher; and these selections have been collected, tested, and culled through a number of years of teaching activity with the purpose of presenting to his students writings which were most helpful in spurring the mind to look at religion critically and constructively. Nevertheless, there has been a constant endeavor to avoid either academic or personal bias, and it is hoped that this collection will represent fairly and adequately the major trends in religious thinking of these last stirring years.

The selections in this anthology are arranged under six headings which represent subjects of primary importance in the field of the philosophy of religion, although the classification is in some cases more or less arbitrary. Under each heading appear articles which present different religious viewpoints or diverse approaches to the subject; and particular voice is given to the various schools of deism, theism, and humanism. In the appendix is a bibliography suggesting further contemporary readings upon each of the six subjects, also a biographical index giving brief information about each writer and a sentence appraisal of his religious position.

THOMAS S. KEPLER

CONTENTS

Part I

THE NATURE OF RELIGION

Part II

THE FINDING OF RELIGIOUS TRUTH

Part III

THE IDEA OF GOD

Part IV
THE PROBLEM OF EVIL

Part V
THE MEANING OF WORSHIP

Part VI
IMMORTALITY

APPENDIX

Part 1

THE NATURE OF RELIGION

WHAT IS RELIGION?

Harry Emerson Fosdick

THE ELUSIVENESS of religion puzzles many people. Once they could describe it with definiteness and finality as identical with their creed and church. With widening horizons, however, religion has become ambiguous. It includes Christ and Buddha, Lao-tse and Mary Baker G. Eddy. It takes in polytheist, monotheist, and humanist. Bishop Manning, Billy Sunday, Gandhi, Professor Whitehead at Harvard, and Voliva of Zion City are all religious. Many, therefore, who began by believing in religion have first fallen into doubt about it, and now are not so much either believing or doubting as wondering what it is.

Science has been described as the art of giving the same name to different things: by which is meant that considering black coal, white paper, red apples, green leaves, and colorless gasoline, it requires science to reveal that they all are chiefly carbon. What, then, shall be said about the strange incongruities which comprehensively are called religion? Fetish-worship in Africa and Fundamentalism in the United States; Hindus chanting "Om" before the vast impersonal Absolute, and Christians seeking gifts from a highly individualized Father; Shinto priests and Mohammedan mahdis; Quakers and popes; William Jennings Bryan and John Haynes Holmes—what common element can make one thing, religion, of such a salmagundi?

When the intelligentsia try to clarify this situation by their definitions they only confound it the more. If anyone, confused about religion's meaning, wishes to make his bewilderment more complete, let him become a connoisseur in definitions of religion. Matthew Arnold called it "morality touched by emotion"; Professor Tylor, "the belief in Spiritual Beings." Professor Whitehead describes it as "what the individual does with his own solitariness"; but Professor Ames calls it "the pursuit on the part of the community, or the individual member of the community, of what are thought to be the highest social values." Professor Stratton defines it as "man's whole bearing toward what seems to him the Best, or Greatest"; while Professor Lowie sees its essence in the "sense of something transcending the expected or natural, a sense of the Extraordinary, Mysterious, or Supernatural." Solomon Reinach thinks it is a "sum of scruples which impede the free exercise of our faculties"; but Professor Haydon exalts it as "the co-operative quest for a completely satisfying life." To George Bernard Shaw religion is "that which binds men to one another and irreligion

From *As I See Religion*, New York, 1932, chap. i. Reprinted by permission of the publishers, Harper & Brothers.

that which sunders"; while Havelock Ellis writes, "Now and again we must draw a deep breath of relief—and that is religion." After which, and a great deal more of the same sort, one moves the previous question: What is religion?

That this inquiry, so far from being merely theoretical, is of practical importance, anyone acquainted with the younger generation in its lucid and serious intervals will testify. One cannot sell them a foregone conclusion in religion any more. . . . . They know too much about the protean exhibitions of religion in history, and the immense and sometimes splendid reaches of spiritual life which the historic Jesus never influenced, to have the old denominational patriotisms or even the old Christian formulas passed off on them as necessarily bona fide religion. Yet they are religious; at least, they are intensely interested in religion; and as they face the world's pot-pourri of faiths, above their mingled belief and doubt one feels their increasing wonder as to what, after all, religion is. . . . .

II

Religion is increasingly dealt with today not in ecclesiastical or theological, but in psychological terms. Increasing numbers of people mean by religion, not first of all a true church or an orthodox system of theology, but a psychological experience. There, they think, lies the germinal nucleus of the matter; and this conviction makes a serious difference between them and many historic definers of religion. . . . .

The envenomed controversy also as to which is the true theology, which for centuries has kept Christianity, in general, and Protestantism, in particular, fighting mad, seems largely futile. . . . . All theology tentatively phrases in current thought and language the best that, up to date, thinkers on religion have achieved; and the most hopeful thing about any system of theology is that it will not last. . . . .

As for doctrine, that always is important. Let a physician get his doctrine about scarlet fever right or he will bungle his task. So in religion we want the best churches and the truest thinking we can get. There are some kinds of theology and ecclesiastical practice in which most certainly we do not believe, and some kinds that seem to us wise, useful, and true. But religion is deeper than these. It created these in the first place, and it will persist long after their present forms have passed. Religion, therefore, cannot be essentially described in terms of its temporary clothes, its churches, and its creeds. Religion at its fountainhead is an individual, psychological experience.

III

Between religion conceived primarily in terms of churches and theologies and religion conceived primarily as a psychological experience, at least one distinction is apparent. Churches and theologies can be inherited; from generation to generation they can be handed on, their doctrines written in books and their institutions passed from the custody of fathers to the custody of sons. Almost inevitably, therefore, churches and theologies become in time objects which believing people try to preserve. How much contemporary religion consists in the earnest, sometimes militant, frequently desperate, endeavor to save the churches and their theologies!

When, however, religion is looked at and sought for primarily as an individual, psychological experience, it at once becomes not so much something which the possessor must save as something which saves him. This distinction is fundamental. We may have a religion toward which the preservative attitude prevails, as though our supreme concern were somehow to save it, or we may have a religion which we do not worry much about saving, because it so vitally and visibly saves us.

Multitudes of people today are trying to preserve the organizations and thought-forms of religion. They are habitual steadiers of the Ark. Often with feverish militancy, always with deadly earnestness, they have made up their minds that religion must be saved. Such an attitude is a sure sign of religion's senility; it has uniformly proceded the downfall of those historic faiths that have grown old and passed away. In a religion's vigorous youth its devotees are not anxious about saving it, because it so powerfully saves them. And this is true because a young religion is not yet a static church or a settled theology to be preserved, but a psychological experience to be enjoyed.

This difference between a youthful and a senescent faith is evident in Christianity. While the early Christians battled stoutly for the things they believed, their major stress was not somehow to save their faith, anxiously defend it, and see it through. Their faith saved them, defended them, and saw them through. It carried them. It was to them health, peace, joy, and moral power. And whenever men thus have a religion which vitally saves them they have a religion which they need not worry much about saving.

The difference today between prevalent attitudes toward science on the one side and religion on the other ought to give us serious pause. Nobody solicitously is trying to save science for the simple reason that in its own sphere science is saving us. That is to say, it saves us from taking a covered wagon to San Francisco when we wish to consult a friend—we can use a telephone. It saves us from being isolated at sea—we can keep in touch with the whole world by radio. It may even save us from bothering about the sea at all when we go to Europe through the air. From many a disease, disability, and fear, science is positively saving us; and so long as science can go on saving us scientists need not worry much about saving it. Science is not yet primarily an organization to be maintained or a final creed to be preserved; it is still in the creative vigor of individual venturesomeness and exploration.

Turn, however, to religion! Read the books! Listen to the sermons! Multitudes of people are out with props trying to shore up religion. . . . . Our real task is to achieve a religion which saves people; and such religion must be primarily an individual, psychological experience. . . . .

IV

The content of such a creative religious experience as we have in mind is not easily described. If it takes various folk from Havelock Ellis to Saint John to make plain what love is, anything that one man writes about religion will surely be segmental. We may note, however, that whenever one finds people enjoying a religion which they do not worry about saving, because it saves them, there are two aspects to their experience, one active, the other receptive.

The gist of the active aspect lies in a basic fact: life faces us not only with things which give themselves to us and serve our interests but also with things to which we should give ourselves and which we should serve. . . . . . In this scientific age when we commonly command law-abiding forces to our practical advantage, we are tempted to suppose that life's glory lies in the things which we master. The fact is, however, that our greatest hours never are associated with the things which we master but with the things which master us. Let a man compare the time when he learned to drive an automobile and felt the thrill of command over harnessed energy, with the day he first heard Beethoven's *Fifth Symphony* and was carried out of himself by something greater than himself, to which he gave himself!

Whenever anybody thus finds any goodness, truth, or beauty concerning which he feels not that it should give itself to him, but that he should give himself to it and be its loyal servant, that man has entered into an authentic religious experience.

That this approach to the meaning of religion is radically different from the common conventions of the churches is obvious. Here, for example, is a youth in straits about his religion. He has been reared in an inherited faith. It has consisted largely of a regimented system of religious opinions. He was drilled in them and consented to them as naturally as he consented to the fashion of his clothes or the articulation of his speech. Now, however, he has come to a university center. He is surrounded by new ways of thinking and fresh methods of dealing with knowledge. His religion begins perilously to disintegrate. At first he desperately tries to defend it, but it falls to pieces. For a long while he clings to the shreds, but now even these have gone. He has lost his religion.

The first thing to be said is that any religion which can be lost like that had something deeply the matter with it from the start, and that the youth would better not worry too much about losing it. What he would better do is to forget, at least for the time being, religion theologically defined and ecclesiastically organized, and go within himself to discover what religion means as a psychological experience. What if that youth, having lost an external and inherited religion, should discover that he is himself incurably religious and so come through to a religion which he will not need to defend, because it defends him, or laboriously carry, because it carries him, no longer weight to him but wings!

Try, then, saying to such a youth, "Your religion lost! Nothing more to live for!" Only recently a fine young fellow, in precisely this situation which I have described, came swiftly back at me when I spoke to him like that. "Nothing to live for?" he said in effect. "Upon the contrary, plenty to live for! Life is rich in things to give oneself to, truth to be discovered, beauty to create, social causes to serve, friendship to claim one's loyalty. I am in love with life because there is so much to be devoted to." . . . .

Some say that the essence of religion is the sense of sacredness. Even the most carnal and insensitive mind must sometime have proved its human quality by feeling the presence of something sacred that ought not to be desecrated. Those things in human history of which the race has most reason to be proud spring from this sense of sacredness at its best. Truth for the scientist is sacred—to violate it is the unpardonable sin. Beauty to the artist is sacred—to wrong it is blasphemy. The rights of personality are to the man of moral insight sacred, and our economic exploitations are sacrilege. Why should man have emerged into this strange, compelling sense of the "holy," possessing rights over us so imperative that at our best we find our glory in serving it to the death? . . . .

Others say that the essence of religion is worship. We truly live, they insist, not by virtue of those things that are beneath us but by virtue of those things that are above us. Our appreciations, admirations, and worships liberate life and give it worth. We spiritually are freed, not by what we enslave and use, but by what we adore. Therefore, the practical mastery over nature's law-abiding forces, which science confers, never can solve our human problem in its depths. Not what we command but what commands us determines destiny. . . . . .

V

Alongside this attitude of active self-committal, a receptive aspect is always present in a vitally saving faith. Inward communion from which come peace and power is characteristic of genuine religion. . . . . Indeed, a great deal of the unconventional religion of our day that has broken free from the orthodox churches is motivated mainly by a desire to recover religion as a resource of power, health, peace, and vitality in daily life. The explanation of the rise of cults like Christian Science and New Thought is obvious. While the old-line churches were largely concerning themselves with dogma, ritual, and organization, multitudes of folk were starving for available spiritual power with which to live. These cults arose to meet this need; and with all their mistaken attitudes toward scientific medicine, and their metaphysics, that to some of us is quite incredible, they have genuinely served millions of people by translating religion into terms of power available for daily use. . . . .

Indeed, here lies one of the major reasons why many youths today, weaned away from orthodox religion, if ever they were suckled on it, still know that religion itself is real. A typical young woman from the university, reared out of touch with organized Christianity and untrained in dogmatic faith, sought membership in the church. I wondered what the religion of this highly intelligent and unconventional young person was like, and was interested to discover that it consisted almost exclusively in the practice of affirmative prayer. That is, prayer did not mean to her reminding an individual called God to do something he had forgotten or urging him to bestow a blessing that otherwise he would not have been good enough to give. Prayer meant fulfilling inward conditions of attitude and receptivity and getting appropriate results in heightened insight, stability, peace, and self-control. Prayer was not magic, but the meeting of real conditions in a law-abiding, spiritual world and getting real results.

When religion means such commerce of the spirit it becomes as indispensable as food and drink. It is the vital center from which life's energies proceed. The possessor of this secret does not live from the teeth out, but taps resources of power that seem at least, as William James put it, to come up through the subconscious into consciousness from origins that are cosmic and not merely individual. . . . .

This experience is of the very essence of religion. It substitutes confidence for fear, a sense of security for a life lived on the ragged edge; it takes people who thought they had to lift twenty pounds with only strength enough to lift ten, and transforms them into people who tackle life as a ten-pound load with strength to handle twenty. It inevitably affects health. Said one of the world's most famous psychologists to a friend of mine, "For complete psychological health mankind requires, either a religion, or some substitute for Religion which has not yet been discovered." Certainly this experience makes a difference to the integration of personality, to the moral drive of character, and to the radiance, tranquility, hopefulness, and power with which men live. . . . .

VI

The present churches and the present theologies have too little to do with this saving experience of genuine spiritual devotion and daily spiritual power. Upon the contrary, a great deal of this vital religious experience has already fled from the churches and shaken off the dust of orthodoxy in order to get air to breathe and room to move about in. What have the differences between Baptists, Methodists, Presbyterians, and Episcopalians to do with such an experience of religion as we have been describing? Moreover, when the modern mind hears the creeds upon which many of the churches still insist, with all the corollaries brought out by controversy and urged as indispensables of religious truth—old cosmologies, doctrines of Biblical infallibility, miracles like virgin birth or physical resurrection—the reaction is not simply incredulity, although incredulity is undoubtedly emphatic—but wonder as to what such things have to do with religion.

As things are now, we cannot gather an ecumenical conference of Christians on church union without having three questions at once walk up stage as major matters of concern: the correct definition of the sacraments, the correct phrasing of ancient dogmas, the correct understanding of apostolic succession—before all of which an increasing number of religious people stand marveling that such things are supposed to be of interest to religion.

What we are driving at, therefore, is not what one writer scornfully calls "gossamer platitudes about the distinction between dogma and experience." We are insisting, rather, that the sort of dogma now enjoying ecclesiastical ascendency has no vital relation with the best spiritual life of our time, and that the sort of churches now existent are often stifling the life out of real religion.

As a matter of fact, we are deeply interested in theology. So far from thinking, for example, that non-theistic humanism is right in supposing that religion, being basically a psychological experience, can get on without God, many of us are vigorous contenders for the opposite. Moreover, we find God very near at hand and visibly operative. Consider the experience, whose individual aspects we have been discussing—a life carried out of itself by something greater than itself, to which it gives itself. Such experience is not merely individual; it is racial. Something greater than humanity has laid hold upon humanity. . . . .

Squirm and twist as we will, we cannot be rid of this experimental fact which, of old, theologians phrased as the sovereignty of God, and which a poet like Francis Thompson calls the Hound of Heaven. . . . . Such a concept must indubitably stop, as David Starr Jordan says about science, "where the facts stop," or thereabouts. But if this narrows its boundaries it also increases its reality. There is a Creative Factor in this universe favorable to personality, or else personality never would have arrived. A Cosmic Power is operative here, propitious to enlarging truth, creative beauty, and expanding goodness, or else they would never have existed. If by the term God one means this, then one does most certainly mean something real and efficient in this universe whereof the picture-thinking of our religious symbolism is only the partial representative.

Some such confidence in God as this, today as always, is characteristic of religion. From Lotze and Höffding on, the interpretation of religion as faith in the conservation of life's spiritual values has been powerfully influential. Indeed, this would better be included in our description of religion as a psychological experience. Such experience begins with devotion to spiritual values; it goes on to confidence in their Conserver; it issues in such communion with him as brings peace and power. . . . .

VII

The tragedy of religion today is that multitudes, hungry amid the conventionalities of our ecclesiasticism, are wandering homeless, like Kipling's cat "by his wild lone." Wanting religion as a saving experience, one sees them on all sides getting help by nibbles, lacking intellectual articulation for their thought or any sense of human companionship in seeking what they desire. They want spiritual homes to which they can belong. They want intellectual justification for sustaining faith. And up through all this uncertain welter come at times sure signs of bona fide religion—folk within the churches and outside them who know what is meant by genuine spiritual devotion, confidence in the Conserver of life's spiritual values, and communion with him that brings peace and power.

The one thing that backward, sectarian, and obscurantist churches need most to fear is such religion. They need not in the least fear the attacks of the irreligious. Religion can whip irreligion on any field at any time. But from the days of Buddha in India and Christ in the Roman Empire, an aged and decrepit religion clinging to its crutches has always needed to fear a youthful movement of the spirit, a vigorous and spontaneous emergence of religious experience in its essential meanings.

The only thing that ever yet has been able to reform religion is religion.

THE NATURE OF RELIGION

Henry Nelson Wieman

RELIGION IS man's acute awareness of the realm of unattained possibility and the behavior that results from this awareness. The acute awareness is religious experience; the consequent behavior is man's attempt to get into right adjustment with the most protecting and sustaining behavior of the universe to the end of escaping the terrible possibilities of evil which have entered his awareness, and to attain the glorious possibilities of good. In many religions this most sustaining and protecting behavior is called God. But whether it is called God or not, every religion either finds or searches for something that will provide these major goods and save from these major evils.

A great deal of religion, the sort we shall later describe as second-hand, consists in living in accordance with some "certified plan of the universe" in which God is accurately defined and the way of adjusting to him is minutely prescribed. Religious people differ greatly with respect to the importance given to the traditional "certified plan" on the one hand, and the searching experimental processes on the other. But unless there is at least some modicum of the latter we maintain that the paraphernalia of religion is a sham. Since this last is perhaps our most controversial point we must devote a paragraph to its clarification.

A "certified plan" can be transmitted only by means of words or other symbols. But symbols do not deposit their meanings miraculously in the mind. We can find what they mean only by searching out that meaning in the actual processes of experimental living. This is peculiarly true of those obscure and most intimately personal adjustments which are involved in religion. Symbols, such as words and the like, serve to suggest experimental processes, i.e., certain mental attitudes and courses of conduct. But unless these experiments are made, unless one cautiously and inquisitively and critically tests these attitudes and courses of conduct with a view to discovering what they reveal, he can never know what the symbols mean. And the chances are a hundred to one that the first thing the symbols suggest is not what they were originally intended to suggest. . . . .

Religion is one way in which we seek to attain good and avoid evil. It differs from all other ways of dealing with value in two respects. First, the field of its search is more inclusive than in any other undertaking. It is concerned not only with all the goods produced and evils averted by the several arts and sciences, but it reaches out beyond them to consider the goods and evils of all time and all space and all possibility. Second, the experimental process by which it prosecutes the search is more radical than

From *The Wrestle of Religion with Truth*, New York, 1927, chap. viii. Reprinted by permission of the publishers, The Macmillan Company.

in any other undertaking. It endeavors to attain the great goods and avoid the great evils not merely by experimental adjustments in some carefully segregated department of life, but by experimenting with the most intimate and personal and ultimate loves and loyalties and hopes and fears, thereby seeking right adaptation to the behavior of the universe which most vitally and profoundly affects human welfare. This radical, intimate, personal form of the experimental process on the one hand, and the inclusive reach of values sought on the other, distinguish religion from all other human ways of promoting the good of life.

The nearest rival to religion in the matter of inclusiveness is morality. But religion reaches out to deal with unexplored possibilities of value, beyond the reach of morals. Morality endeavors to organize life in such a way as to attain the definable goods and avert the definable evils that may befall human life. Morality may go even further than this. It may become highly adventurous and explore the realms of undefined and heretofore unencountered goods. And it may endeavor to guard against undefined and unencountered evils. But when it does this it begins to take on the character of religion. There is no necessary opposition between religion and morality. They often merge, but they can be distinguished.

Morality is not religious when it ignores the more remote and presumably vaster possibilities of good and evil which lie beyond the range of our definite knowledge and mastery, and concerns itself solely with the organization of those goods which we can more directly control and accurately know. Religion is not moral when it becomes so absorbed in the remote and cosmic possibilities of good and evil that it assumes no responsibility for the manifest goods of the various arts and sciences such as those to be found and promoted through association with our fellows, through industrial and political action, the fine arts, scientific procedure, and so forth. But no religion is fully normal and wholesome which is not moral, and no morality is satisfactory which is not religious. The two must merge if either is to fulfil its function as human living requires. . . . .

Religion seeks a love beyond any love that has ever developed between human associates. It seeks a love which, so far as human association is concerned, is only a possibility. But precisely because religion does afford a vision of this possibility, it stimulates love-making between parent and child and David and Jonathan and man and woman to the end of achieving more love between humans. And love-making is one of the great arts of living. Thus does religion inspire the arts to larger achievement by keeping before them the mysterious realm of possibilities. It revives the flagging zeal and widens the horizon. . . . .

Each department of human living, such as each of the several sciences, the fine arts, political and industrial activity and home life, has its own special realm of goods, possible and actual, which it may attain and which it sustains. But unless there is some overarching search after a total good, human living falls asunder. If each department devotes itself to its own separate region of possibility, and ignores all else, confusion follows sooner or later. Maladjustment and conflict inevitably arise among these separate interests. And all vision of the total good of life fades out unless religion supplements the arts; for religion provides this vision of the total good. . . . . Without this religious unification life loses direction and zest; it becomes aimless, barren and stale. . . . .

It has sometimes been thought that philosophy could accomplish this work of integration. It is true that philosophy may develop an integrating theory. But the integration itself must be a certain way of living. And when a philosophic theory becomes an actual way of living (if ever it does) it becomes forthwith a religion and more than philosophy. Every cultured religion involves a philosophy inasmuch as it entertains some theory about the universe as a whole. But religion is more than philosophy; it is an experimental launch of the whole of life by which the possible goods which the theory portrays are brought forth into the actual goods of human living. Philosophy is a theory, while religion is a way of living. Religion is the most complete and full-orbed expression of the striving toward interaction with the widest and fullest environment, physical and social, minute and vast, past, present, and future, near and far, actual and possible. All the arts and sciences peculiar to human living express and promote this endeavor; but they all differ from religion in that they express and promote only some one phase or aspect of the great enterprise. Religion alone is man's attempt to deal with the total problem of increasing to the maximum the intercourse of man with his total environment.

Let us restate the problem which religion undertakes to solve. It is, first, to find that behavior of the universe, and, second, to make that human adaptation to it, which will yield the maximum good. The maximum good for humankind, human nature being what it is, is interaction with the widest and fullest environment, physical and social, minute and vast, present, past, and future, actual and possible. This twofold problem arises inevitably when man becomes acutely aware of the awful, alluring and horrifying realm of boundless possibility. Such awareness is religious experience. Such awareness can reach its maximum when the confining routine of habit is disintegrated under peculiarly intense stimulation. . . . . Consequently religion is the total outreach and farfling of human life toward maximum abundance. When philosophy and the special arts and sciences can help in this great endeavor, it draws upon them or should do so. But when they cannot help, as in wide regions of life they cannot, religion carries on alone. Philosophy investigates the universe as a whole, but life in adaptation to the most important behavior of the universe is more than investigation. It is the total vital process launched upon an undertaking, and not merely the formulation of a theory. A theory is needed, hence philosophy is of greatest assistance. But religion, not philosophy, is the proper name for that enterprise of so conducting the whole of human life as to catch whatever winds and tides there be which may carry human living to its largest possibilities. Religion started the great quest before any of the arts and sciences were born; and it adventures still beyond the bounds of any art or science. Religion is the undying fire of human aspiration.

Its flare searched the Great Dark before our little lamps of culture were ever invented. . . . .

But this valiant, heroic, adventurous character applies only to first-hand religion. It applies only to that human behavior which springs from the innovating religious experience. When religion becomes second-hand, when it becomes institutionalized and traditional, it may take on a character exactly opposite to that which we have portrayed. This distinction between first- and second-hand religion is so important that we must dwell upon it.

These terms, first- and second-hand, merely serve to point out the distinction between the experience which generates religion and the tradition which conserves whatever vision and other achievements of the innovating experience are capable of being perpetuated in the form of doctrines, practices, bibles, institutions and ceremonies.

It is probable that no one has first-hand religion solely. The innovating experience scarcely arises without the stimulus and guidance of some traditional culture; and this culture gives tone and character to the experience. As religion gushes forth from the original experience of the individual it immediately blends with the cultural stream flowing down from the past, so that its own waters are not distinguishable in color, odor or taste from the muddy sediment of other times and experiences. But our figure is not adequate. The interdependence and interpenetration of first- and second-hand religion are even greater than indicated. The spring could not gush if the stream did not flow. . . . .

Second-hand religion does, then, have its value and its rightful place. But if it be not constantly revitalized by the original innovating religious experience it becomes degenerate. This degenerate sort of second-hand religion is very common, and for many people the word religion connotes only this degenerate religiosity. Consequently it is exceedingly important that we distinguish very carefully between it and the sort of thing we are describing under the name of religion. . . . .

All men part of the time, and most men most of the time, shrink from the vast and the unknown, from the unexplored terrors and glories of existence. They strive to shut out all this from their awareness. So they rear great walls of myth and on these walls they paint pictures of what they think, or would like to think, the vast unknown must be. They make these pictures as clear and definite as they can. And they insist that everyone who adopts the cause of religion shall declare himself certain, beyond peradventure of a doubt, that all the vast unknown, all eternity, and God and heaven and hell, is just precisely as these pictures represent. For only in this way can they make themselves feel comfortable. Only in this way can they preserve that complacency which the animal nature of man so persistently craves. Only in this way can they shut out the mystery, the terror, the uncertainty, the groping spirit, that reaches and strives after the unattained. Only by insisting that everyone believe the literal reality of these pictures, and thus support their own belief, can they protect themselves from the discomfort of doubt, from the annoyance of wonder and adventuring. . . . .

In contrast to this degenerate type of religion the genuine thing is man's awareness of the vastness and the terror and the unknown good of that which encompasses him. It is also his endeavor to explore these possibilities of immeasurable degradation and anguish, and glory and blessedness, in order that he may apprehend the best which the universe has to offer and live by it; and to apprehend the worst in order that he may flee it or destroy it or war against it, or otherwise protect himself from it. It is his endeavor to find that adjustment to the most protecting and uplifting Behavior of the universe in order that he may be saved from the worst possibilities and may actualize the best. Religion of this original sort is man's groping into the unexplored possibilities of all being in order to win ultimate salvation and escape ultimate destruction.

THE ORIGIN OF RELIGION

D. Miall Edwards

CHAPTER II: THE ORIGIN OF RELIGION IN THE LIGHT OF ANTHROPOLOGY

ONE OF THE main tasks of the Philosophy of Religion is to explain the nature and function of religion. It has to show what religion *is*, and what religion *does* or what purpose it fulfils in the life of the individual and of society. But the nature and function of religion can only be explained after a careful investigation has been made into the problem of its historical and psychological *origin* and *development*. If we can learn from the anthropologist, the psychologist, and the historian how and why man came to be a religious being, as well as how and why religion developed from its crude beginnings to its highest forms, then we are on the high-road to a solution of the problems as to what religion essentially is and what purpose it answers in human life. First, then, let us take up the question of the origi of religion.

It is necessary, however, to warn the reader at the outset that the ques n of origins is relatively independent of the question of values. If reli ion can be traced back to lowly origins, that should not in itself be regarded as prejudicial to its real value in the higher stages of its development, or to its relative value even at the lower stages, any more than the fact that science, morality, and art have sprung from most crude and unpromising beginnings should discredit the value of the final results or of the painful and often bungling efforts which have contributed to those results. If we are at all justified in judging origin and fulfilment the one in the light of the other, it seems more rational to maintain that the final achievement enhances the worth of the crude beginnings than to say that the crudeness of the beginnings depreciates the value of the result. . . . .

I

The question of the origin of religion was not scientifically studied until modern times. Before we come to consider some modern theories it may be well to refer briefly to two views which were once widely prevalent, but which are now obsolete or obsolescent.

1. The first is the view that traced religion back to a primitive or a special Divine Revelation. This view has held a prominent place in Jewish, Christian, and Mohammedan theologies. It has usually taken the form of a belief in a primeval monotheism of divine origin, from which polytheism in its many forms is a later relapse. In its usual forms the doctrine of revelation has explained the origin of religion in far too intellectual and mechanical a fashion, as if religion began with the impartation to man of a

From *The Philosophy of Religion*, New York, 1930, pp. 29-60. Reprinted by permission of the publishers, Harper & Brothers.

set of ideas, ready-made and finished ideas poured into a mind conceived as a kind of empty vessel. This is a crudely unpsychological view. It makes revelation to be purely an act of God, and does not help us to understand how it was conditioned by the nature and experience of man, how it was psychologically mediated. The criticism of the doctrine of primitive revelation made by Schnelling is pertinent, to the effect that if religion were to be derived from an historical communication from God, men would have to be conceived as without religion before that communication, and that if we admit an original atheism of human consciousness, it would remain inconceivable how such a consciousness could have received a revelation from God. . . . . The theory of evolution has led us to conceive of primitive man as utterly incapable of receiving and retaining the highly developed ideas which primitive revelation was supposed to communicate to him.

2. The other view is that of the so-called English Deists of the eighteenth century. These thinkers rejected the idea of revelation and found the origin of religion in human reason. The fundamental truths of religion, such as the being of God, the immortality of the soul, the authority of the moral law, are truths of reason which can be established with the certainty of mathematical truths and which constitute the natural religion which is the common element in all the varied religions of the world. This religion of reason is natural to man and therefore known to him from the beginning. But through the cunning devices of the priests, whose one object was to exploit the fears and credulity of the masses in order to get them under their control, elaborate superstitious beliefs and ritual practices came everywhere to take the place of the simple religion of reason. Thus religion has a twofold origin—viz., reason as the source of pure natural religion, and wilful deceit on the part of priests as the source of all the actual historical religions. The purest form of religion is thus the religion of primitive man, before the "priestcraft" had commenced its corrupting work. Natural religion existed from the first as a perfected thing, and all additions are not only unnecessary, but false and mischievous. This theory . . . . is now quite obsolete. It has several very serious and obvious defects. (a) It exaggerates the place of reason as the originating source of religion, and ignores that emotional intuitional illumination which is such a fruitful source of religious ideas and experience. (b) It reveals a lack of the historic sense and ignores the principle of historical development which is at work in religion as in all other departments of life. It attributes to primitive man mature ideas which it took untold ages for man to be able to grasp and appreciate. . . . . (c) Most absurd of all is the idea that all the actual religions of history are simply calculating hypocrisies invented by priests in a spirit of selfish greed for power. Doubtless priests have frequently exploited the religious impulses of men to serve their own ends, but they could only exploit what already existed independently of them. The priest avails himself of what is already in existence. His function is not to originate but to conserve, while the real creators are the prophets and apostles, who are little concerned with the outward rites and ceremonies of religion. . . . .

These older and pre-scientific views we may now put on one side and proceed to discuss some of the more important modern theories of the origin of religion. There are two ways in which the question may be approached—the way of the anthropologist and the way of the psychologist. The former is concerned with the historic, or rather prehistoric, origin of religion. How did religion first appear in time and place? In what way did the religious nature of man first express itself? What was the most rudimentary form of religion, from which all other forms may be said to have developed? But the problem of the latter is, What is its source in man's spiritual nature, not at the beginning only, but everywhere and always? What are the constant factors in the inner life of man which, in interplay with the environment, generate the attitude which we call religious? What are the impulses, promptings, motives, felt needs, which lead him to apprehend the supernatural and to adjust his life to it? What is there in his mental make-up that accounts for the fact that wherever man is found he has some form or other of religion? These two sets of questions are really inseparable. The anthropologist needs the help of psychology to enable him to solve his problem, and the psychologist likewise needs the help of anthropology. The anthropologist especially needs to have an insight into the psychology of the primitive mind before he can hope to reconstruct the religion of the primitive man. In fact, we may say that his task is primarily psychological. For there are no records of the oldest forms of religion, either in written documents or in trustworthy traditions. He cannot, therefore, go back in history to the beginnings and there make a study of man in the process of becoming religious, for at the very dawn of history man is already fully religious. But by a sympathetic study of the mind and ways of modern savages and of children, and by constructive imagination on the basis of such study, the anthropologist may rebuild for us the religion of the primitive man. His reconstruction must necessarily be purely hypothetical. Even though scientific investigation has placed at our disposal a great wealth of material with regard to the religion of the savage, it must remain largely a matter of conjecture which, if any, of these low forms of religion can be regarded as the original or parent form, or as the nearest approximation to it. And the truth of the conjecture will largely depend on the measure of psychological insight which is behind it. Hence our main interest will be in the question, What are the roots of religion in man's inner nature? . . . .

II

The Animistic Theory of E. B. Tylor.—This may be said to be the first theory of the origin of religion that was backed up by a thoroughly scientific study of the mind and habits of the savage. It first appeared in Tylor's monumental volumes, *Primitive Culture* (first edition 1871, third edition 1891), where it is shown that at a certain stage of culture men everywhere attribute a kind of soul to the phenomena of Nature—e.g., to trees, brooks, mountains, clouds, stones, stars. Primitive man regarded all he saw as possessing a life like unto his own. He instinctively projected his own experience into the objects around him, making unconscious use of the only prin-

ciple that was available to him—viz., the principle of analogy. The movements of things around him he accounted for on the analogy of his own
movements, which he knew by immediate experience were due to the activity of his spirit or will. To early man, as to the savage today, all Nature
was alive, filled with innumerable spirits. According to Tylor, it was on
the basis of this animistic view of the world that religion arose. Religion
had its origin in the attempt of man to establish a relationship between him
and certain of the spirits with which the world around him was peopled,
and this would lead him to seek to propitiate the powerful spirits and to
exorcise the evil ones. . . . .

Yet as an account of the origin of religion it cannot be regarded as satisfactory. (1) Animism is not rudimentary religion, as it is sometimes loosely
called, but a kind of rudimentary philosophy; "the most elementary of human philosophies," Höffding calls it. Not all the spirits which animate the
objects of Nature are worshipped or evoke religious emotion and action.
Hence it is still necessary to find a psychological motive to explain why
man should seek to establish a relation with some spirits and not with others.
The worshipper must see in the object of his reverence something to stir
up his emotions profoundly, something to evoke his special interest. Worship implies selection, and for the selection a motive must be found. Thus
it is psychology that holds the key to the problem. Religion means man's
response in some way to the supernatural, or to what he conceives as having in some way control over his destiny. But the supernatural is no part of
animism pure and simple, which ascribes human, but not superhuman, powers to non-human beings. . . . . Thus we cannot say that religion arose out of
animism. We can only say that the religion of early man was, like the whole
of his life, dominated by animism. (2) But even as a kind of philosophy
animism is not strictly primitive. It involves the notion of a soul, which
could only have been achieved through considerable reflection extended
over a long period of time. The notion of a soul as a definite thing is a
fairly advanced concept which must have been beyond the mental reach
of primitive man. Nor did he have to wait until he could attribute a separate spirit to each object of Nature before he could have a religion. And so
authorities have come to recognize what is called a pre-animistic stage of religion.

The Ghost-Theory of Herbert Spencer.—. . . . Some awe of the ghosts
of the departed prevails widely among savages, and as far back as we can go
men are seen offering sacrifices to the spirits of their ancestors. This Herbert Spencer believed to be the most primitive form of religion, the one
which accounts for and developed into the other forms. The fear of the
dead who had passed beyond the control of the living was the motive which
led to the observance of religious rites. . . . . Spencer's theory errs on the
side of over-simplicity. The deification of ancestors is far too narrow a
basis on which to rear the structure of religion. "Religion is too complex
a phenomenon to be accounted for by the growth and spread of a single
custom. . . . . Dr. Jevons expresses his view in unqualified terms thus: "It
never happens that the spirits of the dead are conceived to be gods. Man

is dependent on the gods, but the spirits of his dead ancestors are dependent on him. . . . . The worshiper's pride is that *his* ancestor was a god and no mere mortal. . . . . The fact is that ancestors known to be human were not worshipped as gods, and that ancestors worshipped as gods were not believed to be human." . . . .

Totemism as the Simplest and Most Primitive Religion.—. . . . A totem is a species of animal or plant, or more rarely a class of inanimate objects, to which a social group (a clan) stands in an intimate and very special relation of friendship or kinship—frequently it is thought of as the ancestor of the clan—and which provides that social group with its name. The totem is not exactly a god, but a cognate being and one to be respected. It must not be used for common purposes, nor must it be slain or eaten except in some solemn and sacramental way. It is always the species and never an individual animal or plant that is regarded as a totem. . . . .

Durkheim regards totemism as the most simple and primitive religion which it is possible to find. Though he insists that the importance of totemism is absolutely independent of whether it was ever universal or not, yet it is practically assumed as the earliest form of society and of religion everywhere. The substratum of all religious belief lies in the idea of a mysterious impersonal force controlling life, and this sense of force is derived from the authority of society over the individual. It is this sense of the power of the social group over his life that becomes to man the consciousness of a mysterious power in the world. . . . . His real god is society; the power he really worships is the power of society. Durkheim's interest in totemism is determined by his sociological theory of religion as essentially and wholly a social phenomenon. . . . .

III

Pre-Animistic Religion: The Conception of Mana.—Recent anthropology tends more and more to find the origin of religion—in common with magic —in a pre-animistic period or stage characterized by a sense of awe in the presence of a diffused, indefinable, mysterious power or powers not regarded as personal. This power is designated by the Melanesian term *mana*, which is common to a large group of languages and corresponds to what the Algonquin tribes of North America call *manitou*, the Iroquoian tribes *orenda*, and the Sioux *wakonda*. . . . . It is a mysterious or magical—as distinguished from natural—quality or potency hovering between the personal and the impersonal, but more psychical than physical in character, permeating all things, but often concentrated in individual persons or things, an indefinite reservoir of energy in the universe, on which man can draw for good or ill. It is this incalculable power that manifests itself in extraordinary things and persons and unexpected events. "All conspicuous success is a proof that a man has *mana*. . . . . A man's power, though political or social in character, is his *mana*. . . . . If a man has been successful in fighting, it has not been his natural strength of arm, quickness of eye, or readiness of resource that has won success; he has certainly got the *mana* of a spirit or of a deceased warrior to empower him, conveyed in an amulet or a stone around his neck, or a tuft of leaves in his belt. . . . ." The totem animal has power or cunning and is sacred because it has *mana,* and men eat the totem animal sacramentally in order to obtain *mana.* . . . .

CHAPTER III: THE PSYCHICAL ORIGIN AND DEVELOPMENT OF RELIGION

We have now to approach the question of the origin of religion more definitely from the psychological point of view. What, then in the nature of man constitutes him a religious being? Where in his inner life are we to find the springs of religion? . . . .

I

To say that man is religious because he has a *religious instinct* is a cheap and facile way of solving—or of shirking—the psychological problem of the origin of religion. It is perilously easy to multiply indefinitely the number of the instincts in order to account for certain widespread characteristics of human behavior. . . . . It is true that man is endowed with a number of basal instincts, the raw material of personality, but they are few in number and simple in character. They constitute the original outfit with which every man is equipped and which he has in common with other animals. The word "instinct" has come to mean for psychologists something very definite and simple—viz., the inborn, untaught tendency to react in a specific way to a certain kind of object or situation, independently of prior experience. But religion is not a simple, specific reaction to a simple, specific kind of impression. It is rather "a very complex and diversified product of the co-operation of several instincts, which bring forth very heterogeneous manifestations." . . . . Religion is rather the synthetic organization of the elemental instincts and emotions of our being in the pursuit of ideal ends. Such a synthesis is, indeed, the expression of a fundamental and permanent need of our nature. But to attribute it to a religious instinct is to oversimplify a complex phenomenon.

Equally unsatisfactory is it to account for religion by saying that man has a *religious faculty*. Here we have another instance of the old and easy method of explaining a special kind of activity by inventing a special faculty as its organ. But the days of the old "faculty psychology" are gone. To imagine a separate religious faculty functioning apart from the rest of the mind is to ignore the fundamental unity of the human mind. . . . . There is no part of man's psychical nature which can be labeled religious in the sense that it is that part *alone* which functions in his religious life and that it functions *only* in the religious life.

Another instance of a fallacious simplification of the problem is the one that attributes the origin of religion to one single elemental emotion. The most famous example of this is the very old theory which found in the emotion of *fear* the ultimate spring of religion. This view found its classical exponent in the Epicurean philosophers and the Latin poet Lucretius, who identified religion with superstition. It is well summed up in the famous line of Petronius, *primus in orbe deos fecit timor.* . . . . And there can be no doubt that fear does play a predominant part, especially in the lowest religions. A vague terror of the mysterious forces of Nature pervades the life of the savage and leads him to endeavor by acts of propitiation to win over to his side the hostile powers by which he is surrounded. Among un-civilized peoples, while the good spirits are known, much more attention is paid to warding off the wrath of malevolent spirits than to securing the favor of good ones. The tendency is to let alone the good spirits, because, being good, they will do no harm. It is thus fear of the evil spirits that leads to actual religious activities. But it is quite another thing to say that the simple emotion of fear is an adequate cause of religion in general. We have al-ready supported the view that a sense of awe in the presence of the mysteri-ous potencies of the universe is the most fundamental religious emotion. But awe is not to be identified simply with fear, though fear is an ingredient in it. . . . . But even in the mind of the savage there are the germs of trust and hope, and a sense of the positive values which he desires to acquire or conserve. The flower of religion is love, and "perfect love casteth out fear," not, however, in the sense of uprooting and destroying it, but in the sense of sublimating and transfiguring it.

WESTERN SOCIETY AT THE CROSSROADS

Arthur E. Holt

DRAW A LINE between the Scandinavian countries on the west and Russia on the east, let it pass between Denmark and Germany, and follow down to the Mediterranean Sea between France and Germany. On the west side of this line will lie most of the countries which have had an experience with and still profess a belief in the democratic method. On the east of this line will be the countries which have undertaken the solution of social problems through resort to some kind of dictatorship. The line between the countries which are so distinguished will probably become sharper as the days go on.

I

If one were to approach intelligent citizens on the west side of this line and ask them their convictions about social methods, one would receive answers somewhat as follows:

We believe (they would say) that a democracy which trusts the people to co-operate in self-government is worth fighting for. We have no desire to be members of a totalitarian state.

We believe that education which respects individual judgment and does not turn a university into a group of "yes-men" is worth fighting for. We view with apprehension the shift of the center of educational control from standards which are indigenous to educational institutions to those based on the short-time objectives of a racial group or of the state. The dictator who surrounds himself with educators who tell him what he wants to know will ultimately die of ignorance. Our educational institutions believe that they render the best service to the common good in an environment where freedom of research and the right of private judgment are recognized. We will maintain a social order, in which there is willingness to grant this freedom to educational institutions because we desire to have the service of free investigators rather than of intellectual slaves.

We believe that a church which can stand over against the state and look the state in the face and criticize it in the name of the highest good is worth fighting for. Religious institutions are charged with the task of interpreting that which is worthy of supreme devotion. Freedom to do this without first paying obeisance to any of the secondary values of race, class or nation, is an indispensable condition of social health.

We worship a God before whose will every secondary absolute of race, class, or nation must walk humbly. This God is superior to every *Volk* God. The career of the God we worship is marked by successive triumphs over the professed absolutes of empire and race. In early Christianity the

Reprinted by permission from *Christendom*, Summer, 1936.

battle was fought once and for all against emperor worship, and in early Judaism our God ceased to be the God of a preferred people. He cannot now be made to serve the purpose of either a class or a race. They must serve him.

We believe that the state cannot possibly be the final teacher of morals. By its very definition the state is an institution based on power; its objectives must be local and provincial. When it subordinates religion to itself it sacrifices its best friend because it forfeits its most disinterested critic. Likewise the state needs the free criticism of the scientist and the educator. It can trust itself with power only as it disciplines itself through free criticism.

To all this those on the eastern side of the line would probably reply:

It is true that Western democracy has given to the vocations, especially those which flourish in the city—money-lending, trading and manufacturing—their greatest opportunity. They have grown strong but they have grown at the expense of the laborers in the factory and on the farm. The benefits of democracy are one-sided and very limited. Democracy has given to the professions their great opportunity. They have each developed a laudable autonomy. But democracy has not achieved an organic society. Vocational prejudice is almost as acute as class prejudice and race prejudice. The democratic countries are atomistic in their development and unjust in their distribution of rewards.

It is true (those on the east side of the line would say) that education has achieved a remarkable development but this education is practically helpless in the face of great national crises. It does not deal with those issues which are most acute in national life. The universities are filled with loafers to whom education is an opportunity to delve in harmless specialties which have no practical value for suffering humanity. Society must act. It must plan. It must do something about the truth which it possesses. The unlimited accumulation of volumes on library shelves does not justify the vast expenditures on education. Education has not created public-minded citizens.

Those on the east side would continue thus: The claim that the West worships a God of love in a free church is sheer sentimentality. In the first place, the church is not free. It is proving itself subservient to the groups who have paid its bills. It has not lifted the ideals of the people to high service in a world of public evil. It has been provincial, interested in self-preservation, filled with competitive strife. It has operated on the low level of the ethics of self-preservation. It has taught private morality in a world of public evil. In the second place, the West has not worshiped a God of love. The God of the West has been a God of power. No nations have more thoroughly followed his bidding than the democratic nations which have ruthlessly penetrated to the uttermost parts of the earth in search of trade. The claim that a God of love is the central idea in western ethics is sheer hypocrisy. It is well to be rid of such hypocrisy, and this requires that we recognize the sentimentalism and insincerity of all such claims to universality.

While thus disclaiming any loyalty to the ideals of democracy, those on the east side would probably claim to offer an organic society in which there was some attempt to solve those problems which democracy has not yet solved. A dictatorship can at least bring order out of chaos. It is possible for a dictatorship to plan a totalitarian state and thus deal with those large-scale emotions which gather around the regional provincialism and class struggle and which plague the steps of every Western democratic statesman.

II

Before this panorama of battling world forces, Western society stands compelled to make some great decisions. Those decisions require that we reach a better understanding of the past and strive as best we can to envisage the issues involved in various alternatives. The considerations which enter into these great decisions will not be altogether theoretical ones. Ten million unemployed in one nation, with the right kind of leader, may constitute an argument stronger than abstract theory. One thing is certain—humanity is no longer confined to just one way out. Hard-pressed in the midst of a social order which is not providing a satisfactory type of life, Western society now stands at a crossroads where there are multiple alternatives. The remainder of this article will be given to a short attempt to explore the road by which we have come and a still more inadequate effort to make clear the issues with which we are confronted.

The thirteenth century has often been called the greatest century in Western social experience. All social forces seemed at that time to be going in the same direction and there was something of a sense of unity of idea and purpose. The West was then an organic society. With the growth of the towns and the development of a trader economy this sense of organic unity gave way to that set of ideas which have been grouped under the general concept of democracy. For the past three hundred years we have been emphasizing the rights and responsibilities of the individual. Men began to explore human society almost entirely from this angle. They developed certain great slogans—the right of private judgment, the right of free speech, freedom of the press, freedom in education, the right of every religious group to organize as it saw fit, private initiative in business and the right of private property. These principles came to be considered as firmly established; they had been won at great cost and seemed to mark out the pathway of all future progress.

But gradually society has taken another turn. Once more it is beginning to explore the interdependence of life. We are coming to see that the great values of life cannot be gained by us as individuals. We cannot get married by ourselves, we cannot play baseball by ourselves, we cannot get food by ourselves. We must have co-operative agreements with their more or less complex regulations. Collective relationships are now more important to us than individual rights and responsibilities. All the various functions of society which have struggled for their autonomy are now facing the necessity of deciding how much of their autonomy they must give up in order to have satisfactory relationships with other functions which are equally necessary to the social body.

Four great experiments are abroad in the world at the present time, each of which is characteristized by some modification of the principle of autonomy in the vocations. If the Reformation period could be characterized as a period when each of the vocations sought to go its separate way, the present time can be characterized as one in which the vocations are seeking one another for the purpose of effecting an organic inter-relationship. The critical question concerns the nature of that relationship. Over against the values of democracy, new movements are stressing the right of the state to co-ordinate all functions. In economic matters collective control is placed above private control. Education and religion are regimented to make the state more secure. All these new experiments are offering to society some new collective arrangement and they are dealing roughly with the hard won values and virtues which democracy defends.

If the national socialism of Germany were the only experiment which challenged Western idealism it might be dismissed as a symptom of the diseased condition of the Western mind, and many so dismiss it. But whatever its shortcomings, it must be classified as one of those new attempts at a collective society which shares with other social experiments in a distinct departure from Western idealism. The right of the individual is challenged also by communism in Russia and by fascism in Italy. Over against the virtues of democracy all these types of social order are emphasizing the supreme right of the social group over all rights of the individual. In all of them it is the business of education to indoctrinate either for the state or for some dominant class.

Any system such as capitalism, fascism, national socialism, communism, or democratic collectivism has certain persistent factors on the basis of which it can be analyzed and compared with other systems. These persistent factors may be used as windows through which to view large-scale ways of doing things. About each one of these systems it is possible to ask the following questions:

1. Around what values does this system organize itself?

2. Where are the originating sources of these values?

3. What are the ways of social change advocated by this system?

4. What social and economic arrangement between the four major classes is provided for?

5. What basic religious ideas are held and how are these ideas provided for in religious institutions?

III

Let us focus attention on the dominant systems now contending for human loyalty, as they are exemplified in the following countries: Democracy represented in the United States, fascism in Italy, national socialism in Germany, communism in Russia, democratic collectivism in Denmark and Scandinavia, and let us ask of them the proposed questions.

If we ask: What are the basic values? the answers are:

Democracy: the individual, the right of private initiative, private judgment and private property.
National Socialism: the *Volk* and its racial welfare.
Fascism: the state and national supremacy.
Communism: the proletariat mass and dictatorship of proletariat.
Democratic Collectivism: the individual and the group.

If we ask: What are the originating sources of values? the answers are:

Democracy: every man.
National Socialism: the race; the élite.
Fascism: the whole state speaking through the élite.
Communism: the proletariat mass.
Democratic Collectivism: the individual and the group.

If we ask: What are the ways of social change and social control advocated by the systems? the answers are:

Democracy: supremacy of truth, education, popular vote and parliamentary action.
National Socialism: Volk welfare supreme over truth; first emphasis on securing of power; rule through propaganda.
Fascism: religious truth apart by itself; power abides in state rule by state propaganda.
Communism: power first, truth second; rule by power and propaganda.
Democratic Collectivism: freedom for truth and culture, co-operative collectivism; state action is product of parliamentary procedure.

If we ask: What are the ways of social arrangement between the classes? the answers are:

Democracy: laissez-faire in theory, opportunity for the entrepreneur, actually special privilege for the money-lender, trader and manufacturer.
National Socialism: national planning through economic dictatorship; responsible leadership of entrepreneur; much government ownership; agricultural and middle classes privileged.
Fascism: national planning through dictatorship; state control of capitalist system; most business privately owned.
Communism: abolition of capitalist system; state ownership of means of production, and distribution; control largely in interest of urban proletariat, middle classes eliminated; agriculture regimented.
Democratic Collectivism: large growth of co-operative movement; much of private industry still remains; state enters business at point where private industry is least adequate.

If we ask: What are the basic religious ideas held by the systems? the answers are:

Democracy: religious respect for individual; largely Protestant in faith; freedom in worship maintained.
National Socialism: religion to revert to tribal stage, church to be regimented in interest of *Volk* and state; state assumes many functions of church.
Fascism: church and state exist in separated and unrelated functions.
Communism: religion identified as instrument of slavery; state takes over church function of determining that which is worthy of supreme devotion; church abolished.
Democratic Collectivism: church still free to discover and determine that which is worthy of supreme devotion; church, school and state maintain a fellowship of functions.

The change with which Western society is confronted is over-powering in its significance. The reconstruction in ethics will be epoch-making. For three hundred years we have been placing responsibility on the individual. We have insisted that it was impossible to have a society in which the individual did not accept responsibility in those relationships in which he joined with others in the great things he could not do for himself. Our whole system of rewards and punishments has been built up with the idea of enforcing individual responsibility. We are now faced with a reversal of this line of thinking, and are asked to make society responsible and to excuse the individual.

It would be easy to plead over against this new collectivism the advantages of democracy. But democracy has back of it too much bad performance to make it easily defensible. Democracy has not given us an organic society; it has given us an atomistic society, a society full of cleavages. It has not given us a just society; its privileges have been laid at the feet of the capitalist class. Democracy boasts of freedom of speech, freedom of the press and freedom of the pulpit, but these slogans often hide an indefensible selfishness and a bondage which can be easily exposed as such. The question as to whether democracy will survive seems to hinge on the question whether the values of democracy can be maintained while we work out some inter-relationship of functions which shall represent both freedom and organic unity.

If the past epoch was faced with the problem of freeing the institutions of church, family, school, and state, the present generation faces the problem of what is to be done with this freedom in a society which is increasingly organic. If the past epoch was concerned with separating church and state, the present generation must undertake the task of bringing them together without doing violence to the genius of either. If once the public welfare was served by setting free each of these institutions from the domination of each other, it must now be realized that neither can fulfill its true function apart from the other.

It would be easy to plead over against "statism" the excellencies of the Christian religion. But the Christian religion has acquiesced in too much bad performance on the part of various social groups to make its defense an easy matter. Western religion now faces one of its major crises. Either it will once more become the voice of an idealism vigorous and critical enough to state the legitimate objectives of a world-wide society or it will be dragged down and made the servant of the state or of some social class.

The case is not altogether a hopeless one. Criticize the development of the last three hundred years as we will, a very large body of the churches have achieved the ability to support themselves apart from the state and have so broadened the basis of their support that they are not dependent upon any one class. Western religion has come to terms with historical criticism, which offers a scientific method for disentangling itself from society. It has, by social criticism, formulated programs of human brotherhood which are independent of the dictates of the state or of any one race. A certain part of the church has risen above the futility which has characterized the doctrine of separation of the church from the state and has demonstrated the ability of the church to participate in the forming of that super-political conscience which is the most important factor in social control.

The social systems of Europe have broken open. Inside of them we can see a struggle going on as to what is worthy of supreme devotion. Underneath modern politics is the stuff out of which religion is made. The most impressive fact in the present situation is that all the major controversies of Western society have become religious. Men have caught the vision of a new age when, by intelligent planning, a new abundance may be at the disposal of all. But planning involves a decision as to the values around which the planning is to be organized, and that decision lies in the realm of religion and ethics. Whether or not Western religion can survive as an institution of universality will depend upon the church's ability, in the name of its high goals for humanity, so vigorously to define and defend that which is worthy of supreme devotion that the state will be caused to relinquish the totalitarian function wherever it has usurped it or threatens to usurp it.

NEO-THOMISM

Edwin Ewart Aubrey

THE DISEASE OF MODERN SOCIETY

Disunity. Even the casual observer cannot fail to be impressed with the fact that our contemporary society lacks either unity, direction, or depth. Atomism pervades all phases of modern life. The process which began with the emancipation of national monarchies from the universal hierarchy continued with the revolt of the nobility against the crown, and the rise of the bourgeois groups against the nobles, and was consummated in that individualism which threatens our social integrity. In politics it finds ultimate expression in anarchy. But there is anarchy in culture, too. "Art for art's sake," "knowledge for its own sake," "keep government out of business": these are slogans which arise out of the autonomous independence of cultural activities which have no higher synthesis. Such atomism is epitomized for religion in the scores of sects which deprive the term Protestantism of any unitary significance except the negative one of protest. In world relations it emerges in the selfish nationalism which seems to be psychologically estopped from that co-operation which would make the world a brotherhood of men. Indeed, this atomism infects even the personality of men, torturing them with the conflict which spells "dissociation," and leaving unhealed the cleavage between man's spiritual insight and his social life, between what the Germans call *Geist* and *Leben*.

In the last analysis this atomism is secularism; activities of culture which were once pursued in allegiance to the spiritual unity of a common religious faith in God, are now divorced from religion and have gone their separate ways. Philosophy and art were in the Middle Ages allies of Christian faith. With the Renaissance they became subordinate to secular princes. The Enlightenment freed them even from that control. Philosophy, eager to be free from religion, developed an anti-religious bias, so that it ignored the supernatural and attempted to naturalize first the world and then man. Thus human nature was itself secularized, abstracted from its metaphysical spiritual background and reduced to a mechanical rationalist behaviorism. Consequently, revolutionary doctrines of progress appeared which dealt exclusively in materialistic reorganization. The distinction between the natural and the supernatural was over-looked; and in the positivism initiated by Kant and systematized in Comte, philosophy was confused with science. Thus arose a bland optimism resting on the assurance that scientific control of the natural world would bring men to a perfect life. Adjustment came to be the goal even of education, without clear insight into the distinction between being "transformed by the renewing

From *Present Theological Tendencies*, New York, 1936, pp. 120-49. Reprinted by permission of the publishers, Harper & Brothers.

of a right spirit" and being "conformed to this world." Secular education has come to worry about "character education" while it repudiates spiritual realities of a supernatural order; and is concerned about "motivation" of higher conduct while it tries to restrict man's ideals to the natural order.

Lack of direction. Modern culture suffers, further, from lack of direction. For a sense of direction is a unification of experience; and this, we have seen, is lacking. The divorce of nature from the supernatural leaves man in the natural world without a goal beyond his present situation in any profound sense. Proximate objectives for immediate activity he may have; but without some real goal of effort that transcends his physical life and his mundane existence, there can be no unifying direction for his life as a whole. In the same way human society can find direction for its activity only in a real goal that transcends history. Nay, more: the dilemma of human nature that is in nature and yet transcends its natural environment requires for its solution a direction towards the supernatural. It is therefore little wonder that, with an outlook that is naturalistic, man should be driven to a sense of futility and meaninglessness.

But a sense of direction also means that one is emancipated from himself in dedication to that which is beyond him. Accordingly, the mood of subjectivism that characterizes post-Renaissance thought is the enemy of directed living. When the men of the Renaissance and their spiritual progeny, the men of the Enlightenment, sought to throw off all external shackles and to rely on their own reason, they lost touch with the criteria for direction in thought itself. Thus human thought became mired in doubt about itself, that fatal doubt that brings failure of nerve. In Montaigne it had found polite expression. In Hume it attained systematic exposition, tempered only by a healthy sense of humor. Kant accepted its limitations upon metaphysics, and became agnostic about the world-in-itself. Man was left in the restricted area of his own knowledge, and wondered why his life seemed small and meaningless. Losing confidence in his own knowledge, he lost even the basis of his own rational self-direction. The curse of his anti-intellectualism is now upon him. Failing to find guidance for conduct or thought, man's social life is caught in confusion and his mental life in self-contradiction.

Shallowness. Modern man seeks stability yet insists on perpetual flux and absolute relativism. He believes that "Penelope-like, we must undo the work already finished, and begin to weave anew the texture of philosophic thought, only to have it unraveled again by our successors," and still he relies on accumulated knowledge as the basis of stability. On the one hand he restricts knowledge to the subjective area of one's own perceptions, relegating metaphysics to the idle play of human speculative fancy; while, on the other, he maintains a blithe faith in progress. Progress, which implies an appraisal of movement in terms of some standard or criterion of good, is asserted at the same time that men feel "that all moments of human thought . . . . are in themselves venerable." The controversy of the Schoolmen as to the primacy of the intellect or the will (following Thomas Aquinas and Duns Scotus respectively) has been distorted into a conflict between intelligence and will. The reaction against rationalism becomes a declaration that the intellect is ineffectual in the face of the power of the impulses, or the will-to-live (Schopenhauer) or the will-to-power (Nietzsche); and yet the very declaration is elaborated in a philosophic system! This shallow confusion persists because of the failure to cope with the fundamental intellectual problems underlying the concepts employed. The result is modern activism, which tries to smother smouldering doubts and querulous restlessness under a load of preoccupying busy-ness.

This is, then, the predicament of our contemporary culture as the neo-Thomist sees it. Coherence and unity are lost in a confused atomism which appears to the critic like the fragments of a picture puzzle in the hands of a child that will not believe in pictures. Man's hunger for meaning and direction in life satisfactory to his highest aspirations is fed with a stone for bread: a view of nature, of human society, and of his own personality which reduces these to a naturalistic level where the hunger itself is argued out of existence but the ache is left. Bewildered, unhappy, restless, the modern man bemoans his own confusion; and yet smiles bitterly at all proposals for relief because his faith in human thought has been demoralized. These are the symptoms of a disease that has become chronic in "the equivocation that has lasted for three centuries."

THE SOURCES OF INFECTION

Naturalism. We have seen how the Renaissance and the Enlightenment mark the reaction against the later scholastics and the establishment of the foundations of modern thought. The interpretation of this reaction will therefore determine the attitude towards our present cultural problem. Since the historiography of our time is itself a product of the modern spirit in philosophy, it is natural that certain prejudices, developed early in the modern era, should have crept into our accounts of the dawn of our modern age. Thus our prejudices subtly assume the guise of clear historical factuality, and the vicious circle is closed. This is itself one of the sources of our difficulty.

The Renaissance embodies two attitudes: that of the Christian humanists, and that of the pagans. Both derived their impetus from the recovery of ancient learning, and classical literature; but while the Christian humanists saw these new discoveries in relation to Christian faith, the pagans sought a revival of the pre-Christian spirit of lusty naturalism. These latter lost sight of the continuity of intellectual history and hence of the contribution which Christian thought in the Middle Ages had made to their own development. In fact, they secured many of their fundamental principles from Christian sources without being aware of their origin. But so preoccupied were they with the stupidity of late scholastic pedants with their dry and sterile discussions and their barbarous Latin style, that they made the mistake of rejecting along with that pedantry the philosophic principles of the masters of scholastic thought.

The Platonic revival. A prominent phase of the Renaissance was the revival of interest in Plato. While Platonism had exercised an influence in medieval thought through the mediation of Augustine and Eriugena, it was largely under the impress given to it by Plotinus. This neo-Platonic mysticism leans heavily towards an ascetic dualism in which the real world is not the world of physical experience but a realm of pure ideas. Man as an individual is thus left stranded in the world of mere appearances, and for lack of an adequate unifying metaphysics is ethically impotent: for he cannot embody the divine will in his earthly conduct. It was this form of Platonism which helped to furnish a rationale for ascetic mysticism, but which was inadequate for a socially active religion. With the rediscovery of Aristotle in the twelfth century the way was opened to a rational metaphysics and the dominance of Plato over medieval Christian thought was ended. The Renaissance discovered another Plato: not the mystical theologian of the Augustinians but the mathematician.

After the establishment of Aristotelian thought by Albertus Magnus and his greater disciple, Thomas Aquinas, the reappearance of Platonic thought seemed like a revolt. The Aristotelian philosophy had had a deep feeling for quality by its emphasis on the *form* which gives to each individual its essential character. In Platonism this concreteness of the individual is lost in the emphasis on abstract universals; hence his devotion to mathematics which treats of universal and abstract relations. In the Renaissance this mathematical approach seized men's imagination as furnishing the clue to the philosophy of the future. In Descartes and Spinoza all philosophical problems are to be solved *more geometrico*, according to the method of geometry. It is not surprising, therefore, that mechanism replaces teleology in the Cartesian philosophy; and when these mathematical relations are confined to the physical objects themselves the stage is set for modern philosophic materialism.

At the same time, the operation of reason within the limits allowed by the Platonic philosophy leads to preoccupation with the relations of particular, individual, concrete objects, and to abandonment of the search for their essences which are their universal forms. This was the genius of nominalism with its virtual repudiation of metaphysics in the *via moderna* of Occam. From this eventually flowed the stream of positivism, so influential in nineteenth-century thought. Here also empiricism took its rise with its faith in the possibilities of reaching truth by inductive generalization from concrete data of the senses. From Francis Bacon to John Stuart Mill and Herbert Spencer this philosophical current grows steadily into a predominant tendency in contemporary thought.

Subjectivism. The nominalist abandonment of Aristotelian metaphysics had another consequence: the objective world was explained by subjective experience, and this rejection, combined with the platonic theory of ideas, gave rise to modern idealist philosophy. This was the great heresy of Descartes, that he initiated that reduction of objective being to subjective thought, of nature to mind, which gave the subjectivistic bias to modern philosophic reflection.

The modern exaltation of man derives in part from the Renaissance protest against asceticism in the name of Greco-Roman humanism, and in part from this subjectivism which made man the measure of all things.   His assurance of supremacy over nature in which he regards himself as central, is approximated by his self-exaltation in relation to God upon whom man ceases to feel dependent.   Gradually thought shifts from a theocentric world-view to an anthropocentric cosmology; while at the same time man's critical thought turns in upon itself in a corroding attack on reason itself.

Anti-intellectualism. The root of our contemporary difficulty is anti-intellectualism: we are unwilling to undertake the searching examination of the foundations of a rational world-view.   Luther sought escape from dogmatic theology in the "Gospel" as an inward experience.   Descartes sought to find a simple intuitive insight independent of past logical premises, and thus to escape from cumulative thinking.   Romanticism revolted against discursive reasoning in the name of feeling and bequeathed its anti-intellectualism to theology through Schleiermacher.   Behaviorism picked up the evolutionary theory and used it to frame a biological theory of knowledge in which thought is a form of bodily adjustment.   In psycho-analysis the intellect is deprived of its reliability by demonstration of the subconscious drives which determine the alleged free activity of the thinking mind.   Theology witnesses the loss of confidence in the intelligence in the disillusioned anti-rationalism of Karl Barth, who finds no place for syllogistic thought in the achievement of faith.   Even in art there emerges a cult of unintelligibility in the recent French literary super-realism and in the paintings of the post-impressionists.

In a subtler form this anti-intellectualism appears in philosophy itself in the vitalism of Eucken, Bergson, and William James.   It corrupts metaphysics through its naturalistic delimitation of thought by arbitrary truncation of reality and by positivistic abandonment of crucial problems of the speculative mind.

It is now clear that the neo-Thomists are not afraid of modern thought, but are on the contrary dissatisfied with its lack of thoroughness.   Such a criticism, of course, carries its own implications as to the conditions of rehabilitating contemporary religious thought.   This rehabilitation, they insist, can be achieved only by a fundamental reorientation of our thinking —a reorientation through the recovery of certain problems and principles of thought which were lost in the attempt of the Renaissance and the Enlightenment to make a fresh start by ignoring the continuity of Western intellectual development.

The Recovery of Intellectualism

The slogan of the Thomist revival is: back to Thomas Aquinas and from Thomas forward.   But it must be made clear at the outset that this return to Thomistic thought is not an attempt to reinstate medieval pseudo-scientific views of the physical world.   We shall not go back to alchemy or astrology. The recovery of Thomist principles is to be selective: it is to be a "return to his spirit and his method of working."   Since he was an exploring and independent eclectic, the attitude of the neo-Thomist will be far from a romantic idealization of the conclusions of the Angelic Doctor: it will ap-

proach new scientific knowledge and new philosophic developments with
an open mind. And yet the basic principles of Aquinas will be used to examine modern problems. In these principles will be found correctives of
the self-defeating subjectivism, the demoralizing anti-intellectualism, the
shallow positivism which have brought us to the cultural impasse of the
present day. Let us therefore see what they are.

Scholastic metaphysics—change, law, and freedom. First of all, we need
an adequate theory of the relation between natural and spiritual realities—
in other words, a comprehensive metaphysics. Only such metaphysics must
provide an explanation of: (1) the fact of change upon which rests the idea
of natural development according to law; (2) the relation of change to a
permanent ground of existence upon which rests our sense of stability and
security as well as our capacity to distinguish significant from trivial aspects of any object or event; and (3) the conditions of human freedom in
the world of law, as a basic requirement for morality. The clues to this
metaphysics were found by Thomas Aquinas in the philosophy of Aristotle.
Taking these clues he clarified their implications, used them to interpret
the new findings of his day, and thus built up a systematic body of thought
upon all the major problems of human existence. The success of his approach when applied to modern problems justifies for the neo-Thomists the
declaration that he offers a basic philosophy capable of fertilizing investigations in any area of human knowledge and experience.

The primary task of any philosophy, according to both Aristotle and
Aquinas, is to find the essential nature of the things which we experience.
Now a thing may axiomatically be said to be capable of being what it is:
it is, in other words, an actualized potentiality. But it can be what it is and
not something different: it has individuality by virtue of a special end
which it realizes. Thus there is a determinate quality in every object, by
virtue of which it behaves according to law—the law of its being. In interaction with other objects which have their own peculiar individual
tendencies, this object will therefore behave in terms of a complex of determinate conditions: and this is the basis of the formulation of natural laws.
Nay, more, this *is* natural law, which is objective and not merely, as Hume
suggested, a sort of subjective convenience for assorting chaotic impressions.

Change is real in so far as potentiality is real; i.e., a thing changes by
virtue of a power of becoming something which it is not yet. The acorn
can become an oak. It cannot change into a rose. The change is therefore
conditioned by the essential nature of the object: and through the successive
stages of changing this essential nature persists as the constitutive principle
in terms of which the change is orderly and not chaotic. Prior to and
throughout the changes, therefore, there is the essence of the object. This
is what is meant on the one hand by substance and on the other by identity.

There are, then, two sorts of objects of our experience: those that exist
by themselves, and those that exist as modes of something. That is, the
identical character of the acorn, its substance, exists throughout and independent of the successive changes which it undergoes in becoming an oak
tree. But these successive characteristics which it assumes in that process

of development (roots, leaves, bark, growing, etc.) cannot exist except as qualities of this persistent something, hard to name, which is the essential basis of an acorn-becoming-an-oak. Substance, then, is that which exists by itself.

After what seems like a digression from the concerns of religion, we are now ready to see the implications of this brief summary for theology. The important point to note is that the fact of change is not accepted as primary. Changes presuppose a cause, and ultimately we must return logically to an uncaused, self-existent cause: pure essence. Pure essence, to deserve its name, will be independent of determination by other objects; it will be free being. This is God the First Cause, the self-existent Being. God, therefore, is immanent in the world of which he is the constitutive principle; both as the condition of its orderly development, and as the permanent ground of its existence. We may go further, and point out that the very possibility of relations between objects requires an explanation, for without it there is no accounting for the interactions of which the world consists. This structure of possible relations requires some unitary cause and that is God.

We have now offered the basis for an answer to the first two problems of metaphysics listed above; except for the distinction between important and trivial aspects of any object or event. And even here the neo-Thomist answer should now be clearly implicit: we can differentiate between accidental and essential features of reality, between casual, temporary objects of experience and those that are permanent. Here is the foundation offered for a stability, serenity and poise in life: that we in God have found the rock on which our house of human experience in the world is built.

But another important conclusion also flows from this exposition. The supernatural is not set over against the natural as a contradiction (as in Barth), but is that which pervades nature as its constitutive principle and completes nature as its final consummation. Grace is thus continuous with nature, as the process of its perfection. But there is also a definite distinction between the natural and the supernatural. This is more clearly seen if we turn to that part of nature which is also supernatural: human nature.

Man, like every object in the world, has his nature, his essential quality, and also his activities. And man's essence, his soul, gives the body its perfection, its actual existence, its life. Man is thus integrally related to nature, and so "the value, dignity, and perpetuity of the human body" is insisted upon as that in which the soul is expressed. But the inner tendency of human nature is rational, and in this it stands above the rest of nature, for man can grasp the inner nature of the objects of his world as they cannot themselves. This fact sets the peculiar problem of the metaphysics of man himself which Peter Wust declares to be the crucial problem for contemporary thought.

This problem, germane to the whole range of cultural issues of our time, is the freedom of man in a world of natural law. It is the third of our problems stated above. Man is a rational animal, and his intellect is directed toward the inner nature of objects. But this inner nature reveals to him the presence of God; so that the human intellect is capable of knowing that God exists. Thus the human mind can know the source of its own being. Man is accordingly free from the world; but only in so far as he recognizes his dependence upon God. This paradox is to be explained by an understanding of the meeting place of God and nature, intellect and matter, in man. Man is a citizen of two worlds—the natural and the supernatural—and his freedom is found in the resolution of the difference between them. We have indicated that this resolution lies in seeing the natural as infused with the supernatural, and in grasping the determinative control of the supernatural over the natural. Only the spiritual man is the free man; but the spiritual man is expressed in the natural man; and so his freedom in action is never perfect.

This question has brought us already to the main problem with which neo-Thomism deals. Since the exposition of Scholastic thought by non-scholastics stresses so often the subordination of reason to faith, of philosophy to theology, it is important that a movement which uses proudly the appellation "intellectualist" and attacks "anti-intellectualism" should be allowed to clarify its position regarding the relation of intelligence to faith.

Faith and intelligence. We have already seen the insistence which is laid upon the capacity of human intelligence to reach objective reality. The Kantian agnosticism concerning things-in-themselves is vigorously rejected. Since objective reality is knowable, then the scope of science is co-extensive with reality itself. In so far, therefore, as natural theology is concerned—i.e., a religious faith based on reasoning from the facts of our objective natural world—the neo-Thomist is a thoroughgoing inductive thinker. But two other considerations are involved: (1) the rôle of a priori assumptions in the interpretation of nature; and (2) the possibility of revelation.

When we speak of inductive reasoning, the notion is intended to convey the idea that from a series of data we build up a conclusion, a generalization. Now this process was used at times by the Scholastics, though the limitation of observation for lack of instruments made any great development of induction impossible. But the task of science is not complete when facts are gathered: "it must look for the causes of natural phenomena." This search for causes, however, carries its own presuppositions with it: (1) that things are actually held together in such a way that causation is possible as an objective relation; (2) that knowledge gained about causal relations in the past has value in prediction by virtue of the determinate character of reality. Yet both these assumptions are independent of inductive proof, being derived from the metaphysics described above. This is also what is meant by saying that science rests on a faith in the orderliness, the rationality of the universe. Furthermore, the careful inductive generalizations of modern science are ideally expressed in mathematical terms; but mathematics is a deductive science. So that the assumptions of a quantitative statement of inductive, scientific knowledge are of a mathematical, deductive sort.

Revelation. We may now turn to the question of the meaning and possibility of revelation. At the outset let us be reminded of the neo-scholastic insistence that the supernatural does not contradict nature, it is not anti-natural. It is, rather, a completion of the natural. All objects of the natural world have a structure of relationships, and they have an inner character which is an essence realizing itself. But this process of self-realization is metaphysically connected with the self-realizations of other essences; and this connectedness spells the unity of the world. Now, this inter-connectedness is in turn the expression of an essence realizing itself, so that there is a purposive or teleological character to all reality. To gain full knowledge of the world, therefore, it is necessary to see objects not only as they are in themselves but as they are in terms of what they exist for, in terms of their proper ends. Yet when the reason engages in this quest, it is soon brought to a realization of its limitations: proximate ends—or natural functions—it can grasp; but the ultimate ends are not rationally discernible.

Here it is that faith enters, not as a contradiction of reason but as a supplement and consummation of reason. For the pursuit of these ultimate ends leads us up by logical necessity to a Being for whom all ends of all things are present; but it does not tell us what that Being is. This is the meaning of revelation: that that Being communicates itself to man. How can man receive this communication, how can he grasp its meaning, if it is totally estranged from his intellectual faculties? The relations of faith and reason are intimate. Furthermore, by analogy the unification of ends in part rationally perceptible by man argues a rational source of their unity. So that God is a rational being. Yet not rational in our limited sense, since we have admitted such limitations. So that he is supra-rational as he is super-natural. Then, just as every type of experience has its object—the senses point to physical things, and the intellect to abstract relations—so faith points to God.

This summary does not do justice to the detailed dovetailing of the neo-Thomist philosophy; but it suggests the main lines along which its approach to the problems of modern thought is worked out.

The Cure of Modern Social Ills

A world-view. From the foregoing it is clear that any civilization to be worthy of the name must be firmly grounded in a world-view. "True civilization," says Dawson, "is essentially a spiritual order. . . . . In Christianity the idea of spiritual order acquires a yet wider and more profound significance. It is based upon the belief in a divine society which transcends all states and cultures and is the final goal of humanity. . . . . This society exists in the nature of things as 'the republic of all men under the law of God,' although the actual disorder of human nature prevented its effective realization by man."

Such a statement is reminiscent of Thomas Aquinas' discussion of law, which Henry Sidgwick regarded as "the starting-point of independent ethical thought in the modern world." Aquinas differentiated four kinds of law: "eternal law" which is the regulative reason of God which determines the behavior of the whole creation; "natural law" which is the eternal law as applied to rational beings; "human law" which consists of deductions of natural law in terms of actual social situations (here the great Scholastic follows Roman legal theory); and "divine law" which is specially revealed to man in the Scriptures. Now this subordination of human social control to the principles of natural law carries the implication, noted above, that social order is inseparable from a metaphysics of nature. But, as Thomas goes on to say, neither natural law nor human law takes account of that supernatural blessedness which is man's highest end, and so divine law is needed to reveal it, and grace, to attain it. The "primacy of the spiritual" necessarily follows, with its stress upon the subordination of civilization to that spiritual control from which it wandered off in the Renaissance, the Reformation, and the Enlightenment.

The source of progress. In addition, any concept of progress must logically rest on a theory of possibility. The basis of such a concept we have already seen in the discussion of act and potentiality. From the standpoint of social ethical progress this possibility is contained in the Church. "The Church is the embryo of a new world." But the Church (invisible) is also that fellowship in which "the divine life that they possess now by grace is essentially the same as that which will be manifested in the next world in glory. Indeed, the true line of division runs not between Heaven and Earth, but between the natural and supernatural orders in this present world." This explains the radical prophetic function of the Church in the midst of a culture: it sees the social order in terms of the divine order and issues a challenge and an invitation to the social order in the name of the divine order. This is well expressed by Jacques Maritain:

> The world at the moment seems to be in the grip of two opposite forms of barbarism. I have not the least idea whether it will escape. In any event, it must not be forgotten that if the Christian conception has not been the spiritual dominant of civilisation for some centuries past, it has still remained alive, dammed up, not abolished. That such a conception may succeed in dominating culture is still a *possibility* today: whether such a possibility will be realised or not is God's secret. We must therefore work with our whole hearts to bring such a realisation about, no longer, certainly, according to the ideal of the Holy Roman Empire but according to a new ideal, a much less unitary ideal, in which an entirely moral and spiritual activity of the Church shall preside over the temporal order of a multitude of politically and culturally heterogeneous nations, whose religious differences are still not likely soon to disappear. . . . . We may, at any rate, indulge the hope that, in the new world, an authentic Christian culture will arise, "a culture no longer gathered and assembled, as in the Middle Ages, in a homogeneous body of civilisation occupying a tiny privileged portion of the inhabited earth, but scattered over the whole surface of the globe—a living network of hearths of the Christian life disseminated among the nations within the great supra-cultural unity of the Church. . . . .

This pious hope is supported by the belief in the divine purpose realizing itself in history, in Providence. This is clearly expressed by Thomas Aquinas in his argument that since God is pure, unconditioned Being, he has given being to his creatures not by necessity but by choice. God is, therefore, master of his works, and in absolute control of the totality of being. Each created thing therefore has a certain purpose which is the end in view in the will of God. In its movement toward this end the created thing is directed by God, who is himself governed by nothing, so that no part of creation is independent of his control.   Since he is both perfect Being and perfect Cause, his government is also perfect.

But how is man in his weakness to have power to share in this purpose while he lives in the world of nature? The answer to this question is found in the doctrine of the Incarnation:

> This is the claim of the Catholic Faith, that a new power has in fact been brought into the world which is capable of regenerating humanity. . . . . Jesus Christ is to the Catholic not a prophet and teacher like the founders of other great religions, nor even is He only the divine revealer of God to man: He is the restorer of the human race the New man, in Whom humanity has a fresh beginning and man acquires a new nature.

Yet there is also an answer to be found in human experience itself. In contemplation, "which connects the spirit with eternity," man rises above the level of active life. For since the aim of all activity, including moral effort, is toward that beatific vision in which the soul attains its union with God, it follows that activity realizes itself in contemplation, and derives from contemplation its guiding vision. This is the source of ethical power and of morale.

Collectivistic ethics. Finally, let us note a striking emphasis in the social ethical outlook of the neo-Thomists: their emphasis upon collectivism. This was, of course, to be expected from their attack on individualism; but it is striking because of its relation to collectivistic theories in contemporary thought. Indeed, Scholastic thought is closely related to socialistic theory with its emphasis on solidarity. "Christianity," Dawson insists, "was in origin a religion of order and solidarity which throve in an atmosphere of anonymity and collectivism."   The obvious objection of the neo-Thomists to socialism is directed against its materialistic world-view. The collectivism of neo-Thomist thought is a spiritual fellowship.

There are, says Maritain, two sorts of universalism: the one seeking the principle of unity within man himself, which leads to violent despotism; the other finding its unity in God the Father of all men, which is true catholicity. Wust devotes a whole book of his *Dialektik des Geistes* to the problem of solidarity, finding it to consist in the unity of the *nexus animarum*. Men are bound together by their communication with each other, by the common dependence on the physical environment, and by their common will. The aim of Christian ethics is to secure a collectivism based on a dynamic interrelation of human striving through common devotion to God.

THE ETHICAL RESOURCES OF THE CHRISTIAN RELIGION

Reinhold Niebuhr

WHAT HAS RELIGION to offer in an empirical day to the problems of conduct, of social relationship? Those problems of conduct can be solved empirically, can they not? We can say that anything is good which fulfills vital capacity; we can say that men have many impulses and diverse capacities and that any end which fulfills any vital capacity is a good. We can go on rationally and say that since there are many vital capacities the greatest good is that good which fulfills all of them in terms of harmony, which represses no legitimate capacity, which offers room for each one.

Of course this rational solution is not a complete solution, for the question is still with us: If we are going to bring various vital capacities together into terms of harmony, just what relationship are they going to have each to the other? Which is going to be on top and which below, or are they all going to be in a circle? If a circle, what is going to be the center of the circle?

There is no absolute rational solution to the problem of bringing all vital capacities together except the Aristotelian law of measure, "in nothing too much," and I have a suspicion that the rational life can, in matters of conduct, never get beyond Aristotle's "in nothing too much."

We say that we can bring vital capacities into some kind of harmony if we deal with the problem of conduct empirically. Then, however, arises the problem of the capacities of other people. We are living in a world in which we are not alone; others have vital capacities. We cannot express our vital capacities as if we were living a solitary life, and so we come rationally to the solution that that is good which not only fulfills our vital capacities in terms of harmony with one another but which fulfills our vital capacities in terms of harmony with the vital capacities of all people.

We have arrived then, at a solution of rational good which brings us in terms of harmony with all people. This rational good is not one superimposed upon us by reason, for it so happens that in our nature we are related to the whole of our society, with its personalities and social products, and by our impulses we are endowed with social sympathy. All that we get in the rational direction of our life, possibly, is an enlargement of the social sympathy which nature has given us so that we may recognize and make a place for the vital capacities of more and more people of the whole of society.

That is a very rough sketch of the way that empirical people use the

From *Education Adequate for Modern Times*, New York, 1931, pp. 54-66. Reprinted by permission of the publishers, Association Press.

scientific method to arrive at their conception of the good. I see no way
for any modern, intelligent man to depart from the empirical and rational
method. Certainly we cannot go back to some absolute standard or code
of an earlier generation. It is the tragedy of history that each generation
has tried to live its life by a tradition fashioned by a previous generation—a
pattern which probably was not completely true when the generation fashioned it, and which has become less true by shifting circumstance. And
in America today, this industrial America with its vast intricacies and in-
terdependencies, we are trying to govern ourselves by the political and
ethical standards which our pioneer forefathers created. It is a tragedy
of history. I am saying that we are not going back, any of us who count
ourselves modern or intelligent or scientific or empirical, to some absolute
and obsolete standard or code. Empirically we are going about our problems of conduct and behavior. We are going to say, What fulfills vital
capacity? What fulfills all vital capacities—my own and those of my fellow
men?

If we are going to be as empirical as that, what can religion add to the
solution of our moral problem; and more specifically, the Christian religion? I will put my solution briefly: religion adds a touch of madness,
precisely that touch of madness which, when combined with common
sense, produces a compound of wisdom. Without the touch of madness
all ethical life governed by reason sinks deeply into common sense and therefore it degenerates more and more into an enlightened self-interest, a prudent
selfishness.

What is this touch of madness that is added by religion, that Jesus adds,
for instance, to the ethical solution of our problems? It is religion's search
for the absolute, and in the case of the Christian religion, the insistence that
the absolute can be defined in terms of these highest ethical values which
empirically we have discovered in life. Religion does not create a new
moral standard nor does it superimpose one on a rational man or on a
natural man; it takes the social sympathy which is in man, which is en-
larged by reason; it takes that moral standard which is more completely adequate to our whole social situation and it declares that this standard must
be perfected in the direction of an absolute ideal. It searches for the
absolute; it looks upon the contemporary and specific situation from the
perspective of an absolute which it has defined in terms of the highest
moral ideals which humanity has achieved.

It is this absolute reference in religion which gives it the touch of absurdity, but which also puts a kind of sublime madness into its ethic.
Religion cannot be a resource for you if you are so completely empirical
that you are unwilling to look for any pattern behind the flux of circumstance. It is religion's inveterate habit, vice, and genius to look for
the absolute, the transcendent, behind and above the flux of circumstance.
And what makes it still more absurd is religion's tendency to define this
absolute, which is the basis for existence, in terms of the ideal toward which
existence is striving.

I say there is a touch of absurdity in that because you cannot define the ideal except in terms taken out of human life, and to read these ethical terms into cosmic reality has something absurd in it. And yet, since that only is real or since that is most real which is potential, it is not altogether unreasonable to define the basis of reality in the terms of the ideal toward which reality is moving.

Now let us see how Jesus does that, how he builds his metaphysic upon the ethic and the ethic upon the metaphysic. It is a curious circular reasoning that is the central absurdity of religion and at the same time sublime wisdom. Jesus says that we ought to love one another because God loves. Therefore, love your enemies that you may be children of your Father in heaven, for he maketh his sun to shine upon the evil and the good and he sendeth his rain upon the just and the unjust. I don't know whether we have elsewhere in the gospel a more perfect example of religious imagination than exists in that statement. Jesus takes the highest ethical value that has been revealed in human life. He reads it into the heart of God and then he makes the impartiality of nature substantiate it.

Nature cannot possibly be interpreted as being just. Any world of nature which sendeth its rain upon the just and the unjust and maketh its sun to shine upon the evil and the good is not a just nature. But perhaps we may claim that this nature gives us just a glimpse of the idea of love, if not of justice; for it is nature's genius not to be exacting in its rewards and punishment. And Jesus, by this kind of imagination, declares that God loves, that we ought to love as God does, and that God's love is revealed in that world of nature which seems to be inimical to the highest values of man.

On the other hand, Jesus puts it the other way around. He builds his ethical idea on his metaphysics, but again he builds his metaphysics upon his ethics. He suggests we ought to believe in God's love as it has been revealed in human life. "If you, being evil, know how to give good gifts unto your children, how much more will your Father in heaven give good gifts unto you who ask?" A high ethical value is here revealed. Isn't it logical, says Jesus, to assume that there is somewhere in the heart of reality a potentiality, love, which is greater than what has been revealed in your life? There you have your metaphysical assumption based upon ethical achievement.

It is because you have this absolute reference in the religion of Jesus, this suggestion that there is an absolute ideal toward which we are striving and that this ideal is love, that you get a touch of absurdity and madness which has the root of wisdom in it in every specific moral standard that Jesus suggests. The reason that we have not taken these standards seriously is because, from the perspective of any given situation, they seem too absurd to be taken seriously; yet, if we do not take them seriously we will find that in every case our ethic will degenerate into common sense, into the kind of common sense which glorifies self-interest.

Let us look at some of these suggestions of an absolute love ethic as we find it in the Sermon on the Mount. "Resist not evil. If a man smite thee on the cheek, turn to him the other also." Now that is absurd. Jesus is saying that if a man is evil, we ought to be so good that our goodness will finally redeem him, that we ought not to resist his selfishness. From the perspective of any specific problem, that is absurd—because if we do not resist selfishness it will expand indefinitely. We will probably need more social restraints, rather than less, in the years to come. In the kind of world in which we live, men are not imaginative enough and disciplined enough to restrict their expansive desires either by rational or religious discipline and probably they will have to be restricted, more and more.

But while this may be absurd when you deal with a relative situation, isn't it a fact that resistance against evil never changes the evil heart and that in an ultimate sense Jesus is absolutely right? If you resist evil, the evil man has excellent reason to assume that your resistance is not due to a high interest in virtue but to your own selfishness; he assumes that you are setting your selfishness against his. We stand for our rights against somebody else's rights and we say, It is not that I care for myself; it is the principle of the thing. Well, the person who sees you righteously standing for the principle of the thing is just shrewd enough to guess how selfish you really are. Consider the hypocrisies of the nations in the period preceding the World War; they were doing exactly that kind of thing all the time—standing for "principles" and at the same time trying to grab everything within reach.

In an ultimate and final sense Jesus is right. You cannot overcome evil by setting yourself against it. The only real possibility of change of heart in the expansive ego is for goodness to challenge selfishness, and while this ideal may be impossible of achievement in any given situation, anything less than the ideal is, in an ultimate sense, inadequate. In other words, we have here an ideal which leaves us dissatisfied with any particular achievement of ours in the ethical field. We may try to restrain our own selfishness in the hope that our life in some sense may be redemptive, but never can we be sure that we have done it as completely as we might; that had we gone farther we would not have accomplished more.

Take the whole series of suggestions in the Sermon on the Mount, in which Jesus suggested we ought to trust other people absolutely. If they ask us to go a mile we shall go twain. If they ask us for our cloak we shall give our coat also. In each case we shall do more than they ask on the assumption that these people are trustworthy at heart and if we act toward them as if they were they will become more completely trustworthy; that if we are absolutely free with our rights and with our privileges, other people will protect them; or, if they be not protected we will have to count that as a sacrifice for the sake of the ultimate ideal. Here again you have the absurd ideal coming from the assumption that love is an absolute written into the heart of the universe—an ideal which does not work out in each situation from the perspective of a common-sense man and which, at the same time, has all the creative and redemptive power of true moral life in it.

What shall I think of my fellow man? Shall I really trust him? Potentially he is my enemy and I should fear him. If I fear him he will become my enemy more than he is; if I trust him he may violate my trust, but there is just a possibility that to trust him will mean that that which is trustworthy in him will be discovered, revealed, and created.

One reason Jesus can go so far in this absolute love ethic is because there is always another assumption in his approach, not alone the assumption that the ideal of love is real but also that the real man is to a certain extent ideal; that this man, living by the impulses of nature, is to a certain extent a child of God, that his potentialities are infinite beyond anything that he now reveals, that we shall deal with human beings, not as they are, but as they might be and as they are becoming if we believe that they might be that.

The religious approach to personality, therefore, is always this approach of hope and of faith. There is always hope and faith in true love. When we love people we love them not altogether for what they are but for what they are becoming. That is the language of hope and faith as it expresses itself in love. When we deal scientifically with a situation we describe it as it is. When we deal religiously with a situation, we describe it as it ought to be and may be becoming, for the ideal is always implicit in the real.

H. N. Brailsford, in a recent article about India, made this interesting suggestion: "The psychology of conflict exists between India and England. As hatred and fear continue between these two groups—the one that holds power and the one that seeks to destroy this power—the more difficult does it become to arrive at any kind of a solution which will protect the highest values which have been created in the British Empire."

And Brailsford says, further: "If the British people could be imaginative enough to say to the Indian people, We are going to get out of India absolutely; we are not going to have a string attached to any one of your policies; we will get out and then we will say to you, If you want us for anything, if there has been any good in our Empire, if we have made any contribution to your life so that co-operation with us is good for you, if you want us for anything, call upon us and we will go as far as you want us to go—I am convinced the Indian people would ask them for more than the British people will ever be able to get in the way of control when they fight for a place in India."

Don't you think that is true? Doesn't there seem to be real wisdom in that statement? And yet, in spite of the fact that the British people are politically the most imaginative people on the face of the earth, you know they are not going to follow that advice. Common sense will prevent; there is not enough madness in their ethic to make that kind of action possible. But if with their common sense a religious imagination were completely fused they might actually rise to the height of ultimate political wisdom. Yes, the ethics of Jesus are absurd, but in them is the root of wisdom. In any specific situation you can prove they cannot be for your good; yet they are the ultimate good.

Jesus drives this matter a little farther when he says that we must love our enemies and forgive not seven times but seventy times seven. Here Jesus is insisting that not only shall we trust people before they have revealed their capacity for trustworthy action but we shall trust people even after they have shown themselves to be untrustworthy and after they have committed evil against us.

That also is an absurd idea. Psychologically it is impossible to love your enemies, and it may not be just to do so. We are more likely to act on the advice of Confucius to a disciple: "Master, shall we forgive our enemies?" "No," replied Confucius, "that would be unjust to our friends; let us love our friends and be just to our enemies."

What could be more reasonable than that? That is a perfectly rational ethic and no reason will ever carry you beyond it. The only thing that will carry you beyond it is the madness of religion. It is a significant thing that this highly sophisticated, rationalistic, ethical idea of Confucius should be put in just that way in regard to the teaching of Jesus that we shall love our enemies, for if we actually have imagination great enough to look behind the evil that the enemy has committed, to challenge the good that is in him against the immediate evidence to the contrary, forgiving perhaps seventy times seven, we will, of course, finally prove our absurd action to be wise; for the trust, the love and the forgiveness that we show is the creative reality which helps to produce in the heart of the enemy that which we had assumed to be there.

The reason love always justifies itself in the end is because it is not dealing with a static world. It is dealing with a dynamic world and it is itself helping to create that world. Therefore the suggestion of Jesus goes outside of the group. "If ye love those that love you, what thanks have you? Do not even the publicans and sinners also?" Here we have the absurd suggestion that we ought to do violence to our natural parental impulses, let us say. Nature has gathered us together in little groups and has given us a natural affection for the child, for the brother and the sister and the father and the mother. Shall we do violence to these natural impulses of nature? Ought we not to thank God that in one place in life, at least nature supports the ideal values? Yet Jesus suggests that we should be critical of these narrow loyalties and of these restricted sympathies; that until we can extend our sympathy and our imaginative insight into the lives of other people, beyond the barriers of race and class and family, we have not revealed any real spiritual qualities. Do not publicans and sinners also? It is the impulse of nature to love those who love you. But you must go beyond that, and none can say, for another man, just how far the other shall go. Those who do attempt to point the way for others are headed toward an asceticism—and incidentally religion in its most sensitive moments always produces a certain amount of asceticism. I am not sure that asceticism is a virtue; I think it is a vice—but I think it is a suggestion in the direction of virtue, for you cannot have ripe apples on a tree without having a few that are over-ripe. When religion is very sensitive to the problems of life, it will produce a certain amount of over-ripeness, expressed in asceticism.

What the ascetics are telling us is that every loyalty, loyalty to the family, loyalty to the group, is, from the view of the ultimate needs of society, an evil. But is that finally as absurd as at first it seems to be? Isn't it a fact that most of us are anti-social in conduct, not purely because we are selfish, but because we are selfish for our group? We hide our selfishness behind our unselfishness; it is because we seek advantages for our children, for our family, for our race or our nation, for our class, that we are as selfish as we are, and it is for that reason that Jesus' terrible strictures against the family are in an ultimate sense justified: "Who serves father and mother more than me is not worthy of me." You have here, again, an insistence that the love ideal must be made absolute and universal against the forces of history and against the impulses of nature, a suggestion which, if followed to the ultimate conclusion, will issue in an unnatural life—but suggestion, nevertheless, which is continually necessary to save you from the group selfishness which common sense creates.

Jesus said to the rich young man, "Sell all thou hast and give to the poor." Again and again you have in the gospel a critical attitude toward the acquisitive instinct; partly because the acquisitive *per se* is regarded as not attaining the highest spiritual values and partly because Jesus recognized that privilege is always a bar to fellowship and love. If I have things that my fellow man does not possess he will not love me perfectly for he will envy me, and I shall not love him perfectly for I shall hold him in contempt. I have a certain amount of pride as I look down upon him, whether it is privilege or power I now have. If I cannot bring myself into terms of equality with him my love will not be perfect. I shall pity him, perhaps, and think that is love. Pity, however, is simply a compound of contempt and love.

Jesus recognized that fact and so he insisted that if we really want to love our fellow men we must tear down the wall of privilege which separates us from them. But again, if we are going to do that absolutely, we will become ascetic. The only way it can be done in this kind of a world is in ascetic terms; but the absolute reference can save us from being balked by our privileges, and it will help us reduce them to the lowest possible minimum.

Can any of our privileges really be justified except those physical privileges upon which our spiritual values rest? It is a paradox and a tragedy of history that spiritual values do rest upon privileges. The times to pray, to paint, to think—each comes out of physical privilege, and most of us will say, for that reason, that we are not going to drive ruthlessly toward an equalitarian society if it means that the cultural values are going to be destroyed; yet most of us hold privilege beyond the needs of culture and some of us probably should be asking ourselves whether our cultural privileges should not be reduced for the sake of those who have not the bare necessities of life.

If you do not believe that this fanaticism, this touch of madness, is necessary to produce an ethical relationship between man and man, may I ask what are you doing, and what am I doing, to aid the plight of the unemployed? Have we, by reason, by social insight, come to ethical terms with the people who are out of work? Five hundred thousand people in the city of Detroit are living insecure lives because they are partially employed or totally unemployed.

How much have we restricted our incomes in terms of the bitter social need of our day? Can you give any rational solution for the problem of how much we should restrict our income? One person may say, "I will give a third of what I earn for the sake of providing some kind of security for these vast millions." But in New York is a widow about whom I read in the *New York Times* the other day, who had barely enough to live; when a mother in the tenement next to hers died and left four children the widow took the four children in and went back to work as a scrubwoman in order to provide for their needs. What do you think about that action? Was it rational? I wouldn't have done it. Nothing that I have done will equal what that widow has done. There is a touch of madness in what she did, and yet by her action I feel the race of mankind has been ennobled. She has approached the absolute standard of love in the way that all we rational and common-sense people have not approached it.

Jesus finally puts together in a great challenge all of his suggestions about the ethical life: "Be ye therefore perfect even as your Father in heaven is perfect." I ask you what is more absurd than that?—to suggest that these puny little ants, living on this little planet, shall in some way approximate an ultimate standard of morality, shall lift themselves above themselves and be like God! Here in one phrase is stated the central absurdity in the sublime wisdom of religion, for man lives in this world with moral ideas conditioned by time, circumstance, and place. Man is an animal in time and place, yet man is an animal seeking for the absolute and he transcends time and place to a certain degree because he is searching for the absolute. In the gospel story you remember that Jesus said to his disciple, "We are going to Jerusalem. It needs has come to pass that the Son of Man shall suffer many things." He looked forward to the Cross. "Lord," said Peter, "let not that happen unto thee." And Jesus, replying, said, "Peter, you think like a man and not like God."

How can we think like God? Will the time come when every real science, every real history, every honest thought that we put into life, will be an effort to think like God and not like man? We are trying in all our philosophies, in our science and our religion to lift ourselves above the prejudices of our day and the inclinations that are inherent in the impulses of nature. Anything like God prompts man to seek some absolute perspective from which to judge himself and to hold in check the impulses of nature.

That seems to me to be the emphasis put by religion into empirical ethics to save the generation which acts only by common sense. What have we as an alternative to the madness of religion? We have the ethical standards of the conventional church and of the conventional world—a hodge-podge of Biblical standards plus a conglomeration of historical standards read back into the Bible. That is what makes religion dangerous; it takes the relativities of time and place and reads them into the absolute.

There is only one standard that has any business being read into the heart of God, and that is this ultimate standard of love. As another alternative you have the ethics of the modern church—but the modern church of the nineteenth century is inclined to think of the ethics of duty. It is the church that tells its faithful that they must be true to their own highest insights, that they must perform their duty, that they must have pure motives, that whatever their convictions upon any subject, so long as they honestly follow their convictions they will be Christian.

Such creeds make honest men but do not make Christians; people are not imaginative enough to know where their duty lies. Except they are constantly inspired by the resources that come out of the imagination of religion and the experience of life, they will be true to their duty but their duty will be a conception of less than the best.

Your extreme modern church and your school have the absolute empirical answer to your problem. And their answer is not duty. They are saying: "We are looking at the contemporary world and at the immediate situation and are asking ourselves what is the right thing to do. We will discover that reason-guided conduct can arrive at virtue." But a glance into history will reveal that this empiricism, which has some high values in it, never did get beyond enlightened self-interest in the past and is not getting beyond it today.

When you are prudentially selfish usually you are more selfish than prudent—or perhaps you are selfish because you are prudent. One reason why this is so is that the love ethic, which always is wise and rational in retrospect, is never quite wise and rational in prospect.

I have a relation of power, let me say, to my fellow man and if I am altogether wise I will say that I will sacrifice my power for the sake of having a more organic relationship to my fellow man. I will lose myself, then, only to find myself in a larger way. If I would be altogether wise I could do that, but the fact is that this higher self that I find as I lose my immediate self is discovered only after I have lost my immediate self. The thing is always rational as I look back on it. I make a sacrifice of immediate advantage and I gain a more ultimate advantage, but I can never quite gain the ultimate advantage if I focus my eye only upon the ultimate advantage. The fact is, sometimes the ultimate advantage does not reveal itself until the deed has been committed. That is why a prudent selfishness never gets to the heart of the moral problem.

It seems to me that there is no way out except to be empirical, but finally to have a standard which will put content into the ultimate standard. Be as empirical as you want in regard to the details of specific moral problems, but if you keep on pushing the problem back with questions— What is that good for? What it that good for?—you come to the ultimate question, What is the ultimate good? It must be something in the heart of reality itself, something in the direction of which the whole of the world is striving.

Now what Christianity does—at least the religion of Jesus as you and I have been uncritically identifying Christianity and the religion of Jesus today—is to interpret the ultimate good in terms of love and to press the ideal of love until it becomes absurd from the perspective of any immediate situation but wise in terms of the total problem.

RELIGION VERSUS THE RELIGIOUS

John Dewey

THE HEART of my point, as far as I shall develop it in this first section, is that there is a difference between religion, *a* religion, and the religious; between anything that may be denoted by a noun substantive and the quality of experience that is designated by an adjective. It is not easy to find a definition of religion in the substantive sense that wins general acceptance. However, in the *Oxford Dictionary* I find the following: "Recognition on the part of man of some unseen higher power as having control of his destiny and as being entitled to obedience, reverence and worship." . . . .

I can illustrate what I mean by a common phenomenon in contemporary life. It is widely supposed that a person who does not accept any religion is thereby shown to be a non-religious person. Yet it is conceivable that the present depression in religion is closely connected with the fact that religions now prevent, because of their weight of historic encumbrances, the religious quality of experience from coming to consciousness and finding the expression that is appropriate to present conditions, intellectual and moral. I believe that such is the case. I believe that many persons are so repelled from what exists as a religion by its intellectual and moral implications, that they are not even aware of attitudes in themselves that if they came to fruition would be genuinely religious. I hope that this remark may help make clear what I mean by the distinction between "religion" as a noun substantive and "religious" as adjectival.

To be somewhat more explicit, a religion (and as I have just said there is no such thing as religion in general) always signifies a special body of beliefs and practices having some kind of institutional organization, loose or tight. In contrast, the adjective "religious" denotes nothing in the way of a specifiable entity, either institutional or as a system of beliefs. It does not denote anything to which one can specifically point as one can point to this and that historic religion or existing church. For it does not denote anything that can exist by itself or that can be organized into a particular and distinctive form of existence. It denotes attitudes that may be taken toward every object and every proposed end or ideal. . . . .

Those who hold to the notion that there is a definite kind of experience which is itself religious, by that very fact make out of it something specific, as a kind of experience that is marked off from experience as aesthetic, scientific, moral, political; from experience as companionship and friendship. But "religious" as a quality of experience signifies something that may belong to all these experiences. It is the polar opposite of some type of experience that can exist by itself. The distinction comes out clearly

From *A Common Faith*, New Haven, 1934, pp. 3-87. Reprinted by permission of the publishers, Yale University Press.

when it is noted that the concept of this distinct kind of experience is used to validate a belief in some special kind of object and also to justify some special kind of practice. . . . .

The difference between an experience having a religious force because of what it does in and to the processes of living and religious experience as a separate kind of thing gives me occasion to refer to a previous remark. If this function were rescued through emancipation from dependence upon specific types of beliefs and practices, from those elements that constitute a religion, many individuals would find that experiences having the force of bringing about a better, deeper and enduring adjustment in life are not so rare and infrequent as they are commonly supposed to be. They occur frequently in connection with many significant moments of living. The idea of invisible powers would take on the meaning of all the conditions of nature and human association that support and deepen the sense of values which carry one through periods of darkness and despair to such an extent that they lose their usual depressive character. . . . .

Let us then for the moment drop the term "religious," and ask what are the attitudes that lend deep and enduring support to the processes of living. I have, for example, used the words "adjustment" and "orientation." What do they signify?

While the words "accommodation," "adaptation," and "adjustment" are frequently employed as synonyms, attitudes exist that are so different that for the sake of clear thought they should be discriminated. There are conditions we meet that cannot be changed. If they are particular and limited, we modify our own particular attitudes in accordance with them. Thus we accommodate ourselves to changes in weather, to alterations in income when we have no other resource. When the external conditions are lasting we become inured, habituated, or, as the process is now often called, conditioned. The two main traits of this attitude, which I should like to call accommodation, are that it affects *particular* modes of conduct, not the entire self, and that the process is mainly *passive*. It may, however, become general and then it becomes fatalistic resignation or submission. There are other attitudes toward the environment that are also particular but that are more active. We re-act against conditions and endeavor to change them to meet our wants and demands. . . . .

Faith and Its Object

The idea that "God" represents a unification of ideal values that is essentially imaginative in origin when the imagination supervenes in conduct is attended with verbal difficulties owing to our frequent use of the word "imagination" to denote fantasy and doubtful reality. But the reality of ideal ends as ideals is vouched for by their undeniable power in action. An ideal is not an illusion because imagination is the organ through which it is apprehended. For *all* possibilities reach us through the imagination. In a definite sense the only meaning that can be assigned the term "imagination" is that things unrealized in fact come home to us and have power to stir us. . . . .

The aims and ideals that move us are generated through imagination. But they are not made out of imaginary stuff. They are made out of the hard stuff of the world of physical and social experience. The locomotive did not exist before Stevenson, nor the telegraph before the time of Morse. But the conditions for their existence were there in physical material and energies and in human capacity. Imagination seized hold upon the idea of a rearrangement of existing things that would evolve new objects. The same thing is true of a painter, a musician, a poet, a philanthropist, a moral prophet. The new vision does not arise out of nothing, but emerges through seeing, in terms of possibilities, that is, of imagination, old things in new relations serving a new end which the new end aids in creating. . . . .

Interaction between aim and existent conditions improves and tests the ideal; and conditions are at the same time modified. Ideals change as they are applied in existent conditions. The process endures and advances with the life of humanity. What one person and one group accomplish becomes the standing ground and starting point of those who succeed them. . . . .

These considerations may be applied to the idea of God, or, to avoid misleading conceptions, to the idea of the divine. This idea is, as I have said, one of ideal possibilities unified through imaginative realization and projection. But this idea of God, or of the divine, is also connected with all the natural forces and conditions—including man and human association—that promote the growth of the ideal and that further its realization. We are in the presence neither of ideals completely embodied in existence nor yet of ideals that are mere rootless ideals, fantasies, utopias. For there are forces in nature and society that generate and support the ideals. They are further unified by the action that gives them coherence and solidity. It is this *active* relation between ideal and actual to which I would give the name "God." . . . .

The Human Abode

The individual believer may indeed carry the disposition and motivation he has acquired through affiliation with a religious organization into his political action, into his connection with schools, even into his business and amusements. But there remain two facts that constitute a revolution. In the first place, conditions are such that this action is a matter of personal choice and resolution on the part of individuals, not of the very nature of social organization. In the second place, the very fact that an individual imports or carries his personal attitude into affairs that are inherently secular, that are outside the scope of religion, constitutes an enormous change, in spite of the belief that secular matters *should* be permeated by the spirit of religion. Even if it be asserted, as it is by some religionists, that all the new movements and interests of any value grew up under the auspices of a church and received their impetus from the same source, it must be admitted that once the vessels have been launched, they are sailing on strange seas to far lands.

Here, it seems to me, is the issue to be faced. Here is the place where the distinction that I have drawn between a religion and the religious function is peculiarly applicable. It is of the nature of a religion based on the supernatural to draw a line between the religious and the secular and profane, even when it asserts the rightful authority of the Church and its religion to dominate these other interests. The conception that "religious" signifies a certain attitude and outlook, independent of the supernatural, necessitates no such division. It does not shut religious values up within a particular compartment, nor assume that a particular form of association bears a unique relation to it. Upon the social side the future of the religious function seems pre-eminently bound up with its emancipation from religions and a particular religion. Many persons feel perplexed because of the multiplicity of churches and the conflict of their claims. But the fundamental difficulty goes deeper.

In what has been said I have not ignored the interpretation put, by representatives of religious organizations, upon the historic change that has occurred. The oldest organization, the Roman Catholic church, judges the secularization of life, the growing independence of social interests and values from control by the church, as but one evidence the more of the apostasy of the natural man from God: the corruption inherent in the will of mankind has resulted in defiance of the authority that God has delegated to his designated representatives on earth. This church points to the fact that secularization has proceeded *pari passu* with the extension of Protestantism as evidence of the wilful heresy of the latter in its appeal to private conscience and choice. The remedy is simple. Submission to the will of God, as continuously expressed through the organization that is his established vicegerent on earth, is the sole means by which social relations and values can again become coextensive with religion.

Protestant churches, on the contrary, have emphasized the fact that the relation of man to God is primarily an individual matter, a matter of personal choice and responsibility. From this point of view, one aspect of the change outlined marks an advance that is religious as well as moral. For according to it, the beliefs and rites that tend to make relation of man to God a collective and institutional affair erect barriers between the human soul and the divine spirit. Communion with God must be initiated by the individual's heart and will through direct divine assistance. Hence the change that has occurred in the social status of organized religion is nothing to deplore. What has been lost was at best specious and external. What has been gained is that religion has been placed upon its only real and solid foundation: direct relationship of conscience and will of God. Although there is much that is non-Christian and anti-Christian in existing economic and political institutions, it is better that change be accomplished by the sum total of efforts of men and women who are imbued with personal faith, than that they be effected by any wholesale institutional effort that subordinates the individual to an external and ultimately a worldly authority.

NATURAL AND REVEALED RELIGION

Paul Tillich

NATURAL RELIGION is a religion which belongs to man by nature. The contrasting concept is "revealed religion" which man receives from a supernatural reality. "Supernatural" in this connection is not human mind or human reason, for they belong to man's natural equipment. The supernatural reality transcends human nature in *every* direction, man's body as well as his mind, his vitality as well as his reason. Natural religion is the necessary consequence of human nature. Supernatural religion is not the consequence of human nature in any way; it transcends human nature entirely; it is entirely contingent from the point of view of human nature. In revealed religion human nature is exclusively receptive, not productive at all.

In natural religion human nature alone is productive. Human nature is characterized by human reason, that is, by the power of man to have a meaningful world and a meaningful self, namely, a world which is built up by understandable categories, laws, and concepts and a self which has these categories and laws as the categories and laws of its own mind. Consequently natural religion is a religion which develops with the natural development of human mind or with the natural development of reason. Natural religion can have a very low degree corresponding to a very low stage of the development of reason, and it can have a very high degree when reason has developed to a high stage. The highest degree in principle is reached when reason understands itself as reason, when it explains itself consciously, and purifies itself from all the remnants of imagination, feeling, passion and mere belief. On this level natural religion becomes rational religion and expresses itself in a rational doctrine of God, in a so-called "natural theology." . . . .

Natural theology presupposes that the contents of religion are to be found in human reason, consequently that the development of human reason is at the same time the development of religion; that God is manifest for man within the historical process of religions. It makes no difference from our point of view whether this process has the character of a continuous progress or whether the highest religion is to be sought in the past or whether there are different types of religion each one of which is perfect in itself. In each of these interpretations human nature is decisive for the development of religion; and there is nothing in it but human nature, because human nature in having a world and a self implies having God. . . . .

I

It is understandable that with respect to this situation, transcendentalism,

Reprinted by permission from *Christendom*, Autumn, 1935.

represented by Karl Barth, has attacked not only the pure natural theology without any theology of revelation, but also every theology of revelation which keeps a natural theology as substructure. The history of theology has shown—this is his argument—that the theology of revelation is lost at the moment when it presupposes a natural theology. For if man has by his nature a God who is really God, he does not need revelation. But he needs revelation because he is separated from God. Therefore human nature only can produce imagination of a demonic character and the corresponding attitude of fear and superstition—as every natural religion in the interpretation of Barth does. Natural religion has demons, not God. Therefore theology is not allowed to use it as a substructure for the theology of revelation.

Natural theology—this is the basic point of view of Barth and the whole dialectical theology—gives man the power of determining to a certain extent his relation to God. Man's relation to God in this way is dependent to a certain extent on man's intellectual or moral activity, and that implies the presupposition that God in his relation to man is dependent to a certain extent on man. But a God who depends in any way on man is not God. He is a demon. Natural theology is an attack upon the majesty, the absoluteness of God; it is idolatry. . . . . The God of natural theology is not able to give the religious certainty which is called "forgiveness of sins" or "grace." Since man by nature is in guilt, every one of his activities, every one of his thoughts, has an element of guilt in itself. And it is a contradiction in terms to assume that guilty thinking and guilty acting can overcome guilt. Guilt cannot be conquered by guilt and that means it cannot be conquered by human nature which is perverted by guilt. So from every point of view natural theology is to be denied. It is idolatry, because it makes God dependent on man; it destroys religious certainty, because it makes our knowledge of God dependent on man's fallacious insight, it destroys the certainty of salvation, because it makes grace dependent on our guilty activities. God can be known only by God himself, that is, by revelation. God's perfection can be reached only by God himself, that is, by salvation. And both revelation and salvation transcend human nature entirely. They are matters of faith and not of self-development; they presuppose that man is gripped by a transcendent power and thrown upon something beyond himself and all the possibilities of his nature.

In defending itself against this attack which is launched by Karl Barth with a really prophetic force, natural theology emphasizes that revelation presupposes that character of man which is called in the old tradition: "the image of God." If man is the image of God he must be able to have some idea of God in having an idea of himself and of his world. . . . .

Barth replies to this argument that the similarity with God is an eschatological concept, that it is a commandment rather than an experience; that sin makes it impossible for us to derive anything from our similarity to God and from the idea of creation in general. Man in the stage of innocence perhaps could have a natural relation to God. The world in its genuine stage of creation could give an idea of God. But this possibility never can become reality because the stage of innocence and genuine creation has been lost and we do not know anything about it. Therefore it is impossible to derive any laws of natural justice, of politics and social order, from the doctrine of creation. We do not know a divine order of social life; neither nation nor family nor classless society, neither feudalism nor democracy, neither liberalism nor collectivism are orders of creation. They are human possibilities, and no natural theology is able to give them the validity of divine commandment. And in the same way no natural theology is able to give the validity of divine truth to any philosophy or world-view including every philosophy of religion. From this point of view the philosophy of religion is challenged in general by Karl Barth. Philosophy of religion, if it is more than a description of historical and psychological facts, is natural theology and is impossible for the same reason that natural theology is impossible.

Natural theology in its defense presents another argument. It points to the problem of receiving revelation. How is it possible that revelation is received by man if it transcends man entirely? In the first place: Why is man alone capable of receiving a revelation, why not animals? Does not this faculty of man imply a certain capacity for the knowledge of God? Is not man nearer to God by nature if his nature makes revelation possible? . . . .

Natural theology defends itself by indicating the fact that revelation must be received by the human mind if it is to be a revelation to *man*. Consequently the human mind must have an element of identity with the truth which is communicated by revelation. Mind cannot receive a content which is entirely strange to it. . . . .

Barth replies that man can receive revelation only in so far as he has become a new creature; revelation occurs in the human mind beyond human mind, in human history beyond human history. Not the old creature but the new creature, not human nature but a reality beyond human nature, receives revelation. The Holy Spirit creates a new spirit in man, and he beareth witness to this new spirit. . . . .
ence. . . . .

II

Since the tool of revelation is human language, and since language is meaningful only through the common experience which is incorporated in it, revelation is not possible without the preceding religious experience of mankind in past, present and future. Revelation is more than religious experience. It is the divine criticism and transformation of religious experience. But the material of revelation, the matter so to speak which receives a new transcendent form by revelation, is religious experience. Without the historical process of religion there would not have been the event of revelation, nor the prophetic criticism and transformation of a pagan tribe religion into the people of God and the church of Christ. . . . .

But now we have to ask, How can we explain this problem today? Is it allowable for us to go back to the old formulas in which on the substructure of a natural theology a superstructure of theology of revelation arises? I do not think so. . . . .

First of all, we have to reject the category "natural" itself in this connection. Not nature, but history of man, is the place in which revelation as well as religious experience occur. . . . . Human existence, activity, development, history are the consequences of human essence, of the necessity of man's nature. Human religious existence, the whole history of religion, flows out of the necessity of man's religious nature. Therefore there is no more content in human history actually than there is in human nature potentially; there is no more religious content in the history of religion than there is in man's religious nature; history does not produce new contents, there is no such thing as freedom to transcend human nature, there is no freedom to contradict oneself and one's own nature.

But it is just this freedom which makes man man, and it is this which is the basis of his history. Man's existence is not determined by man's essence; man's history is not determined by man's nature. History cannot be understood from the point of view of natural necessity. Since freedom is the special quality of human nature, man can produce an existence which transcends his essence: he can produce history. For the problem of natural religion, this means that there is no religion by nature, but by history; that there is no natural theology and no supernatural theology. There is only *one* theology—it is a theology which interprets human religious experience by revelation as criticism and transformation of human religious experience. . . . .

III

I know that this idea is not without danger and that it can be distorted by the interpretation that history of religion in itself is revelation. I want to deny this error emphatically. It is the error of idealism and theological liberalism. It is natural theology, not the theology of historical revelation. Revelation for us, in correlation to us, revelation which grips us and gives us the ultimate criterion for our existence, is confined to one moment. For contrasting revelations are not revelation at all. Revelation for us is exclusive, it gives us the criterion for everything in acting and thinking, and there cannot be another criterion above it or beside it. On the other hand, this moment has meaningful content only because and in so far as the contents of preceding revelations are implied in it. Those preceding revelations are not revelations for us; they are not directly decisive for our existence; they are material presuppositions and effective indirectly as being implied in the actual and decisive revelation.

So, if Christ is revelation for somebody, in the picture of Christ is implied the religion of the Jewish people and the revelation given them in their history; but this history and its document, the Old Testament, is revelation for him only indirectly, it is not criterion itself, it is criticized and transformed by the criterion. And if the prophetic word is revelation for somebody, the priestly religion which is criticized and transformed by the prophetic word is implied in this revelation, but not as revelation, only as material of revelation. And if the message of Paul is revelation for somebody, the mysticism and the morals of the surrounding world are implied, but as criticized and transformed. . . . .

Man in history never is without revelation and he never is without questioning for revelation. The latter implies that man never can boast that he has the God who is really God; the former implies that man never is left by God and separated from him; and both imply that there is no natural relation to God which could be developed in history and which could be derived from human reason. Every doctrine of God is theology of historical revelation in so far as it is rooted in a revelation received in history. Every doctrine of God presupposes faith; for faith is correlated to revelation. Natural theology without preceding faith is nonsense, while natural theology which has the foundation in faith and revelation is not natural theology at all but theology of historical revelation, the only theology which is possible. . . . .

Thus we replace the mechanistic scheme of natural substructure and supernatural superstructure by a living interdependence between question and answer, answer and question. Natural theology must be denied, but its intention can be saved. I try to save its intention through explaining a theology of historical revelation in which nature is replaced by history, essential necessity by existential freedom, in which the cleavage between natural and supernatural religion and theology is overcome through the *one* theology which has *two* poles: the question of human existence and the answer of divine revelation.

TWENTY MINUTES OF REALITY

Margaret Prescott Montague

I DO NOT really know how long the insight lasted. I have said, at a rough guess, twenty minutes. It may have been a little shorter time, it may have been a little longer. But at best it was very transitory.

It happened to me about two years ago, on the day when my bed was first pushed out of doors to the open gallery of the hospital. I was recovering from a surgical operation. I had undergone a certain amount of physical pain, and had suffered for a short time the most acute mental depression which it has ever been my misfortune to encounter. I suppose that this depression was due to physical causes, but at the time it seemed to me that somewhere down there under the anaesthetic, in the black abyss of unconsciousness, I had discovered a terrible secret, and the secret was that there was no God; or, if there was one, He was indifferent to all human suffering.

Though I had hardly re-established my normal state of faith, still the first acuteness of that depression had faded, and only a scar of fear was left when, several days later, my bed was first wheeled out to the porch. There other patients took their airing and received their visitors; busy internes and nurses came and went, and one could get a glimpse of the sky, with bare gray branches against it, and of the ground, with here and there a patch of melting snow.

It was an ordinary cloudy March day. I am glad to think that it was. I am glad to remember that there was nothing extraordinary about the weather, nor any unusualness of setting—no flush of spring or beauty of scenery—to induce what I saw. It was, on the contrary, almost a dingy day. The branches were bare and colorless, and the occasional half-melted piles of snow were a forlorn gray rather than white. Colorless little city sparrows flew and chirped in the trees, while human beings, in no way remarkable, passed along the porch.

There was, however, a wind blowing, and if any outside thing intensified the experience it was the blowing of that wind. In every other respect it was an ordinary commonplace day. Yet here, in this everyday setting, and entirely unexpectedly (for I had never dreamed of such a thing), my eyes were opened, and for the first time in all my life I caught a glimpse of the ecstatic beauty of reality.

I cannot now recall whether the revelation came suddenly or gradually; I only remember finding myself in the very midst of those wonderful moments, beholding life for the first time in all its young intoxication of loveliness, in its unspeakable joy, beauty, and importance. I cannot say ex-

Reprinted from *The Atlantic Monthly*, May, 1916, and November, 1932, (as a booklet, New York [E. P. Dutton & Company], 1916) by permission of Margaret Prescott Montague.

actly what the mysterious change was. I saw no new thing, but I saw all the usual things in a miraculous new light—in what I believe is their true light. I saw for the first time how wildly beautiful and joyous, beyond any words of mine to describe, is the whole of life. Every human being moving across that porch, every sparrow that flew, every branch tossing in the wind, was caught in and was a part of the whole mad ecstasy of loveliness, of joy, of importance, of intoxication of life.

It was not that for a few keyed-up moments I *imagined* all existence as beautiful, but that my inner vision was cleared to the truth so that I *saw* the actual loveliness which is always there, but which we so rarely perceive; and I knew that every man, woman, bird, and tree, every living thing before me, was extravagantly beautiful, and extravagantly important. And as I beheld, my heart melted out of me in a rapture of love and delight. A nurse was walking past; the wind caught a strand of her hair and blew it out in a momentary gleam of sunshine, and never in my life before had I seen how beautiful beyond all belief is a woman's hair. Nor had I ever guessed how marvelous it is for a human being to walk. As for the internes in their white suits, I had never realized before the whiteness of white linen; but much more than that, I had never so much as dreamed of the mad beauty of young manhood. A little sparrow chirped and flew to a near-by branch, and I honestly believe that only "the morning stars singing together, and the sons of God shouting for joy" can in the least express the ecstasy of a bird's flight. I cannot express it, but I have seen it.

Once out of all the gray days of my life I have looked into the heart of reality; I have witnessed the truth; I have seen life as it really is—ravishingly, ecstatically, madly beautiful, and filled to overflowing with a wild joy, and a value unspeakable. For those glorified moments I was in love with every living thing before me—trees in the wind, the little birds flying, the nurses, the internes, the people who came and went. There was nothing that was alive that was not a miracle. Just to be alive was in itself a miracle. My very soul flowed out of me in a great joy.

No one can be as happy as I was and not have it show in some way. A stranger passing paused by my bed and said, "What are you lying here all alone looking so happy about?" I made some inadequate response as to the pleasure of being out-of-doors and of getting well. How could I explain all the beauty that I was seeing? How could I say that the gray curtain of unreality had swirled away and that I was seeing into the heart of life? It was not an experience for words. It was an emotion, a rapture of the heart.

Besides all the joy and beauty and that curious sense of importance, there was a wonderful feeling of rhythm as well, only it was somehow just beyond the grasp of my mind. I heard no music, yet there was an exquisite sense of time, as though all life went by to a vast unseen melody. Everything that moved wove out a little thread of rhythm in this tremendous whole. When a bird flew, it did so because somewhere a note had been struck for it to fly on; or else its flying struck the note; or else again the great Will that is Melody willed that it should fly. When people walked, somewhere they beat out a bit of rhythm that was in harmony with the whole great theme.

Then, the extraordinary importance of everything! Every living creature was intensely alive and intensely beautiful, but it was as well of a marvelous value. Whether this value was in itself or a part of the whole, I could not see; but it seemed as though before my very eyes I actually beheld the truth of Christ's saying that not even a sparrow falls to the ground without the knowledge of the Father in Heaven. Yet *what* the importance was, I did not grasp. If my heart could have seen just a little further I should have understood. Even now the tips of my thoughts are forever on the verge of grasping it, forever just missing it. I have a curious halffeeling that somewhere, deep inside of myself, I know very well what this importance is, and have always known; but I cannot get it from the depth of myself into my mind, and thence into words. But whatever it is, the importance seemed to be nearer to beauty and joy than to an anxious morality. I had a feeling that it was in some way different from the importance I had usually attached to life.

It was perhaps as though that great value in every living thing were not so much here and now in ourselves as somewhere else. There is a great significance in every created thing, but the significance is beyond our present grasp. I do not know what it is; I only know that it is there, and that all life is far more valuable than we ever dream of its being. Perhaps the following quotation from Milton may be what I was conscious of:

> "What if Earth
> Be but the shadow of Heaven, and things therein
> Each to other like more than on Earth is thought!"

What if here we are only symbols of ourselves, and our real being is somewhere else—perhaps in the heart of God? Certainly that unspeakable importance had to do with our relationship to the great Whole; but what the relationship was I could not tell. Was it a relationship of love toward us, or only the delight in creation? But it is hardly likely that a glimpse of a cold Creator could have filled me with such an extravagant joy, or so melted the heart within me. For those fleeting, lovely moments I did indeed, and in truth, love my neighbor as myself. Nay, more: of myself I was hardly conscious, while with my neighbor in every form, from windtossed branches and little sparrows flying, up to human beings, I was madly in love. Is it likely that I could have experienced such love if there were not some such emotion at the heart of Reality? If I did not actually see it, it was not that it was not there, but that I did not see quite far enough.

Perhaps this was because I was still somewhat in the grip of that black doubt which I had experienced, and of which I have spoken. I think it was owing to this doubt also that afterwards I had a certain feeling of distrust. I was afraid that all that beauty might be an uncaring joy. As if, though we were indeed intensely important in some unguessed way to the great Reality, our own small individual sorrows were perhaps not of much moment. I am not sure that I actually had this feeling, as it is very difficult, after the lapse of almost two years, to recapture in memory all the emotions of so fleeting and so unusual an experience. If I did, however, I comfort myself, as I have said, with the thought of the intense joy that I experienced. The vision of an uncaring Reality would hardly have melted me to such happiness. That the Creator is a loving Creator I believe with all my heart; but this is belief, not sight. What I saw that day was an unspeakable joy and loveliness, and a value to all life beyond anything that we have knowledge of; while in myself I knew a wilder happiness than I have ever before or since experienced.

Moreover, though there was nothing exactly religious in what I saw, the accounts given by people who have passed through religious conversion or illumination come nearer to describing my emotions than anything else that I have come across. . . . .

Mine was, I think, a sort of accidental clearing of the vision by the rebirth of returning health. I believe that a good many people have experienced the same thing during convalescence. Perhaps this is the way in which we should all view life if we were born into it grown up. As it is, when we first arrive we are so engaged in the tremendous business of cutting teeth, saying words, and taking steps, that we have no time for, and little consciousness of, outside wonders; and by the time we have the leisure for admiration life has lost for us its first freshness. Convalescence is a sort of grown-up rebirth, enabling us to see life with a fresh eye.

Doubtless almost any intense emotion may open our "inward eye" to the beauty of reality. Falling in love appears to do it for some people. The beauties of nature or the exhilaration of artistic creation does it for others. Probably any high experience may momentarily stretch our souls up on tiptoe, so that we catch a glimpse of that marvelous beauty which is always there, but which we are not often tall enough to perceive.

Emerson says, "We are immersed in beauty, but our eyes have no clear vision." I believe that religious conversion more often clears the eyes to this beauty of truth than any other experience; and it is possible that had I not still been somewhat under that black cloud of doubt, I should have seen further than I did. Yet what I did see was very good indeed. . . . .

In what I saw there was nothing seemingly of an ethical nature. There were no new rules of conduct revealed by those twenty minutes. Indeed, it seemed as though beauty and joy were more at the heart of Reality than an overanxious morality. It was a little as though (to transpose the quotation)

> "I had slept and dreamed that life was duty,
> But waked to find that life was beauty."

Perhaps at such times of illumination there is no need to worry over sin, for one is so transported by the beauty of humanity, and so poured out in love toward every human being, that sin becomes almost impossible. . . . . And all the beauty is forever there before us, forever piping to us, and we are forever failing to dance. We could not help but dance if we could see things as they really are. Then we should kiss both hands to Fate and fling our bodies, hearts, minds, and souls into life with a glorious abandonment, an extravagant, delighted loyalty, knowing that our wildest enthusiasm cannot more than brush the hem of the real beauty and joy and wonder that are always there.

This is how, for me, all fear of eternity has been wiped away. I have had a little taste of bliss, and if Heaven can offer this, no eternity will be too long to enjoy the miracle of existence. But that was not the greatest thing that those twenty minutes revealed, and that did most to end all dread of life everlasting. The great thing was the realization that weariness, and boredom, and questions as to the use of it all, belong entirely to unreality. When once we wake to Reality—whether we do so here or have to wait for the next life for it—we shall never be bored, for in Reality there is no such thing.

Chesterton has pointed out the power for endless enjoyment of the same thing which most children possess, and suggested that this is a Godlike capacity; that perhaps to God His creation always presents itself with a freshness of delight; that perhaps the rising of the sun this morning was for Him the same ecstatic event that it was upon the first day of its creation. I think it was the truth of this suggestion that I perceived in those twenty minutes of cleared vision, and realized that in the youth of eternity we shall recapture that Godlike and childhood attribute which the old age and unreality of Time have temporarily snatched from us.

No; I shall have no more fear of eternity. And even if there were no other life, this life here and now, if we could but open our dull eyes to see it in its truth, is lovely enough to require no far-off Heaven for its justification. Heaven, in all its springtide of beauty, is here and now, before our very eyes, surging up to our very feet, lapping against our hearts; but we, alas, know not how to let it in!

Once again, when I was almost recovered, I had another fleeting visitation of this extreme beauty. A friend came into my room dressed for the opera. I had seen her thus a great number of times before, but for a moment I saw her clothed in all that wild beauty of Reality, and, as before, my heart melted with joy at the sight. But this second occasion was even more transitory than the first, and since then I have had no return. Tagore's illumination, he says, lasted for seven or eight days, and Jacob Boehme knew a "Sabbath calm of the soul that lasted for seven days," during which he was, as it were, inwardly surrounded by a divine light. "The triumph that was then in my soul," he says, "I can neither tell nor describe; I can only liken it to a resurrection from the dead."

And this miraculous time was with him for a whole week, while I have only tasted it for those few short minutes! But he was a saint, and had really ascended to the holy hill of the Lord through clean hands and a pure heart, while I was swept there momentarily, and, as it were, by accident, through the rebirth of returning health. But when the inspired ones testify to a great beauty I too can cry, "Yes, I have seen it also! Yes, O Beauty, O Reality, O Mad Joy! I too have seen you face to face!" And though I have never again touched the fullness of that ecstatic vision, I know all created things to be of a beauty and value unspeakable, and I shall not fail to pay homage to all the loveliness with which existence overflows. Nor shall I fear to accord to all of life's experiences, whether sad or gay, as high, as extravagant, and as undismayed a tribute of enthusiasm as I am capable of.

Perhaps some day I shall meet it face to face again. Again the gray veil of unreality will be swirled aside; once more I shall see into Reality. Sometimes still, when the wind is blowing through the trees, or flowers, I have an eery sense that I am almost in touch with it. The veil was very thin in my garden one day last summer. The wind was blowing there, and I knew that all that beauty and wild young ecstasy at the heart of life was rioting with it through the tossing larkspurs and rosepink Canterbury bells, and bowing with the foxgloves; only I just could not see it. But it is there —it is always there—and some day I shall meet it again. The vision will clear, the inner eye open, and again all that mad joy will be upon me. Some day—not yet perhaps—but some day!

GENERAL CHARACTERISTICS OF MYSTICISM AND PROPHETIC RELIGION

Friedrich Heiler

Mysticism is that form of intercourse with God in which the world and self are absolutely denied, in which human personality is dissolved, disappears and is absorbed in the infinite unity of the Godhead. The lofty type of religion, standing at the opposite pole from mysticism, does not come under this definition. It is, therefore, better treated not as a special form of mysticism but as something quite different and independent. A simple, unambiguous description of this type in which its essential nature is clearly outlined is difficult. It is best characterized by the terms used by Söderblom, "prophetic religion" and "religion of revelation" whereby, of course, light is thrown on only one aspect of the problem; by the first term on the activity of the religious vocation, by the second on the peculiarity of the idea of God. Since this type of piety is especially represented by the Old and New Testaments and receives in the Gospel of Jesus its classical form it can also be called simply "biblical" or "evangelical" religion.

Seldom only has mysticism been carried out to its strict logical consequences, as in the Upanishads, in the Vedanta of Sankara, in the Hinayana school of Buddhism, Plotinus, the Areopagite, Eckhart, Tauler, Angelus Silesius, and Molinos. It loses for the most part, under the influence of the prophetic experience or of the popular religion, its non-personal character and takes on a more personal coloring. The Tao mysticism of Lao-tsze, the Hindu Bhakti mysticism (as it appears in the *Bhagavadgîta,* and still more clearly in the Râmânuja, Tulsi Dâs, and the Tamil mystics), the cultural mysticism of the Hellenistic mystery-religions, the mystical piety of Philo the Jew, the Sufist mysticism of Islam, the Christian God-mysticism, show through all the centuries personal warmth and fervor, enthusiastic power and devotion, as opposed to the sobriety, coldness, and monotony of pure mysticism. Nevertheless, even this more personal mysticism in its inner structure is clearly separate from purely prophetic religion and agrees with logical mysticism in the goal of all its efforts after salvation. The structural difference of the two types must be, in the first place, worked out so that the diversity of prophetic and mystical prayer may be better understood. And here also it is necessary to make clear the definite, fundamental religious conceptions which always recur in our exposition of prophetic and mystical prayer, as for example, faith, love, ecstasy, sin, salvation, and so forth. . . . .

1. The Fundamental Psychic Experience in Mysticism

In times when a highly developed civilization is in a state of decay,

From *Prayer*, New York, 1932, chap. vi. Reprinted by permission of the publishers, Oxford University Press.

as in ancient India, the Graeco-Roman world, mediaeval Germany, and France of the sixteenth and seventeenth centuries, the feeling of life and self, the healthy will to live is weakened in gifted and noble-minded persons, and joyous faith in the future, in the concrete values, aims, and tasks of life, collapses. A vehement dislike of the world and civilization seizes them, a burning desire for an infinite Good gives them no rest and violently urges them to free themselves from the world, civilization and society.

The pious man, dissatisfied with the world and its glory feels himself a stranger on the earth, he is conscious that he is dreadfully fettered by the body, he sees in it a wretched prison, a dark grave. The thought of the ancient Orphic play on the Greek word for "body," (sōma-sēma) "body-prison," which Plato has appropriated, runs through the mystical literature of all the Christian centuries. The fettered soul yearns for freedom from the bonds of the physical organism, in order to soar to heavenly heights, to return to the infinite and the divine from which it sprang. It is only through man's inner being that the way to redemption is to be found. This means to tear oneself forcibly from all the ensnaring charms of the outer world, to close the gates of the senses, to turn wholly inwardly, "to withdraw oneself into oneself," as Albertus Magnus puts it, to plunge into the lowest deeps of the soul.

But it does not suffice that the pious man hungering for redemption is freed from the outer world of things, he must rather escape from his own ego, from all selfish wishes and desires. He must stifle the natural psychic impulses which call forth disquietude in man, especially the clamant and importunate tendencies of the will. He must drive out of the soul the creations of the imagination which perpetually rise up out of the depths of the emotional life; nay, he must even be free of concern about and appreciation of all worldly objects. The entire natural life of the soul is consciously and intentionally hemmed in, cut off from the outer world, all vital inner life and endeavor "done away," "brought to rest," "killed"; "the senses must be blinded," "man must sink away from himself and all things," as Suso phrases it.

Thus in the mystic's soul is achieved a great negative process, "a systematic letting die of all the propensities of life." Plato designates this process by the old Orphic term "purification," the neo-Platonists call it "simplification," an expression which passed into the language of the Christian mystics. Eckhart in a remarkable linguistic creation of his own characterizes it as an *Entwerden*, "a ceasing to be"; Suso names it a "ceasing to be a creature"; the Indian, like the western mystics, describes it bluntly as "annihilation," "the becoming nothing." This negative process carries the mystic out of the customary state of mind into a supernormal state of intense concentration, to complete "withdrawal" and "inwardness," to deep peace, blessed quiet and passive "not doing," to complete *abandon*, painless and joyless indifference.

This complete emptying and denudation of the psychic life, this stripping off to the uttermost of everything earthly and human, this introversion or perfect turning in upon oneself is only a preparation for exclusive concentration on the infinite, the divine, the eternal. . . . .

Mystical love is a straining and striving after the Highest but it is not yet its possession; it is only a movement toward the lofty goal but it is not yet the goal itself. Mystical love is perfected in ecstasy, it is, as it were, "the mother of ecstasy," as Dionysius the Areopagite says. But even the chill, non-emotional mysticism to which the glow of mystical passion is quite foreign, knows an exaltation akin to ecstasy, that is, *Nirvana. Ecstasy* and *Nirvana* are two inexpressible mystical secrets. In psychological language both are supernormal states of the soul which presuppose a perfect cessation of the normal conscious life; both occur relatively seldom in mystical experience. Both exhibit an experience of unity and value of such height, purity, and blessedness as would be impossible in the normal life of the soul. But in spite of the similarity of their inner structure they stand at opposite poles from each other. Ecstasy is boiling point, Nirvana is freezing point, ecstasy is a positive height, Nirvana is a negative height (and as "height" something positive); ecstasy is infinite fulness, Nirvana is infinite emptiness. Ecstasy is the highest pitch of emotion. . . . .

The ecstatic experience is for him who has been awakened from ecstasy incomprehensible and indescribable. The ordinary conscious life was broken in upon and therefore the mystic, having returned to this life, is not able to declare and explain what he really experienced. But the marvelous power and greatness of his experiences constrain him to interpret it. The strange, limitless, supreme, holy thing that he has experienced must have been a divine thing with which his soul has become united in an inconceivable and ineffable fashion. For Lao-tsze this highest experience of the mystic is the *tao*, the eternal world-order; for the men of the Upanishads it is *Brahma*, the universal divinity; for Plotinus, it is the One, the Illimitable, from which streams forth all the diversity of existence; for the theistic mystic of the East and the West it is the divine Lord and Saviour who condescends to the devout soul. The incomprehensible paradox that the small human "I" has become an infinite "I" the mystic can understand only as meaning that he himself has become God. As Plotinus says, the ecstatic "has become God, nay, rather he is God." Catherine of Genoa declares joyfully: "My 'I' is God, and I know no other 'I' but this my God." And Madame Guyon expresses herself in a similar fashion. Other mystics do not venture to speak of the soul's identity in essence with God, but content themselves with speaking of the indwelling of God in the soul. Plato expressly emphasizes the fact that the soul is not God but only in the image of God, or "related to God" or the "divine." Many Christian mystics in their humility describe the ecstatic union with God not as a union of essence, but as a union of married love; the soul does not disappear in God but fuses with Him in deepest unity. "God is in me and I am in Him. He is mine and I am His." So writes Elsa of Neustadt. But in spite of this milder and weaker formula which is in harmony with personal theism, the fundamental psychological character of the ecstatic experience is the same in the one as in the other. "The mystic's soul turned inwards experiences God in itself in its innermost essence and deepest ground," as Koepp remarks. God and the soul are bound together in indissoluble unity.

2. THE FUNDAMENTAL PSYCHIC EXPERIENCE IN PROPHETIC RELIGION

The fundamental psychic experience in *mysticism* is the denial of the impulse of life, a denial born of weariness of life, the unreserved surrender to the Infinite, the crown and culmination of which is ecstasy. The fundamental psychic experience in *prophetic* religion is an uncontrollable will to live, a constant impulse to the assertion, strengthening and enhancement of the feeling of life, a being overmastered by values and tasks, a passionate endeavor to realize these ideals and aims. Paul, for example, speaks of "being led by the Spirit," of being "fervent in spirit," of the "power of the Spirit." Mysticism is passive, quietist, resigned, contemplative; the prophetic religion is active, challenging, desiring, ethical. The mystic aims at the extinction of the emotional and volitional life, for the delight of ecstasy can be purchased only at the price of killing the will to live. In prophetic experience the emotions blaze up, the will to live asserts itself, triumphs in external defeat, and defies death and annihilation. Born of a tenacious will to live, faith, immovable confidence, reliance and trust firm as a rock, bold, adventurous hope break forth at last out of the bosom of tribulation and despair. The mystic is one who renounces, resigns, is at peace; the prophet is a fighter who ever struggles upwards from doubt to assurance, from tormenting uncertainty to absolute security of life, from despondency to fresh courage of soul, from fear to hope, from a depressing consciousness of guilt to the blessed experience of grace and salvation. He is no happy possessor but must ever establish his confidence in life in a creative act, in a free, moral deed, "in hope believing against all hope," "rousing himself against despair," as Luther says. No one has expressed in such pithy words as Paul the continuous emergence of trust and power out of anxiety and distress. "As dying and behold we live," he writes; "as chastened and not killed; as sorrowful yet always rejoicing." The feeling of absolute security in spite of all external uncertainty, to which the pious man struggles, has been described by the psalmist in a very remarkable way. "Yea, though I walk through the valley of the shadow of death I will fear no evil; for Thou art with me."

Thus faith is the basic experience of prophetic piety, of course not in the intellectualist sense of mere assent to truth, but in the sense of a fundamental feeling of confidence in life. Hence it is no mere hoping and seeking but an immovable having and possessing. . . . .

"Faith," "trust," "confidence"—that is the *leitmotif* which sounds through the entire literature of the Old and New Testaments and resounds anew in the writings of the reformers. If "love" and "union" are the central conceptions of mysticism, "faith" is the watchword of prophetic religion. Faith is that religious power which the oldest historical books of Israel report in praise of the patriarchs. "And Abraham believed Jahve and it was counted to him for righteousness." The great men of God in Israel again and again demand from their people a trusting faith in Jahve. Isaiah is pre-eminently the prophet of faith. "In quietness and confidence shall be your strength," is his exhortation to his people. Daring trust is that lofty mood of the soul which the adepts of prayer—Jeremiah and the exilic and post-exilic psalmist —won in a hard inner conflict. It is Jesus who has spoken the most powerful and the most paradoxical words about faith: "All things are possible to him that believeth." . . . .

The contrast between this prophetic vital feeling and the mystical is as sharp as possible. Mysticism flees from and denies the natural life and the relish of life in order to experience an infinite life beyond it; prophetic piety, on the contrary, believes in life and affirms it, throws itself resolutely and joyfully into the arms of life. On the one side we have an uncompromising denial of life, on the other an unconquerable belief in life.

3. The Idea of God in Mysticism

In ecstasy the mystic experiences himself as a complete unity; so also the God of mysticism is an undifferentiated unity, the "Simple," the "most simple," the "One without a second," the "only, pure, clear One, free from all duality." In ecstasy all the variety of psychic experience as also of the external world ceases. For the mystic who awakens out of the bliss of ecstasy, out of the experience of unity to the normal, conscious life, the objective world in its diversity is deception and illusion, *mâyâ*, or at least the dim emanation or dark shadow of the only genuine reality. Ecstasy is the final stage in the depersonalizing achieved in the mystical life; the God of the speculative mystic is non-personal, wholly devoid of anthropomorphic features. Thought, will, and self-consciousness are extinguished in ecstasy; likewise "the One" neither thinks nor wills nor is self-conscious. The ecstatic condition is perfectly empty of all concrete content, "perfect emptiness," "unconditioned negation." The absolute Unity is also completely without any quality; one can assert nothing of it; it is the "No, No," as it is called in the Upanishads, "exalted above being," as Plotinus says. Ecstasy is a hidden, incomprehensible mystery. It can never be grasped in thought and described in words, since it is beyond conscious experience. . . . .

The mystical conception of God is therefore, thoroughly static. He who is sunk in ecstasy is beyond all values; in the words of Plotinus, "he has left behind him the beautiful as he has passed beyond the circle of virtues." The God of extreme mysticism possesses neither ethical nor aesthetic predicates; He is "higher than virtue, higher than goodness, higher than beauty," says Philo; or as Plotinus puts it, He is the "super-good," the "super-beautiful." The ecstatic experiences an infinite Value, the Supreme Blessedness; the God of the mystic is, therefore, the Highest Good, the *Summum Bonum*, a term which was coined by Plotinus following Plato and which, through Augustine, became most frequently used as descriptive of God. It meets us also in the Song of Songs of Indian mysticism, the *Bhagavadgîta*, nay, even in the *Tao-teh-King* of Lao-tsze.

Clearer and more concrete is the idea of God in personal mysticism which interprets ecstatic experience in mysticism not speculatively but in a simple, imaginative fashion. God is not the non-personal, unqualified Unity beyond reality and values, but the highest Value conceived as a personality. He is the living Lord, the lovable Savior who stoops to man's petty soul in order to raise it up to Himself. The Infinite assumes an earthly form, the *summum bonum* becomes a human Redeemer-God, the Vishnu-Krishna-Râma in the Indian Bhakti religion, Jesus Christ in western mysticism, especially since Bernard of Clairvaux. Nay, so deep in the condescension of the heavenly Savior-God, that He as a living bridegroom draws near to the yearning soul, woos it with His love, and with a tender embrace unites Himself with it. Since here the personal features of the naive idea of God are living we call this mysticism by a term coined by Rudolf Otto, "mysticism of personal theism" in contrast to "mysticism of the Absolute." But even in this personal mysticism God is not the living, active Will, but the changeless, still Majesty, the statically conceived perfect Ideal, "the eternal Rest of the Saints," as à Kempis writes.

4. The Idea of God in Prophetic Religion

As the idea of God in mysticism exhibits the hypostatizing of ecstasy, so the idea of God in prophetic religion is the reflex of the dominance of the will in the experience of faith. "Faith is the creator of the Deity," says Luther in a paradoxical but striking phrase. God is not the immobile, infinite Unity, but the living, energizing Will, not the quiet Stillness but the active Energy, not always at rest but ever in action, not the highest Being but the supreme Life—so run the contrasting terms of Augustine. "My Father worketh hitherto," says the Johannine Christ. The experience of the mighty power of God becomes in prophetic spirits an anxious dread before the inescapable wrath of the living God. "Jahve is the true God; He is the living God and an everlasting King: at His wrath the earth trembleth" is the word of Jeremiah. On the power of the living God prophetic spirits feel themselves absolutely dependent; in His hands are weal and woe, blessing and cursing, life and death. "No sparrow falls to the ground without your Father." But trustful faith, immovable confidence, produces the wonderful paradox that the angry, jealous, and judging God is at the same time the giving and forgiving God, the Helper and Deliverer, that the Almighty Power in its inmost essence is nothing but wisdom, compassion and goodness. God is the "Father of mercies and God of all comfort." "God is love."

The mystic experiences in absolute silence the presence of the Infinite and draws into his deepest being the gentle breath of divine peace. The prophetic feeling of God's presence is an experience of the activity of God and possesses a far greater dynamic; everywhere and always he traces His living nearness and consuming power; not even in the underworld can he escape it.

Extreme mysticism strips the idea of God of all personal attributes until it arrives at the "bare," "pure" Infinite. The God of prophetic spirits, on the contrary, has unmistakably the features of a human personality, in whom primitive anthropomorphism lives on, spiritualized indeed, but in all its original power. God is Lord, King, Judge, and when trust has cast out all fear, He is Father.

Part II

THE FINDING OF RELIGIOUS TRUTH

THE RELIGIOUS SITUATION

Richard Niebuhr

PAUL TILLICH'S *Die religiöse Lage der Gegenwart* is one of the most important of the many attempts which has been made in modern Germany to achieve the orientation of thought and life in the new world of the twentieth century. It is not a book about the religion of the churches but an effort to interpret the whole contemporary situation from the point of view of one who constantly inquires what fundamental faith is expressed in the forms which civilization takes. Tillich is more interested in the religious values of secularism, of modern movements in art, science, education, and politics than in tracing tendencies within the churches or even in theology. Back of this book is the conviction that modern civilization is not only on trial but that it has been judged and found wanting and that in the struggle for a new world more is at stake than the discovery of new political and economic organizations which will enable the West or humanity, for that matter, to survive a while longer. The book is an earnest and profound attempt to discover where we stand and to ascertain whether there are creative forces at work in the catastrophes of the time.

Briefly, Tillich argues that what we are witnessing and participating in is not the decline of the West but a revolt against the spirit of capitalist society. Capitalist society, however, is not a scheme of economic organization only; it is also a culture with a definitely religious character. Its civilization is based upon faith in the self-sufficiency of the human and finite world; its hope and purposes is the establishment of human control over the world of nature and mind. Natural science, technique and capitalist economy—a trinity of powers which re-enforce each other—support and control the civilization. The spirit of human and finite self-sufficiency is expressed in painting, sculpture, education, politics, and religion and gives rise everywhere to an attitude of human domination over things in which there is no respect for the given and no true appreciation of human or any other kind of individuality.

The revolt against capitalist civilization has not been confined to communism. On the contrary, communism in its later phase, since it has lost the prophetic character of its early years, has adopted much of the spirit of capitalism so that the Russian Revolution may be regarded as one of the greatest triumphs of the spirit of capitalist society. The revolt against this spirit became manifest first of all in art. Its precursors were Cezánne, van Gogh and Gauguin. In literature Strindberg and Nietzsche were its earliest prophets. In science Einstein, Planck and Bohr and other founders of

"Translator's Preface" to *The Religious Situation*, by Paul Tillich, translated by Richard Niebuhr, New York, 1932, pp. vii-xxii. Reprinted by permission of the publishers, Henry Holt & Company.

the new science of the twentieth century, in philosophy Bergson, Simmel, and Husserl, in psychology Freud, in education a multitude of reformers, in morals the youth movement—all are representative of the revolt. Tillich attempts to interpret the significance of these tendencies as protests against the spirit of capitalist society and as prophecies of a new attitude.

The new attitude which is developing in consequence of these revolutions may be described in religious terms, he believes, as an attitude of "belief-ful realism." The term is strange and paradoxical and it is intended to be so. Religion for Tillich is "direction toward the Unconditioned." It is the reference in all life to the ultimate source of meaning and the ultimate ground of being. This ultimate transcends experience and knowledge though it is that to which all experience and knowledge refer. It is apprehended only indirectly through the symbols of the finite world. Nothing temporal, nothing finite, no one object among other objects, or no one value among other values can be designated as the ultimate. It is always transcendent and therefore unknown, yet the reference to it is implicit in life and wherever there is any meaning this reference to an ultimate source of meaning is present. The religious reference may be present in culture, in art, science, politics, education and the economic life, but in these spheres it does not become explicit. It is taken for granted; it is an unacknowledged presupposition. In religion in the narrower sense of that term the reference to the Unconditioned becomes explicit. Since the Unconditioned is forever hidden, transcendent and unknowable, it follows that all religious ideas are symbolical. They are good symbols when they point unambiguously to the transcendent; they become false symbols when they are regarded as possessing an intrinsic meaning or when they claim absolute value for themselves. A belief-ful realism is first of all an attitude in which the reference to the transcendent and eternal source of meaning and ground of being is present. This reference has been absent from capitalist society with its reliance on intra-worldly, intra-temporal sources of meaning, its exaltation of the finite into an absolute.

In the new movements of revolt the reference to the Unconditioned is once more making itself manifest or, at least, the negative conditions for the rise of the religious reference are being created. Where this reference to the ultimate is present there the first term of the paradox, the element of belief, asserts itself. But belief or faith must be mated with a realistic attiude toward things. A belief-ful idealism tends to spiritualize its objects, to regard them no longer as symbols of the ultimate or as deriving their meaning from the Unconditioned but as significant in and of themselves. A belief-ful realism, on the other hand, does not idealize or spiritualize its objects. It is the skeptical, unromantic, unsentimental attitude which accepts the objects in their stark givenness. It sees the world with the sober eyes of the scientist or realistic artist, accepting it at the same time as symbolic of the eternal and unconditioned source of all meaning and ground of all being.

"Belief-ful realism," Tillich writes, "is a total attitude toward reality. It is not a theory of the universe, neither is it a kind of practice but it belongs to a level of life which lies underneath the cleavage between theory and practice. It is not a particular kind of religion or theology. In fact it is not any kind of separate, particular thing. By the connection of *belief-ful* and *realism* the most fundamental of all dualisms is called into question and if it is justly called into question, it is also overcome. Faith is an attitude which transcends every conceivable and experienceable reality; realism is an attitude which rejects every transcending of reality, every transcendency and all transcendentalizing. In view of the antithesis of these attitudes it is natural that the mind should be inclined to evade the tension which results from their union. Evasion is possible in one of two directions, either in the direction of a beliefless realism or in the direction of idealism. Beliefless realism forbids all trespassing over the boundaries of experienceable reality. Its noblest form is to be found in positivism, which needs by no means to be irreligious but can assign religious objects to the realm of experienceable reality. Pragmatism proceeds in this fashion, very consistently in America, less consistently in the empirical theology of Germany. In the case of idealism even one's feeling for what is linguistically permissible resists the suggestion that the adjectives *belief-ful* or *beliefless* might be added to that term. This is due to the fact that idealism transcends experienceable reality and cannot therefore be designated as beliefless so that the antithesis disappears. Consequently idealism can claim, with apparent justification, to be in itself and immediately belief-ful. But this formulation of the claim contains implicitly the criticism that is to be made. To say 'in itself and immediately' is to omit just that which faith means—the transcending of reality, that is an attitude which cannot be reached on the basis of reality and which must therefore stand in unconditioned tension with reality. From the point of view of faith idealism also is a beliefless realism, from the point of view of realism it is too transcendental or transcendentalized. In this double attack from faith and realism idealism is destroyed. It is overcome by one side or the other, historically and systematically, in life and in thought. Its excellence lies in its effort to reconcile the necessity of abiding in the real with the necessity of going beyond the real. Its limits and its tragedy lie in the fact that it transcendentalizes rather than transcends the real and so is unable to do justice either to realism or to faith.

"Hence we are led to the surprising result that faith and realism, just because of the tension which prevails between them, belong together. For in faith the unconditioned tension is present and no attitude which weakens this tension can be associated with it. Idealism weakens it, beliefless realism cancels it, belief-ful realism expresses it."

Tillich has been quoted at length on this subject because the concept is central in his thought. The idea is inherently difficult and the difficulty of translating the finer nuances of his expression does not improve the intelligibility of the definition. The reader will do well, however, to think of the realism of art and history rather than of the realism of epistemology in the first place in attempting to understand Tillich's position. The belief-ful realism which he recommends and finds developing in the modern movements is the antithesis to a "technical" realism which is interested in reducing things to their general and utilizable terms. This realism seeks to fit things into the scheme of rational concepts and to identify their actuality with those elements in them which can be handled in thought and practice. A belief-ful realism, on the contrary, is willing to concede individuality and uniqueness to things. It sees them as independent of the human mind, as purely given things, which may indeed be analyzed in part for purposes of control, which, however, never reveal the whole secret of their being to generalizing analysis but only to sympathetic intuition. Hence Tillich finds greater religious value in a still-life by Cezánne or a tree by van Gogh than in a picture of Jesus by Uhde.

Belief-ful realism is closely related to a theory of history in which the decisive importance of the present is emphasized. Tillich, following Troeltsch, Rickert and Dilthey as well as many great historians who concerned themselves with the problem of the meaning of history, is an historical realist who emphasizes the category of individuality in history. He has abandoned the liberal myth of unending progress and it is impossible for him to accept the old orthodox mythology of history. Whatever values these conceptions may have had in the past they are not useful today. The myth of progress has been destroyed not only by the realism which the events of the time have taught, but also by the realism of historical research, which discovers that the uniqueness and unrepeatability of historical events are quite as significant as the general sociological laws which may be represented in them. The myth of progress, furthermore, expresses that sense of the self-sufficiency of the temporal order which Tillich finds characteristic of the whole capitalist civilization. It does not recognize that all time receives its meaning from its relation to eternity, to the Unconditioned. Orthodox mythology on the other hand finds the meaning of history not in the secular process, even with its reference to the ultimate, but in a super-history or a sacred history of this world. Tillich, rejecting both of these views, turns to the conception of *Kairos* for the adequate symbol with which to express his sense of the meaning of time. "Kairos is fulfilled time, the moment of time which is invaded by eternity. But Kairos is not perfection or completion in time. To act and to wait with the sense of Kairos is to wait upon the invasion of the eternal and to act accordingly, not to wait and act as though the eternal were a fixed quantity which could be introduced into time, as a social structure which represents the end and goal of history, for instance. The eternal is that which invades; it is not something tangible and objective. There are societies which are turned away from the eternal, which rest content in time and finitude, and there are others which are turned toward the eternal and which express in their forms the judgment that they have experienced as proceeding from the eternal. But there are no societies which possess the eternal." Every period of time is related to the eternal but not every period is aware of this relation. Consciousness of the relation arises only when the sacred symbols which have lost their symbolic character as pointers and have come to claim meaning in their own right or the social structures and forms of civilization which have become self-sufficient are subjected to an ultimate criticism and shaken by catastrophe. When the prophetic spirit arises, when the relation of all existence to the ultimate source of meaning and existence becomes apparent in judgment, then the consciousness of Kairos and of the responsibility of man come to their climax.

Kairos is in a sense the antithesis of both Utopia and the Golden Age. A conservative theory of history finds all the meaning of history concentrated in the past; the present is significant insofar as it is related to the past. Utopianism finds the significance of the present in its relation to the future. But historical realism and relativism cannot make the significance of Greece and Rome depend on the contribution which they have been able to make to modern Western civilization or to some future Utopia. Neither can it find the significance of the present in the relative judgment which some future point in time will make of this period, or in the elements of modern culture which may survive or be selected by that future. It must see every period as somehow having its own meaning; yet its meaning cannot be intrinsic. It lies rather in the relation of an era to an ultimate that is beyond every point of time. The conception of Kairos expresses for Tillich both the negative meaning of historical relativism and the positive sense of the significance and responsibility of the present moment.

It is his conviction that we now stand in the Kairos, in the moment when the judgment of the eternal upon time and all things temporal and the responsibility of the temporal to the eternal become evident in the events of the period. We are facing not merely a transition from one stage of culture to another, from one religion to another. The problem of the present is not whether a communistic civilization will take the place of a capitalistic culture or whether a new faith will supplant Christianity. We are rather in a situation in which the whole question of the meaningfulness of existence is brought before us in such a fashion that we cannot escape it, a period in which every social institution and religious symbol is challenged as to its right to existence. The eternal invades time and places every temporal form in question. There is in this not only judgment but also challenge to create such forms, such a culture and religion as will express the meaningfulness derived from the relation to the ultimate.

Tillich expects no reconstruction of life from sudden revolution. "When we look upon the actual events of our time," he writes, "must we not say that it seems as though a frost had fallen upon all of the things of which we have spoken, whether it be the youth movement or the philosophy of life, whether it be expressionism or religious socialism? Was not all of this romanticism, intoxication, utopianism? One thing is certain: all of these things, and that means all of us also, are once more being subjected to the judgment. What was not real in what we did and thought is being consumed by fire. . . . . And this means that the spirit of capitalist society is far too strong to be conquered by romanticism, longing and revolution. Its demonic power is too great. It means in the second place that the judgment which comes from the Unconditioned is not a dialectic but an extremely real power which drives us again and again to the verge of despair. And it means in the third place that in every sphere we must return to painstaking labor in the concrete situation."

It is evident that Tillich's interest in the philosophy of history is a practical interest. He is particularly active in the religious socialist movement and the practical as well as theoretic problem which he faces is the problem of combining socialism and religion. What he is seeking is not merely a coalition between a Christian idealism—which he would reject—and socialist utopianism but a fundamental reinterpretation of the bases of socialism and a fundamental definition of the ethical task of religion. Like Barth and Brunner and other members of the dialectical school Tillich begins with the ethical question, What shall I do? The theologians of crisis also began their course as religious socialists and remain socialists to a large extent to the present day. But the ethics to which the logic of their theological position leads them appears to become more and more conservative. They are in danger, as Tillich points out, of becoming supporters of things as they are, not because all things are good but because all reforms are also bad. Tillich on the other hand continues to assert the radical consequences of the religious position and his whole theology and philosophy must be approached from this point of view among others. He is seeking for an adequate social ethics.

His importance for English and American readers lies largely in this fact. The ethics of the "social gospel" of the past were mated with naïve faith in progress and with a thoroughly humanistic and anthropocentric religious attitude. The decline of the liberal philosophy has called the whole social gospel into question. A change in the theological climate is evident. Will it be simple reaction, involving also the reaction to the orthodox conservative ethics? Liberalism and fundamentalism are equally intolerable, both in their theology and in their ethics. The struggle for a new theology and a radical ethics of the Christian life is inevitable in England and America as well as in Germany. In this struggle Tillich's point of view can be very helpful. The crisis is naturally more acute and the problems are more sharply defined in Germany than elsewhere, not only because the German temper runs to sharp antitheses and exclusive definitions but also because that country has been visited by a severer fate in our time than the other countries of the West have been. Nevertheless the problems of religious socialism, of the reconstruction of Protestantism and of the religious foundations of the new culture are pressing for solutions in England and America also.

AN ANTHOLOGY OF DOUBT

Will Durant

I. THE PROBLEM

I HAVE SENT the following letter, with variations, to certain famous contemporaries here and abroad for whose intelligence I have high regard.

NEW YORK,
July 15, 1931.

DEAR —————

Will you interrupt your work for a moment and play the game of philosophy with me?

I am attempting to face a question which our generation, perhaps more than any, seems always to ask and never able to answer—What is the meaning or worth of human life? Heretofore this question has been dealt with chiefly by theorists, from Ikhnaton and Lao-tse to Bergson and Spengler. The result has been a kind of intellectual suicide: thought, by its very development, seems to have destroyed the value and significance of life. The growth and spread of knowledge, for which so many idealists and reformers prayed, has resulted in a disillusionment which has almost broken the spirit of our race.

Astronomers have told us that human affairs constitute but a moment in the trajectory of a star; geologists have told us that civilization is but a precarious interlude between ice ages; biologists have told us that all life is war, a struggle for existence among individuals, groups, nations, alliances, and species; historians have told us that "progress" is a delusion, whose glory ends in decay, psychologists have told us that the will and the self are the helpless instruments of heredity and environment, and that the once incorruptible soul is but a transient incandescence of the brain. The Industrial Revolution has destroyed the home, and the discovery of contraceptives is destroying the family, the old morality, and perhaps (through the sterility of the intelligent) the race. Love is analyzed into a physical congestion, and marriage becomes a temporary physiological convenience slightly superior to promiscuity. Democracy has degenerated into such corruption as only Milo's Rome knew; and our youthful dreams of a socialist Utopia disappear as we see, day after day, the inexhaustible acquisitiveness of men. Every invention strengthens the strong and weakens the weak; every new mechanism displaces men, and multiplies the horrors of war. God, who once was the consolation of our brief life, and our refuge in bereavement and suffering, has apparently vanished from the scene; no telescope, no microscope discovers him. Life has become, in that total perspective which is philosophy, a fitful pullulation of human insects on the earth, a planetary

From *On the Meaning of Life*, New York, 1932, pp. 3-25. Reprinted by permission of the publishers, Julian Messner, Inc.

eczema that may soon be cured; nothing is certain in it except defeat and death—a sleep from which, it seems, there is no awakening.

We are driven to conclude that the greatest mistake in human history was the discovery of "truth." It has not made us free, except from delusions that comforted us and restraints that preserved us. It has not made us happy, for truth is not beautiful, and did not deserve to be so passionately chased. As we look on it now we wonder why we hurried so to find it. For it has taken from us every reason for existence except the moment's pleasure and tomorrow's trivial hope.

This is the pass to which science and philosophy have brought us. I, who have loved philosophy for many years, now turn back to life itself, and ask you, as one who has lived as well as thought, to help me understand. Perhaps the verdict of those who have lived is different from that of those who have merely thought. Spare me a moment to tell me what meaning life has for you, what keeps you going, what help—if any—religion gives you, what are the sources of your inspiration and your energy, what is the goal or motive-force of your toil, where you find your consolations and your happiness, where, in the last resort, your treasure lies. Write briefly if you must; write me at length and at leisure if you possibly can; for every word from you will be precious to me.

Sincerely yours,

WILL DURANT.

I would not have this letter taken as expressing very accurately my own conclusions on the meaning of our existence; I cannot find it in my nature to be so despondent. But I wished to confront at the outset the bitterest possibilities, to load the dice against my own desires, and to put the problem in such a way as to guard against the superficial optimism with which men are wont to turn aside the profounder issues of life.

And since no one deserves to believe unless he has served an apprenticeship of doubt, I propose to state at some length the case against the worth and significance of human affairs. Later we shall consider the replies which have come to this letter from various nations and continents; and in the sequel I propose to answer the question for myself with whatever sincerity a half-century of life has left me in the face of the greatest of all temptations to lie.

II. RELIGION

The natural condition of humanity, and even of philosophers, is hope. Great religions arise and flourish out of the need men feel to believe in their worth and destiny; and great civilizations have normally rested upon these inspiriting religions. Where such a faith, after supporting men for centuries, begins to weaken, life narrows down from a spiritual drama to a biological episode; it sacrifices the dignity conferred by a destiny endless in time, and shrinks to a strange interlude between a ridiculous birth and an annihilating death. Reduced to a microscopic triviality by the perspective of science, the informed individual loses belief in himself and his race, and enterprises of great pith and moment, which once aroused his effort and imagination, awaken in him only scepticism and scorn. Faith and hope disappear; doubt and despair are the order of the day.

This is the essential diagnosis of our time. It is not merely the War of 1914 that has plunged us into pessimism, much less the economic depression of these recent years; we have to do here with something far deeper than a temporary diminution of our wealth, or even the death of 26,000,000 men; it is not our homes and our treasuries that are empty, it is our "hearts." It seems impossible any longer to believe in the permanent greatness of man, or to give life a meaning that cannot be annulled by death. We move into an age of spiritual exhaustion and despondency like that which hungered for the birth of Christ.

III. SCIENCE

When the eighteenth century laid the foundations of the nineteenth, it staked everything upon one idea—the replacement of theology with science. Given science, and there would soon be wealth, which would make men happy; given science, and there would be truth, which would make men free. Universal education would spread the findings of science, liberate men from superstition, and make them fit for democracy; a century of such universal schooling, Bentham predicted, would solve all major problems, and bring Utopia. "There is no limit to the progress of mankind," said Condorcet, "except the duration of the globe upon which it is placed." "The young are fortunate," said Voltaire, "for they will see great things."

They did. They saw the Revolution and the Terror, Waterloo and '48, Balaklava and Gettysburg, Sédan and Mukden, Armageddon and Lenin. They saw the growth and triumph of the sciences; of biology with Darwin, of physics with Faraday, of chemistry with Dalton, of astronomy with Laplace, of medicine with Pasteur, of mathematics with Einstein. All the hopes of the Enlightenment were realized; science was free, and was remaking the world. But while the technicians were using science to transform the earth, philosophers were using it to transform the universe. Slowly, as one science after another reported its findings, a picture was unfolded of universal struggle and death; and decade by decade the optimism of the nineteenth century yielded to the pessimism of today.

The astronomers reported that the earth, which had been the footstool of God and the home of the atoning Christ, was a minor planet circling about a minor sun; that it had had its birth in a violent disruption, and would end in collision and conflagration, leaving not a shadow of man's work to tell his tale. The geologists reported that life was tolerated transiently upon the earth at the pleasure of ice and heat, at the mercy of falling lava and failing rain; that oceans and mountains were engaged in a perpetual warfare of encroachment and corrosion, and alternating victory; that great continents had been destroyed by earthquakes and would be again. The paleontologists reported that a million species of animals had lived on the earth for a paltry eon or two and had disappeared without leaving anything more than a few bones and imprints in the rocks. The biologists reported that all life lives at the expense of other life, that big things eat little things and are eaten in turn; that strong organisms use and abuse weak organisms in a hundred thousand ways forever; that the ability to kill is the ultimate test of survival; that reproduction is suicide, and that love is the prelude to replacement and death.

Here, as example and symbol of all life, is my dog Wolf, who owes her existence to the olfactory attractiveness of her police-dog mother to her collie sire. She eats greedily and drinks abstemiously (she is a teetotaler, and despite the pressure of current fashions refuses all alcoholic beverages); she chases whatever we throw, takes the cosiest seats in the house, receives our affection as a matter of course, falls into a rut, and lures to our porch half a hundred lovers. All night long our neighbor's Airedale waits at our door, and moans like a Troubadour. What but bad poetry is the difference between this and love?

Later Lady Wolf, after much commotion, suffering, and mute inquiries as to the sense and meaning of it all, litters the house with pups. She suckles them patiently, protects them growlingly against all danger, and nearly dies of their simultaneous voracity. At times she laps up milk from a bowl while her babies tug at her breasts, and then the apparently aimless circularity and repetitiousness of life leaps to the eye. One by one the pups are given away; Wolf looks for them for a day, and then forgets them. The final pup exploits and maltreats her, stealing her food and snapping at her legs; she permits it all graciously, like any Madonna with her babe. When this last surviver goes in his turn, Wolf gives no sign of bereavement; she falls back into her maiden routine, and lives happily until the love-fever agitates her—and the village—again. Then she mates, breeds, and the cycle of life comes full turn once more.

Is not this also the essence of human life? Take away the frills, and what greater significance than Wolf's has our own merry-go-round of births and deaths? Hidden away in the small type of our daily press, under the captions of "Births," "Marriages," and "Deaths," is the essential history of mankind; everything else is ornament. Looked at in this canine perspective the sublime tale of Héloise and Abélard, or the lyric of Wimpole Street, are but incidents in Nature's fanatical resolution to carry on. All this hunting of a man after a maid, all this anatomical display, this revealing concealment, these luring perfumes, these graceful movements, this stealthy scrutiny, this gynecological wit, these romances and dramas and films, all this money-making, tailoring, clothes-brushing, preening, dancing, singing, tail-spreading, prattling, itching—all are part of the ritual of reproduction. The ceremony becomes more complex, but the end is as before: unto them a little child is born.

Once the child had an immortal soul; now it has glands. To the physicist it is only a bundle of molecules, or atoms, or electrons, or protons; to the physiologist it is an unstable conjunction of muscles, bones, and nerves; to the physician it is a red mass of illnesses and pain; to the psychologist it is a helpless mouthpiece of heredity and environment, a rabble of conditioned reflexes marshaled by hunger and love. Almost every idea this strange organism will have will be a delusion, almost every perception will be a prejudice. It will rear fine theories of free will and immortal life, and from hour to hour it will "rot and rot"; it will construct great systems of philosophy, in which the drop of water will explain the sea. The thought will seldom occur to this "forked radish" called man that it is just one species among a billion, a passing experiment of Nature, who, as Turgeniev said, entertains no preferences as between men and fleas. Only science gives us at last the gift which Robert Burns unwisely begged of the gods—to see ourselves as others see us, even as other species see us. In the end we perceive that to the dog we are but irrational praters, making much noise with the tongue; and that to the mosquito we are merely meals. Some of us reach the stage of objectivity, and surrender our final prejudice, the judgment of beauty; we admit that something may be said for the Zulu's idolatry of adipose mates, and that a Martian might conceivably admire, next to the beauty of collies and mares, the loveliness of woman. Slowly we cease to be the center and summit of the universe; we and our species, in the scientific eye, are trivial fragments, flying off at a tangent towards destruction.

IV. History

The nineteenth century was the age of history as well as of science; the hunger for facts turned with a concerted fury upon the past, dismembered and dissected it, and discovered the rise and fall of nations. The resultant picture is a panorama of development and decay; history, as Bacon said, is the planks of a shipwreck, and nothing seems certain in it except decadence, degeneration, and death.

A thousand varieties of man—Piltdown, Neanderthal, Chellean, Acheulean, Mousterian, Aurignacian, Cro-magnon, Rhodesian, Pekin man—lived for thousands of years, fought, thought, invented, painted, carved, made children, and left no more to posterity than a few flints and scratches, forgotten for millenia and found only by the picks and spades of our inquisitive day. A thousand civilizations have disappeared under the ocean or the earth, leaving, like Atlantis, merely a legend behind; Turkestan, Mohenjo-Daru, Ur of the Chaldees, Samarkand of Tamerlane, Angkor of the Khmers, Yucatan of the Mayas, and the Incas' Peru—these are the mausolea of cultures almost completely lost. They are among the few which we have unearthed; calculate, then, the number of dead civilizations of which history preserves no vestige at all. And of the pitiful minority that have clung to some place in human memory—like Babylon and Egypt, Persia and Crete, Greece and Rome—consider their grandeur and decadence, and see how uncertain a thing history is, how its greatest names are writ in water, and how even Shakespeare may become to his countrymen, within a century of his death, a half-forgotten barbarian given to melodramatic fustian and bad puns.

All things, said Aristotle, have been discovered and forgotten many times over. Progress, he assured us, is a delusion; human affairs are like the sea, which on its surface is disturbed into a thousand motions, and seems to be headed somewhere, while at its bottom it is comparatively changeless and still. What we call progress is, perhaps, mere superficial change, a succession of fashions in dress, transportation, government, psychology, religion; Christian Science, behaviorism, democracy, automobiles, and pants are not progress, they are change; they are new ways of doing old things, new errors in the vain attempt to understand eternal mysteries. Underneath these varying phenomena the essence remains the same; the man who uses the steam shovel and the electric drill, the tractor and the tank, the adding-machine and the machine-gun, the airplane and the bomb, is the same sort of man as those who used wooden ploughs, flint knives, log wheels, bow and arrows, knot writing, and poisoned spear-heads; the tool differs, the end is the same; the scale is vaster, the purposes as crude and selfish, as stupid and contradictory, as murderous and suicidal, as in phehistoric or ancient days; everything has progressed except man.

All history, then, all the proud record of human accumulations and discoveries, seems at times to be a futile circle, a weary tragedy in which Sisyphis man repeatedly pushes invention and labor up the high hill of civilization and culture, only to have the precarious structure again and again topple back into barbarism—into coolies, ryots, fellaheen, moujiks, and serfs—through the exhaustion of the soil, or the migrations of trade, or the vandalism of invaders, or the educated sterility of the race. So much remains of Condorcet's "indefinite perfectibility of mankind." Indefinite indeed.

V. Utopia

All the dogma that in the last one hundred years gave to earthly life something of the significance which the hope of heaven brought to medieval man, seems to have lost countenance in this skeptical century. "Progress," "universal education," "popular sovereignty"—who is now so poor in doubt as to do them reverence? Our schools are like our inventions—they offer us new ideas, new means of doing old things; they elevate us from petty larceny to bank wreckages and Teapot Domes. They stake all on intellect, only to find that character wins in the end. We taught people how to read, and they enrich the "tabloids" and the "talkies"; we invented radio, and they pour out, a hundred times more abundantly than before, the music of savages and the prejudices of mobs. We gave them, through technology and engineering, unprecedented wealth—miraculous automobiles, luxurious travel, and spacious homes; only to find that peace departs as riches come, that automobiles over-ride morality and connive at crime, that quarrels grow bitterer as the spoils increase, and that the largest houses are the bloodiest battlegrounds of the ancient war between man and woman. We discovered birth-control, and now it sterilizes the intelligent, multiplies the ignorant, debases love with promiscuity, frustrates the educator, empowers the demagogue, and deteriorates the race. We enfranchised all men, and find them supporting and preserving, in nearly every city, a nefarious "machine" that blocks the road between ability and office; we enfranchised women, and discovered that nothing is changed except clerical expense. We dreamed of socialism, and find our souls too greedy to make it possible; in our hearts we too are capitalists, and have no serious objection to becoming rich. We dreamed of emancipation through organized labor, and find great unions working hand in hand with corrupt machines and murderous gangs; these are the instruments with which we poor intellectuals planned to build Utopia. We turned at last to Russia, and find it conquering poverty at the cost of that freedom of body and mind, of work and thought, which has been the soul of liberalism and radicalism from Godwin to Darrow, from Emerson to Kropotkin, from Rabelais to Anatole France.

And over all the drama hovers, like a many-armed Shiva, the merry god of war. The grandeur of Egypt is the child of brutal conquest and despotism; the glory of Greece is rooted in the mire of slavery; the majesty of Rome is in its triremes and its legions; the civilization of Europe rises and falls with its guns. History, like Napoleon's God, is on the side of big Bertha; it laughs at artists and philosophers, destroys their work in a moment of patriotism, and gives its honors, its statues, and its pages to Mars. Egypt builds and Persia destroys it; Persia builds and Greece destroys it; Greece builds and Rome destroys it; Islam builds and Spain destroys it; Spain builds and England destroys it; Europe builds and Europe destroys it. Men kill one another at first with sticks and stones, then with arrows and lances, then with phalanxes and cohorts, then with cannon and musketry, then with dreadnoughts and submarines, then with tanks and planes; the scale and grandeur of construction and progress are equaled by the scale and terror of destruction and war. One by one the nations rear their heads in pride, and one by one war decapitates them. "Look on my works, ye mighty, and despair," reads the proud inscription on the ruined and desolate statue of Ozymandias, builder of buildings and "King of Kings"; but the traveler reports, simply,

> "Nothing beside remains. Round the decay
> Of that colossal wreck, boundless and bare
> The lone and level sands stretch far away."

VI. THE SUICIDE OF THE INTELLECT

In the face of this impartial destructiveness of history, this neutrality of nature between good and evil, life and death, the soul of man, in the past, has strengthened itself with faith in a juster world to come. There all these wrongs would be righted, and the poor man in heaven would have the pleasure of letting a drop of water fall upon the rich man's tongue in hell. There was something ferocious in the old faiths; the gentle gospels of Buddha and Christ were blackened by time into holy orgies of revenge; every paradise had its inferno, to which good people fervently consigned those who had succeeded too well in life, or had adopted the wrong myth. In those "happy days" men agreed that life was evil: Guatama called the extinction of individual consciousness the greatest good, and the Church described life as a vale of tears. Men could afford to be pessimists about the earth, because they were optimists about the sky; behind those clouds they saw the isles of the blest, the abode of everlasting bliss.

As I write a song comes up from the street below. A black-garbed lass, accompanied by a tremulous brass band, is singing *The Rock of Ages*. Silently I join in the refrain; and all the idealized memories of my pious youth surge up within me. I slip down and pass among the impromptu congregation that has gathered about the singers. The uniformed men in the official band do not impress me; without exception they are hard-looking, practical fellows; long since, I fear, religion has become a business with them. The uniformed women, whose shrill voices carry the burden of the song, are pale and thin, empty in body and soul; everything spiritual dies when it is sold, or made a motley to the view.

But in the crowd itself the faces are not hard. These men seem for the most part destitute—jobless and penniless; the exploitation and poverty that are a part of life have fallen heavily upon them; they are one moment in the eternal wastage of selection. Yet they are not bitter; they listen patiently to the harangue of the preacher calling them violently to the gentle Christ. Despite his invectives and denunciations some of them seem comforted; for a while they catch a glimpse of another world than their daily round of unemployment and fruitless search, of burning hunger and weary feet. In a dark doorway an old woman listens hopefully, sheds a tear, and mumbles a prayer. But for the most part the men smile incredulously; their poverty does not seem to them to declare the glory of God. When the song is renewed not one of them joins in it; one by one they walk quietly away. Even into these simple souls the scepticism of our time has entered. How shall I, fortunate and comfortable, ever fathom the despair of these men, shorn not only of the goods of life but of a consoling faith as well?

For today science, which, because of its marvelous creations, they have learned to trust as once they trusted the priest, has told them that the sky which of old promised them happiness, is mere blue nothing, cold and empty space, and that those clouds among which the angels frolicked are only the steaming perspiration of the earth. Science does not offer consolation, it offers death. Everything, from the unwinding universe of the astronomers to the college girl irradiating life with beauty and laughter, must pass away; this handsome youth, erect and vigorous, fresh from athletic victories, will be laid low tomorrow by some modest, ingratiating germ; this noble pianist, who has dignified his time with perfection, and has taught a million souls to forget themselves in beauty, is already in the clutch of death, and will, within a decade, be rotting in the tomb.

The greatest question of our time is not communism vs. individualism, not Europe vs. America, not even the East vs. the West; it is whether men bear to live without God.

Religion was profounder than philosophy, and refused to root human happiness in the earth; it based man's hopes where knowledge could never reach them—beyond the grave. Perhaps Asia was profounder than Europe, and medievalism profounder than modernity; for they kept at arm's length this science that seems to kill whatever it touches, reducing soul to brain, life to matter, personality to chemistry, and will to fate. Perhaps some confident and stoic race, still strong in religious enthusiasm, will engulf and absorb these disillusioned peoples of the West, so scientifically in love with death.

This then is the final triumph of thought—that it disintegrates all societies, and at last destroys the thinker himself. Perhaps the invention of thought was one of the cardinal errors of mankind. For first, thought undermined morality by shearing it of its supernatural sanctions and sanctity, and revealing it as a social utility designed to save policemen; and a morality without God is as weak as a traffic law when the policeman is on foot. Second, thought undermined society by separating sex from parentage, removing the penalty from promiscuity, and liberating the individual from the race; now only the ignorant transmit their kind. Finally it undermined the thinker by revealing to him, in astronomy and geology, biology and history, a panorama in which he saw himself as an insignificant fragment in space and a flickering moment in time; it took from him his belief in his own will and future, left his fate nude of nobility and grandeur, and weakened him into despondency and surrender.

And here, in the *macabre finale*, philosophy joins hands with science in the work of destruction. That total perspective which it preached so proudly and so eagerly pursued is apparently the most dangerous—though the rarest—foe of resolution and joy; for what meaning or dignity can the individual have in a world so vast, among species without number, and in time without end? He that increaseth knowledge increaseth sorrow, and in much wisdom is much vanity.

VII. Finis

This is the challenge which confronts our age, and dwarfs all other problems of philosophy and religion, economics and statesmanship; beside it the apparent ruin of our economic system becomes a transitory trifle unworthy of serious concern. If the reader has been disturbed by these pages, it is good; let him now find in his own mental resources some basis for his faith; let him honestly formulate his own reply to this philosophy of despair. For those of us who wish to live consciously, to know the worst and praise the best, must meet all these doubts if we are to maintain any longer our pretense to the life of reason.

THE PROBLEM OF UNBELIEF

Walter Lippmann

1. WHIRL IS KING

Among those who no longer believe in the religion of their fathers, some are proudly defiant, and many are indifferent. But there are also a few, perhaps an increasing number, who feel that there is a vacancy in their lives. This inquiry deals with their problem. It is not intended to disturb the serenity of those who are unshaken in the faith they hold, and it is not concerned with those who are still exhilarated by their escape from some stale orthodoxy. It is concerned with those who are perplexed by the consequences of their own irreligion. It deals with the problem of unbelief, not as believers are accustomed to deal with it, in the spirit of men confidently calling the lost sheep back into the fold, but as unbelievers themselves must, I think, face the problem if they face it candidly and without presumption.

When such men put their feelings into words they are likely to say that, having lost their faith, they have lost the certainty that their lives are significant, and that it matters what they do with their lives. If they deal with young people they are likely to say that they know of no compelling reason which certifies the moral code they adhere to, and that, therefore, their own preferences, when tested by the ruthless curiosity of their children, seem to have no sure foundation of any kind. They are likely to point to the world about them, and to ask whether the modern man possesses any criterion by which he can measure the value of his own desires, whether there is any standard he really believes in which permits him to put a term upon that pursuit of money, of power, and of excitement which has created so much of the turmoil and the squalor and the explosiveness of modern civilization.

These are, perhaps, merely the rationalizations of the modern man's discontent. At the heart of it there are likely to be moments of blank misgiving in which he finds that the civilization of which he is a part leaves a dusty taste in his mouth. He may be very busy with many things, but he discovers one day that he is no longer sure they are worth doing. He has been much preoccupied; but he is no longer sure he knows why. He has become involved in an elaborate routine of pleasures; and they do not seem to amuse him very much. He finds it hard to believe that doing any one thing is better than doing any other thing, or, in fact, that it is better than doing nothing at all. It occurs to him that it is a great deal of trouble to live, and that even in the best of lives the thrills are few and far between. He begins more or less consciously to seek satisfactions, because he is no

From *A Preface to Morals*, New York, 1929, pp. 3-14. Reprinted by permission of the publishers, The Macmillan Company.

longer satisfied, and all the while he realizes that the pursuit of happiness was always a most unhappy quest. In the later stages of his woe he not only loses his appetite, but becomes excessively miserable trying to recover it. And then, surveying the flux of events and the giddiness of his own soul, he comes to feel that Aristophanes must have been thinking of him when he declared that "Whirl is King, having driven out Zeus."

2. FALSE PROPHECIES

The modern age has been rich both in prophecies that men would at last inherit the kingdoms of this world, and in complaints at the kind of world they inherited. Thus Petrarch, who was an early victim of modernity, came to feel that he would "have preferred to be born in any other period" than his own; he tells us that he sought an escape by imagining that he lived in some other age. The Nineteenth Century, which begat us, was forever blowing the trumpets of freedom and providing asylums in which its most sensitive children could take refuge. Wordsworth fled from mankind to rejoice in nature. Chateaubriand fled from man to rejoice in savages. Byron fled to an imaginary Greece, and William Morris to the Middle Ages. A few tried an imaginary India. A few an equally imaginary China. Many fled to Bohemia, to Utopia, to the Golden West, and to the Latin Quarter, and some, like James Thomson, to hell where they were

> "gratified to gain
> That positive eternity of pain
> Instead of this insufferable inane."

They had all been disappointed by the failure of a great prophecy. The theme of this prophecy had been that man is a beautiful soul who in the course of history had somehow become enslaved by

> "Scepters, tiaras, swords, and chains, and tombs
> Of reasoned wrong, glazed on by ignorance,"

and they believed with Shelley that when "the loathsome mask has fallen" man, exempt from awe, worship, degree, the king over himself, would then be "free from guilt or pain." This was the orthodox liberalism to which men turned when they had lost the religion of their fathers. But the promises of liberalism have not been fulfilled. We are living in the midst of that vast dissolution of ancient habits which the emancipators believed would restore our birthright of happiness. We know now that they did not see very clearly beyond the evils against which they were rebelling. It is evident to us that their prophecies were pleasant fantasies which concealed the greater difficulties that confront men, when having won the freedom to do what they wish—that wish, as Byron said:

> "which ages have not yet subdued
> In man—to have no master save his mood,"

they are full of contrary moods and do not know what they wish to do. We have come to see that Huxley was right when he said that "a man's worst difficulties begin when he is able to do as he likes."

The evidences of these greater difficulties lie all about us: in the brave and brilliant atheists who have defied the Methodist God, and have become very nervous; in the women who have emancipated themselves from the tyranny of fathers, husbands, and homes, and with the intermittent but expensive help of a psychoanalyst, are now enduring liberty as interior decorators; in the young men and women who are world-weary at twenty-two; in the multitudes who drug themselves with pleasure; in the crowds enfranchised by the blood of heroes who cannot be persuaded to take an interest in their destiny; in the millions, at last free to think without fear of priest or policeman, who have made the moving pictures and the popular newspapers what they are.

These are the prisoners who have been released. They ought to be very happy. They ought to be serene and composed. They are free to make their own lives. There are no conventions, no tabus, no gods, priests, princes, fathers, or revelations which they must accept. Yet the result is not so good as they thought it would be. The prison door is wide open. They stagger out into trackless space under a blinding sun. They find it nerve-racking. "My sensibility," said Flaubert, "is sharper than a razor's edge; the creaking of a door, the face of a bourgeois, an absurd statement set my heart to throbbing and completely upset me." They must find their own courage for battle and their own consolation in defeat. They complain, like Renan after he had broken with the Church, that the enchanted circle which embraced the whole of life is broken, and that they are left with a feeling of emptiness "like that which follows an attack of fever or an unhappy love affair." "Where is my *home?*" cried Nietzsche: "For it do I ask and seek, and have sought, but have not found it. O eternal everywhere, O eternal nowhere, O eternal in vain."

To more placid temperaments the pangs of freedom are no doubt less acute. It is possible for multitudes in time of peace and security to exist agreeably—somewhat incoherently, perhaps, but without convulsions—to dream a little and not unpleasantly, to have only now and then a nightmare, and only occasionally a rude awakening. It is possible to drift along not too discontentedly, somewhat nervously, somewhat anxiously, somewhat confusedly, hoping for the best, and believing in nothing very much. It is possible to be a passable citizen. But it is not possible to be wholly at peace. For serenity of soul requires some better organization of life than a man can attain by pursuing his casual ambitions, satisfying his hungers, and for the rest accepting destiny as an idiot's tale in which one dumb sensation succeeds another to no known end. And it is not possible for him to be wholly alive. For that depends upon his sense of being completely engaged with the world, with all his passions and all the faculties in rich harmonies with one another, and in deep rhythm with the nature of things.

These are the gifts of a vital religion which can bring the whole of a man into adjustment with the whole of his relevant experience. Our forefathers had such a religion. They quarreled a good deal about the details, but they had no doubt that there was an order in the universe which

justified their lives because they were a part of it. The acids of modernity
have dissolved that order for many of us, and there are some in consequence
who think that the needs which religion fulfilled have also been dissolved.
But however self-sufficient the eugenic and perfectly educated man of
the distant future may be, our present experience is that the needs remain. In
failing to meet them, it is plain that we have succeeded only in substituting
trivial illusions for majestic faith. For while the modern emancipated man
may wonder how anyone ever believed that in this universe of stars and atoms
and multitudinous life, there is a drama in progress of which the principal
event was enacted in Palestine nineteen hundred years ago, it is not really a
stranger fable than many which he so readily accepts. He does not believe
the words of the Gospel but he believes the best-advertised notion. The
older fable may be incredible today, when it was credible it bound together
the whole of experience upon a stately and dignified theme. The modern
man has ceased to believe in it but he has not ceased to be credulous, and the
need to believe haunts him. It is no wonder that his impulse is to turn back
from his freedom, and to find someone who says he knows the truth and
can tell him what to do, to find the shrine of some new god, of any cult
however newfangled, where he can kneel and be comforted, put on man-
acles to keep his hands from trembling, ensconce himself in some citadel
where it is safe and warm.

For the modern man who has ceased to believe, without ceasing to be
credulous, hangs, as it were, between heaven and earth, and is at rest nowhere. There is no theory of the meaning and value of events which
he is compelled to accept, but he is none the less compelled to accept the
events. There is no moral authority to which he must turn now, but there
is coercion in opinions, fashions, and fads. There is for him no inevitable
purpose in the universe, but there are elaborate necessities, physical, political,
economic. He does not feel himself to be an actor in a great and dramatic
destiny, but he is subject to the massive powers of our civilization, forced
to adopt their pace, bound to their routine, entangled in their conflicts.
He can believe what he chooses about this civilization. He cannot,
however, escape the compulsion of modern events. They compel
his body and his senses as ruthlessly as ever did king or priest. They do
not compel his mind. They have all the force of natural events, but not
their majesty, all the tyrannical power of ancient institutions, but none of
their moral certainty. Events are there, and they overpower him. But
they do not convince him that they have that dignity which inheres in
that which is necessary and in the nature of things.

In the old order the compulsions were often painful, but there was sense
in the pain that was inflicted by the will of an all-knowing God. In the
new order the compulsions are painful and, as it were, accidental, unnecessary, wanton, and full of mockery. The modern man does not make his
peace with them. For in effect he has replaced natural piety with a
grudging endurance of a series of unsanctified compulsions. When he believed that the unfolding of events was a manifestation of the will of God,
he would say: Thy will be done. . . . . In His will is our peace. But when

he believes that events are determined by the votes of a majority, the orders
of his bosses, the opinions of his neighbors, the laws of supply and demand,
and the decisions of quite selfish men, he yields because he has to yield. He
is conquered but unconvinced.

3. Sorties and Retreats

It might seem as if, in all this, men were merely going through once
again what they have often gone through before. This is not the first age
in which the orthodox religion has been in conflict with the science of the
day. Plato was born into such an age. For two centuries the philosophers
of Greece had been critical of Homer and of the popular gods, and when
Socrates faced his accusers, his answer to the accusation of heresy must
certainly have sounded unresponsive. "I do believe," he said, "that there
are gods, and in a higher sense than that in which my accusers believe in
them." That is all very well. But to believe in a "higher sense" is also to
believe in a different sense.

There is nothing new in the fact that men have ceased to believe in the
religion of their fathers. In the history of Catholic Christianity, there has
always existed a tradition, extending from the author of the Fourth Gospel
through Origen to the neo-Platonists of modern times, which rejects the
popular idea of God as a power acting upon events, and of immortality as
everlasting life, and translates the popular theology into a symbolic statement of a purely spiritual experience. In every civilized age there have been
educated and discerning men who could not accept literally and simply the
traditions of the ancient faith. We are told that during the Periclean Age
"among educated men everything was in dispute: political sanctions, literary
values, moral standards, religious convictions, even the possibility of reaching any truth about anything." When the educated classes of the Roman
world accepted Christianity they had ceased to believe in the pagan gods,
and were much too critical to accept the primitive Hebraic theories of the
creation, the redemption, and the Messianic Kingdom which were so
central in the popular religion. They had to do what Socrates had done;
they had to take the popular theology in a "higher" and therefore in a
different sense before they could use it. Indeed, it is so unusual to find an
age of active-minded men in which the most highly educated are genuinely
orthodox in the popular sense, that the Thirteenth Century, the age of
Dante and St. Thomas Aquinas, when this phenomenon is reputed to have
occurred, is regarded as a unique and wonderful period in the history of
the world. It is not at all unlikely that there never was such an age in the
history of civilized men.

And yet, the position of modern men who have broken with the religion of their fathers is in certain profound ways different from that of
other men in other ages. This is the first age, I think, in the history of
mankind when the circumstances of life have conspired with the intellectual
habits of the time to render any fixed and authoritative belief incredible to
large masses of men. The dissolution of the old modes of thought has gone so
far, and is so cumulative in its effect, that the modern man is not able to

sink back after a period of prophesying into a new but stable orthodoxy. The irreligion of the modern world is radical to a degree for which there is, I think, no counterpart. For always in the past it has been possible for new conventions to crystallize, and for men to find rest and surcease of effort in accepting them.

We often assume, therefore, that a period of dissolution will necessarily be followed by one of conformity, that the heterodoxy of one age will become the orthodoxy of the next, and that when this orthodoxy decays a new period of prophesying will begin. Thus we say that by the time of Hosea and Isaiah the religion of the Jews had become a system of rules for transacting business with Jehovah. The Prophets then revivified it by thundering against the conventional belief that religion was mere burnt offering and sacrifice. A few centuries passed and the religion based on the Law and the Prophets had in its turn become a set of mechanical rites manipulated by the Scribes and the Pharisees. As against this system Jesus and Paul preached a religion of grace, and against the "letter" of the synagogues the "spirit" of Christ. But the inner light which can perceive the spirit is rare, and so shortly after the death of Paul, the teaching gradually ceased to appeal to direct inspiration in the minds of the believers and became a body of dogma, a "sacred deposit" of the faith "once for all delivered to the saints." In the succeeding ages there appeared again many prophets who thought they had within them the revealing spirit. Though some of the prophets were burnt, much of the prophesying was absorbed into the canon. In Luther this sense of revelation appeared once more in a most confident form. He rejected the authority not only of the Pope and the clergy, but even of the Bible itself, except where in his opinion the Bible confirmed his faith. But in the establishment of a Lutheran Church the old difficulty reappeared: the inner light which had burned so fiercely in Luther did not burn brightly or steadily in all Lutherans, and so the right of private judgment, even in Luther's restricted use of the term, led to all kinds of heresies and abominations. Very soon there came to be an authoritative teaching backed by the power of the police. And in Calvinism the revolt of the Reformation became stabilized to the last degree. "Everything," said Calvin, "pertaining to the perfect rule of a good life the Lord has so comprehended in His law that there remains nothing for man to add to that summary."

Men fully as intelligent as the most emancipated among us once believed that, and I have no doubt that the successors of Mr. Darrow and Mr. Mencken would come to believe something very much like it if conditions permitted them to obey the instinct to retreat from the chaos of modernity into order and certainty. It is all very well to talk about being the captain of your soul. It is hard, and only a few heroes, saints, and geniuses have been the captains of their souls for any extended period of their lives. Most men, after a little freedom, have preferred authority with the consoling assurances and the economy of effort which it brings. "If, outside of Christ, you wish by your own thoughts to know your relation to God, you will break your neck. Thunder strikes him who examines." Thus spoke

Martin Luther, and there is every reason to suppose that the German people thought he was talking the plainest common sense. "He who is gifted with the heavenly knowledge of faith," said the Council of Trent, "is free from an inquisitive curiosity." These words are rasping to our modern ears, but there is no occasion to doubt that the men who uttered them had made a shrewd appraisal of average human nature. The record of experience is one of sorties and retreats. The search for moral guidance which shall not depend upon external authority has invariably ended in the acknowledgment of some new authority.

IS BELIEF OUT OF DATE?

André Bremond

I SHOULD like to expose a few ideas which were suggested to me by Mr. Vanderlaan's article in the *Journal of Religion* for April, 1935, entitled "Is Unbelief Out of Date?" I think I may sum up the main ideas of that article in three points: first, whatever may have been said or thought to the contrary, the recent discoveries and theories in physics do not supply the believer with a scientific proof of the existence of God. Consequently, unbelief remains the rational attitude of the modern and scientific man in the question of God; second, the question of a cosmological God, a prime mover, or supreme architect and engineer of the material world, without any interest in man's well-being or in his moral life, is purely academic; and, third, a belief in a "moral" God as a ground of human morals is useless and futile, since man finds in humanism, or the study of human nature as a fact of experience, both the rule and the means of moral conduct. Therefore the implied conclusion in the article of Mr. Vanderlaan is not only that unbelief is out of date, but that belief is out of date now as it has been ever since the beginning of the modern scientific age.

My intention is to show that, on the contrary, belief in God is not and can never be out of date to the moral man; in other words, that some explicit or implicit assertion of a transcendent or supernatural value and reality is necessary as a rational ground of man's moral life. And by supernatural I mean what is above the natural experimental science of man. To the scientist's dogma of the self-sufficiency of man, theoretical and moral in everything that pertains to rational activity, I oppose the natural need in man of something above nature. I hold, as Father H. Steuart puts it, that

considered by himself as a being who should be able, without involving any other being, to give a fully satisfying account of himself, man is a failure. . . . . Man, studied by the methods which prove so successful when applied to the rest of creation, stubbornly refuses to be explained. He comes under many categories, but under none of them completely; he partakes of many natures but transcends them all.

Before proceeding farther I must explain in a few words the believer's attitude with regard to science: its meaning, its scope, its progress, and its recent discoveries, in relation to his beliefs. That attitude, I am sorry to say, is altogether misrepresented by Mr. Vanderlaan when he suggests that the theist finds in certain scientific theories a decisive argument for the existence of God, and even that there is no other proof; and that the certitude that God exists is bound up with Eddington's interpretation of the most recent data of physics.

From *The Journal of Religion*, April, 1936. Reprinted by permission of the publishers, The University of Chicago Press.

The alleged positive argument thus established could be put in this form: Where science fails to explain the facts of nature, supernatural will and power are required as a cause. But we have of late found in the first elements of matter and their motion an indetermination and a spontaneity such that science is unable to foresee and explain what may or may not happen in the future. Therefore it is necessary to postulate a supernatural will and power which we call God. But, says Mr. Vanderlaan, exposing the weakness of the supposed argument: "Ignorance cannot be the open door to certitude. If science cannot tell us as well as once it claimed, what reality is, that is more reason, not less, for agnosticism. A time when science is in difficulties is precisely not the time to say it has discovered God."

To that I answer, and I am sure that any theist who knows the grounds of his belief would answer the same. First, the reasons for belief in God are independent of science, positive or experimental, with its postulates and self-appointed limits, since they are of a different and superior order. Science has for its object observable facts and their laws, or relations of necessary sequence or simultaneity. That there is between phenomena such a necessary sequence is not an a priori evidence, nor can it be scientifically demonstrated. It is a postulate which can be interpreted in many different senses. And it is a fact that when men of science care to investigate the grounds and value of their principles, the greatest diversity prevails among them. We must bear in mind the essential difference between science which has for its object the laws of phenomena but remains abstract and hypothetical as to the existence of things, and philosophy which starts from the fact of existence as such, and seeks the causes of that existence. Not only, then, the theist does not conclude the existence of God from any scientific fact or theory, but he is sure that scientific investigation and reasoning, if it be careful not to transgress its own rules, cannot possibly interfere with his own conclusions. Second, I answer that it often happens that certain scientists and unbelievers of the "scientist" type do transgress those rules and make their negation of God dependent on scientific determinism, taken as an absolute and necessary law of things. For them the sequence of events of any observable order is ruled by the same necessity as mathematics; and as mathematics excludes all consideration of efficience and finality, so does the knowledge of nature.

Consequently, if it happens that the very progress of scientific investigation throws some doubt on the absolute character of determinism in physics, and points to indetermination and spontaneity in the inmost heart of nature, the dogmatic unbeliever and scientist will have some reason to be genuinely distressed. The believer, on the other hand, will have some reason to rejoice, not for himself but for the sake of the unbeliever; not that science has proved the existence of God, for it can neither prove nor disprove it, but because science itself has removed a prejudice which was for some of its devotees an obstacle to the rational belief in the existence of God.

Let me now discuss the main point at issue: the necessity to the moral man of the belief in God. Kant speaks of two facts of inexhaustible wonder: the starry heavens above our heads and the moral law in our souls.

Each testifies to the divine. But I pass over the starry heavens and the order of the physical universe to consider only the fact of moral consciousness. Indeed, I am convinced that there is a valid cosmological argument for the existence of God, but I am ready to concede to Mr. Vanderlaan that, if from nature, outside man, we could infer only a cosmological God, as Aristotle, for instance, seems to do—a God without a relation to man's moral life—such a question of God would be merely academic. But I maintain, moreover, that man finds in his very conscience the evidence of a God, of the soul, etc. That this God of man's moral world is the God of the material universe can, I think, just as truly be demonstrated. But it is a different question altogether, one into which I need not enter now.

Therefore, I argue that man's, any man's, moral life, his idea of duty, of a good transcending any kind of private gratification, of a supreme and an absolute good, the only good which makes life worth living—in a word, everything which makes up the moral life of man—is all bound up with the explicit or implicit belief in a God—a moral, personal God, a God who is our living law, our living Providence and love: the perfect expression of such divine reality which is none other than the Christian dogma of the divine fatherhood.

Against such a view Mr. Vanderlaan holds what we may call the dogma of the moral self-sufficiency of man. He writes in the beginning of his article: "It ought by now to be clear that idealistic strivings contain their own rewards, and that valid moral imperatives correspond to basic desires of human nature." Now what I do not find perfectly clear in that sentence is how Mr. Vanderlaan makes any distinction between the fact of basic desires and the idea and validity of a moral imperative; whether the idea of duty has for him any value beside the fact of our instinctive strivings; whether our basic desires or instinctive strivings are truly idealistic, and what the scientific meaning of ideal and idealistic really is; and finally, what those moral imperatives which correspond to our basic desires are.

We have a partial answer to these questions, but they are only partial. Mr. Vanderlaan writes:

These moral imperatives which spring from innate impulses, like the love of justice and the hate of suffering, need no superhuman support, nor could they be more commanding if uttered by a voice from Sinai. It is needless to inquire why we ought to care about our neighbor or about future generations. The fact is that normal humanity has those interests. If altruism formed no part of our natural constitution, it could be no more binding on us than it is on stones. But the fact that sheer brute selfishness does not satisfy our full body of desires forms an adequate basis for morality, regardless of academic questions about the universe.

There is still, to my mind, some obscurity there. But I take it to mean that altruism or unselfish devotion to other people's good, or to a common good, has become a part of man's nature; that the question of duty or of moral imperative, of an "ought," beside the fact of instinct, is not merely academic but altogether idle and meaningless, as it is idle to inquire why we should eat or sleep, since normal humanity eats when it is hungry and goes to sleep when it is tired. Just as the man made out of brute humanity by Dr. Moreau in Wells's tale had to repeat to himself the command to walk on two legs. But whatever may be thought, said, or guessed about our animal ancestry, it is a fact that the actual human biped, the normal biped, walks on two legs, and has not the least sense of a duty of doing so. Fact is, indeed, stronger than duty!

Therefore Mr. Vanderlaan acknowledges an actual opposition between instinct, some natural instincts, and the moral imperative or the instinct of altruism. Consequently, he is bound to give some reason why normal humanity should follow one instinct rather than another. At any rate, he cannot dismiss the question as idle and academic. Moreover, there is a certain lack of precision, a vagueness in the definition of those moral imperatives, which have become natural impulses, as justice and the hate of suffering, which our author puts side by side. Justice and the hate of suffering—that is rather perplexing for me. The hate of suffering, as such, is very human, but it does not strike me as bearing an essential relation to justice or to altruism. It seems to me that it is, on the contrary, strongly individualistic if not selfish. It begins at home, and too often ends at home. Now the idea that suffering, and especially bodily suffering, is such an absolute evil that it must be avoided at any price—that I consider as simply immoral.

Pain, Socrates would say, is foreign to good or evil, irrelevant to virtue. Pain may be good, and pleasure, especially sensual pleasure, may be bad. It is certainly bad, and is the source of all injustice if pursued as an end for its own sake. Pain is given us with pleasure to make virtue out of it. Indifference to pain is a condition of moral virtue. I should say more: That pain is, in the actual state of man, the condition of moral progress; it has a purifying and strengthening effect which, if borne bravely, makes the human heart stronger and more compassionate as well. As Coventry Patmore has so well put it:

> "O Pain, love's mystery
> Close next of kin,
> To Joy and heart's delight,
> Low pleasure's opposite,
> Choice food of sanctity
> And medicine of sin. . . . ."

Whatever certain scientists may think, such a sense of the value of pain is a fact in certain souls, and these the most noble souls. What a pity it would be, indeed, if ever it becomes out of date!

But that is, after all, only a secondary point. And I suppose the fault is rather in the expression than in the actual thought itself. Consequently, I shall confine myself to what is, no doubt, the essential part of morality, or of moral instinct, according to Mr. Vanderlaan: care about our neighbor or about future generations, or, as we say in common parlance—altruism.

Is such altruism a dominant fact, an instinct normally prevailing over other contrary instincts? Is modern man more altruistic than selfish? Or if instinct is not yet strong enough, does positive science supply what is wanting, and afford a clear and effective rule of social good conduct? It may be so in some secret paradise, at Los Gatos, or in the immediate neighborhood, perhaps; but what strikes the observer is the rather alarming progress of individualism, the questioning of altruistic principles, which in a less enlightened age were not, at least as rules of conduct, open to discussion, but were admitted unreservedly.

I will not deny that there is an instinct of altruism or self-devotion. There always has been. A thoroughly selfish, self-centered individual could not live. A certain generosity has always been a law of life. But the individualistic instinct is, to say the least, as strong—the will to live, to persevere in one's being by whatever means nature puts at our disposal. But shall we say that such an instinct to live has been superseded by altruism? I doubt it, as I see no evident signs of it; but, on the contrary, an alarming revival of rational individualism. The devotion of self to any common cause, to any social group, has never been so freely open to discussion and doubt as at the present time. All social and national bonds seem to be relaxed and the individual left to himself to find his own individual happiness, and to use to that effect the resources of modern civilization. What still binds nations or social groups together is rather a community of fear and hate, not a common ideal of good, not a spontaneous mutual love.

Certainly the instinct to reason out principles and dogmas and impulses has never been stronger than now in this enlightened twentieth century. Man is, indeed, a rational animal, and reason has the power to weaken irrational instincts. And once we begin to reason out our altruistic instinct, a multitude of questions arises on the meaning of altruism itself. We have all heard that man must love his neighbor as himself. But what does love of my neighbor mean? The precept has a clear sense in Christian theology and practice; not so in a strictly scientific society, and from the point of view of positive science. And who is my neighbor? What individual or group or common ideal has a claim to my love? Does the parable of the good Samaritan express an instinct of the modern man? Outside of Christianity I do not see that there is a unanimous answer to the momentary question: What is that man, that human nature, whose perfection and whose welfare I have perpetually—and shall I say instinctively?—at heart, even though it be against my individual interests? What is "man" for the modern man? Merely a name conveniently applied to beings who are more or less like myself in bodily structure and the faculty of speech. But is mere likeness sufficient to stir in me an instinct of special consideration, respect, and benevolence? Has the most modern man the same consideration for all men alike, whatever be their race or their color? Is the Negro, for instance, always and everywhere a "neighbor," a brother to the white man? What is the value of a brown-skinned anthropoid, gifted with articulated speech, compared to the value of a good horse or of my old faithful dog? I may need a faith, a strong faith—I do not mean to make a difference between the two but to decide in favor of the grinning anthropoid. It is not a question of what we feel to be a duty, though opposed to impulse, but rather of the instinctive impulse which it is my duty to resist and conquer. But, omitting the doubts arising from the difference of race or color, there is the question among civilized men of the qualities one must fulfil to be

entitled to the respect of other men, to be accounted a man with the full
rights of humanity, or even with any right at all. What, for instance, must
be the attitude of men (of the state or of the individual) toward the helpless, the apparent cases of humanity, which, through disease, are altogether
inefficient, useless, a mere burden to society, even a danger, for disease, any
disease, is in some degree contagious? Is it healthy for man to devote his
life to the service of such degraded humanity, of the lepers, for instance?
Is it rational and scientific to follow such an impulse for the poor and the
helpless? In a word, is there still outside Christianity a living idea, an instinct, of the dignity of man as man?

There is still another question which does not appear to be solved either
by instinct or by scientific reason: which of the two forms of altruism, the
love of the living, individual man, or the love of humanity in the abstract,
are we to practice? or how reconcile them? Have future generations, men
as yet unborn, the same right to our care, nay more, even a greater right,
than the actually living man who is soon to die? There have been, and there
are still even now, fanatics all the more dangerous for the sincerity of their
altruism, in whom the idolatry, the worship, of some abstract, ideal super-
man has destroyed all regard for the well-being of their immediate, actually
living and suffering neighbor. The priest, or the Levite, who looked on the
poor man lying wounded by the wayside and passed on, may have been
such an idealist. Each instinct if not exclusive is right: love of mankind
and the progress of mankind and of future generations, love of my fellow-
traveler in the present ways of life, even self-love are all right. And self-
love is good, fundamental, and necessary. But the harmonious and living
synthesis of these impulses is not effected by any scientific reason. Rather,
I maintain that it needs a higher and a divine principle: a real unity binding the individual with the whole, not absorbing and losing it in the whole.

Let us look at the problem more closely. Kant's formula of duty was good
but incomplete: "Always treat humanity, both in your person and in the
persons of others, as an end and never merely as a means." But the real
spring of morality is respect and love, not alone respect, but respect joined
with love; love and respect not of an abstract principle such as "law," but of
something real which makes man worthy, both of reverence and of love,
such as I should not hesitate in certain cases to sacrifice my pleasure and
interest to his well-being, even to risk my life for his.

But what makes a man, any man, an object of reverence to another man
must be something superior to mere human nature, a more than human
value. That more than human value I call divine. It must be an essential
relation to a reality which claims absolute reverence or adoration. In other
words I revere God in man, and any man ought to revere God in his poor
human self, however naturally faulty and defective.

But, again, mere reverence without love will achieve nothing. Self-devotion requires love; I must love my neighbor as myself. But why? Because that essential relation to God in man is one of sonship. God is the
father of all men. That divine fatherly love of all and each is the principle
of a divine equality between men: a veritable bond of brotherly love. Con-

sequently, it might be shown that such dogma of divine fatherhood or a more or less distinct anticipation of that dogma is at the basic origin of religion, the very essence of religion; and that it is at the same time the bond of human society and the principle of individual freedom. It cannot be scientifically proved or disproved, and it does not run the risk of becoming obsolete, so long as the conflict in the human soul between the autonomy of self-love and altruism, between the devotion to human society and the love of and devotion to the individual human person, has been solved by science or philosophy.

In a word, if belief is out of date, morality is out of date as well; and we see no sign of instinctive agreement between men on these essential points of morality—now less than ever before. I can only suggest here that the consideration of the meaning of human life from the point of view of death would bring us to the same conclusion on the subject of belief.

We may agree with Spinoza that philosophy, the philosophy implied in any rational life, ought to be a meditation not on death but on life. But still the fact of death cannot be overlooked. On the contrary, if we are in earnest, if we do not want to deceive ourselves, we must look the hateful fact in the face, and our meditation ought to be of life in death and through death—how death can be conquered and how immortality secured. It might be shown that there is no instinct which makes the idea of death the absolute end beyond which there is no hope of survival tolerable to the modern man; that such meditation is beyond the scope of experimental science, is rather of the supernatural order; and that, consequently, the belief in the personal and living God as the guaranty of our own life beyond death is not and never shall be out of date.

METHODS OF MYSTICISM

Henry Nelson Wieman

THE WORD MYSTICISM means very different things as used at different times and by different people. Often it is used without any clear distinction between several different meanings. Sometimes the meanings are so divergent as to make it absurd to use the same word at all. This is one of the chief reasons for the extremely diverse valuations placed upon it. . . . .

We shall consider eleven different kinds or aspects of experience which are frequently referred to as mystical. We shall exclude from our present consideration the philosophies which go by the name of mysticism since we are interested in mystical experiences, not philosophies.

The eleven experiences we have divided into three groups of six, three, and two. The first six consist of experiences which we think are worthless. They certainly do occur and are frequently called mystical. But in our esteem they are not only bereft of value; they are in some cases positively vicious. The experiences of the second group, on the other hand, are of some value when rightly conducted. But it is only when we come to the last two experiences to be described that we find the kind of mysticism which we hold to be of outstanding importance.

I. WORTHLESS TYPES OF MYSTICISM

(1) The first kind of mystical experience we would mention, and the one lowest in our scale of value, is the experience of being muddleheaded or confused in thinking. Perhaps no one makes mysticism identical with all confused thinking. But if the thinking has to do with high themes, or assumes to do so, and especially if the confused thinker is led by his addled brain to adopt some mistaken notion which fills him with enthusiasm or ecstasy, then some critic who is especially irritated by such thinking, may apply to it the term of mysticism in a derogatory sense, saying: "That is nothing but mysticism," in scornful tone.

(2) A second kind of experience or belief which goes by the name of mysticism is occultism. It involves certain esoteric practices, and, presumably, certain weird experiences. We include under this head spiritualism as well as much theosophy and new thought and the like. We do not claim that these are alike in other respects but they do have in them something of the occult. We lump them all together as constituting a modern form of superstition. . . . .

(3) In the third place mysticism may be applied to almost any very unusual state of consciousness, for example, the feeling that we are experiencing in a given situation what we experienced before. Or the feeling that

From *Methods of Private Religious Living*, New York, 1929, pp. 163-195. Reprinted by permission of the publishers, The Macmillan Company.

sometimes comes to some people that their experience is unreal. The sights, sounds, what they touch are a dream, a sham, a mask, a bit of stage play, concealing the true reality. Other bizarre experiences might be added, such as may be induced by certain drugs or diseases or psychic trance.

(4) A fourth kind of mysticism is hallucination. Under this head we include the voices heard by Socrates warning him of what will be the consequences of some anticipated course of action; or the voices heard by Joan of Arc; the vision of Christ walking the fields of Flanders, seen by soldiers in the Great War; the vision of the Virgin Mary seen by the wounded soldier; the ghosts seen in the graveyard. This is a very common form of mental pathology. It is not commonly called mysticism when found in an insane asylum; but if the subject is an individual of great prestige, especially if he is a religious leader, and above all if his voices are the psychological ornamentations added to some profound insight, the hallucinations are likely to be considered mystical. George Fox was much addicted to them.

Now there seems to be no question but that individuals of marked intellectual ability, innovators and thinkers, men and women of enormous powers of leadership, have had such hallucinations. When we say that this kind of mysticism is worthless we are not suggesting in any way that the insights and achievements and abilities of such persons are diminished in value because they had them. We are only saying that the hallucination added nothing whatever of value to their achievement or their insight. Neither did it subtract anything. . . . .

(5) A fifth kind of mysticism is what is sometimes called the "inner conviction" or the "inner light." It is the holding of some belief as precious and true simply because one feels it must be so but without any adequate support of reason or experimental evidence. For example one may say: I know this is the thing I should do. I feel it here. Then he strikes himself somewhere in the region of the breast or the abdomen. Or. one cries: I know I am saved, I feel it here. He also indicates roughly the region of the viscera as the source of his assurance.

Here again we must remember that such "inner conviction" is sometimes a kind of profound insight. But the fact that we "feel it here" throws no light whatsoever on the question whether it is true or false. Only the tests of reason and experiment can answer that question. Therefore, to pick out the inner feeling and the absence of all reason and experimental evidence as the one feature in such an experience which makes it mystical, is to pick out precisely the feature in it which is weakest and most dangerous. The insight is good, if it is insight; but the absence of explicit reason and evidence is bad. . . . .

(6) The sixth kind of mysticism is one of the most widely recognized forms of it. Its chief distinguishing characteristic is loss of volitional control. The stream of consciousness and the bodily behavior continue but the individual does not exercise any control over them. He thinks it must be God in him who acts, talks and thinks, since the acting, talking and thinking go on without any conscious control on his part. Hence devotees

ardently seek to induce the experience in themselves and others, for thus do they join themselves with God according to their belief.

There are various methods by which this loss of control can be brought about without loss of consciousness and often with intensified vividness of conscious states. The use of certain drugs will do it and among primitive peoples it is a very common practice to use these drugs to bring about divine possession of this sort. Sometimes excessive fasting will do it. Furious dancing, shouting, striking one's self will for some produce the desired state. The yoga system is a special technique developed for this purpose. Dervishes have their method of rhythmic movement, and prescribed words. The powerful stimulus of a crowd will greatly augment any or all of these effects, especially if the assembled people are expecting to go into a trance or lose control of themselves, talk with tongues or leap about without conscious direction. The tremendous suggestion of crowd expectation plays a great part in reducing a person to a state wherein he talks, feels, and acts without volitional control. Some people may have a nervous constitution of such kind that they can pass into this state without help of any unusual stimulus. According to Leuba the suppression and distortion of powerful sexual impulses may play a great part in producing this trance-like state of mind and body. The most widespread manifestation of this kind of mysticism in recent times is perhaps "talking with tongues."

Needless to say we do not think divinity is any more fully operative in these states of uncontrolled consciousness and behavior than in others. If anything deity is less manifested here, for these conditions often seem to be disintegrating, hence opposed to the working of God. . . . .

II. Better Types of Mysticism

These better types of mysticism are not necessarily in each case an unadulterated good. They may be practiced in such a way as to be worthless or harmful. But when properly treated they minister in some measure to the good life.

(7) The seventh type of mysticism, and the first of the better kinds, is that experience which ensues when some belief or ideal is held fixedly before the mind until it has exercised a powerful influence upon the individual. The value of this depends in part upon the kind of belief or ideal so held. It has been suggested that the Christlike stigmata of St. Francis of Assisi did actually appear and that they were produced by prolonged and recurrent fixation of the mind upon the idea of Christ as he was known to men of that time. Whether or not that be true, it would seem that the life and character of St. Francis developed in the way it did partly at least because of his personal absorption in what he knew about Jesus. Another example is the case of a man who believes in transubstantiation and holds that belief before his mind with such concentration and self-surrender to it that when he partakes of the bread and wine of the communion service he is transported into an ecstasy and possibly the bent of his mind permanently modified. . . . . Or, to take another example, one may hold before the mind the thought that the world is very shortly to come to an end and

the millennium be ushered in. If this is done with sufficient fixation it may produce a state of mind that is called mystical.

We place this kind of mysticism lowest in this group because, in the first place, so much depends on the kind of idea which is the object of contemplation. Secondly, it is likely to produce dissociation or hypnosis and that is not, generally speaking, we believe, a wholesome thing. Through this self-hypnosis one can quiet all doubts and establish unshakable conviction of the truth of anything he would like to believe and do it without the pain and labor of intellectual inquiry. In fact he can do it far more readily than can ever be done by inquiry, for intelligent inquiry might force him to cast the belief aside as illusory. . . . .

This kind of mysticism, which is really a species of auto-suggestion, may be one of the greatest evils, although, under rightly controlled conditions, it may be very valuable.

(8) The eighth type of mysticism is awareness of mystery. Without doubt mysterious realms, that is unexplored realms, of existence and possibility constantly encompass us; but for the most part we are not conscious of them. The little realm of common things with which we have become familiar and which stand out in the clear light of our cognition, holds our attention to the exclusion of mystery. The encompassing mysteries which sustain us or frustrate us, which hover over us and waver through us, are not even imagined by us. But when occasionally some one does become strongly conscious of this mystery which enshrouds our little day he has an experience which is rightly called mystical. Otto's sense of the "numinous" belongs to this type of mysticism, although he gives to it an interpretation of his own which we do not accept and which takes all the value away from the experience. According to him the mystery which reaches us in this experience pertains to another realm of being wholly outside of that with which we deal in ordinary life of common things. Such interpretation of the experience makes it a source of error; for the mystery discerned, we believe, is simply the mystery which is involved in the common things with which we deal. All things are mysterious in the sense that we know them so imperfectly. . . . .

The awareness of mystery may be engendered by any unusual experience. A savage who saw a locomotive for the first time might have it. A little child seeing one for the first time probably always does. Most of the symbols used in religious worship serve to suggest those mysterious realities with which we constantly deal but know it not save as these symbols bring them to mind. . . . .

Now it is plain that we cannot strive to explore the realms of mystery, if we have no sense of mystery. Hence the kind of mysticism which consists in sense of mystery is needful to keep us groping, questing, growing; to keep us plastic; to prevent us from developing a hard shell beyond which aspiration and imagination cannot venture. . . . .

But this kind of mysticism has its danger. The value of it just described may be perverted. The sense of mystery may be cultivated as a luxury, as a voluptuous experience, and not as a stimulus to further growth. We are afraid that Otto's treatment of it tends in this direction. A perverted mystic of this kind may cling to his mystery in such manner that he resents all investigation and extension of life which would render no longer mysterious the particular thing which seems mysterious to him.

Another way in which the sense of mystery may be perverted is through myths. The sense of mystery naturally leads to myth-making, which is the first tentative venturing of the human mind out into these unexplored realms. But a later generation, and even contemporaries who lack the mystic sense of mystery, may accept these myths as a charted map and accurate description of the unexplored realms. Thereafter anyone who ventures to explore this region by more profound thought and stronger imagination and deeper capacity for experience, is denounced or stoned for disturbing the sacred myths. . . . .

The man who has no sense of mystery (and perhaps that includes most of us during most of the time) is a man whose conscious experience is sharply delimited and confined to the artificial, conventional molds and images of things. He cannot pierce beyond this veil of conventional imagery to the things as they exist. . . . .

(9) The ninth kind of mysticism is the sudden inflooding of the sense of peace and power which comes to most people in some measure at some time or other. The value of this experience depends on what it signifies. If it indicates an achieved integration of personality, a resolution of inner conflict, and the organization of impulses about some dominant trend, it may be a very good thing. Stanley Jones in his *Christ of the Indian Road* seems to have had such an experience. It is not at all uncommon. William James in his *Varieties* has many instances of it; also Harold Begbie in his *Twice Born Men*.

But it is important to note that the state of consciousness as such does not always betoken such a transformation of personality. The sense of peace and power may be brought on by physiological conditions which have nothing to do with unification of personality. Some pleasant illusion will cause it. Certain drugs will produce it. In fact when this peculiar state of consciousness is set up as the essential feature of the mystical experience, as it often is, we have something which is not necessarily good and may be evil. Here again we have the case of taking a very untrustworthy feature of a total experience and identifying it with mysticism, thereby rendering mysticism of doubtful value.

We should go further still and say that even integration of personality is not always good. If integration is attained or preserved by narrowing the scope of interests, by being indifferent and stupid and selfish, by sharing less in the lives of others and in the process of history, then it is not good. Better have inner conflict due to assuming responsibilities and sharing interests which one has not yet been able to integrate, than to have the peace that comes from stolidity, indifference and inertia. Better Socrates unhappy than a pig happy. . . . .

The peace and joy that arise from achieving some richer integration than the individual life has thus far attained, is a great good. But the good is in the integration; the mental state is merely registration in consciousness of the value attained. . . . .

III. Best Types of Mysticism

We now come to the discussion of the last two types of mysticism. These two we hold to be of towering importance, far exceeding the value of anything we have thus far discussed. Hitherto we have been describing kinds of mysticism which were either harmful or worthless or of vacillating and doubtful value. . . . . However, some of the types of experience we have described may often enter in as facets or adjuncts to these last two kinds of experience.

(10) To get the tenth kind of mysticism before us consider an example. Augustine struggled for years with the rich data of experience which teemed upon him, unable to find an adequate integration. But finally he did discover a way of living in which the stormy impulses of his heart, the longings of his mother, the total cultural situation of his day, the movement of history and the cosmic process so far as it discernibly affected him, could all be brought into an organic unity in which he was himself one organic member. The unity which he thus discovered he called the City of God. It fascinated the minds of Europe for a thousand years. In so far as the City of God was a fact (and it was not wholly made up of error) it was not something Augustine invented, but an integrating process which he discovered and to which he joined himself. The experience was not merely an integration of his own personality; it was discovery of a process with which and in which he could be united as one member to an organic body. Before he made this discovery the experiences of life had been to Augustine like diverse sounds, some pleasant, some not, but through which no harmony was discerned that could transform them into music. The cravings of his heart, the movements of the age, the problems of the time, had been pulling him this way and that. He did not discern the integrating principle and so could have no peace until he found the way of life in which all these could fit together into an organic whole. When he did make the discovery he yielded himself to this organic whole, crying: "O God, thou didst make our hearts for thee and they are restless till they rest in thee."

The mystic experience we are here describing is experience of discerning how things which were made for one another fit together. One's own personality is one of the things thus found to fit into a unity with other things. The thinking, feeling, willing of the self is found through this experience to inhere in a large whole made up of other processes going on in the world. It is often said that conversion is the experience of achieving integration of personality after it has suffered from inner conflict. That may be all there is in some conversion; but it is only a part, and the less important, of the experience we are here considering. In the mystic experience we now have before us, the integration of the personality of the subject is incidental to his discernment of a much wider integration, far exceeding the bounds of his own personality, but to which he can unite himself as one organic member. . . . .

(11) The eleventh kind of mysticism is a method of solving problems. . . . . When one discerns the most inclusive integration of which he is capable he has no problem to solve. It is an experience of a problem solved, not an experience of problem solving. It is not a seeking but a finding, not striving but attainment. . . . .

But now we are to give our attention to the opposite kind of experience, a kind of mysticism which struggles with a problem, which seek an integration not yet discerned. It is a striving to escape from a disintegrated situation; not the appreciative discernment of a situation already integrated. It is a striving to escape from that condition in which various unreconciled demands are made upon the individual and divergent interests lay hold on him. This conflict threatens either to tear his life asunder or force him for the sake of his own integrity to fall back to a narrower, more meager way of living. Or it may be not threatened disruption nor impoverishment of life but simply the feeling that there is some richer integration he has not yet attained, which leads him to resort to the problem-solving method of mysticism.

Whenever we can solve a problem by putting old ideas together, by drawing inferences from old premises, by experimenting with hypotheses already discovered, the method of mysticism is of no avail. One had far better spend his time putting his ideas together, drawing his inferences and experimenting with his hypotheses. But the kind of problem which requires the method of mysticism for its solution is the one for which we need some new idea that cannot be formed by merely putting old ideas together. It is a problem the solution of which requires discernment of some integration of the data of experience more inclusive and rich in content than any we have thus far apprehended and for which we do not yet have the principle. We must get started on some wholly new lines of thinking.

How can we go about finding an entirely new line of thought? Here is where the problem-solving mysticism we are now considering serves its purpose. It consists in facing the problematical situation without any formulated thought but in a state of receptivity and responsiveness, waiting for some clue that will lead on to a new line. It is a state of waiting but without preconception of what one is waiting for. The mind is in a fluid, unorganized state. It is a kind of disorganization, for the old organization of thoughts and attitudes has been cast off, but it is a disorganization which is seeking some new organization. The mind is divested of all other plan and purpose. Before one enters this state he will have plans and purposes and theories about the problem with which he is dealing. But in this state he divests his mind of its formulated content so far as possible and exposes his total unbiased capacity for response to the problematical situation in the groping endeavor to hit on some clue that will put him on the right track. . . . .

It should be clear that the mystical experience we are here describing is not one in which the mind is a blank. The mind is not empty of everything, but it is empty of distinct ideas. The content of consciousness, as Dewey says, is formless, fluid, ineffable. One is reacting to the problem but without any stateable idea or established mental set. One is in a state of stimulation but without any formulated purpose save a vague groping. . . . .

If the problem which is being treated in this way has to do with making adjustment of human living to the vast processes of God (and this is what all major human problems ultimately involve) the experience we have described is a kind of worship. It is one of the most profound kinds of worship. It is a problem-solving worship out of which has emerged the great revolutionary insights of history and also the great revolutionary insights which have transformed individual lives.

One important requisite for the practice of this kind of mysticism is patience. Sometimes it may lead quite quickly to the discernment of the required integration. But more often, perhaps, especially if the problem is very complex, the solution may require months or years. After intervals of struggle with the problem one may return again to this state of mysticism and may continue this alternation between mental effort and mystic waiting for months or even years before the long-sought integration is discerned.

There are three further prerequisites that should be noted besides patience. First, one must be struggling earnestly with the problem with whatever ideas he has at his command, only resorting to this method of mysticism when he has found all these ideas to be inadequate. Secondly, he must have a mind richly stored with the experiences of life. Third, he should have his problem as well formulated as possible before he enters the mystic state. . . . .

The kind of problem for which this method is adapted is one requiring some advance beyond the frontiers of human living, at least so far as concerns the experience of that individual. Hence it is peculiarly fitted for those most complex and serious problems which arise in our dealings with other people, since intimate association with unique individuals and complex social situations generally demand of us radical readjustments and introduce us to rich realms of unexplored experience. But the greatest use of this method lies in seeking better adjustment of individual habits and social institutions to that progressively integrating process of widest scope with which one can deal. The great religious and moral and artistic insights of history have come in this way, we believe. The great founders and innovators of religion seem to have proceeded by this method of mysticism.

The cosmic process in which and with which we live, when we live well, far exceeds any powers of comprehension we have thus far achieved. All our ideas are inadequate for making adjustment to it. Hence we must ever strive for more inclusive integrations in dealing with it. To this end we must periodically turn aside from our routine activities and wait in mystic quietude in order that more adequate insights may come to us. In this way we are able to pierce more deeply into the mystery that encompasses us, explore the unexplored, and imagine the unimagined. This is the great task of religion. It is the way man learns to live more intimately with God.

THE RATIONAL AND THE NON-RATIONAL

Rudolf Otto

IT IS ESSENTIAL to every theistic conception of God, and most of all to the Christian, that it designates and precisely characterizes Deity by the attributes Spirit, Reason, Purpose, Good Will, Supreme Power, Unity, Selfhood. The nature of God is thus thought of by analogy with our human nature of reason and personality; only, whereas in ourselves we are aware of this as qualified by restriction and limitation, as applied to God the attributes we use are "completed," i.e., thought as absolute and unqualified. Now all these attributes constitute clear and definite *concepts*: they can be grasped by the intellect; they can be analyzed by thought; they even admit of definition. An object that can thus be thought conceptionally may be termed *rational*. The nature of deity described in the attributes above mentioned is, then, a rational nature; and a religion which recognizes and maintains such a view of God is in so far a "rational" religion. Only on such terms is Belief possible in contrast to mere *feeling*. . . . .

All language, in so far as it consists of words, purports to convey ideas or concepts—that is what language means—and the more clearly and unequivocally it does so, the better the language. And hence expositions of religious truth in language inevitably tend to stress the "rational" attributes of God.

But though the above mistake is thus a natural one enough, it is none the less seriously misleading. For so far are these "rational" attributes from exhausting the idea of deity, that they in fact imply a non-rational or suprarational Subject of which they are predicates. They are "essential" (and not merely "accidental") attributes of that subject, but they are also, it is important to notice, *synthetic* essential attributes. That is to say, we have to predicate them of a subject which they qualify, but which in its deeper essence is not, nor indeed can be, comprehended in them; which rather requires comprehension of a quite different kind. Yet, though it eludes the conceptual way of understanding, it must me in some way or other within our grasp, else absolutely nothing could be asserted of it. And even Mysticism, in speaking of it as τὸ ἄρρητον, the ineffable, does not really mean to imply that absolutely nothing can be asserted of the object of the religious consciousness; otherwise, Mysticism could exist only in unbroken silence, whereas what has generally been a characteristic of the mystics is their copious eloquence.

Here for the first time we come up against the contrast between Rationalism and profounder religion, and with this contrast and its signs we shall be repeatedly concerned in what follows. We have here in fact the first

From *The Idea of the Holy*, London, 1924, pp. 1-12. Reprinted by permission of the publishers, Oxford University Press.

and most distinctive mark of Rationalism, with which all the rest are bound up. It is not that which is commonly asserted, that Rationalism is the denial, and its opposite the affirmation, of the miraculous. That is manifestly a wrong or at least a very superficial distinction. For the traditional theory of the miraculous as the occasional breach in the casual nexus in nature by a Being who himself instituted and must therefore be master of it—this theory is itself as massively "rational" as it is possible to be. Rationalists have often enough acquiesced in the possibility of the miraculous in this sense; they have even themselves contributed to frame a theory of it—whereas anti-Rationalists have been often indifferent to the whole controversy about miracles. The difference between Rationalism and its opposite is to be found elsewhere. It resolves itself rather into a peculiar difference of *quality* in the mental attitude and emotional content of the religious life itself. All depends upon this: in our idea of God is the non-rational overborne, even perhaps wholly excluded, by the rational? Or conversely, does the non-rational itself preponderate over the rational? Looking at the matter thus, we see that the common dictum, that Orthodoxy itself has been the mother of Rationalism, is in some measure well founded. It is not simply that Orthodoxy was preoccupied with doctrine and the framing of dogma, for these have been no less a concern of the wildest mystics. It is rather that Orthodoxy found in the construction of dogma and doctrine no way to do justice to the non-rational aspect of its subject. So far from keeping the non-rational element in religion alive in the heart of the religious experience, orthodox Christianity manifestly failed to recognize its value, and by this failure gave to the idea of God a one-sidedly intellectualistic and rationalistic interpretation. . . . . .

And so it is salutary that we should be incited to notice that Religion is not exclusively contained and exhaustively comprised in any series of "rational" assertions; and it is well worth while to attempt to bring the relation of the different "moments" of religion to one another clearly before the mind, so that its nature may become more manifest.

This attempt we are now to make with respect to the quite distinctive category of the holy or sacred.

"Numen" and the "Numinous"

"Holiness"—"the holy"—is a category of interpretation and valuation peculiar to the sphere of religion. It is, indeed, applied by transference to another sphere—that of Ethics—but it is not itself derived from this. While it is complex, it contains a quite specific element or "moment," which sets it apart from the Rational in the meaning we gave to that word above, and which remains inexpressible—an ἄρρητον or *ineffabile*—in the sense that it completely eludes apprehension in terms of concepts. The same thing is true (to take a quite different region of experience) of the category of the beautiful.

Now these statements would be untrue from the outset if "the holy" were merely what is meant by the word, not only in common parlance, but in philosophical, and generally even in theological usage. The fact is we have come to use the words *holy*, *sacred* (heilig) in an entirely derivative sense, quite different from that which they originally bore. We generally take "holy" as meaning "completely good"; it is the absolute moral attribute, denoting the consummation of moral goodness. In this sense Kant calls the will which remains unwaveringly obedient to the moral law from the motive of duty a "holy" will; here clearly we have simply the *perfectly moral* will. In the same way we may speak of the holiness or sanctity of Duty or Law, meaning merely that they are imperative upon conduct and universally obligatory.

But this common usage of the term is inaccurate. It is true that all this moral significance is contained in the word "holy," but it includes in addition—as even we cannot but feel—a clear overplus of meaning, and this it is now our task to isolate. Nor is this merely a later or acquired meaning; rather, "holy," or at least the equivalent words in Latin and Greek, in Semitic and other ancient languages, denoted first and foremost *only* this overplus; if the ethical element was present at all, at any rate it was not original and never constituted the whole meaning of the word. Anyone who uses it today does undoubtedly always feel "the morally good" to be implied in "holy"; and accordingly in our inquiry into that element which is separate and peculiar to the idea of the holy it will be useful, at least for the temporary purpose of the investigation, to invent a special term to stand for "the holy" *minus* its moral factor or "moment," and, as we can now add, minus its "rational" aspect altogether.

It will be our endeavor to suggest this unnamed Something to the reader as far as we may, so that he may himself feel it. There is no religion in which it does not live as the real innermost core, and without it no religion would be worthy of the name. It is pre-eminently a living force in the Semitic religions, and of these again in none has it such vigour as in that of the Bible. Here, too, it has a name of its own, viz. the Hebrew *qādôsh*, to which the Greek ἅγιος and the Latin *sanctus*, and, more accurately still, *sacer*, are the corresponding terms. It is not, of course, disputed, that these terms in all three languages connote, as part of their meaning, *good, absolute, goodness*, when, that is, the notion has ripened and reached the highest stage in its development. And we then use the word "holy" to translate them. But this "holy" then represents the gradual shaping and filling in with ethical meaning, or what we shall call the "schematization," of what was a unique original feeling-response, which can be in itself ethically neutral and claims consideration in its own right. And when this moment or element first emerges and begins its long development, all those expressions (*qādôsh*, ἅγιος, *sacer*, etc.) mean beyond all question something quite other than "the good." This is universally agreed by contemporary criticism, which rightly explains the rendering of *qādôsh* by "good" as a mistranslation and unwarranted "rationalization" or "moralization" of the term.

Accordingly, it is worth while, as we have said, to find a word to stand for this element in isolation, this "extra" in the meaning of "holy" above and beyond the meaning of goodness. By means of a special term we shall the better be able, first, to keep the meaning clearly apart and distinct, and second, to apprehend and classify connectedly whatever subordinate forms or stages of development it may show. For this purpose I adopt a word coined from the Latin *numen. Omen* has given us *ominous,* and there is no reason why from *numen* we should not similarly form a word "*numinous.*" I shall speak then of a unique "numinous" category of value and of a definitely "numinous" state of mind, which is always found wherever the category is applied. This mental state is perfectly *sui generis* and irreducible to any other; and therefore, like every absolutely primary and elementary datum, while it admits of being discussed, it cannot be strictly defined. There is only one way to help another to an understanding of it. He must be guided and led on by consideration and discussion of the matter through the ways of his own mind, until he reach the point at which "the numinous" in him perforce begins to stir, to start into life and into consciousness. We can co-operate in this process by bringing before his notice all that can be found in other regions of the mind, already known and familiar, to resemble, or again to afford some special contrast to, the particular experience we wish to elucidate. Then we must add: "This X of ours is not precisely *this* experience, but akin to this one and the opposite of that other. Cannot you now realize for yourself what it is? In other words our X cannot, strictly speaking, be taught, it can only be evoked, awakened in the mind; as everything that comes "of the spirit" must be awakened.

The Elements in the "Numinous": Creature-Feeling

The reader is invited to direct his mind to a moment of deeply-felt religious experience, as little as possible qualified by other forms of consciousness. Whoever cannot do this, whoever knows no such moments in his experience, is requested to read no further; for it is not easy to discuss questions of religious psychology with one who can recollect the emotions of his adolescence, the discomforts of indigestion, or, say, social feelings, but cannot recall any intrinsically religious feelings. We do not blame such a one, when he tries for himself to advance as far as he can with the help of such principles of explanation as he knows, interpreting "Aesthetics" in terms of sensuous pleasure, and "Religion" as a function of the gregarious instinct and social standards, or as something more primitive still. But the artist, who for his part has an intimate personal knowledge of the distinctive element in the aesthetic experience, will decline his theories with thanks, and the religious man will reject them even more uncompromisingly.

Next, in the probing and analysis of such states of the soul as that of solemn worship, it will be well if regard be paid to what is unique in them rather than to what they have in common with other similar states. To be *rapt* in worship is one thing; to be morally *uplifted* by the contemplation of a good deed is another; and it is not to their common features, but to those elements of emotional content peculiar to the first that we would have attention directed as precisely as possible. As Christians we undoubtedly here first meet with feelings familiar enough in a weaker form in other departments of experience, such as feelings of gratitude, trust, love, reliance, humble submission, and dedication. But this does not by any means exhaust the content of religious worship. Not in any of these have we got the special features of the quite unique and incomparable experience of solemn worship. In what does this consist? . . . .

It is easily seen that, once again, this phrase, whatever it is, is not a *conceptual* explanation of the matter. All that this new term, "creature-feeling," can express, is the note of self-abasement into nothingness before an overpowering, absolute might of some kind; whereas everything turns upon the *character* of this overpowering might, a character which cannot be expressed verbally, and can only be suggested indirectly through the tone and content of a man's feeling-response to it. And this response must be directly experienced in oneself to be understood. . . . .

Rather, the "creature-feeling" is itself a first subjective concomitant and effect of another feeling-element, which casts it like a shadow, but which in itself indubitably has immediate and primary reference to an object outside the self.

Now this object is just what we have already spoken of as "the numinous." For the "creature-feeling" and the sense of dependence to arise in the mind the "numen" must be experienced as present, a "numen praesens," as in the case of Abraham. There must be felt a something "numinous," something bearing the character of a "numen," to which the mind turns spontaneously; or (which is the same thing in other words) these feelings can only arise in the mind as accompanying emotions when the category of "the numinous" is called into play.

The numinous is thus felt as objective and outside the self.

THE AUTHORITY OF THE OLD TESTAMENT

Julius A. Bewer

THE OLD TESTAMENT was originally a Jewish book, the sacred Bible of the Jewish temple and synagogue. It became the Bible of the Christian church before any part of the New Testament was written and it remained authoritative for the Christians even after their separation from the Jews and in spite of their fierce conflict with them, in the course of which the Jews defined more closely the extent of their sacred canon. The Christians made it the first part of their larger Bible, placing it side by side with the New Testament after that had been completed and canonized; and they bound both frequently together in one single volume.

The church never forgot that the Old Testament had been the Bible of Jesus, which he read and studied, which gave to him strength and inspiration because he found in it the word of God. The whole New Testament is full of Old Testament references. Paul and the apostles, the writers of the Gospels, the whole church read and knew and used the Old Testament as divinely inspired and authoritative. All through the Christian ages, in Catholicism and Protestantism, the Old Testament was revered, and everywhere it exerted a profound influence. It is easy to see that its high veneration, due in many instances to remarkable spiritual blessings obtained from reading it, should lead to a doctrine of divine inspiration. But it was most unfortunate that the harmful doctrine of verbal inspiration which asserted that every word of the Old Testament had been divinely inspired and that every bit of it was infallible should have been appropriated by the Christians.

To us that is simply an impossible doctrine. When we read the stories and histories of the Old Testament and find again and again contradictions, errors, impossible or distasteful statements; when we read the law sections, not merely the ceremonial and sacrificial law, but the moral law, and compare the moral practice, "an eye for an eye, a tooth for a tooth," the cruelties and barbarities advocated and practiced; when we read the prophecies and find many of them unfulfilled and mistaken, though given in the name of God, some cruel, narrow, and egotistic; when we study the Psalms and find so much hatred and vengefulness in many of them; when we read the Wisdom literature and find an ethic not always on a high level—we cannot believe that God has inspired all this, that all this is the word of God. For we see that it is not infallible, not always truly spiritual, not everywhere highly moral, not always edifying. The Old Testament sanctions polygamy and easy divorce; hatred, revenge, and ruthless extermination of enemies; non-intercourse and non-marriage with foreigners; exclusion of certain

From *The Journal of Religion*, January, 1936. Reprinted by permission of the publishers, The University of Chicago Press.

foreigners from ever gaining citizenship; extreme nationalism in politics and religion.

These matters did not escape the earlier generations, but they could make use of the methods of allegorical and typological interpretation and thus they overcame these difficulties. But when these methods were discarded as false and as obviously doing no justice to the Old Testament, Christian scholars began to study this amazing literature in a true literary and historical manner. And the work of these devoted men during more than a century and a half has done much to give us a truer understanding of the Old Testament, of its origin, growth, and final canonization. It has shown that it is not all on the same level, that it started from low beginnings morally and religiously and went on and on to ever higher levels, that one age stood on the shoulders of the preceding and grew in the knowledge of God and of his will, sometimes a later age sharply denying the beliefs or actions which a former generation had sanctioned as divine. The result was a new view of the Old Testament, fascinating and inspiring. The whole of it became once more full of interest and life. And many people who had begun to doubt with the divine origin of the Old Testament also the truth of divine revelation altogether, regained their faith and devotion to God and his Christ, and their love for the Old Testament.

That was a vast gain for the Christian church, which it was, however, slow to perceive and still is reluctant to acknowledge. The ultimate reason for this is not far to seek. There is a danger in it of which the church is sorely afraid: In the eager study of the ever changing and passing human side of this amazingly fascinating development of religion by means of literary, historical, and psyhcological criticism one is liable to forget the imperishable divine element, to neglect the reality and truth of the revelation of God in these pages. And even when this is not forgotten there remains the question: If the divine revelation in history is so relative that what is divine and authoritative for one age is no longer so for the next, where is the enduringly divine element in this book whose origin is so human and whose pages are so full of lower elements? How can it have any authority for us? That is a fair and a serious question, and it is no wonder that the church is full of concern. She must be aware that no decree of her own or any pronouncement of theology, however high sounding its claims may be, can restore the authority of the Old Testament to the modern man when once he has read the Old Testament in this new way.

For the thinking man only that can really be authoritative which compels his inward assent, obedience, and homage by virtue of its truth. Truth alone possesses moral and spiritual power over us; and only those moral and religious teachings which we have recognized as truth or which become clear to us as truth, can have authority for us. Since truth is divine, only that which evidences itself to us as the word of God is authoritative for us.

That the Old Testament as a whole is not the word of God and therefore not authoritative for us we have already seen, and we must now ask, Is there anything in the Old Testament that partakes of such an authoritative character that we may say "while indeed the Old Testament as a whole is not the word of God, it nevertheless contains the word of God"?

In view of the wonderful influence it has exerted all through the history of the church down to our own day we should expect that this is so. But if it is really so, what is to be the distinguishing principle which will enable us to separate the imperishable divine from the ephemeral human? To the Christian the only norm and standard is the spirit of God as revealed in Jesus. Whatever is not in harmony with that spirit cannot be authoritative for him. If we apply this test we see at once that whole books, such as the Book of Esther and the Song of Songs, and most, if not all, of the prophetic books of Nahum and Obadiah, as well as large sections of other prophetic books, together with the ritual and sacrificial law books and a good many Psalms, notably the imprecatory Psalms, fall far short of the spirit of Jesus; also many stories and legends in the so-called historical books, together with the pragmatic view of history taught in them. Besides these, which are obviously out of harmony with the spirit of Jesus, there are others which have no particular spiritual meaning to us: genealogies, hero tales, such as Samson's; stories of petty wars, and the like. It would be a mistake to think that all these, or as a matter of fact that any of them, are without value. The century-long earnest and devoted critical study of the Old Testament by the use of the literary, historical, and pyschological method has brought out the importance of every one of these books and of all their parts, so that we would not miss a single one of them, for each detail fills a certain definite place in the long, varied, and fascinating history of this people to whom God granted the wonderful prerogative of becoming the bearer of the central line of his revelation to mankind.

But our point just now is that all those parts of the Old Testament which are contrary to the spirit of Jesus, or which have no direct spiritual meaning to us, are for us without authority.

It would seem that it should be possible for Christians to reach a consensus on those parts that are to be regarded as spiritually valuable and authoritative. At any rate, it is the duty of the Christian church to make it perfectly clear that the Old Testament as whole is not on a level with the New Testament, and that a sharp discrimination must be made within the Old Testament writings between the spiritually and morally valuable and the spiritually and morally harmful or indifferent parts. The church should no longer say, "the Old Testament is the word of God," but only that it contains the word of God. This divine element alone can be placed alongside of the New Testament as having authority for us Christians. This alone can be canonical: the external, objective authority, the standard, the rule of faith and practice for us as far as the Old Testament is concerned.

If, however, this is to have real meaning for the individual Christian, the external authority must become an internal authority: the word of God in the Old Testament must become the word of God to him, to his own heart and conscience. Only when I become aware that God is addressing me, speaking directly to me as I read and ponder those words in the Old Testament, and compels my assent, obedience, homage, and adoration—

only then is this the word of God to me, affecting, molding, changing, and directing my life.

It is along three lines that the word of God in the Old Testament finds us, strikes home, touches our hearts, justifies itself to our minds, commands our consciences:

1. Along the line of some of its moral teachings and precepts, whether they are given in the form of moral commandments, as in the Decalogue, or in sage and sane moral advice, as in proverbs and stories, or in the impassioned addresses of the prophets. The righteousness of God finds powerful utterance here and lays its compulsion upon our consciences.

2. God makes himself real to us in the spiritual experiences of the prophets. His reality, his character, his demands, his work among Israel and among the nations, as well as in the individual soul, are most impressively presented to one who reads and ponders the words of these prophets which they were conscious of having received by divine inspiration. He who meditates deeply upon Amos, e.g., on the historic situation and this shepherd's experience, becomes aware of a suprahistorical, a divine element, stands with him in the presence of God, and knows that he, too, must take off his shoes, for he stands on holy ground. And who that ponders profoundly the mightly inaugural vision of Isaiah and enters sympathetically into his experience does not feel with throbbing heart the divine mystery, and is filled with holy awe at the sense of the divine nearness? "Holy, holy, holy is the Lord God of Hosts, the whole earth is full of His glory." This holy awe in the presence of the divine mystery is one of the primal elements of true religion, the experience of which brings with it the sure conviction of the reality of God and of his overwhelming greatness. We may enter into it by studying the prophets and we shall be forever grateful to them for this priceless gift. Not only the sense of awe and fear at the reality and presence of the tremendous, overpowering, divine mystery may be aroused by a deep contemplation of the prophets, but also the sense of that inexpressible longing for communion with God that ever draws us to him in spite of his majesty, that feels that it can never be satisfied without him who is so highly exalted and so distant, and yet also, so gracious and so near. Who, that enters into the pathos of Hosea's life, does not feel with him the love of God behind and in the human tragedy of the prophet's heart and of the nation's history? And who can become Jeremiah's spiritual friend without experiencing something of the divine fellowship which he had been found worthy to have so completely? When God speaks to him and through him to his people, "Yea, I have loved thee with an everlasting love, therefore with lovingkindness have I drawn thee," we hear God speak to us, addressing our own soul, "Yea, I have loved thee with an everlasting love, therefore with lovingkindness have I drawn thee," and our heart responds: "O Love that wilt not let me go, I yield my hungry soul to Thee."

3. There is, I believe, a third line along which God's revelation comes to us in the Old Testament. The revelation of the reality and activity of God and of his character and his demands, God's way of coming to us, is

complemented by the revelation of our way of coming to him. The search of the human heart for God is the needed complement of the search of God for the human heart. Here the Old Testament gives marvelous illustrations of the deep mystery of the prayer of the Holy Spirit in our hearts. When we read such words as the beginning of Psalm 42: "As the hart panteth after the water brooks, so panteth my soul after Thee, O God," or "Out of the depth I cry unto Thee, O Lord; Lord hear my voice," or "Create in me a clean heart, O God, and renew a steadfast spirit within me. Cast me not away from thy presence, and take not Thy Holy Spirit from me," or again "The Lord is my Shepherd, I shall not want" and the rest of this precious psalm, or "The Lord is our refuge and strength, a very present help in time of trouble," or "The Lord is my light and my salvation, whom shall I fear, He is the strength of my life, of whom shall I be afraid?"— and scores and scores of other words equally wonderful, great, and gracious, we feel that they have been uttered by God-inspired personalities through whom his Spirit himself gave utterance to the divine longings, hopes, and trusts of the human heart in words charged with the power of eternity, and we gratefully and joyfully or penitently and trustfully use them in our own prayers to God—even as we use our Lord's prayer in which he revealed the true expression of human longings and needs. These, also, have the touch of divine authority upon them.

It is thus along these three lines that the Old Testament still has for us Christians today divine authority: (1) in its highest and truest moral and social teachings, (2) in the revelation of God in the spiritual experiences especially of the prophets, and (3) in the prayers and longings, so purely and so amazingly uttered, that we still take them as a gift of the hand of God himself.

All this, however, is authoritative only to him who believes, and more precisely only to him who believes himself directly confronted and addressed by God, to whom God himself and his personal interest in him and concern for him are deeply real, to whom, therefore, God's demands and commands and unfoldings come with inescapable directness in these words of his messages of old. To him who has no such faith the Old Testament, even in the limited scope of which we have spoken, is not and cannot be authoritative. That is one of the reasons—perhaps the most important one— why the Old Testament is regarded as having no or but little authority even by some who read and study it, critically and professionally: they read it without ever realizing that God has a direct message to them, too, in these words; their intellect is keenly alive, but their heart and their conscience are unconcerned.

Per contra, there have been and are Christian believers who have read the Old Testament with their heart and conscience only and not also with a discriminating intellect. They have read the entire gospel into the Old Testament and have found the whole of it, even the Book of Leviticus, full of Christ. We do not argue with them, but for ourselves we plead for a reading with the whole personality alive and concerned, with a discriminating mind, a keenly responsive conscience, and a warm and eager heart.

That was the way in which Jesus read his Bible; he found in it God's word, which helped and strengthened and illumined him. But he discriminated sharply between the temporal and the eternal. "It was said to them of old"—in the Old Testament—"but I say unto you" something higher, truer, diviner. We take his Bible which he used and thereby hallowed for us, and we are deeply grateful to him for it. We are grateful also to his church throughout the ages that it has ever—against all attacks from without and within—kept this sacred heritage and bound it together with the Christian Bible of the New Testament. For, as we have seen, the Old Testament really contains in its pages the Word of God, full of life and power and grace to him who reads it with a believing mind, an eager heart, and a sensitive conscience: he knows the true authority of the Old Testament.

We are at the end of our disquisition. It may be well to summarize the important points in a series of propositions:

1. Only that is authoritative for the Christian which compels his inward assent, obedience, and homage.

2. The Old Testament becomes thus authoritative for the Christian only when he becomes aware that God is addressing him directly as he reads in it and feels the inward compulsion to assent, obey, and adore.

3. The Old Testament as a whole cannot be authoritative for him because as a whole it is not the word of God. Only certain parts contain the word of God which shows to him God's way of coming to men (his revelation of himself to men) and man's way of coming to God (the way of salvation).

4. These parts are determined by their conformity to God's highest self-revelation in the New Testament, more precisely, to the spirit of God as revealed in Jesus.

5. The parts which measure up to this standard are found to contain (a) the highest moral teachings, or (b) men's deepest religious experiences of God, or (c) the purest expressions of man's longings for God.

6. Within these limits the Old Testament has life-giving power and is of enduring significance. But it can have divine authority only to him who believes in God and his self-revelation to men.

THE STRANGE NEW WORLD WITHIN THE BIBLE

Karl Barth

WE ARE TO ATTEMPT to find an answer to the question, What is there within the Bible? What sort of house is it to which the Bible is the door? What sort of country is spread before our eyes when we throw the Bible open?

We are with Abraham in Haran. We hear a call which commands him: Get thee out of thy country, and from thy kindred, unto a land that I will show thee! We hear a promise: I will make of thee a great nation. And Abraham believed in the Lord; and he counted it to him for righteousness. What is the meaning of all this? We can but feel that there is something behind these words and experiences. But what?

We are with Moses in the wilderness. For forty years he has been living among the sheep, doing penance for an over-hasty act. What change has come over him? We are not told; it is apparently not our concern. But suddenly there comes to him also a call: Moses, Moses!—a great command: Come now therefore, and I will send thee unto Pharoah, that thou mayest bring forth my people, the children of Israel, out of Egypt!—and a simple assurance: Certainly I will be with thee. Here again are words and experiences which seem at first to be nothing but riddles. We do not read the like either in the daily papers or in other books. What lies behind?

It is a time of severe oppression in the land of Canaan. Under the oak at Ophrah stands the farmer's son, Gideon. The "angel of the Lord" appears to him, and says, The Lord is with thee, thou mighty man of valor. He sees nothing amiss in protesting, if the Lord be with us, why then is all this befallen us? But "the Lord" knows how to bring him to silence: Go in this thy might, and *thou* shalt save Israel from the hand of the Midianites: have not *I* sent thee?

In the tabernacle at Shiloh lies the young Samuel. Again a call: Samuel, Samuel! And the pious priest Eli, to whom he runs, wisely advises him to lie down again. He obeys and sleeps until, the call returning and returning, he can no longer sleep; and the thought comes to the pious Eli: It might be. . . . ! And Samuel must hear and obey.

We read all this, but what do we read behind it? We are aware of something like the tremors of an earthquake or like the ceaseless thundering of ocean waves against thin dikes; but what really is it that beats at the barrier and seeks entrance here?

We remember how Elijah felt himself called of "the Lord" to offer defiance to the whole authority of his king, and then himself had to make the acquaintance of this "Lord," not in the wind and storm but in a "still, small voice"—how Isaiah and Jeremiah wished not to speak but had to speak the

From *The Word of God and the Word of Man*, Grand Rapids, Michigan, 1935, pp. 28-50. Reprinted by permission of the publishers, Zondervan Publishing House.

secrets of divine judgment and divine blessing upon a sinful people—how, later, during the deepest humiliation of this people there stood up strange and solitary "servants of God" who struggled ever more fiercely with the question, Where is now thy God? and forever gave the answer, Israel hath yet God for consolation!—how in the midst of all the wrongdoing and misery of the people they could but blare out, as it were, the announcement: Arise, shine, for thy light is come, and the glory of the Lord is risen upon thee! What does it mean? Why do these men speak so? Whence is kindled all the indignation, all the pity, all the joy, all the hope and the unbounded confidence which even today we see flaring up like fire from every page of the prophets and the psalms?

Then come the incomprehensible, incomparable days, when all previous time, history, and experience seem to stand still—like the sun at Gibeon—in the presence of a man who was no prophet, no poet, no hero, no thinker, and yet all of these and more! His words cause alarm, for he speaks with authority and not as we ministers. With compelling power he calls to each one: Follow me! Even to the distrustful and antagonistic he gives an irresistible impression of "eternal life." "The blind receive their sight, and the lame walk, the lepers are cleansed, and the deaf hear, the dead are raised up, and the poor have the gospel preached to them." "Blessed is the womb that bare thee," cry the people. And the quieter and lonelier he becomes, and the less real "faith" he finds in the world about him, the stronger through his whole being peals one triumphant note: "I am the resurrection and the life! Because I live—ye shall live also!"

And then comes the echo, weak enough, if we compare it with that note of Easter morning—and yet strong, much too strong for our ears, accustomed as they are to the weak, pitiably weak tones of today—the echo which this man's life finds in a little crowd of folk who listen, watch, and wait. Here is the echo of the first courageous missionaries who felt the necessity upon them to go into all the world and preach the gospel to every creature. Here is the echo of Paul: "The righteousness of God is revealed! If any man be in Christ, he is a new creature. And he which hath begun a good work in you will finish it!" Here is the deep still echo of John: "Life was manifested. . . . . We beheld his glory. . . . . Now are we the sons of God. . . . . And this is the victory that overcometh the world, even our faith."

Then the echo ceases. The Bible is finished.

Who is the man who spoke such words and lived such a life, who set these echoes ringing? And again we ask: What is there within the Bible? What is the significance of the remarkable line from Abraham to Christ? What of the chorus of prophets and apostles? and what is the burden of their song? What is the one truth that these voices evidently all desire to announce, each in its own tone, each in its own way? What lies between the strange statement, In the beginning God created the heaven and the earth, and the equally strange cry of longing, Even so, come, Lord Jesus! What is there behind all this, that labors for expression?

It is a dangerous question. We might do better not to come too near this burning bush. For we are sure to betray what is—behind *us*! The Bible gives to every man and to every era such answers to their questions as they deserve. We shall always find in it as much as we seek and no more: high and divine content if it is high and divine content that we seek; transitory and "historical" content, if it is transitory and "historical" content that we seek—nothing whatever, if it is nothing whatever that we seek. The hungry are satisfied by it, and to the satisfied it is surfeiting before they have opened it. The question, What is within the Bible? has a mortifying way of converting itself into the opposing question, Well, what are you looking for, and who are you, pray, who make bold to look?

But in spite of all this danger of making embarrassing discoveries in ourselves, we must yet trust ourselves to ask our question. Moreover, we must trust ourselves to reach eagerly for an answer which is really much too large for us, for which we really are not yet ready, and of which we do not seem worthy, since it is a fruit which our own longing, striving, and inner labor have not planted. What this fruit, this answer, is, is suggested by the title of my address: within the Bible there is a strange, new world, the world of God. This answer is the same as that which came to the first martyr, Stephen: Behold, I see the heavens opened and the Son of man standing on the right hand of God. Neither by the earnestness of our belief nor by the depth and richness of our experience have we deserved the right to this answer. What I shall have to say about it will be only a small and unsatisfying part of it. We must openly confess that we are reaching far beyond ourselves. But that is just the point: if we wish to come to grips with the contents of the Bible we must dare to reach far beyond ourselves. The Book admits of nothing less. For, besides giving to every one of us what he rightly deserves—to one, much, to another, something, to a third, nothing—it leaves us no rest whatever, if we are in earnest, once with our shortsighted eyes and awkward fingers we have found the answer in it that *we* deserve. Such an answer is something but, as we soon realize, not everything. It may satisfy us for a few years, but we simply cannot be content with it forever. Ere long the Bible says to us, in a manner candid and friendly enough, with regard to the "versions" we make of it: "These may be you, but they are not I! They may perhaps suit you, meeting the demands of your thought and temperament, of your era and your 'circle,' of your religious or philosophical theories. You wanted to be mirrored in me, and now you have really found in me your own reflection. But now I bid you come seek *me*, as well. Seek what is here." It is the Bible itself, it is the straight inexorable logic of its on-march which drives us out beyond ourselves and invites us, without regard to our worthiness or unworthiness, to reach for the last highest answer, in which all is said that can be said, although we can hardly understand and only stammeringly express it. And that answer is: A new world, the world of God. There is a spirit in the Bible that allows us to stop awhile and play among secondary things as is our wont—but presently it begins to press us on; and however we may object that we are only weak, imperfect, and most average folk, it presses us on to the primary fact, whether we will or no. There is a river in the

Bible that carries us away, once we have entrusted our destiny to it—away from ourselves to the sea. The Holy Scriptures will interpret themselves in spite of all our human limitations. We need only dare to follow this drive, this spirit, this river, to grow out beyond ourselves toward the highest answer. This daring is *faith*: and we read the Bible rightly, not when we do so with false modesty, restraint, and attempted sobriety, for these are passive qualities, but when we read it in faith. And the invitation to dare and to reach toward the highest, even though we do not deserve it, is the expression of *grace* in the Bible: the Bible unfolds to us as we are met, guided, drawn on, and made to grow by the grace of God.

What is there within the Bible? *History!* The history of a remarkable, even unique, people; the history of powerful, mentally vigorous personalities; the history of Christianity in its beginnings—a history of men and ideas in which anyone who considers himself educated must be interested, if for no other reason than because of its effects upon the times following and the present time.

Now one can content himself for a time with this answer and find in it many true and beautiful possibilities. The Bible is full of history; religious history, literary history, cultural history, world history, and human history of every sort. A picture full of animation and color is unrolled before all who approach the Bible with open eyes.

But the pleasure is short-lived: the picture, on closer inspection, proves quite incomprehensible and flat, if it is meant only for history. The man who is looking for history or for stories will be glad after a little to turn from the Bible to the morning paper or to other books. For when we study history and amuse ourselves with stories, we are always wanting to know: How did it all happen? How is it that one event follows another? What are the natural causes of things? *Why* did the people speak such words and live such lives? It is just at the most decisive points of its history that the Bible gives no answer to our Why. Such is the case, indeed, not only with the Bible, but with all the truly decisive men and events of history. The greater a crisis, the less of an answer we get to our inquisitive Why. And *vice versa:* the smaller a man or an era, the more the "historians" find to explain and establish. But the Bible meets the lover of history with silences quite unparalleled.

Why was it that the Israelitish people did not perish in the Egyptian bondage, but remained a people, or rather in the very deepest of their need, became one? Why? There was a reason! Why was it that Moses was able to create a law which for purity and humanity puts us moderns only to shame? There was a reason! Why is it that Jeremiah stands there during the siege of Jerusalem with his message of doom, an enemy of the people, a man without a country? Why Jesus' healing of the sick, why his messianic consciousness, why the resurrection? Why does a Saul become a Paul? Why that other-worldly picture of Christ in the fourth gospel? Why does John on the Isle of Patmos—ignoring the Roman Empire in its very heyday—see the holy city, new Jerusalem, coming down from

God out of heaven, prepared as a bride adorned for her husband? There was a reason!

How much trouble the Bible makes the poor research workers! There was a reason (with an exclamation point)! is hardly an adequate answer for a history; and if one can say of the incidents of the Bible only, There was a reason! its history is in truth stark nonsense. Some men have felt compelled to seek grounds and explanations where there were none, and what has resulted from that procedure is a history in itself—and unhappy history into which I will not enter at this time. The Bible itself, in any case, answers our eager Why neither like a sphinx, with There was a reason! nor, like a lawyer, with a thousand arguments, deductions, and parallels, but says to us, The decisive cause is God. Because God lives, speaks, and acts, there was a reason. . . . !

To be sure, when we hear the word "God," it may at first seem the same as There was a reason! In the leading articles of our dailies, and in the primary history readers of our Aargau schools one does not expect to have events explained by the fact that "God created," or "God spoke!" When God enters, history for the while ceases to be, and there is nothing more to ask; for something wholly different and new begins—a history with its own distinct grounds, possibilities, and hypotheses.

The paramount question is whether we have understanding for this different, new world, or good will enough to meditate and enter upon it inwardly. Do we desire the presence of "God"? Do we dare to go whither evidently we are being led? That were "faith"! A new world projects itself into our old ordinary world. We may reject it. We may say, It is nothing; this is imagination, madness, this "God." But we may not deny nor prevent our being led by Bible "history" far out beyond what is elsewhere called history—into a new world, into the world of God.

We might also say, There is morality within the Bible. It is a collection of teachings and illustrations of virtue and human greatness. No one has ever yet seriously questioned the fact that in their way the men of the Bible were good representative men, from whom we have an endless amount to learn. Whether we seek practical wisdom or lofty examples of a certain type of heroism, we find them here forthwith.

And again in the long run we do not. Large parts of the Bible are almost useless to the school in its moral curriculum because they are lacking in just this wisdom and just these "good examples." The heroes of the Bible are to a certain degree quite respectable, but to serve as examples to the good, efficient, industrious, publicly educated, average citizen of Switzerland, men like Samson, David, Amos, and Peter are very ill fitted indeed; Rosa of Tannenburg, the figures of Amicis' "Courage" (*Il Cuore*), and the magnificent characters of later Swiss history are quite different people. The Bible is an embarrassment in the school and foreign to it. How shall we find in the life and teaching of Jesus something to "do" in "practical life"? Is it not as if he wished to say to us at every step "What interest have I in your 'practical life'? I have little to do with that. Follow after *me* or let me go my way!"

At certain crucial points the Bible amazes us by its remarkable indifference to our conception of good and evil.   Abraham, for instance, as the highest proof of his faith desires to sacrifice his son to God; Jacob wins the birthright by a refined deception of his blind father; Elijah slays the four hundred and fifty priests of Baal by the brook Kishon.   Are these exactly praiseworthy examples?

And in how many phases of morality the Bible is grievously wanting! How little fundamental information it offers in regard to the difficult questions of business life, marriage, civilization, and statecraft, with which we have to struggle!   To mention only a single problem, but to us today a mortal one: how unceremoniously and constantly war is waged in the Bible! Time and again, when this question comes up, the teacher or minister must resort to various kinds of extra-Biblical material, because the New as well as the Old Testament almost completely breaks down at this point.   Time and again serious Christian people who seek "comfort" and "inspiration" in the midst of personal difficulties will quietly close their Bibles and reach for the clearer-toned lyre of a Christian Fürchtegott Gellert or for the books of Hilty, if not toward psychoanalysis—where everything is so much more practicable, simple, and comprehensible.   Time and again the Bible gives us the impression that it contains no instructions, counsels, or examples whatsoever, either for individuals or for nations and governments; and the impression is correct.   It offers us not at all what we first seek in it.

Once more we stand before this "other" new world which begins in the Bible.   In it the chief consideration is not the doings of man but the doings of God—not the various ways which we may take if we are men of good will, but the power out of which good will must first be created—not the unfolding and fruition of love as we may understand it, but the existence and outpouring of eternal love, of love as God understands it—not industry, honesty, and helpfulness as we may practice them in our old ordinary world, but the establishment and growth of a new world, the world in which God and *his* morality reign.   In the light of this coming world a David is a great man in spite of his adultery and bloody sword: blessed is the man unto whom the Lord imputeth not iniquity!   Into this world the publicans and the harlots will go before your impeccably elegant and righteous folk of good society!   In this world the true hero is the lost son, who is absolutely lost and feeding swine—and not his moral elder brother. The reality which lies behind Abraham and Moses, behind Christ and his apostles, is the world of the Father, in which morality is dispensed with because it is taken for granted.   And the blood of the New Testament which seeks inflow into our veins is the will of the Father which would be done on earth as it is in heaven.

We may have grasped this as the meaning of the Bible, as *its* answer to our great and small questions, and still say: I do not need this; I do not desire it; it tells me nothing; I cannot get anywhere with it!   It may be that we really cannot get anywhere with it on our present highways and byways—on our byways of church and school, for example, and, in many instances, on the byway of the personal life which we have been traveling with such perseverance. There are blind alleys of a thousand types, out of which the way into the kingdom of heaven can at first lead only backwards. And it is certain that the Bible, if we read it carefully, makes straight for the point where one must decide to accept or reject the sovereignty of God. This is the new world within the Bible. We are offered the magnificent, productive, hopeful life of a grain of seed, a new beginning, out of which all things shall be made new. One cannot learn or imitate this life of the divine seed in the new world. One can only let it live, grow, and ripen within him. One can only believe—can only hold the ground whither he has been led. Or not believe. There is no third way.

Let us seek our way out on still another side: let us start with the proposition that in the Bible we have a revelation of true *religion*, of religion defined as what we are to think concerning God, how we are to find him, and how we are to conduct ourselves in his presence—all that is included in what today we like to call "worship and service" (Frömmigkeit). The Bible as a "source-book for godly living"—how much has been said and written upon this theme in the last years! And such the Bible is. It is a treasury of truth concerning the right relation of men to the eternal and divine—but here too the same law holds: we have only to seek honestly and we shall make the plain discovery that there is something greater in the Bible than religion and "worship." Here again we have only a kind of crust which must be broken through.

We have all been troubled with the thought that there are so many kinds of Christianity in the world—Catholic Christianity and Protestant, the Christianities of the various communions and of the "groups" (Richtungen) within them, the Christianity of the old-fashioned and the Christianity of the modern—and all, all of them appealing with the same earnestness and zeal to the Bible. Each insists, *Ours* is the religion revealed in the Bible, or at least its most legitimate successor. And how is one to answer? Does it not require a generous bit of effrontery to say, We Protestants, or we members of such and such a communion or society are right, for such and such reasons; and all the others are wrong? When once one knows how easy it is to find "reasons," the pleasure of participating in this eternal game begins to pall.

Then shall we take the position that fundamentally we are all right? Shall we dip our hands into that from which the spirit of the Bible silently turns away, the dish of tolerance which is more and more being proclaimed, especially in our national church, as the highest good?

Or may we all, jointly and severally, with our various views and various forms of worship, be—wrong? The fact is that we must seek our answer in this direction—"Yea, let God be true, but every man a liar." All religions may be found in the Bible, if one will have it so; but when he looks closely, there are none at all. There is only—the "other," new, greater world! When we come to the Bible with our questions—How shall I think of God and the universe? How arrive at the divine? How present myself?—it answers us, as it were, "My dear sir, these are *your* problems: you must not ask *me!* Whether it is better to hear mass or hear a sermon, whether the proper form of Christianity is to be discovered in the Salvation Army or in 'Christian Science,' whether the better belief is that of old Reverend Doctor Smith or young Reverend Mr. Jones, whether your religion should be more a religion of the understanding, of the will, or of the feelings, you can and must decide for yourself. If you do not care to enter upon *my* questions, you may, to be sure, find in me all sorts of arguments and quasi-arguments for one or another standpoint, but you will not then find what is really here." We shall find ourselves only in the midst of a vast human controversy and far, far away from reality, or what might become reality in our lives.

It is not the right human thoughts about God which form the content of the Bible, but the right divine thoughts about men. The Bible tells us not how we should talk with God but what he says to us; not how we find the way to him, but how he has sought and found the way to us; not the right relation in which we must place ourselves to him, but the covenant which he has made with all who are Abraham's spiritual children and which he has sealed once and for all in Jesus Christ. It is this which is within the Bible. The word of God is within the Bible.

Our grandfathers, after all, were right when they struggled so desperately in behalf of the truth that there is revelation in the Bible and not religion only, and when they would not allow facts to be turned upside down for them even by so pious and intelligent a man as Schleiermacher. And our fathers were right when they guarded warily against being drawn out upon the shaky scaffolding of religious self-expression.

The more honestly we search the Scriptures the surer, sooner or later, comes the answer: The right forms of worship and service?—"they are they which testify of *Me!*" We seek ourselves—we find God; and having done so stand before him with our religions, Christianities, and other notions, like blundering scholars with their ABC's. Yet we cannot be sad about it but rejoice that we have found, among all lesser considerations, the chief one, without which every form of religion, even the most perfect, is only a delusion and a snare. This chief consideration contains, again, the living grain of seed out of which a right relation to God, a service of God "in spirit and in truth," necessarily must issue, whether we lay stress more upon this detail or that. The word of God! The standpoint of God!

Once more we have every liberty of choice. We may explain: "I cannot get anywhere with this: the conception of the 'word of God' is not part of my philosophy. I still prefer the old ordinary Christianity of my kind of 'worship' and my own particular standpoint." Or we may be willing to hear what "passeth all understanding"; may desire in the power of God and the Saviour to let it grow and ripen within us according to the laws of the great life process set forth in the Bible; may obey the spirit of the Book and acknowledge God to be right instead of trying to prove ourselves right; may dare—to believe. Here we find ourselves faced once more by the question of faith. But without anticipating our answer to it, we may rest assured that in the Bible, in both the Old and the New Testaments, the theme is, so to speak, the religion of God and never once the religion of the Jews, or Christians, or heathen; that in this respect, as in others, the Bible lifts us out of the old atmosphere of man to the open portals of a new world, the world of God.

But we are not yet quite at an end. We have found in the Bible a new world, God, God's sovereignty, God's glory, God's incomprehensible love. Not the history of man but the history of God! Not the virtues of men but the virtues of him who hath called us out of darkness into his marvelous light! Not human standpoints but the standpoint of God!

Now, however, might not a last series of questions arise: Who then is God? What is his will? What are his thoughts? What is the mysterious "other," new, greater world which emerges in the Bible beyond all the ways of men, summoning us to a decision to believe or not to believe? In whom did Abraham believe? For whom did the heroes fight and conquer? Whom did the prophets prophesy? In whose power did Christ die and rise again? Whose name did the Apostles proclaim? The contents of the Bible are "God." But what is the content of the contents? Something "new" breaks forth! But what is the new?

To these questions there is a series of ready answers, serious and well-founded answers taken from the Bible itself, answers to which we must listen: God is the Lord and Redeemer, the Saviour and Comforter of all the souls that turn to him; and the new world is the kingdom of blessedness which is prepared for the little flock who escape destruction. Is not this in the Bible? .... Again: God is the fountain of life which begins its quiet murmuring when once we turn away from the externalities of the world and bow before him in silence; and the new world is the incomparable peace of such a life hid with Christ in God. Is not this also in the Bible? .... Again: God is the Lord of the heaven which awaits us, and in which, when our journey through the sorrows and imperfections of this life is done, we are to possess and enjoy our citizenship; and the new world is just this blessed other life, the "still eternity" into which the faithful shall one day enter. This answer also comes directly from the Bible.

These are true enough answers. But are they *truth*? Are they the whole truth? Can one read or hear read even as much as two chapters from the Bible and still with good conscience say, God's word went forth to humanity, his mandate guided history from Abraham to Christ, the Holy Spirit descended in tongues of fire upon the apostles at Pentecost, a Saul became a Paul and traveled over land and sea—all in order that here and there specimens of men like you and me might be "converted," find inner "peace," and by a redeeming death go some day to "heaven." Is *that* all? Is *that* all of God and his new world, of the meaning of the Bible, of the content of the contents? The powerful forces which come to expression in the Bible, the movements of peoples, the battles, and the convulsions which take place before us there, the miracles and revelations which constantly occur there, the immeasurable promises for the future which are unceasingly repeated to us there—do not all these things stand in a rather strange relation to so small a result—if that is really the only result they have? Is not God—greater than that? Even in these answers, earnest and pious as they may be, have we not measured God with our own measure, conceived God with our own conceptions, wished ourselves a God according to our own wishes? When we begin to read the Bible carefully, must we not grow beyond these answers, too?

Must we not also grow beyond the strange question, Who is God? As if we could dream of asking such a question, having willingly and sincerely allowed ourselves to be led to the gates of the new world, to the threshold of the kingdom of God! There one asks no longer. There one sees. There one hears. There one has. There one knows. There one no longer gives his petty, narrow little answers. The question, Who is God? and our inadequate answers to it come only from our having halted somewhere on the way to the open gates of the new world; from our having refused somewhere to let the Bible speak to us candidly; from our having failed somewhere truly to desire to—believe. At the point of halt the truth again becomes unclear, confused, problematical—narrow, stupid, highchurch, non-conformist, monotonous, or meaningless. "He that hath *seen* me hath *seen* the Father." That is it: when we allow ourselves to press on to the highest answer, when we find God in the Bible, when we dare with Paul not to be disobedient to the heavenly vision, then God stands before us as he really is, "Believing, we shall receive!" God is *God*.

But who may say, I believe?—"Lord, I believe; help thou mine unbelief." It is because of our unbelief that we are so perplexed by the question, Who is God?—that we feel so small and ashamed before the fullness of the Godhead which the men and women of the Bible saw and proclaimed. It is because of our unbelief that even now I can only stammer, hint at, and make promises about that which would be opened to us if the Bible could speak to us unhindered, in the full fluency of its revelations.

Who is God? The heavenly Father! But the heavenly Father even upon *earth*, and upon earth really the *heavenly* Father. He will not allow life to be split into a "here" and "beyond." He will not leave to death the task of freeing us from sin and sorrow. He will bless us, not with the power of the church but with the power of life and resurrection. In Christ he caused his word to be made flesh. He has caused eternity to dawn in place of time, or rather upon time—for what sort of eternity were it which should begin "afterwards"! He purposes naught but the establishment of a new *world*.

Who is God? The Son who has become "the mediator of my soul." But more than that: He has become the mediator for the whole world, the redeeming Word, who was in the beginning of all things and is earnestly expected by all things. He is the redeemer of my brothers and sisters. He is the redeemer of a humanity gone astray and ruled by evil spirits and powers. He is the redeemer of the groaning creation about us. The whole Bible authoritatively announces that God must be all in all; and the events of the Bible are the beginning, the glorious beginning of a new *world*.

Who is God? The Spirit in his believers, the spirit

"by which we own
The Son who lived and died and rose;
Which crystal clear from God's pure throne
Through quiet hearts forever flows."

But God is also that spirit (that is to say, that love and good will) which will and must break forth from quiet hearts into the world outside, that it may be manifest, visible, comprehensible: behold the tabernacle of God is with men! The Holy Spirit makes a new heaven and a new earth and, therefore, new men, new families, new relationships, new politics. It has no respect for old traditions simply because they are traditions, for old solemnities simply because they are solemn, for old powers simply because they are powerful. The *Holy* Spirit has respect only for truth, for itself. The Holy Spirit establishes the righteousness of heaven in the midst of the unrighteousness of earth and will not stop nor stay until all that is dead has been brought to life and a new *world* has come into being.

This is within the Bible. It is within the Bible for us. For it we were baptized. Oh, that we dared in faith to take what grace can offer us!

I need not suggest that we all have need of this. We live in a sick old world which cries from its soul, out of deepest need: Heal me, O Lord, and I shall be healed! In all men, whoever and wherever and whatever and however they may be, there is a longing for exactly this which is here within the Bible. We all know that.

And now hear: "A certain man made a great supper, and bade many; and sent his servant at suppertime to say to them that were bidden, Come, for all things are now ready! . . . ."

THE HEROIC AND RECONCILING WORD

Lynn Harold Hough

LIFE IS ALWAYS coming to a state of tension. Life is always finding a fashion by which this tension is wrought into harmony. In this is the preacher's bewilderment. And in this is the preacher's opportunity. At its best life is always like a Gothic cathedral whose arches and flying buttresses achieve their poised harmony not in static stillness, but in the dynamic stillness of such integrated tensions that sometimes if you strike a column in a Gothic cathedral it will give forth a musical note.

The thinker of today needs profoundly to realize that this state of tension which could be made into harmony has been characteristic of every vital and seminal age in the life of man. There is no more odd and naïve notion than that which regards the present as the first age when men have felt the clash of the clenched antagonisms of supremely difficult mental struggles. Perhaps no man alive today faces so subtly difficult a situation as that which confronted the most sensitive spirits of the Italian Renaissance. Each age while it lasts seems the age of supreme crisis. Only the man with the rare gift of historic imagination in the things of the mind can realize how desperate the strain and how heroic the victory has been age after age.

At the very beginning of our study we will view quickly, but I trust not superficially, some of the great historic tensions of the mind of man and the fashion of their resolution into harmony through a commandingly heroic and reconciling word.

I

By the time fifth-century Athens had lived its life, spoken its restrained yet living words, created its works of art, asked its probing questions, and given its clear-edged answers, the world as far as it was ready to follow Hellenic leadership had been taught the meaning of life as harmony. That highly integrated loveliness, that sense of "nothing too much," that "passionate pursuit of passionless perfection" which we associate with the Attic spirit, had given the deepest and most commanding sanctions to every mind upon which Athens had cast its spell. But all the while—at least since eighth-century Jerusalem—something else had been going on in the world. A group of grim and passionate men with a blazing fire in their hearts had looked upon life and had drawn back with a kind of bitter and tortured pain at the sight. Their only hope was in moral reconstruction. Their only happy expectation was in a God who could say, "Though your sins be as scarlet, they shall be as white as snow." The Greek saw in life a flower ready to bloom, with astonishing capacity to respond to the garden-

From *Whither Christianity?* New York, 1929, pp. 1-17. Reprinted by permission of the publishers, Harper & Brothers.

er's care. The Hebrew saw in life a flower stunted by some malignant disease which robbed it of the loveliness of bloom and the allurement of fragrance.

It was a decadent Greece and an Israel of waning spiritual vitality in which the two interpretations met. But meet they did, and meet they must. For the Greek and the Hebrew are always doing battle for the possession of the mind of man. Perhaps the deepest tension among all the disturbances which have strained the muscles of the minds of men is this fundamental battle between the Greek and the Hebrew view of life.

It was Jesus himself who spoke the heroic and reconciling word in respect of this tension. And here, as so often, he was more interested in the reconciliation as a matter of vital experience than as a matter of formal dialectic. His own clear mind with its gift of coolness amid the hectic thoughts of men could not fail to appropriate the central insight of the Greeks. "Ye are the light of the world," he said to his disciples. Here he was speaking Greek pure and undefiled. The light which calls forth latent possibilities, the light which illuminates and shows everything clearly in its true nature, is to come with all its gracious ministry to men. There is an unseen harmony which light will call forth. The way of Jesus was to fulfill the Greek hopes which by this time had become dim and wistful in as far as they were noble hopes. He himself was to be the light of the world.

But he was also profoundly aware of that dark and tragic moral cleavage which rent its way across the life of man. He was aware of hard and bitter elements in man's experience which Greek eyes had not quite dared frankly to face. There were strange depths of moral passion back of the cool surface of his understanding. He was too honest to refuse to face the decay of the roots of goodness in the lives of men. "Ye are the salt of the earth," he said to his disciples. Here he was speaking pure Hebrew. He saw in the fifty-third chapter of Isaiah a picture of his own supreme achievement. He put a cross in his heart even while the sunlight was shining in his eyes. He used strange, abrupt, and baffling phrases to tell the tale of his own spiritual grapple with the corrosive poison at the heart of human life. He saw himself as a Prince of Rescue even as he was a Prince of Light. But the very point of it all is that he was both Greek and Hebrew. It was not a matter of salt or light. It was a matter of salt and light. If the Greek and Latin theologies entered upon divergent paths, they surrendered what had been united in the life of their master. He was perfectly Hebrew in order that he might become perfectly Greek. He dealt with the malignant diseases, but bloom and fragrance were always glorious in his expectation even in the hour of grim suffering. "For the joy that was set before he endured." The Prince of Rescue was indeed the Prince of Light.

II

In the later days of the Roman Empire a new tension came into being which was profoundly concerned with the Christian religion itself. The new religion had become so powerful that it was not possible for the sword of persecution to kill Christians as fast as new Christians were made. It became evident at last that Christianity was the most potent force in the Empire. Constantine, part pagan, part shrewd politician, part dimly reverent spirit in the presence of unseen realities, decided to utilize the mighty forces held by the new religion for the purposes of the state. The Roman eagle itself surrendered to the cross, not, however, without danger to the cross upon which the Roman eagle was now to perch. Christianity was to be a religious action dominating and giving unity to the life of the world. But within the church another and very different movement was going on. Athanasius in his *Life of Anthony* and in his personal interpretation had introduced monasticism to the West. And monasticism was an escape from the world in lonely and fruitful spiritual meditation. "Good-by, Proud World; I'm Going Home." Egypt was dotted with its homes of spiritual quiet to which men fled from the evils of life. The life of lonely and brooding thought in the presence of the great God of the inner life became the dream and aspiration of multitudes of the best spirits among men. Not only in Africa, but all about the West, monasteries sprang up.

Here there was a new tension in the church itself. On the one hand, Christianity was seen as a force in action mastering the world. On the other hand, it was seen as a proud spirituality in retreat from a world condemned to sterility and death. It was Augustine who spoke the heroic and reconciling word in respect of this tension. On the one hand he was a great churchman. The stately and lordly leadership of Ambrose in Milan had had much to do with his capitulation to the Christian religion. When Rome shuddered and was about to fall he saw the City of God—*De Civitati Dei*—permanent and potent over against the fragile and falling city of man. If the Christian Church was ready to take the scepter from palsied Roman hands, to tame the Barbarians, and to create modern Europe, it was that high view of the church above all human lordliness which captured men's imagination and made this achievement possible. On the other hand, Augustine knew the strange vicissitudes of the inner life. He had spent years with the Manichaeans who felt with unbelievably dramatic consciousness the contrast between good and evil. The battle had waged fiercely in his own soul. The Augustine of the *Confession* understood every spiritual experience which made monasticism possible. So the great churchman was also the prophet of the inner life and understood the experiences of the lonely soul when it escaped from evil into the presence of the friendly and forgiving God. The tree branches apart in centuries after Augustine, but he is the trunk with divergent tendencies, one in a great unity of life and purpose.

III

By the eleventh century another tension was making itself felt. The Roman Empire had gone the way of empires—even the greatest—and the chaos had spread about the earth. The old Roman roads fell into decay and there was lawlessness everywhere. The recovery of civilization seemed to be the matter of most urgent importance. Little groups of weak men gathered around strong men, giving loyalty in return for protection and leadership, and so feudalism was born. Leaders gave loyalty to stronger and mightier leaders and so feudalism became a far-flung power in the world. The recovery of civilization was well on the way.

But there was a higher and indeed an eternal loyalty which insisted on making itself heard. The passionate and ferocious feudal leaders had their own lawlessness, even though they were journeying in the direction of the reign of law. And the high and commanding sanctions of religion often fell athwart their selfish plans. Why should God be allowed to stand in the way of a feudal lord. "Because," said Anselm, in effect, "God is the greatest feudal lord of all—the greatest of overlords" and in *Cur Deus Homo* he used the very sanctions of feudalism to establish the verities of religion. So he spoke the strong and unifying word. So he made religion authentic and potent in the days of feudal authority.

IV

By the sixteenth century two other principles had come to clenched antagonism. On the one hand, there was the conception of life as a surrender to high authority. On the other, there was the conception of life as a personal spiritual adventure. The clash was seen in a way in the twelfth century, in Abelard's *Sic et Non*. A preliminary reconciliation seemed to be achieved in the *Summa* of St. Thomas in the thirteenth century, but the tension continued, and by the sixteenth the stage was set for a world-wide battle. The conception of an institution more real than any of the individuals who gave their loyalty to it had the distinguished support of the realistic philosophy of the Middle Ages, which traced its ancestry to Plato himself. The sense of the individual as an entity with a life of his own came to vigorous expression in Nominalism and this conception, too, traveled into Middle Ages from a remote past. So religion as authority and religion as personal adventure entered the lists for deadly combat. Oddly enough, when we remember how he seemed to be the leader of one group, Luther himself uttered a reconciling as well as an heroic word in this time of tension. In the living God and his word of grace the reign of authority was to continue. In the vast adventure of the individual spirit accepting the divine grace each man was to find manifold ways of liberty. So freedom and authority met in a kind of beautiful wedlock.

V

The seventeenth century revealed a tension having its own far reaching significance. The court of Louis XIV was the most distinguished expression of social grace and dignity the modern world had seen. All Europe felt the allurement of the new social grandeur. Life became a gesture of noble grace in France and every court in Europe tried to attain the authentic movement of lofty dignity bending into curves of lovely charm. It was an age of splendid and glittering externals. And over against this there was the sense of life as a matter of moral and spiritual power. Within the lovely shell the voice of the infinite sea insisted on sounding. An age of politeness in-

stinctively shrank from that august reality which had a way of revealing
the tinsel in what had been supposed to be gold. In France, such distinguished preachers as Bossuet essayed to speak the unhesitating and unifying word. They embodied the very powers of social grace and distinction
upon which the age prided itself. But the ancient moral and spiritual
grandeur of the Christian religion spoke in their voices. "Thou art the
man" cried a distinguished court preacher pointing an accusing finger
at the Grand Monarch. "The preacher has done his duty. It remains for
us to do ours," said Louis, quietly, while the court listened breathless. To
give a body of grace to ancient austerities and to give a soul of moral
grandeur to lovely social amenities was the lofty endeavor of the great court
preachers of Louis XIV.

VI

In eighteenth-century England the tension came upon a new quality of
stress and strain. The world-wide empire was being won and an expansive individual prosperity was giving color to the life of the nation. Secular enterprise sat on the throne of men's minds. Great navies moved over
the Seven Seas. Great battles were fought far in the East and far in the
West. The merchant princes moved toward places of power. Deep religious feeling became a thing from which men shrank. The manifestation of enthusiasm was thought to prove that a man was not a gentleman.
God ceased to be a dominant motive in men's thoughts and their actions.
The age of triumphant and capable secularity had arrived. Yet over against
this there were the stirrings of a deep spiritual longing and the masses
swept into the glow of a tremendous religious experience. That quality
which the builders of the eighteenth century had rejected claimed to be the
very head of the corner. Preachers like Whitefield turned words into swords
to smite the consciences of men. The very age of triumphant secularity
became the age of great storms of spiritual passion which swept over the
life of the nation. And it was one of the leaders of the Evangelistic movement who spoke the harmonizing word. The sound practical mysticism of
Wesley joined the shrewd sagacity of the secular temper of the age to a
deep and throbbing experience of the things of the spirit. The age which
produced political empire-builders had produced an empire-builder of the
spirit. So Wesley takes his place among the massive men of the British
tradition and the spiritual rulers of the race.

VII

The years of empire-building produced a temper which was capable of
an entirely material expression. There was a grim possibility that the empire which Englishmen were building might be a gigantic body without a
soul. Some of the empire-builders had small enough interest in the things
of the spirit. But the deeper elements which had entered into English life
were moving in quiet and fruitful fashion beneath the brilliant surface of the
achievements of the age. Wyclif and the Lollards had not lived in vain.
Puritanism had not lifted its white banner only to draw it down in defeat.

The eighteenth-century revival had not spent its force. All these influences and many another drew together to oppose the hard materialism which might have made an empire without a soul. In the midst of the clash of the Napoleonic era when England was girded for one of its most terrible conflicts —the twenty years' struggle with the little Corsican—the heroic and reconciling word was spoken by those who inaugurated the modern missionary movement. Every step in the building of a political empire was to be paralleled in the building of a great world empire in the realm of the spirit. The Kingdom of God was actually seen as an empire embracing all mankind.

VIII

The nineteenth century saw the coming of Darwin and Spencer and the emerging of the masterful principle of the reign of law. The tension became astonishingly acute. For over against the conception of the reign of law the personal view of life armed to do battle for the conquest of the mind of man. As the contest raged there were often more sound and fury than light and understanding. All the while the brilliant generalization of evolutionary science marched forward supported by an increasing body of facts. And all the while the profound personal experiences of men made a place for themselves in a world whose physical uniformities were seen to be so wide-lying and potent. The heroic and reconciling word managed to get itself uttered in the conception of an ultimate person as the source of the order of the universe. And the laws of nature were conceived of as the habits of God.

Of course there have been many more tensions during the passing of the belligerent years than those to which we have referred. But at least it has become evident that life is very largely an experience of successive tensions and their resolution into an inclusive harmony.

IX

It is not, however, entirely a matter of the past. Contemporary life and thought confront us with a strange and baffling series of tensions.

The study of the biological process has made us familiar with very lowly origins and very long processes of development. The delight in following the tenuous trails of investigation which lead to an understanding of the long biological process has given a deep satisfaction to many minds. Such study and such knowledge have almost claimed to be ends in themselves. On the other hand, there are the great sanctions of the Kingdom of God, sharp and clear and spiritual, standing forth with august claims in their own right. In certain minds the tension between the two views becomes extreme. In this regard the harmonizing word must reveal the biological process as itself on the road to the great moral sanctions of the Kingdom of God. The long journey has its end in the triumph of these very sanctions. As Professor Simpson has put it, "Jesus Christ is the goal of the evolutionary process."

Another tension in contemporary thought has to do with the interpretation of life as behavior and the interpretation of life as intention. No end

of brushwood of the mind seems to be cast aside if we refuse to be be-
guiled by dark metaphysical mysteries and set about observing behavior
as we find it, classifying the types of action and so coming to a clear picture of experience as it lies all about us. On the other hand, the view of
life as intention determining the direction which we give to the will refuses
to be put out of court. The sense of life as intention is so fundamental
that even the brilliant catalogue of types of behavior seems oddly empty
without it. So the tension becomes acute and we wait for the unifying
word which finds behavior in the last analysis an expression of intention and
in intention the instrument by means of which we may give direction to
behavior.

A somewhat similar tension grows out of the thought of life as an experience in the conservation of values, and that of life as an experience involving the action of creative personality. Here again the approach to
life through values temporarily simplifies our problem very much. We
do not ask baffling questions. We seize upon values as they emerge, accept
them for their own worth, and view life quite happily as an experience in
the conservation of values. On the other hand, the sense of creative personal powers insists on securing a hearing. Just when we have made our
neat classification of values the powerful person arrives and upsets all our
carefully built structure. The tension becomes intense enough. We wait
for the reconciling word which sees that values emerge only in personal
relations and declares that personality finds its ultimate fulfillment in the
expression of values.

Then there is the grim tension between those who find the meaning
of life in a study of the subconscious and those who find the secret of life
in conscious decision. The subconscious is a treasure house full of priceless
possessions. It is also a deadly den full of wild and poisonous things. And
emerging from the subconscious are influences which have the most far-
reaching effect upon our lives. On the other hand, men of destiny have a
way of being men of will. Triumphant volition has a history which is the
best story in the life of the race. So the two interpretations of life join
in battle array. The unifying word must declare that there is a cold and
grim will upon which the subconscious often has deadly revenge. There
is also a joyous and creative will which rules the subconscious with its own
unhesitating power. If we fight our way through to joy in a good decision
the subconscious ceases to be a menacing foe and becomes a friendly slave.

In our time there has come to men a new vision of the great society.
Social wrong has fallen with a vast shock upon the minds of men, and that
social order in which ancient wrongs will be righted had commanded the enthusiastic allegiance of multitudes of noble men and women. In the thought
of many of them the individual has been almost lost in the dream of the
great society. On the other hand, the appreciation of the strong and creative individual has insisted upon its own place in the thought of powerful
men. The perception that the great and commanding and creative individual is the finest flower of civilization has made itself felt with vigorous
insistence. So the age of Socialism has been the age when Nietzsche has won

a wide hearing and the tension between the two has become menacing. The understanding and unifying word must declare the day of the powerful and creative individual using his high endowments for social ends and the great society flowering perpetually into lives of individual distinction as well as producing a lifted level of common good.

There is a type of spirituality in every age—our own included—which comes at last to be a denial of life. Its fear of evil becomes a fear of vital experience, and its loftiness comes at last to be a withdrawal from the full experience of life. On the other hand, in our own time there is a passionate assertion of the desire to taste life fully, to follow the body as well as the spirit—especially the body—to the very limit of every intense and passionate experience. The tension here may seem to be final and capable of no resolution into a higher harmony. Yet here, too, there is a heroic and reconciling word. The perception that the body is the instrument of personality, that the material is the vehicle of the spiritual, may lead to a sacramental view of life where it is seen that the body helps the soul even as the soul must dominate the body. Things are not to be in the saddle and ride mankind. Things are to wear the proud livery of the spiritual Kingdom.

The development of one aspect of contemporary psychology and philosophy leads to the emergence of another tension. That universe of values of which we have already spoken is easily taken as a final goal. Over against it the call for personal fellowship rings clear and imperative. On the one hand, there is a world of values without fellowship. On the other, it is possible, temporarily at least, to have a world of fellowship without values. The harmonizing word with respect to this tension speaks in the name of fellowship with a conscious and loving father in which the very meaning of the fellowship comes to light in the values which emerge as we become conscious of the quality of the character of that loving Father who is the Lord of all.

It is easy to see that each of these contemporary tensions moves about great matters which are central for religion and fundamental for Christianity. Perhaps the hints we have already thrown out at least suggest that, in this complex situation in which Christianity deals with contemporary intelligence, it will be able to speak the understanding and unifying word.

MODERNISM SEEKS DEPTH

Thomas S. Kepler

RELIGIOUS MODERNISM as a general approach has a fairly clear-cut connotation for most us us. We think of it as an attempt to frame lasting verities in a structure of thought and data which will rule out no contemporary note of valid interpretation of reality. Modernism is always seeking to recapture the religious values that count most in the language of the day; it reveres the past, not because of its time element, but rather as a continuing era of struggle which has given the present age a perspective of the perennial values that validate human experience. The centuries refine ideas more carefully than the hours: consequently a wise modernism is indebted to history for her contribution to the onward progress of truth.

Post-war modernism, not unlike other periods of history, found many of her interpreters so drunk with estrangement from orthodoxy that with glad abandon (perhaps!) they sought intellectual holidays. The behaviourists "made up their glands that they had no minds." The anti-theological humanists became enamored with the idea of belittling "God" into corporate man, failing to see in perspective how the great minds of Europe in the nineteenth century listened for awhile to Comte and Feuerbach, only to say, "Interesting, but superficial." Many a historian tried to interpret life psychologically rather than to give objectivity to the historical tradition, or if he retained the objective note he listened more intently to Spengler than to Hegel, crying out, "Progress is an illusion; all will end in decay." To many science became a hybrid of a cosmic Santa Claus and a Baal which would give man the gifts needed to make life significant—maybe!

Modernism did swing far away from a constructive note in these extreme feelings; perhaps they were only growing pains that needed expression, but certainly they were not ends of thought traditions. They were cries of distress that our age needed intellectual panaceas if she were to reach maturity, instead of attaining either sophomoric sophistication or senile debility.

No person possessing honest, courageous sanity can be other than a "modernist." However, no person with a desire for an élan vital in his search for the abundant life wishes the type of modernity that robs him of the drive for the adventure modernity can give him; nor does he need to be satisfied with such. The tragedy of modernity is that it too often becomes a temporary caustic rather than a permanent impulse. When people cry out, "Let us get back to orthodoxy" or "we want theology" they are giving cries of pain that they lack in their religious structures the drive for great living.

It takes time to make a new thought structure in which to embed modern

---

Reprinted by permission from *The Journal of Bible and Religion*, February, 1939.

tenets and I doubt if any era in history has reshaped both its tenets and its structure so rapidly as this post-war generation. For this reason our age is so distressing. The thesis of pre-war orthodoxy, in which many were reared, and the antithesis of post-war modernity, into which they were shifted, knew so little of one another that the "man-on-the-street" and the student in the classroom found themselves reaching for maturing religious help with little satisfaction. But like all processes of the dialectic, the synthesis for a constructive modernism is beginning to form. It may give to a new generation a religious foundation basic for an intellectually tempered religious revival unparalleled in history! Its structure I am here suggesting.

Some Light from the New Cosmology

The new cosmology not only silences mechanism; it causes positivism to re-evaluate its position. When scientists, using their method of analytical observation, tell us the universe is organic, of mind-stuff, possessing indeterminacy, the positivists have an awareness that the world contains more than they saw with their tools. A new part-whole relationship in this organic philosophy brings to religion a unique tenor—the self "repeats in microcosm what the universe is in macrocosm." This idea is not new, for it is merely what much religious idealism has been uttering for centuries; but the idea takes on a new impression when the results of modern science substantiate the intuitive-rational findings of philosophic idealism.

Man is the *key* to his universe qualitatively; the relation of his mind to his body is but a miniature of the Spirit in the universe in relation to natural phenomena. Man's real freedom saves this view from becoming pantheistic, giving to the system a theistic note. Personal idealism thus takes on deep meaning. To follow the implications of such an organic philosophy cannot help but bring to modernity the warmth of ethical mysticism which in turn will give to contemporary man a new urgency in religion. Religion becomes for one a means of feeling a part of the whole.

The tendency of the cosmic quality being of mind-stuff is vividly expressed by both Eddington and Jeans. Eddington writes, "The stuff of the world is mind-stuff. . . . . The mind-stuff of the world is, of course, something more general than our individual conscious minds, but we may think of its nature as not altogether foreign to the feelings in our consciousness. . . . . We liken it (world stuff) to our conscious feelings because, now that we are convinced of the formal and symbolic character of the entities of physics there is nothing else to liken it to." (*The Nature of the Physical World.*) In like fashion Jeans concludes *The New Background of Science* by saying, "Idealism has always maintained that, as the beginning of the road by which we explore nature is mental, the chances are that the end will also be mental. To this present-day science adds that, at the farthest point she has so far reached, much, and possibly all, that was not mental has disappeared, and nothing new has come in that is not mental."

Those who follow the thoughts of Whitehead feel a similar suggestion. His description of God's primordial nature as the impersonal spirit of concretion may be meaningful as an objective hypothesis true to scientific discovery. But the religious value of Whitehead's concept of God accrues in his depicting this primordial deity as also consequent in a personal, immanent manner; in a Hegelian sense God's consciousness is involved in the world process.

The main import of such hypotheses is, that they express with greater adequacy a meaningful cosmos than did the older cosmological doctrines which lacked an organic relationship between God and the world. They indicate that the natural order is not alien to the spiritual order, that God's personal nature is a part of the cosmic drift, and that teleology is rooted in the universe. Thus religion for the modern man possesses an ethico-mystical drive that could not be felt in the mechanistic, impersonal order depicted by a former science.

Many have uttered in recent years, "Naturalism does not satisfy." Now they can add, "Naturalism is not true to reality as neo-science describes it."

God and the World

The problem of evil has driven man to diverse interpretations of God's relationship to the world. Pantheism has stressed God's immanence as the reality composed of "an impersonal something" into which man could flee from an illusory evil world. Naturalism, on the other hand, has defined "God's" immanence in terms of the objects known by physical and human sciences which consequently places man's purposes and ideals as a part of nature. Even when a thinker like Ames speaks of God as "idealized reality," such an expression is only a *symbol* of God's immanence in the tangible; or when Dewey defines God as that which ties the real to the ideal, God is still only immanent as something which man projects from his imagination. Unlike pantheists who have tried to escape evil by denying the reality of the world, naturalists have accepted a real world in which corporate love and courage become means of diminishing sin and suffering.

Contemporary deism has resorted to a dualistic means of relating God and the world. For Crisis theologians the fall of Adam was more than myth; man, originally related organically to God, became separated by sin. Thus there has existed a dichotomy between a good God and a fallen world, and because of man's guilt he has no way of access to God. Even though Emil Brunner may explain God's transcendence as epistemological rather than cosmological, the utter transcendence of God over the world has a vacuum in either case for man in both his individual worship and his social hope for the world. Only pessimism can result, and permanent pessimism is never a nourishment for the soul, even though momentary attitudes of pessimism have remedic value.

Theism, stressing both God's immanence and transcendence, patterns itself best into modern religious thought. It not only is supported by modern cosmological descriptions; it also is authenticated by contemporary metaphysics.

From the angle of one's metaphysics, the results of the new cosmology force one either to accept the relation of microcosm to macrocosm (which is basically theistic) or to deny the validity of the findings of modern science. To do the latter would be to negate the results of man's most certain objective tool of understanding.

Theism not only accepts both the reality of God and the world; it holds also to their organic relationship. In so doing theism does not deny the reality of evil nor does it face evil merely in a Stoical sense. It accepts evil as a purposive necessity by which man understands more profoundly the partnership man and God have in realizing the part-whole nature of an organic, growing universe. Christianity especially in its symbol of the cross seems akin to reality, as man and God strive together toward a cosmic purpose.

COSMIC SIGNIFICANCE OF JESUS CHRIST

Modern portraits of Jesus Christ have varied from those depicting him as a pallid Jewish rabbi reiterating a good ethic to those portraying him as an apocalyptic figure whose passion was a thoroughgoing eschatology. Neither view supports his unique cosmic significance.

Ordinary categories lack adequacy in describing Jesus. That he belongs organically to history none would deny; both his prophetic continuity with Jewish tradition and his integral relationship to the last nineteen hundred years establish this note. Yet Jesus transcends history both in his relation to God, and in the way he has inspired man; to rule out this qualitative transcendence is to lack historical perspective. Jesus belongs organically to the universe in a manner we all do; it is his *degree* of relationship which causes his difference from us. Each of us in a microcosmic manner is a distorted impression of the macrocosm; Jesus, on the other hand, is the cosmic event wherein the eternal values of God are momentarily envisaged in a spatio-temporal world. To develop the spirit of Jesus Christ in one's life is to evolve a mystical feeling of real unity with God.

Constructive modernism believes Christianity to be true to reality. Where individuals have made decisions akin to those Jesus made, they have felt a new kinship with God. Each religious advance in history has shown afresh the validity of Christ. The further the Christian message has gone into the world, the more clearly have men seen its universal import. "After many centuries of historical vicissitudes His word is still current, and fertile of truth."

That God is like Christ is not a *dogmatic, non-experiential* assertion for moderns to make; rather, to follow Jesus Christ with utter abandon is to understand in the twentieth century what "spiritual rebirth" may mean, to discern the way by which disintegration between man and God may resolve itself into organic harmony, and not only to feel with a sense of mystical ecstasy a new vitality for pulsating living, but also to know with experiential certainty that the God-without becomes more clearly realized as the God-within.

To say that Jesus Christ is the saviour of the world is not mere verbosity, it is the most modern realistic expression conceivable. That the cross was answered by the resurrection of Christ in the lives of his followers is not only the gospel of salvation for the first century; it is the "good news" for any era. He who struggles with God for Christian hopes will understand its efficacy with greater certainty than will he who logically proves it by way of careful dogmatics; even more, he will begin to understand the cosmic significance of Jesus Christ.

ESCHATOLOGY AND HISTORY

This cosmic drama for most people is heavily weighted with tragedy. Jesus at Golgotha, Kagawa in Kobe, Milton gone blind, Beethoven deaf, Nietzsche insane—even the great actors bring little more than heartaches tempered with inspiration to those who admire them. Life so often is a perplexing, baffling dilemma. Yet in spite of the bruises it leaves on man's soul, he cannot but feel (or hope) that some day the real will become the ideal. Even one like Thomas Hardy, steeled almost to despair for a grinding universe, could pen a tone of hope,

> "And they shall see what is, ere long
> Not through a glass but face to face,
> And Right shall disestablish Wrong;
> The Great Adjustment is taking place."

What the world is and what it ought to be are far apart; the real and the ideal do not coincide. Furthermore, how can they? Will they ever? The pantheist has no answer for he denies the reality of the world (the real); the naturalist is also silent for he negates the validity of an objective ideal. Religions like Islam, Zoroastrianism, and some interpretations of Judaism and Christianity have given promise of the ideal on a cataclysmic judgment day. However, these attempts to relate the real and the ideal have given little satisfaction to the intelligent modern devotee of religion.

The Old Testament in prophecy and apocalypse did look quite consistently toward the *eschaton* when the real would become the ideal. Then the new age would arrive, evil powers would be overthrown, and God's glorious reward would come to those who kept His will; on "the day of the Lord" history would give way to suprahistory. Naturally this ultimate hope which lay beyond history inculcated meaning for individuals within the structure of history. Christianity, however, offered a unique solution, even though closely related in an organic sense to the Old Testament.

As a person weaves his way through the apocalyptic accretions of the gospel in the New Testament and applies a functional interpretation, he finds history there taking on a new significance. History, affected by the motif of Jesus Christ, has become the vehicle of eternal values; the day of the Lord has become a present realization; demonic powers have been overthrown; eternal life qualitatively has come into the world; *the* divine event inaugurated by Jesus Christ has taken place; in fact, that which always lay beyond history is now a historical realization.

The gospel in the New Testament is an attempt to tell us that the new age is no longer a future hope; it is a present realization; it is "realized eschatology." Even though the world may present a conflict between God and "demons" the Christian fact is an avenue whereby those who understand its power possess eternity qualitatively in time. The statement that "God was in Christ reconciling the world unto himself" becomes the real belief of those who through the ages have found the power of God via Christ as a means of appreciating the ideal in the real.

"History in its relationship to transcendent fulfilment and decision receives absolute seriousness. It is not the realm where man acts without relationship to God. There is no such realm. History is the realm where the ultimate is intended." So writes Paul Tillich. The gospel attempts to express the fact and to show the way by which the "intended ultimate" is a reality in history.

But how then does this reality eventuate in history? By empathizing ourselves with the spirit of Christ and the cross. Ecstasy must be preceded by pain and struggle—it is the framework of a struggling universe. Just as Dante was attaching symbol to the fact of reality when he groped through hell and purgatory before he found the sublime secrets of heaven, so the cross and the resurrection become the aperture by which one sees eternity joined to time as well as the climactic moment in which the *eschaton* is realized as a present reality. This planet and its members belonging organically to God have all the potentialities of becoming the Kingdom of God on earth.

Let Us Follow Through These Implications

Such a structure for a modernism of depth has many implications. It needs intelligent exploration, careful translation for the lay mind, progressive reinterpretation as developments accrue. It lacks completeness. Scholars working along these lines of thought, however, may discover the avenue to a new vitality for modernism. Such an impetus lies somewhere if our era is to play its religious rôle.

Part III

THE IDEA OF GOD

THE PASSING OF THE GODS OF OLD

A. Eustace Haydon

IN SOME CULTURES the idea of God acquired such an exaggerated emphasis that the whole meaning of religion seemed to be oriented there. This was particularly true of Christianity because of the historic stress upon doctrinal authority. In a less marked degree it was true of Judaism and Islam. God gathered into himself the whole meaning of the universe for all three, though the Jewish law and the Moslem Shariah were more important practically than doctrine. In the religions of India and China theology was a matter of relative indifference. The all-important thing was the proper behavior in established social relationships of family, community, caste, or guild. It would be utterly impossible to define Hinduism in terms of creed. Religion is dharma, the ideal pattern of daily duty. "Hinduism is that which the Hindu does." The ease with which India and China make adjustment to modern scientific thinking as compared with the long anguish of the last three centuries in Christendom is a reflection of this difference of emphasis in the religions. It is a contrast between rigidity of custom and rigidity of dogma. The growing-pains in theology are largely Western.

To keep a correct perspective one must remember that until most modern times intellectual anxiety about the nature of God was limited to a very few people. The slow drift of time and social evolution rather than logical thinking made changes in the meaning of gods for the folk. The stream of human living runs on a level lowlier than logic. The comradeship of men and women, the love of little children, the loyalties of friends, the homely familiarity of the natural world, the shared tasks, sorrow and defeat, fears and hopes, the common life with its bonds of cozy custom, its safe habits and close, comfortable contacts—these are the things which make up the realities of experience for the masses of men. The gods are like members of the group, unseen but always within call. Among some peoples they are represented by picture or image. . . . . For the plain and simple people it has always been sufficient that their gods were vouched for by church and teacher, by the tales of marvelous deeds, by sacred drama and Scriptures, or by their own mystical experiences. Even when the intellectuals of Hinduism and Buddhism pushed out beyond the personal gods to the Absolute, the people were not disturbed. The god of the intellectuals was not a jealous god. There was no theological intolerance. The gods of the common folk were too intimately integrated in the patterns of life to be lost, and there was no reason to trouble them for the sake of an Eternal Reality which included them all.

In Christianity it was different. The intellectuals worked with more

From *The Quest of the Ages*, New York, 1929, pp. 98-125. Reprinted by permission of the publishers, Harper & Brothers.

intractable materials. God was solitary, personal, and transcendent. This was the heritage from Judaism. The dualism between the natural and supernatural was more sharply drawn. There was a difference in essence between God and man. This was the heritage from Plato and the Greeks. Through all the centuries of Christian theology it was necessary to bridge the gulf between the world of man and matter, and the transcendent spiritual realm of God. During the ages of uncritical faith the task was not difficult, for there were many ladders leading up to God. One by one they came down as Christianity moved from the mediaeval to the modern world.

First to fall was the trusted revelation authority of the Church, which crumbled under the challenge of the Protestant reformers. It was a loss more serious than men then realized, for in the final analysis the real authority of Scriptures and creeds was Church authority. Both were products of the Church.

There was an old belief that miracles were God's way of setting his seal upon his messenger. The attack of eighteenth-century Rationalism destroyed that form of assurance. Later centuries found it easier to believe in God unproven than to believe in the proofs for miracles. In their turn the deists and rationalists had what they considered a more scientific certainty of God. The Creator had attuned human nature to religion, and at the beginning there was an original natural religion of mankind. Consequently, all men have an innate idea of God. But the facts of history of religions were too well-known and Hume's criticism was too devastating. Their ladder to the unseen was quietly taken down.

There was still left the revelation in sacred Scripture. It was not long, however, until the devoted labors of scholars in historical criticism made of the Bible a living, human book. It was given vital significance as a historical record of a religious quest, but at the same time emptied of its authority as an inspired revelation.

Though all other proofs of God might be shaken, both churchman and philosopher had been confidently certain that his existence at least, if not his nature, could always be demonstrated by reason. Hume first and then Kant took up the arguments one by one and returned the verdict in the negative. From that time, men turned for certainty in religion to the facts of human experience. Kant himself began with man. Because of the absolute quality of the moral imperative in man, he felt it necessary to postulate the existence of God. Kant was too early to know the natural history of morality and the social source of his awed respect for the moral law.

For many men of the last generation, a sufficient evidence of God was given in the experience of Christ. The argument from God to Christ, from the unknown to the known, was reversed. Christ was felt to have the value of God and to be an evidence in time and history of the nature of Deity. To Christians reared in the old tradition this was very appealing. Jesus they knew and loved. There would be complete security in a universe ruled by a God like him. But when the facts of the natural and social history of the world were faced in their stark nakedness, faith was not so easy. The difficulty was voiced in the words of Professor George Burman Foster, who once held this position—"Oh, if we could only believe that God is as good as Jesus!"

A final resort lay in the assurance of mystical experience. For the mystic there was no need for external authority of Church, or Scripture or creed. His assurance was personal and self-sufficient. But once more the proof failed to stand objective analysis. The knowledge given in the mystic's experience was found to be no greater than that of his social environment. Joy, peace, and an untroubled confidence are the qualities of the mystic state. There is a feeling of at-homeness in the universe. This is true whether the mystic be atheist, theist or polytheist. The experience has genuine religious value, but brings back no report from the unseen. . . . .

But there was change. The fact that man felt the need of ceaseless reconstruction was an indication that the issues of life were forcing their claims upon theology. The influences at work were of several kinds. During the century a new vision of the nature of the world and of the development of life emerged. Man's increasing control over the material order and his success in achieving the goods of life awakened a hope that he might win mastery over the most crying evils of the natural world and of society. He was no longer willing to "accept the universe," nor to think the worst of human nature. He dared to challenge in practice all finalities and unseen teleologies. A more sensitive response to the finer, spiritual ideals arising in an increasingly individualistic and democratic age, led to a refusal to accept in resignation either ideas or conditions which blocked the door of opportunity for developing the higher life. There came also an enlargement of mind, by more adequate knowledge of the history of human cultures. The world of man's life in time and space passed in panorama before the eyes of the thinker. It was possible as never before to appreciate the function of religions in human history and the place of the gods in religion. Finally, there came an awed realization of the danger of drift. Science, practically applied, was a greater threat to religious values than science, as knowledge, had been to the old ideas. Man began to feel responsibility for putting intelligent purpose into history, which was a very different thing from trusting that it was already there. All these factors played their part in the transformation of the idea of God during the last hundred years. . . . .

In the discussion of recent years, the paramount place has been given to the values of human life. Even those thinkers who still defend the Almighty and the Absolute, have their eyes turned not to the heavens, but upon the mundane scene. The reconstruction of the Absolute by Royce showed the influence of social idealism. Professor Lyman's god, as Eternal Creative Good Will, is a compromise with the old theology, but at every point oriented to the problems of the everyday world. Increasingly our modern systems are compelled to give central place to human needs, struggles, and ideals. Instead of trying to prove the existence of God, or to reduce to reasonable terms an inherited idea, the fashionable thing today is to ask in what ways the reality, in which we are immersed as living beings, gives us help in the attainment of the good life. . . . .

Changing gods are no novelty to the student of religions. But it is evident that the change which is taking place in the modern world is different from and more fundamental than that of any previous age. The gods of the past are vanishing. Modern men are seeking to know the real nature of the reality which determines their destinies. Instead of the agnosticism which takes the form of faith in an ineffable unknown, there is the more humble effort to know what the real and effective aids to the worthiest life may be. The idea of god meant help for man in his quest for the ideal, but it can no longer be assumed that men of the olden, long-dead days had captured the true nature of that help in the net of their theologies. Instead of asking, "Does God exist?" meaning one of the well-known gods of yesterday, instead of rationalizing and denaturing the vital concepts of an earlier generation, the question is asked direct, "What support does the universe give to our moral ideals?" Answered frankly, without bias or presupposition, in the light of the best available knowledge, this question should reveal what for modern men may function as did the ancient gods. . . . .

When the question is put in this way, the answer is at once clear and assuring. If some of the consolations of the past disappear, their very loss is valuable for a living religion. The elements of support and security, of hope and promise, which come to man from his cosmic and social environment are real and effective. They may some day be the means for the realization of his long-deferred dream.

First of all is the support of the stable balance of the natural world. This may be understood in two ways. Man himself is one phase of the natural order, the result of aeons of cosmic development—an earthchild, molded and trained in body and mind, by constant interaction with environment. The human races have been so thoroughly adjusted to the nature of which they are a part, that man may justly claim to be the form of life most capable, not only of survival, but of mastery on the planet. He has achieved sufficient harmony with the forces of nature to feel secure. He is indeed the planet itself, come to consciousness and capacity for intelligent self-direction. For modern man the physical world has become for the most part a kindly or controllable environment. Natural evils still remain an ominous shadow; but they are by far the least of the great problems of human life. Man's being is so attuned to the nature from which he sprang, and which has nursed his long racial infancy, that some of the finest emotional experiences he has are rooted in the unconscious past. Love of nature is not an affair of reason, but deeper, a more sensuous appreciation of unity with the whole of things. A modern understanding of our relation to all the manifold phases of the patterns of life borne by the great Earth Mother may add to the mystic feel of oneness. But the simple reactions are older— the joy of springtime, the soft peace of moonlit nights, the ever-new exultation at the dawn, the homely love of memory-haunted landscapes, the beauty of sunsets, or the fresh green of sunlit fields after rain. Under the starry heavens, in the presence of the grandeur of nature forces, man feels still the thrill of awe; but the waterfall sings to him, and all living, growing things answer in his own nature the pulse beat of unconquerable life. These appreciations may be socially meditated, but they are the heritage of the age-old experiences of other generations in the winning of a place in the sun and a record of joy in achievement. A mystical naturalism has its roots here.

The other phase is more prosaic and practical. Man, as a product of nature, could not be what he is, were the environment not as it is. On this earth alone could we really be at home. All our bodily functions are a part of its nature. The corollary of this is that a more complete understanding of the ways of nature, and of the orderliness of the material world may make it possible for man to overcome still hostile factors and to mold the natural environment into a more completely satisfying background for his social ideas. Allowed to live, where thousands of life forms failed, through his ability in blind adjustment, he may now consciously complete the physical harmonizing of nature and human nature.

A second element of support for the human quest lies in man's secure biological heritage. It is a continuation of the significance of the first, interpreted in terms of racial history. As we have already seen, the psycho-physical heritage of the normal newborn babe is the accumulation of the experience of millions of years in the development of living organisms. The child is only mediated by the existing generation. He is unspoiled human potentiality, capable of embodying the habits, attitudes, and culture of any social milieu. Decadent civilizations are merely deterrents for the hope of mankind as a whole. Tirelessly, the immortal life cells initiate in every generation an old-fresh creation. The whole of humanity is always ready for a new start, with each successive wave of child life. This also is one of the wise ways of nature, grounded in the pattern of reality, and beyond the control of any single generation. Given the possibility of a social science that shall know how to create an ever richer and more complete cultural environment, this fresh life of each new age may rise at once to the new level, with the opportunity for progressive creative advance. In this there is hope for humanity, though it carries only a pathetic consolation and no help for the destroyed individuals of a disordered age. For the philosopher of religion, however, it is one of the habits of nature that holds out radiant promise of a happier and nobler future.

A third and, for the individual, more important phase of cosmic structure is the enfolding social environment. This is, in the final analysis, his real support, master, guide, and guarantor. It, too, is older than the individual and the generation. It is the continuously growing and conserving continuum of racial experience in civilization and culture. Thousands of years of weary toil and creative effort have entered into the tapestry of some human cultures. In the patterns are conserved the life achievements of the long-forgotten followers of the quest. The web is colored by the loyal devotion, love, and sacrifice of untold multitudes of unnamed and unknown men and women. The social purposiveness of man, seeking always the more abundant life, gives the motif. The individual is born into this enfolding milieu. He is molded by it, given his character by its varied groupings, guarded by its hard-won securities, protected by its accepted modes, mellowed and enriched by the treasured heritage of ages of human contributions to the common store of knowledge, technique, and art, supported and challenged by the embedded ideals toward which the current of the social stream ever runs. The nature of this cultural environment varies with the people, place, age, and civilization, but, such as it is, it performs the function of support and guaranty for every individual who yields himself to its control.

It is in this social mode of cosmic life that the values and ideals of the religious quest have their secure place. Even a superficial knowledge of the gods is enough to show clearly that the human and social structure is the source from which they have always derived character and definition. Spiritual values are the tried, transformed, and tested fruitage of long centuries of experience in social living. They are evolutionary products. They, too, belong to the very nature of the world. Not from any supernal or external source, neither from above nor behind the world, do they come. They are beacons, lit by human aspiration, to lead the way to a better and more beautiful life for man. Safely held in cosmic actuality, enshrined in the heart of a group, they exercise a dominant authority over individuals—commanding loyalty, giving assurance and hope. . . . .

The promise lies in an organization of human society in such a way as to yield to its members a full opportunity for growth into joyous living, freedom, economic security, providential care, consolation in the crises of life, wise training and guidance, a share in the racial heritage of culture now denied to the millions, escape from the tragedies of strife and war, and the recognition which flows from creative contribution to the common life. So the value of god, in the multiform quest of the ages, would become realities. To a degree which we have only recently come to realize, the gods were the anchorage of our wishes and hopes. When in social structure there may actually exist the means for attainment of the shared hopes of the group, the values would become tangible and available for man. In social organization, if anywhere, must come the progressive mastery of evils. There, too, is lodged responsibility for assurance of full and satisfying life to every individual allowed to enter upon the adventure of living. There alone can be won the control of material and technological resources for the service of spiritual ends. There, individuals must find the guaranty of knowledge, of encouragement, of joy in creation, recognition of work well done, and comradeship in the common quest. . . . .

This is the age of all ages when it is necessary to challenge youth and the intellectuals to loyalty in the service of the ancient quest of man. Lucent sincerity and intellectual honesty are essential. The gods have had their high place as companions of the way. In the brilliant light that floods the winding paths of the historic religions, we are now able to understand and to appreciate them. By the same vision it is possible also to enter with sympathy into the religious attitudes of the multitudes for whom the gods performed their beneficial services through storm-swept centuries. But there is a deeper understanding. It is the realization that gods and institutions alike were incidental to the end they served. More fundamental than either was, and is, the undeviating thrust of life in the human line for complete fulfillment. Modern man bears responsibility for carrying the torch of that daring dream in a world wide awake to the real nature of the task. To refuse to face the light would be disloyalty. Heroic spirits, whose names live in the hearts of men, died to break the bonds of a decadent orthodoxy in olden times. What God meant he can no longer mean. To rest in compensatory securities would be betrayal. Heir of the quest of the ages, man feels upon his mind and heart the burden of cosmic purpose. The goal is not guaranteed. No longer is it safe to wait in patient expectation that time will show the way, and to trust that "somehow good will be the final goal of ill." A good world is an achievement not a gift. Nature and the structure of society, the real bases of man's security, wait to be molded to the service of his nobler ideal. The values of God, to be actual, must be woven into the warp and woof of the organized life of the world.

THE SEARCH FOR GOD IN A SCIENTIFIC WORLD

Kirtley F. Mather

PRIMITIVE PEOPLES, WHETHER in ancient times or in places remote from modern civilization, have quite generally assumed that supernatural beings dwelt in every object which they saw. Each tree or river, mountain or valley, rock or swamp, had its own spirit or soul, which might prove either vindictive or helpful toward man. A boulder which rolled down a steep hillside and crashed through a man's hut, did so because the being or spirit residing in that boulder was for some reason offended by the person whose property was thus destroyed. The spirit of the river must be bribed or placated, perhaps by a human sacrifice, in order that in flood-time its waters would not sweep away the village. Or more powerful, friendly spirits must be summoned by incantation or burnt offering to subdue or disperse the spirits whose wrath against men had been aroused unwittingly or who were constantly and naturally determined to make human life unpleasant and difficult. That answer to the question concerning the nature of God is called animism. Inanimate objects were believed to be really animated by some unseen power; everything was imagined to possess an "anima," that is, a soul or spirit. . . . .

But with the progressive discovery of the facts of nature and more extended consideration of human experiences, rational minds soon saw the inconsistencies in the animistic answer to the question concerning the character of the administration of the universe. If there were many independent spirits, each one absolutely free to do just what it pleased, there could be no harmony in the world. Instead there would be anarchy, and it does not take a very high degree of intelligence to discover that although there is occasional conflict between the various units in our surroundings, there are also a smoothness and regularity of operation which necessarily bespeak the harmonious nature of the universe. Out of the animistic conception there naturally developed the thought of one supreme administrator, the all-powerful overlord who ruled the lesser spirits and thus brought order out of chaos. Under his direction, the mob became a well-drilled army.

Primitive Judaism and medieval Christianity gave much the same answer to the question concerning the nature of the administration of the universe. God was a person of majestic power, residing high above the earth, who was in direct and immediate control of all things which happened on this lower level. Having made the world and all its inhabitants, he had withdrawn from it and was now watching from above. When he pulled the strings, the puppets danced; occasionally he stooped down to make an

---

From *Science in Search of God*, New York, 1928, pp. 56-79. Reprinted by permission of the publishers, Henry Holt & Company.

adjustment in the machinery. If something went wrong, down here upon this earthly plane, the only recourse for suffering injured humanity was through appeal to the remote power, high above in inaccessible distance. The appeal might be phrased in magic words, or it might be strengthened by burnt offerings. It might be fortified by ritual or ceremonial, but man could do nothing more; the power to change the mechanism resided wholly in its maker. When God became ready to act, things would be changed; man was helpless and could only await the will of God.

That answer to the inquiry concerning God is technically known as deism. God is the transcendent Creator, but not the immanent Administrator. His task is finished or his labors have wearied him, so that he is now resting in some distant place, entirely outside of his creation. Only occasionally does he intervene and alter the operations of the world mechanism.

But modern science has scanned the heavens with its telescopes and has reported that there is no place where the deistic God may dwell. In a scientific age we know that everything happens in an orderly way in obedience to law; there is no outside interference whatsoever. Every effect is produced by an adequate cause, discoverable within the universe; every cause is followed by its effect. Deism is today absolutely unsatisfactory to the man of science. But so also is it to the intelligent man of religion. If God is deistic, all-powerful, and in direct and immediate control of affairs, how can he, at the same time, be all-wise and all-loving? Why does he permit the suffering and sin, the unhappiness and distress, which is so obviously a part of the life which we know? There are, of course, many ways which have been used by theologians to extricate themselves from this dilemma, but they are too devious to be satisfactory. For the most part they are a tribute more to the cleverness than to the wisdom of their authors.

Dissatisfied or even repelled by deism, many persons proclaim themselves as atheists. Most of modern atheism is merely a reaction to this particular idea concerning the nature of God. Still does the heart of man long, as of old, for an answer to its fundamental need. In this perplexity, it is not surprising that an appeal should be made to science for aid in the search for God. Surely, if science has been so successful in discovering the facts of nature, it ought to have something to say concerning nature's God. It is reasonable to hope that the method of research which has proved successful in revealing the secrets of the material universe ought to prove of value also in the study of spiritual realities. Granted that the man of science has to go outside of his own field and even trespass beyond the pale of natural science, he is somehow expected to have peculiar aptitude for making the venture out into the unknown, where there is neither path for our guidance nor ground for our feet to tread. . . . . .

The philosophical implications of the analytical view of the universe are obvious. The world of sense perception is a manifestation of energy. There is "something back of the universe." Matter is neither eternal nor ultimate; it is a temporary and local expression of energy. If there is anything which is ultimate, eternal, absolute—and our minds somehow seem to expect that there is—that something must be energy. Analysis seems to lead inevitably to the conclusion that energy is the ultimate reality, the eternal verity. Could we know its nature in its entirety, we would have at last the complete answer to the quest of Job.

Here again we turn to the methods of science. How did the scientist discover that there were electrons in the atom? No man ever saw an electron; yet every well-trained scientist is ready to stake his reputation on the fact that electrons are. He knows that electrons are, because he has observed what they do. The results of their activities indicate their nature. Radio impulses are speeding through the air all 'round us, most of the time, whether we are aware of them or not. Although they are quite imperceptible to human senses we become aware of their presence when proper mechanisms are provided to catch them in motion and translate them into sounds which are audible to the human ear. We know that this particular sort of energy is a reality, because of its effects upon certain forms of matter. Even so the nature of Eternal Energy, the Ultimate Reality, may be discovered by observing what it does. . . . .

Man, a product of the energy which fills and thrills the universe, is different from other organisms. He is of course an animal; but there are many grades of existence and man seems to stand alone upon his own level. He is unique, in ways which can be discovered only by observation, experiment, and experience, not by any process of *a priori* reasoning. Nothing concerning man can be taken for granted as a result of observation of other animals. When the cow pauses on the hilltop at sunset to admire the view, or the dog ceases baying at the moon to construct a system of astronomy, we will welcome the cow and the dog into the category of rational aesthetic creatures, in which category man is rightfully placed. Somehow, out of the continuity of the process, real differences have emerged. Even though we may not understand how these differences arose, the facts are there. Knowledge and mystery have a habit of existing side by side; but mystery does not invalidate the fact.

Thus in a scientific age the search for God leads to a new answer to the ancient question. The answer is theism. God is a power, immanent in the universe. He is involved in the hazard of his creation. He is striving mightily to produce a perfect display in the world of sense-perception, of his own true nature. "The whole creation travaileth," because only so can it achieve that purpose. . . . .

Science makes another contribution to our knowledge of God. At last we are beginning to understand that he is spirit. The etymology of that term is interesting and suggestive. It comes from the same classical root which gives rise also to the words, inspiration and respiration. Breath, to the ancients, was the most attenuated form of matter concerning which there was any general knowledge. Breath and spirit were analogous concepts. And to many modern folk, spirit still means an attenuated form of matter, a ghost. To the scientist, spirit is no form of matter whatsoever; it is the antithesis of matter. Matter is that something, no two parts of which can occupy the same place at the same time. A satisfactory definition of matter is necessarily phrased in terms of time and space. There is no satisfactory definition of spirit, known to me; it transcends definition. But surely any definition of spirit must indicate that spirit has no limitations of space or time. . . . . In the meantime, we have the encouragement that God is no longer hiding behind the gaps in our knowledge. . . . .

God is partially revealed by inanimate nature, with its law-abiding planets and its orderly chemical reactions. The crystal with its remarkable internal architecture and its beautiful external forms suggests something of the characteristics of the motive power which has brought the minerals into existence. But we find that power on a distinctly higher plane when we consider the lilies of the field or behold the fowls of the air. Thus we learn something of the attributes of the energy that can produce an organism as well as a crystal, that can induce living cells to emerge from non-living matter. Then when we investigate humanity and inquire into the nature of man we greatly enlarge our estimate of the forces that can produce personality as well as organism, that can induce the reasoning mind to emerge from mere consciousness. The scientist studying nature in strict accordance with the rigid methods which he has developed, cannot fail to have a profound respect for the motive powers of the universe. The farther he advances in his discovery of facts and his understanding of human experiences, the better able is he to guide in the ordering of human conduct toward the goal of a richer and fuller life for man. That is, by discovering the methods of nature we may truly associate ourselves with God in the task of creative evolution.

There is, however, another way of discovering God which ,although at present outside the field of natural science, is in all probability a valid approach to him. The mystical experience of the human spirit brought face to face with the reality that transcends knowledge is a most enticing field for investigation, and psychologists are already making progress there. Some of the experiences of the great prophets may be tested in our own experience. In that way we can appraise the qualifications which they possess to serve as experts in the field of spiritual realities. . . . .

Knowledge concerning God, therefore, becomes a matter of human experience which includes both contact with the physical world of sense-perception in which he is the motive power, and also direct, though mysterious, contact with him, when spirit meets with Spirit. The human soul reaching out into the darkness becomes aware of spiritual realities and through personal contact with the Eternal discovers something of the heights and depths which cannot be measured. The experiences of other men enlarge and enrich our own experiences and thus we become the heirs of all the ages. The response of the universe to the lives of great and good men is an expression of the creative energy which has likewise called us into being, and that response when fully understood is quite sufficient to satisfy our deepest yearnings. In a scientific age, the search for God bids fair to give mankind the wisdom which is more than knowledge.

GOD IN HISTORY

Ernest Fremont Tittle

Is THERE ANY REAL hope of a better world? May we venture to look
forward to a time when the institutions of society will at least offer no
resistance to the human spirit in its attempt to rise above sensuality, greed,
and cruelty; when the practices by which man secures his daily bread will
not interfere with any desire he may have to love his neighbor as himself;
and when his membership in a nation, to which he is bound by strong ties of
tradition and affection, will not prevent him from cherishing a lively
concern for the welfare of other nations?

The present outlook, it must be confessed, is not very encouraging.
European observers remark upon the optimism which is still to be found
in the United States, where, as one of them has said, "Christians still believe
in the efficacy of constructive effort." A European, this same observer
declares, "cannot help be somewhat suspicious" of any belief "in the value,
the power, and the efficacy of human or Christian efforts" to improve the
world. It is, apparently, a fact that in continental Europe almost everywhere
Christians have become passive in the presence of threatening disaster. They
will not consent to deny their faith. Rather than do that, they will suffer
the loss of all things. But they do not suppose that there is much, if
anything, which they can do about the external order of the world. They
cherish the hope, nursed by early Christians, of a divine interference from
without our bourne of time and place; yet as events move on toward
apparent catastrophe and nothing happens to divert their course, they feel
ever more constrained to suppose that a world which has sinned can now
expect nothing save the just but awful retribution of God. Nor do they
suppose that the social conditions of human life on earth will ever be very
much better than they now are. As they see it, any hopeful view of the
future of this world is, to say the least of it, pathetically superficial. Indeed,
they are not a little inclined to brush it aside as being quite unworthy of any
serious consideration.

What is the explanation of so great a divergence from a common faith
as that which appears between Christians in "the efficacy of constructive
effort" and Christians who believe that human effort to improve the world
is futile and foolish? It is tempting, because easy, to suppose that it is
largely a matter of geography: American Christians live in a land that is
three thousand miles away from that boiling cauldron of hates and fears
which is the European inheritance; and the land they live in is overflowing
with oil and iron and other natural resources. But this explanation, although
there is, no doubt, some truth in it, is certainly no adequate account of the

From *Christians in an Unchristian Society*, "Hazen Books on Religion" series, New
York, 1939, pp. 1-12. Reprinted by permission of the publishers, Association Press.

situation. There are Christians in America who are by no means convinced of the possibility of any radical kind of social improvement. There are Christians in Europe who, notwithstanding the desperate character of their situation, still believe in "the efficacy of constructive effort." Is it, after all, quite fair to assume that human faith is largely, if not wholly, conditioned by circumstances? Is it true that the pessimism which is characteristic of European Christianity, as also the optimism which colors American Christianity, is but the natural, if not the inevitable, result of earthly conditions? ....

For my own part, I am driven to the conclusion that the most telling of all reasons why some Christians are pessimistic and others are optimistic as regards the future of the world is to be found in the fact that they hold quite different views of the activity of God in history.

All Christians, of course, reject the view that history is but a continuation of the biological process that operates in nature; that man is nothing more than an animal, "higher," it may be, than all other animals yet not essentially different from them. All Christians reject the view that history is meaningless; that all man's hopes and efforts, all his struggle and pain, are but a phantasmagoria of fleeting appearances that have no significance whatever. With one accord, Christians reject the view of the ancient world, revived in our time by Nietzsche and Spengler, that history is but a futile cycle of birth and decay; that civilizations, like individuals, appear only to die and be buried; that there is, in fact, no future for the world save a tragic repetition of what has already been. Also, with one accord, Christians reject the view of Aristotle, and of some modern philosophies of the absolute, that what happens in history is of no concern to God; that God, indeed, is not even aware of what is going on in the world; that human laughter and human tears, the experience of individuals and the fate of nations, have simply no place in the consciousness of God. And all Christians reject the view that God's relation to history is only that of a spectator, who watches, it may be, with lively interest the successive moves of the game but himself takes no part in it. As all Christians see it, history is "the disclosure of spiritual reality"; it is shot through with meaning and significance; it is the theater of creative power, which brings into existence new conditions and values: not only above history but in it is God, who, indeed, is the only Actor who never disappears from the historic stage.

Up to this point there is universal agreement among Christians, all of whom believe that God is not only aware of man's predicament but concerned to do something about it. All Christians, however, do not hold the same view of God's activity in history. Some believe that God works in history to save individuals *from* the world, allowing the world for the most part to shift for itself. Others believe that God's concern for the salvation of individuals leads him to work, also, for the salvation of the world, that is, of political institutions, social customs, and economic practices. The first of these views is characteristic of European Christianity, especially on the continent, but it is by no means confined to Europe. The second, since the beginning of the present century, has become increasingly influential in American Christianity, but it is not simply an American development. It is now to be found, at least in some Christians, in almost every part of the world—a fact which came to light at Oxford in the summer of 1937 during a conference that included representatives of forty-three nations and 119 Christian communions. Hence, it cannot be said of these differing views of God's activity in history that they are but the product of different temperaments and conditions. It can be said of them that they are themselves productive of profound differences in human outlook, attitude, and conduct.

The first view makes for pessimism as regards the future of the world. God himself is not greatly concerned about the world; he is concerned only to deliver men from the toils of an earthly existence and to prepare them for entrance into that unseen world where alone his kingdom is or ever can be. In the eyes of God, history is important only in so far as it provides a training ground for eternal life. Across the field of history pass the many generations of men, and as they pass God is not greatly concerned about the external conditions of their pilgrimage, whether there be freedom or bondage, justice or injustice, peace or war. Under any conditions, is not his grace sufficient to deliver the trusting soul from its earthly foes and to secure for it some blessed fortaste of eternal bliss? No doubt, the historic field is violently different from what it would have been if man had not sinned. With its revolting injustices, its sickening brutalities and occasional catastrophes, it is not as God meant it to be. It is what man has caused it to be. But not even God is now undertaking to transform it, his one great concern being, as has been said, to bring human beings safely out of a world such as this into a world that is unseen and eternal. . . . .

Now, there must be something wrong with a view of God which leads men to believe that any attempt to correct outrageous conditions is not only futile but presumptuous. What *is* wrong with this traditional view of God's activity in history? Is it not the assumption, which underlies it, that the human soul is quite independent of its earthly environment? It is believed that God profoundly cares for the human soul. It is not believed that he is very much concerned about the social conditions in which the soul is placed; for it is assumed that social conditions of whatever kind can neither promote nor obstruct the soul's salvation. But is this true? It certainly is not true if what is meant by salvation is a spiritual condition which manifests itself in active good will toward men—all men—and in unswerving trust in God. . . . .

If, as all Christians believe, God is profoundly concerned for the human soul, it cannot be that he is unconcerned about the social conditions in which the soul is placed. Hence, that other view of divine activity in history which holds that God's very concern for the salvation of individuals necessarily leads him to work, also, for the salvation of the world itself, those political institutions, social customs, and economic practices that so largely condition the spiritual development of men.

From this it does not follow that there are in the world unseen forces that are making automatically and inevitably for the improvement of society. . . . .

Nor is there any "process of history" that is making inevitably for a condition of social justice, human brotherhood, enduring prosperity, and enduring peace. . . . .

To believe that God in history is seeking alike the redemption of the individual and the redemption of society is *not* to believe that the progress of civilization is inevitable. It *is* to believe that the issues of history are not merely in the hands of natural forces productive of climatic changes, nor merely in the hands of human forces such as the inventions of man's hands and the desires of his heart. It is to believe that the issues of history are finally in the hands of God, who transcends both nature and man. Given the Christian faith concerning the nature of God, it is to believe that the incalculably greatest of all forces now at work in the world is a power that is Christlike in character.

Now one can hardly hold this view of God's activity in history and oneself remain passive in the presence of outrageous conditions. The traditional view allowed comfortably situated Christians to *feel comfortable* in social conditions that afforded *them* many delightful opportunities but which *for the multitude of men* provided only a bare existence fraught with insecurity, misery, and fear. How very different this view which forbids a Christian to remain at rest in a situation that spells loss for his neighbor even though it may spell gain for himself! *God* is not content with that situation. *God* is attempting to correct it. And he is calling for volunteers to help him correct it. When it comes to the maintenance of a cosmic order, God requires no man's assistance; but when it comes to the achievement of a historic justice and peace, he is necessarily dependent, to some extent, upon human co-operation. Hence, this view of God's activity in history leaves the Christian with a goading conviction that, confronted with a situation that is plunging millions of his fellows into a black abyss of misery and despair, he simply cannot look on and do nothing, *unless he is capable of deserting and betraying God.*

Attempting to do something, the Christian will need to maintain an attitude of profound humility in the presence of God, allowing him to reveal his plan of action. All too often, well-meaning men have supposed that their idea of what ought to be done was, of course, God's idea of the true course of history. To how many participants in the World War did it ever occur that their own idea of Christ, in khaki, seeking with a bayonet to impose democracy and peace upon the world might be not a little abhorrent to God? Nor is this the only historic case in which, as we now have abundant reason to suppose, God's idea of what ought to be done was something quite different from the idea that well-meaning men had. Again and again, as Saint Paul observed, "God has chosen that which is foolish in the world to shame the wise; he has chosen what is mean and despised in the world--things which are not to put down things that are." (I Corinthians 1: 27, 28. Moffatt's translation.) He has acted contrary to the expectations of reputed authorities, distinguished ecclesiastics, and professional reformers.

No doubt, we should be prepared to discover that some of the things we are eager to preserve—our own privileges, for example—are not the major concern of God; and that some of the things we are anxious to prevent, including, it may be, a more equitable distribution of material goods, are firmly imbedded in the purpose of God. We should even be prepared to discover that God's way out for China, for Spain, for all of Europe, and, indeed, for all mankind, is something different from the way out that we conceive. It may even be discovered that God's purpose for the human race does not call for the preservation of "civilization" as we now know it, although one may confidently suppose that it calls for the preservation of the highest achievements of human culture and of methods and means of cultural achievement.

A clear view of God's activity in history is certainly conducive to a sense of humility. It is *not* conducive to a sense of dismay. After all, it is God who is concerned for the improvement of the world, not merely a handful of human idealists; and God, although he does of necessity employ human agents in the field of history, is by no means wholly dependent upon the insight and effort of men.

It is God, not man, who creates and maintains a cosmic order in which human existence is possible.

It is God, not man, who provides natural resources, over which nations now fight like dogs over a bone, but which surely might become, as they no doubt were intended to be, the necessary foundation of an all-inclusive world culture.

It is God, not man, who is responsible for a moral order in the nature of things which places limits upon the power of men to do evil in the world. The existence of a moral order which no nation nor civilization can successfully defy is at once the insight of religion and the experience of history. The individual, it is true, may do evil and get away with it. He may spread himself like a green bay tree, acquiring riches, prestige, and power. When his brief day on earth is over, he may die comfortably in bed at peace with himself, and the local press may make out that he was but little lower than the angels. The fact, however, requires to be noted that under modern conditions even the evil-doing individual may be unable entirely to escape the social consequences of his acts. In a closely knit and high-powered civilization such as we now have, the time-span between economic cause and economic effect is far shorter than it once was, so that the economic freebooter, although he may still die in his bed, may not die either with his worldly possessions or with his worldly reputation completely intact.

But let that be as it may. What greatly concerns us is the undeniable fact that evil institutions, evil customs and practices, encounter at last a moral order which leaves them in the condition of a jerry-built house after a Kansas cyclone. In the fourth century, the peoples of the West, including Christians, could not believe that their society was going to pieces, weakened though it was by many internal and external strains; any more than we can believe that our society is in process of dissolution. But this, at least, history has made abundantly clear: no society which countenances greed, injustice, violence, and cruelty can permanently endure. And it does look as if God were saying to our generation, "You had better mend your ways; you had better start building a co-operative society in which as individuals and as nations you can work together for the common good of all." The "stars in their courses" do fight against evil, and it is God, not man, who has created them.

It is God, moreover, who is ultimately responsible for the conversion of men. It is the Hound of Heaven who tracks men down and brings them to their senses. It is the Light of the World who opens men's eyes to saving truth, so that they, in turn, bring light to their fellows. The world-embracing vision that is now the possession of growing numbers of men; the insight into world conditions, why they are as they are; whole-hearted devotion to the world's improvement and the very faith which supports such devotion—all this is a result of God's activity in history. It is he who has profoundly helped to bring about these human achievements of vision, of understanding, of Christlike devotion—of which, almost certainly, there are more to be found in our time than in any period of the past. And it remains to be seen what God can do with such human instrumentalities as are now presented to him by enlightened and determined minorities.

This view of God's activity in history knows no despair. It cannot abide a defeatist spirit. Holding this view, the Christians can believe with Isaiah that in the hands of God "the nations are as a drop of a bucket"; he can ask with Saint Paul, "If God be for us, who can be against us?"; he can look straight at the worst in the world of today and be fortified to know that the future of mankind is in the hands of God, not in the hands of proud and selfish men.

HOW I THINK OF GOD

Henry Sloane Coffin

GOD IS TO ME THAT creative Force, behind and in the universe, who manifests himself as energy, as life, as order, as beauty, as thought, as conscience, as love, and who is self-revealed supremely in the creative Person of Jesus of Nazareth, and operative in all Jesus-like movements in the world today.

In the physical universe I see Him as energy—the energy of whirling electrons which compose light, and which build up the planets, of which our earth is one. I see Him in upsurging life, which assumes innumerable forms in plants and creatures, forms that change in adaptation to changing conditions. And in this vast and unceasing outflow of energy and life I see Him in universally present order and beauty. Electrons disclose a law of their being, and science makes the assumption of faith that everywhere everything is intelligible and methodical. Were the universe capricious, it could neither be known nor depended on. But it is inherently systematic, and belief in this regularity is the faith which underlies all our scientific investigation. The "laws of nature" which we discover and formulate are our descriptions of the ways in which we find that God consistently works. Further, energy and life assume lovely forms—witness the crystals in a snowflake and the shapes and colors of plants. This beauty may be due to our perceptive senses, but it also seems to inhere in the objective world, where nature eliminates the ugly as monstrosities and establishes the fair. Poets, artists, and musicians, who are "priests of the wonder and bloom of the world," are to me interpreters of God, who is Beauty, as well as Energy, Life, and Order.

In plants and animals there is a rudimentary intellectual and moral life—the life of instinct. In that upreaching mind I see God, but God imprisoned and craving more complete self-expression. In man, so closely linked with the subhuman creation and the heir of the long history and development of life through myriads of forms during millions of years, I see God in thought and conscience and affection, God revealing Himself as Truth to be known, as Right to be obeyed, as Love to be trusted. Wherever a man's intelligence is persuaded, there I think of God as touching him and claiming his allegiance. Wherever a man's conscience is laid hold on, there I think of God as in contact with him and demanding his loyalty. Wherever a man's heart is appealed to, there I think of God as present and asking his service. So I think of God as in dwelling in men, and able to reveal more of Himself through them by so much as humanity exceeds the infra-human creation.

From *My Idea of God*, edited by Joseph Fort Newton, Boston, 1926, pp. 125-133. Published by Little, Brown & Company. Reprinted by permission of Joseph Fort Newton.

Looking back across the ages, one sees man, from his most primitive days until now, aware of a Presence in the world, whom he has variously conceived: now as a host of spirits inhabiting trees and stones and clouds, now as gods presiding over tribes or ruling some region of the universe or sphere of human life (the sea or the thunder, childbirth or war or death), and again as the one Lord of earth and heaven, or the one all-pervasive Spirit of life. Amid these kaleidoscopically changing conceptions of Deity, there abides the sense of the Unseen as akin to man, and so to be wooed by him as an ally. And to man's various approaches to the Invisible there has always been a response sufficient not only to afford present satisfaction but also to whet his desire for more. Out of every generation men witness that in fellowship with One beyond their sight or touch or hearing they find something of supremest worth. The spiritual results which they itemize in various epochs differ; but there is a body of concordant testimony to the refreshment and power and cleansing and illumination and serenity which are gained in communion with the Divine.

Of all these seekers after God, He who seems to have found most and best in Him is Jesus of Nazareth. What He Himself was and said and did He attributed to this unseen Presence whom He called Father and Lord, and of whom He thought as controlling the universe and inspiring His own soul. To thousands in the Christian centuries Jesus has communicated His faith. God is to them the response from the unseen which answers the trust of Jesus, or the self-revealing Father who imaged Himself fully in this dutiful and companionable Son. As one who was brought up in Christian surroundings, who from infancy learned prayers and hymns and the Bible, I caught the faith of the Church. God is for me the Father who unveils Himself in Jesus. It is of God so conceived that I think in all my intercourse with the Unseen. It is this Christ-like Father to whom I pray, on whom I depend for re-enforcement and guidance, of whom I think as forgiving my sins and prompting every generous and useful impulse and resolve within me. He is the Spirit manifest in the energy and life and order and beauty of the universe, and in the thought and conscience and love of men, who comes to full self-expression in the Man Christ Jesus.

I think of God as essentially self-imparting. He puts Himself into His universe at every stage in its evolution. But, like all artists, the medium in which He works limits the amount of His possible self-utterance. He expresses as much of Himself through the inanimate creation as it can manifest; but it cannot embody His conscience and heart. He expresses as much of Himself through mankind at every stage in human history as He can succeed in inducing them to receive and incarnate in their personal and social life. But men have never shown themselves fully obedient to the truth which they acknowledged or entirely responsive to the right which they recognized. Only One has seemed completely to understand and accord with His purpose; and in Jesus God has expressed Himself fully. To me Jesus is the adequate picture of God's character.

I try never to think of God as inharmonious with the mind of Jesus. If there be much in the ways of the brute creation which seems unchristian, I interpret it as not yet completed after God's heart and as waiting for Christians to subdue it nearer to their own and their Father's desire. As scientists assume that the world is to be understood and mastered to serve the needs of humanity, so Christians assume that anything in the universe which is hostile or indifferent to the purpose of Jesus is to be conquered and brought under the sway of His Spirit. I do not read God's character in cosmic happenings or charge Him with the results of human greed and folly. I see His character in Jesus and believe it is His purpose that the forces of nature and the wills of men should be made to accord with the aims for which Jesus lived and died and ever liveth.

My thought of God is defined in Jesus, but it is not confined to what I see in Him. I do not think of God as doing aught that is incongruous with Jesus; He deals with men as Jesus dealt with those whom we meet on the pages of the Gospels; He forgives and empowers, redeems and selects as did Jesus. He suffers with and for His children, as Jesus suffered with and for His brethren. But there is more in God than can be incarnated in any human life. The whole universe is pervaded and controlled by Him; the entire race of men is begotten of Him and reflects something of His image. Every religion has its message of God, and can contribute elements to the fellowship of men with Him. Science, art, ethics, philosophy, all bring their discoveries of God as the True, the Beautiful, and the Good. God is to me Christlike and more—the Spirit who rules and fills this and all worlds.

Is God a person? I prefer to put it that He has personal relations with us. Personality is the loftiest product of the world's evolution, and it would be degrading to God to conceive Him in subpersonal terms. We do not wish to lower God to our level or restrict Him within our limitations, and personality as we know it is only embryonic. We men are tadpoles of persons. Further, we cannot conceive a Person who is also the immanent Spirit of the universe, and we posit more in God than the phrase "a person" connotes. Christian thinkers in their doctrine of the Trinity often attribute to God social relations within His selfhood. But the finest religious experience of the race, and supremely the faith of Jesus, discloses a God who has intercourse with His children which we can only describe as personal.

I have so stressed the revelation of God in Jesus that one may ask: Do you think of Jesus as Himself God, or as a man to whom God was fully disclosed? I answer that to me He is both. I grant that it is difficult to combine these two aspects of Jesus—that in which we envisage Him as man, made in all points like ourselves, whose faith discovers God, and that in which we picture Him as coming from God and embodying Him. At the moment physicists are facing a similar difficulty in defining light. They have thought of it as waves of energy which move through a hypothetical ether—"the nominative of the verb, to undulate." But recently they have discovered that light exerts a pressure which can be weighed, and they are computing the tons of sunshine per annum which our earth receives. They are working with both the undulatory and the emission theories of light, but without successfully combining them. The theological problem is similar. As in the undulatory theory of light, God is that Spirit who responds with inspirations and re-enforcements to the faith of Jesus, across the medium which interlies the here and the yonder. As in the emission theory, God is that Spirit who comes in Jesus with the pressure of His love upon our world's woe and sin.

And while I have stressed the full self-disclosure of God in Jesus, I do not think of Him as having nothing more to impart. On the contrary, I think of Him as the indwelling Spirit who has ever been revealing Himself to faithful souls; and that Spirit is the Spirit of Christ. I commenced by saying that God is to me a creative Force. A force can be seen only in action: the Spirit of Christ can be watched in operation—in a Paul, counting all things but loss that he may be found in Christ and present others perfect in Him; in an Augustine, putting off the sensual life and devoting his powers to building up the City of God; in a Francis of Assisi, espousing poverty and claiming glad kinship as a child of God with sun and moon, beasts and birds, and with every man to whom he can minister the happiness of obedience to Jesus; in a Luther, discovering that a Christian is the most free lord of all and subject to none, and the servant of all, bound to be to them what Christ has been to him; in a Lincoln, with malice toward none, with charity for all, with firmness in the right as God gave him to see the right, setting free the bondmen and preserving the unity of a nation; in an Edith Cavell, finding that patriotism is not enough, and that she must die without hatred or bitterness for anyone. In all Jesus-like movements in current thought and life, in the trend toward co-operative fellowship in industry, toward a commonwealth of free nations, maintaining peace and promoting human well-being, toward a comradeship of mutual reverence and mutual help of the races—in every advance in science and art and commerce and education I think of God as imparting more of Himself to the sons of men. He is to me the Living God, a Contemporary, unveiling Himself to His children in the life of each generation, and recognizable as the present Spirit of Christ.

MY CONCEPTION OF GOD

Edward Scribner Ames

MY IDEA OF GOD IS the idea of the personified, idealized whole of reality. If man and his works are included in the conception of nature, then God is the personification and idealization of nature. In that view nature is not set off as the realm of mere weather, or of dead matter, or of blind force, but is qualified by the living forms which appear in her, including man and his life of thought and feeling. The personification of the world is in this case not an arbitrary addition of an entirely foreign element, but the enlargement and emphatic recognition of that aspect which is felt by human beings to be most important and most real. God is thus for me actual, objective; but he is also near and intimate.

It is not difficult to pray to God. Prayer is natural and spontaneous conversation, easy and familiar when life runs smoothly, anxious and searching when trouble comes. As in conversation with a man I try to get his point of view and to see as he sees, so in prayer I find that habit operative. I try to see my problem as a wise, unbiased mind would see it. The very attitude of prayer implies this effort to attain rapport, just as talking with a friend involves sharing what I try to know to be his thought. Into the idea of God go all the factors which I imagine to belong to ideal personality—wisdom, kindliness, power, informality, charm, mystery, orderliness, beauty, and whatever else may be demanded. The sense of such a being has been about me from my infancy, inherited no doubt from my pious parents, but also from the common thought of the general culture in which I was nourished. The men who wrote the Psalms and the men who wrote our great literature impress me as having had such an intimate and vital sense of God.

Upon reflection, I have come to think that my idea of God is analogous to my idea of my Alma Mater. She is a benign and gracious being toward whom I cherish deep gratitude for her nurture and her continuing good will and affection. She received me in my tender years and led me through wonderful ways of learning and happy comradeships of youth. When I return to her halls or foregather with her sons elsewhere, we sing songs in her praise and pledge to her our continuing devotion. She is not a mere imaginary being, but has objective and tangible reality. Part of her is earth, the solid ground she stands on; part of her is brick and mortar; part of her is gold or bonds in banks; part of her is human—trustees, faculty, alumni, students, and supporting friends; part of her is the lore of the world, in her libraries; part of her is a tradition of ideals and memories, an airy thing of song and story. She has a character which is so well defined that we

From *My Idea of God*, edited by Joseph Fort Newton, Boston, 1926, pp. 237-250. Published by Little, Brown & Company. Reprinted by permission of Joseph Fort Newton.

know at once whether certain policies would be in keeping with her spirit. The thought of her comforts and inspires me, as it may at times rebuke and challenge me. She reminds me of standards to be maintained, and she shares with me, as with all her children, whatever good name or fame she achieves.

My idea of Uncle Sam is of the same character. Certainly it would be a great error to identify Uncle Sam with the drawing which the cartoonist makes, or with the paper picture setting forth his quaint form and visage. Uncle Sam is the personified reality known also as the United States of America. This reality is made up of all the domains, mountains, plains, forests, highways, cities, citizens, traditions, institutions, and whatever else belongs to the nation. Uncle Sam is a recognized personal entity. He is morally responsible. He legislates and negotiates. He deliberates, makes plans, executes his will, builds great works, employs servants, and holds the power of life and death over millions of people. In the last ten years he has grown immensely rich and has become more than ever a world figure.

In similar fashion God is the personified reality of the world. He is not a mere idea; He has substance, energy, power. He is the common will, the spirit of mankind; He is seen in men, especially in their belevolent corporate life. His image marks the humblest souls, and is more clearly revealed in the great leaders and saviours of the race. It was no theological dogma but a simple fact, true in some measure of every man, that was expressed in the saying of Jesus, "He that hath seen me hath seen the Father." It is upon the character of the individuals we know that we construct our conceptions of the ideal personages of our faith. The most orthodox contention that it is important to believe that the Son conforms to the nature of the Father, is valid only if we first establish the nature of the Father from knowledge of the Son.

I have been interested to discover that the history of the idea of God shows it to be of this nature. The pattern in which it is woven is the pattern of the life of the people, of their social organization, largely fashioned in their interaction with their environment. In the lower stages of culture the totem objects are species of animals and plants; the chief spirits are those things in which are felt to center the issues of life. Rice-growing tribes have rice gods; fishing tribes have fish gods; the Toda ceremonials focus on the buffaloes; many American Indian ceremonials have to do with maize. "There are no rice gods where there is no rice; there are no tiger gods where there are no tigers." The early Hebrews were shepherds and their great feast was the Passover. When the social organization is developed, it is reflected in the character of the gods. A king on earth calls for a king on high; warrior kings trust in warrior gods; peaceful kings revere peaceful gods. There is always a communal nature about the gods. The fortunes of the tribe are the fortunes of its god. Thus in the Old Testament the names Israel and Jehovah are used almost synonymously. When the nation won a battle. it was a victory for Jehovah. When nations were conquered, their gods were made vassals of the conqueror. If a people was destroyed, its god disappeared, or at best lived only in myth and legend.

While the patterns of the divine beings are human and earthly, yet there is present an idealizing tendency in the minds of men, which magnifies the gods into superheroic size and power. Their prowess in battle is miraculous, their wisdom is clairvoyant, their life is immortal. Hence the gods are normally superior to the people and represent their traits in magnified and impressive proportions. When groups within the national life advance beyond the common level of intelligence and morality, as was true of the philosophers in Greece and of the prophets of Israel, then the gods change for these progressive groups and are correspondingly refined and idealized. This process continues throughout the history of civilization. God, to Jesus and the early Christians, embodied a new measure of compassion and of concern for his children, regardless of concern for his children, regardless of race or moral status. The individual had gained greater dignity and value. In our time the struggle still goes on between the older and the newer ideals of social justice. In the midst of such confusion and stress it is difficult to recognize clearly the divine will, for "we behold the face of God reflected in troubled waters."

Considering these facts and related problems, I have come to believe in God as growing and as finite. The traditional teaching has insisted upon a perfect and changeless deity, but that teaching has never been able to reconcile such perfection with the evil in the world. In my view, man's intelligence and the human social order represent growing points in the real world. This is a phase of "emergent evolution"; and if God is the personified, idealized order of reality, he himself shares in this development. There are obviously conflicts, warfares, between the idealistic trends and the concrete evils of existence, and men are summoned to fight in the armies of the Lord. But if the battle is unaffected by their blood and struggle it becomes a sham battle, most tragic and hideous. I believe men may be co-workers with God in moral and spiritual enterprises. There is tang and urgency in tasks which dip into the real world. But if the perfect thing is already existent, waiting only for the fiat of its own inscrutable decrees to work its miracles, then the human drama becomes a mere shadow picture on the walls of fate.

Sharing in the creative process, even in the slightest degree, gives men moral responsibility from which, on the other assumption, they are inevitably excused. Exhortations to participate in a moral order already prearranged and inevitably destined to arrive at its goal, sound formal and unreal. They do not seem to justify so small a thing as a passive "conversion." To conceive God as the Common Will, experimenting through the deliberations and ventures of social organizations and incarnating himself in institutions, gives him concreteness and accessibility. Professor Coe, expounding the idea that God is love, says: "Where is God? Wherever a mature man or a little child faces the problem of the mutual adjustment of two or more lives to each other, there he meets God." [1]

A growing God must also be finite; but that does not mean small or negligible. God is vast with the vastness which modern science discovers

---

[1] *Social Theory of Religious Education*, p. 112.

in the starry spaces and the aeons of time, and with the majesty which Kant beheld in the heavens above and the moral law within. The attributes of infinite wisdom, power, and goodness—omniscience, omnipotence, and absolute perfection—can be understood as honorific expletives expressing affection, reverence, and devotion, but not as comprehensible statements of fact. It is very common in human speech to employ superlatives to express measureless admiration and loyalty. Thus we speak of a "perfect lady," of a "divine poet," of a "spotless life." Much more therefore is it to be expected that the descriptive terms applied to God should be of the highest and the best. . . . .

My idea of God, it will be plain, is not that which the mystics usually profess. They deny the validity of our imagery and of our thought when employed to represent or understand deity. Because our thinking is finite and relative, it is for them inapplicable to God. Therefore they resort to intuition as an avenue of assurance above the plane of sense and reason. Undoubtedly they have real and vivid experiences, but they are not psychologically different from those which lovers and patriots display. Mysticism is an attempt at an explanation of the mystery of religion by denying the power of the human mind to make explanations in the realm of religious experience! It arose in a pre-scientific age, and continues to make its claim on the basis of its rejection of the validity of science in its field. It is surprising that this should still be the resort of minds which seek to understand and vitally interpret religion in an age whose thinking is so largely dominated by scientific methods. The earnestness and the emotional experience of the mystics cannot be questioned, but it is the doctrine and not the experience which constitutes it mystic*ism*.

It is far more satisfying to me to recognize that human beings are born into a personal relationship; that they attain the essentially human traits through interaction with groups of persons; that their minds are so shaped and fashioned in conversation that it is with difficulty and the most arduous training that they ever approximate genuinely "abstract" thinking, and then only in a very limited field of reflection, and only for short periods of the day; that in their families and among their friends and as members of social organizations they are living in vivid personal ways and thinking in the imagery of persons; and that in religion they tend to dramatize their relation to Life itself, and to regard themselves as in communion with the great heart of the world, humanized and personified in the character of God.

My idea of God enhances for me a sense of friendliness in the universe, which often extends to Nature in her most physical aspects. I get sometimes the "sense of presence" which Wordsworth felt. The approval of conscience in important decisions, the reality of an ideal companionship in devotion to a new or an unpopular cause, encouragment in adherence to plans unexpectedly deferred, confidence in hoping for the recovery of loved ones from illness or an attitude of acceptance when death comes, are often felt as gifts of God. The world is so complex, and every deed carries such a wealth of implications that, when for the time being I have done all I can,

I find comfort and the mood of a "half holiday" in leaving the case with God.

It is obvious that such an idea of God is not capable of logical proofs and cannot be established or imposed by argument, yet it is not fanciful nor subjective. It is like the idea of life itself, which is not demonstrable, yet carries the form and substance of immediate, indubitable experience. It has the appeal of known and felt reality; for the idea of God is the personified idealization of just this experienced reality. The more this reality is known and described by science the richer and more adequate it is possible to make that personification and idealization, and the more the idea serves to release and quicken the imagination. The idea dramatizes our moral values, and provides a setting and a scale commensurate with the felt importance of our most ideal endeavors.

The idea of God is not the source of religion, nor is belief in it the sole test of religious experience. Religion arises out of the will to live, and its symbols spring from the projective, creative energy of the imagination. The idea of God reveals the form and the direction which that energy takes, and guides and sustains its fulfillment. Therefore the idea changes from one culture to another, yet continues through history, and sums up for any age or group the spiritual forces and ideals of our human faith and hope.

TRUTH AND REVELATION

Emil Brunner

CAN WE OR CAN WE NOT know God? This question is not one among many others; because it is not concerned with a truth among other truths. It is the question out of which all other questions originate, from which all values derive their worth, all meanings their content. It is the supreme question, because it aims at the heart of all existence, as the meaning and destiny of all life. It is the primary question even for those who are not aware of it, because it also includes their destiny, and the destiny of all science and culture, which perhaps seems more important to them. For all culture, including science, has grown and still grows out of the faith that human existence has a meaning. And this belief is an outgrowth of religion.

Culture may for a season liberate or emancipate itself from religion. But, if it does, its dissolution has begun.

It is not mere chance that we cannot ask the question about God, the question whether or not we can know him, without passion and with a cool resolve to seek only that which is objective. We cannot and must not ask, save with all the earnestness our hearts are capable of: "Can I know God?"

Two answers seem to be possible. One affirms that we can know Him on the ground of divine immanence; the other asserts it on the ground of divine transcendence. The first answer assumes, on the strength of inward and outward experience, a divine essence in the world. I should call this the way of interpretation. The second answer rests its affirmation on a self-manifestation of God, penetrating and contradicting the world and human experience. I should call this the way of revelation.

In considering the first of these answers, a vital question seems to present itself: "Does the experience of a divine essence in the world originate outside of us or within us?" Now this question has no basis in reality: there is no real difference here. Even the mythological nature-religions of paganism are not actually an interpretation of an external experience of nature. They are rather a projection of an inner experience into the world. What the most modern theology, especially in America, calls *experiencing* God, is in fact an *interpretation* of the world, based on inner spiritual experiences; or, to state it more definitely, based on inward spiritual conditions. It is an interpretation of the universe from the point of view of a self-interpreting mind. In fact this so-called realism and idealism, as well as mystical religion, are intrinsically the same thing. They are a religion of immanence. Man finds God in the depths of nature, be it human or sub-human nature; in the depth of his soul. God is the essence or substance of the empirical world; he is not other-than-the-world, other-than-I.

From *The Theology of Crisis*, New York, 1929, pp. 27-42. Reprinted by permission of the publishers, Charles Scribner's Sons.

Man finds God in existing things. He is merely another name for the essence of existence. A religion based on such a conception of God is monistic and optimistic. It asserts an unbroken unity and continuity of God and the natural existence of man. God and world-experience are not contradictory; nor are the experience of the world and the Ego different from God. There is a way of passing from one to the other. The world in its being is divine and the essence of the Ego is God-like. If God is to be known, as one of your theological leaders puts it, by the "behavior of the universe," he cannot possibly be known as one who is different from, or even in contradiction to, the nature of the world.

Against this doctrine of immanence grave philosophical doubts may be urged. But we pass them by and consider still graver religious objections.

1. A God who is identical with the depths of the world or the soul is not really God. He is neither the sovereign of the world nor of man. He is too close to both of them to be really their Lord. Indeed, he is merely another aspect, the hidden portion, as it were, of the world and of myself. Such a religion, in its final analysis, is nothing but ancient paganism, a deification of the world and self.

2. Such a God is not really personal. What is not personal cannot be my superior but must be my inferior. For the personal is above the impersonal. A God whom I shall have to know through an interpretation of the world or of myself is less than I because I give utterance to him who himself is dumb, as it were. He becomes a personality only through me.

3. This religion of immanence is not really based upon faith. Faith is an answer to a call, a response to a challenge. An immanent God, however, neither calls nor challenges me. He does not demand a decision. In fact a decision is not even possible. The religion of immanence excludes decision because the Divine is supposed to be identical with the deepest self of man. Man is not asked to choose one or another alternative, for man is already in God and God in him. Man is on the safe side before he makes a decision.

4. But, for this very reason, man never becomes a real personality. For decision is the essence of personality. Only when man comes to a crisis and is compelled to choose between life and death does he become a personality. At the very moment when God challenges him to make his decision man is given personality. Faith and personality are identical. Apart from faith, which constitutes man's decision, personality is not to be found. Man becomes personal when his own will is broken into by the will of the Lord.

An impersonal God and an impersonal man are the necessary and inevitable consequences of a religion of immanence. A personal God and a personal faith are not possible when our knowledge of God is the result of an interpretation of the world and the Ego. Personal faith and knowledge of a personal God who is Lord of the world can be gained only when God reveals himself personally. The mysterious God, whom the world neither knows nor shows, whom I do not know and whom the inner man does not reveal, must reveal his mystery to the world—must tell his own name—by "piercing" into the world. He must assert himself over against the world as a being who is not-world, not-ego; who reveals his true name, the secret of his unknown will which is opposed to the world, contrary to our experience and, above all, to the thoughts and intents of our own heart. He is the God of whom it has been said: "No man has seen God at any time; the only begotten Son, which is in the bosom of the Father, he hath declared him." Indeed, we are in a position to criticise the conception of revelation as held by adherents of the religion of immanence, only because and in so far as we know the revelation in Christ. We recognize the illusiveness of every religion of immanence and its doctrine of revelation because we know, through the revelation of Jesus Christ, the reality of God, the reality of man, and the reality of decision. Revelation accordingly means that God no longer speaks *out of* us, but *to* us; we do not know him as being *in* the world, and therefore we do not know him *through* the world, but we know him as the One who comes *into* the world. For he himself is an other than the world, an other than the content of the soul. He is the *Other One*, the mysterious and unknowable One, who has his own proper name and whom we do not know because he is *person*. Personality is a secret; a mystery is hidden in it. Knowledge of a person is possible only through revelation, and he reveals himself through his word. Through the word the mystery of the person is communicated. So God reveals himself in the word because he is spirit, the only true personal spirit.

For this reason revelation and faith must be interpreted and understood in a way different from that by which we obtain knowledge of existing things. The will of God is not identical with that which happens; if it were, God would be identical with fate. He would be so bound as to be in complete bondage to the world. Such a "revelation" would be the discovery of something already existing; it would mean either the unending permanence of the contradictions in the world or the negation of them as mere illusions. Reality, as it now exists, is not only not divine; on the contrary, its centre, that part of it which we really know, our will, is anti-divine. God, therefore, can reveal himself only as One who is in contradiction to the present world and breaks through its immanent order or law. God's will is antagonistic to the course of the world, but through revelation he declares his purpose to overcome the antagonism. The religion of immanence must either optimistically deny or minimize it; otherwise it is forced to acknowledge it as necessary to God's world; and so religion becomes wholly pessimistic and would better give up the name of God. The self-revelation of God means that he reveals himself in spite of and in contradiction to a world which is antagonistic to him. His revelation, therefore, means that his will becomes known as the will which the world neither has nor knows, and that his truth, which is not immanent in the world, is brought into it. He reveals himself as the unheard-of, unrecognized, mysterious person, who cannot be discovered anywhere in the world. His revelation is a communication, through his personal word, of what no one knows and no one has. Through his word God reveals his personality. We ourselves become persons when, through his revelation, he requires us to make a decision between his will and ours. This choice is the essence of faith.

But one more differentiation needs to be made. What is the meaning of "the personal Word?" We may be thinking of the word of the prophets, and not without some justification. But the word of the prophets is not in itself the Word of God; it is merely a word concerning the Word of God. It is not the perfect divine self-manifestation, because it is not itself wholly personal. God's personal word exists and is heard only when he who speaks and what he speaks are one; when the person of the speaker and the authority of his word are inseparable. It must be a word that does not need a prophet as an instrument, but that is present in person, that is, *in persona*. A person then, in space and time, is himself the Word. The Word of God, because it is a personal word, is present as a person. This is what the Christian calls revelation; "the Word was made flesh and we have seen his glory."

Let me further explain what is *not* meant. Revelation is not a miraculous theophany. Paganism knows theophanies, that is, direct appearances of the Deity. The pagan does not know what spirit is. Therefore he does not know that spirit-communication itself is indirect. He wants to see; not to hear. His relation to the Deity is an aesthetic one; not the word, but the sight, gives him his god. It is not direct but indirect communication that constitutes true revelation; and indirect communication is communication through the word. Thus the historical appearance of the human personality of Jesus is not, as such, revelation; it is revelation only in so far as in this historical, human personality the eternal Son of God is recognized. The *incognito* of his historical appearance can be pierced only by the eye of faith. The Christ according to the spirit who must be discerned in the Christ according to the flesh, the eternal Son of God who must be seen by faith as the mystery of the man Jesus, is the incarnate Word of God.

Again, Jesus is not meant to be the teacher, the religious genius, the champion and "revealer" of the highest moral code, and the example of the purest religious and ethical life. A teacher, as Socrates shows, teaches only what is latent in the student. He says nothing essentially new and, therefore, cannot be the bearer of true salvation. Even the loftiest example of religious morality does not help us. He may lead us on a step but he never can lead us out of godlessness. The teacher and the example belong to us, and not to God. Jesus as the most perfect embodiment of the highest religious idea—as modern theology regards him—is not revealer and therefore not Saviour. For as such he does not come *to* the world; he is *of* the world, a product of its immanent possibilities. This conception of Jesus merely adds another to the many religious possibilities. How Jesus found God, how he prayed, how he lived, is not divine revelation for us; then he would be merely a religious man who differs from others because he represents a higher degree of religion. The so-called historical Jesus is not as such the Christ; and that which the historian sees in him is not the saving revelation of God. We mean by revelation what the New Testament and the Church expressed in the doctrine of the incarnation of the eternal Word of God. Any doctrine of Jesus that says less than this, that the Word of God became man, falls below the true fact of revelation. It is, in the final analysis, an aspect of the religion of immanence.

If Jesus is merely a teacher, example, genius, then it does not matter whether he lived or not, whether the world remembers or forgets him. Then we get no further with Jesus than without him. Christian faith has nothing in common with such a religion of immanence. It may claim Jesus for itself; but in reality it is only another form of the religion of the Stoics, who were much more successful than the New Testament in coining the slogans which are said to be characteristic of the Gospel; that is, the fatherhood of God and the brotherhood of man. Christian faith, faith in contradistinction to the religion of immanence, must abide by the assertion: "Jesus Christ, the incarnate Word, God become man." Acknowledgment of the living Word of God constitutes the Christian faith.

You may answer: "But are you sure you are right? Granted that this alone would constitute real revelation and granted that this conception of revelation is the foundation of Christian faith, is this conception and faith true?" We have come to the place where innumerable questions are put to us. Before I begin answering some of the most important ones in the short time available, let me say that the storm of opposition against the affirmation of the incarnation, that is, of real revelation, is not at all unexpected; in fact it is altogether in order. For the assertion of such revelation does more than prick the puffed-up pride of reason. But let me observe that all these questions are asked by outsiders; we are all, at the start, outsiders, spectators. But let me assure you that an outsider's question can never be answered unless he ceases to be an outsider. If God speaks to me, I can hear him only by letting him speak to me. Every theoretical understanding is in its very inception a misunderstanding. The majority of the most difficult questions which Christian theology must deal with arise from an attempt to comprehend and appreciate its message from the standpoint of the spectator. But it can be demonstrated *a priori* that from this point of view the Christian message will be found foolish and absurd from the very start. Its absurdity, however, is not to be sought in the message itself; but rather in the fact that a word, which ought to be heard and appreciated as a challenge to us, is accepted theoretically, that is, from the spectator's standpoint. With these introductory remarks, let us now take up some of the questions that must be in your mind.

1. "How can you prove that Jesus Christ is the Son of God, the incarnate Word?" Here you have the question of the spectator *par excellence*. Let me in turn ask you this question: "Would a revelation which is capable of proof still be a revelation?" In proving an assertion we link it up with higher relations. What kind of a revelation would it be that is subordinate to a superior principle? Say, to reason? What manner of God is he who can be proved? Revelation means that what is said here is truth recognized as being true only by him who permits it to be told to him. It is truth

carrying its trustworthiness within itself, just as all rational truth carries its trustworthiness in itself. It is, as Calvin expresses it *autopistic*. Looking at it from the human angle, what manner of faith is the faith that must be propped up by proof? It would be something like a suitor who, on the point of asking the lady of his choice for her heart and hand, were to employ a detective to spy out her character. Faith is the venture by which one trusts the truth of a word, not because one is courageous and tries it out for once, but because one cannot do otherwise under the constraint of the word.

2. "Every religion basing itself on revelation says the same thing. The claim of Christianity to be the revealed religion is not unique; but it contradicts every other religion." This is not a new objection, but its falsity can be demonstrated. No religion knows the concept of revelation as Christianity holds it. In all other religions revelation relates itself to singulars and is therefore an aggregate of many single revelations which may go on to the end of time. No religion ever dared to affirm seriously that God became man. In the mythological theophanies similar assertions are seemingly made. But they are events which are repeated almost at will and their historical character is as uncertain as their content is dubious. The one word of our confession of faith—crucified under Pontius Pilate—together with the apostle's ἐφάπαξ, "once for all"—fixes the fundamental difference between Christianity's claim of revelation and the claims made by other religions. Revelation, in the sense of the Christian faith, differs wholly from revelation in the meaning of other religions by reason of its "onceness." Christianity takes the concept revelation with absolute seriousness, while the other religions to a larger or smaller degree play with it mythologically.

3. "Christian faith in revelation contradicts modern science; for it presupposes a miracle." Surely it does; not only *a* miracle but *the* absolute miracle. The time has passed when science may speak with authority on the possibility or impossiblity of miracles. Let me point out to you in a few words what needs to be said here. The thought of a continuous causality which dominated the seventeenth and eighteenth centuries has been discarded in our day. Those who know that many, but by no means all, phenomena can be explained by the law of causality have long refused to consider it universal. Within the circle of what is explicable by causality, if that holds good, there are smaller circles which certainly defy explanation under the causal law, as, for example, the circle of the organic, of consciousness, of human freedom. The smallest of these circles is the last named. Man alone belongs to it. Let me put it positively. Let it be granted that the physical is not miraculous; then the organic is the least, and the human the greatest, miracle within the world known to us. In acknowledging the miracle of freedom or of the human mind, the discussion between science and faith ends, or becomes a discussion between reason and faith. But we shall consider the latter discussion later. When an understanding of the nature of spirit has undermined the dogma of causality, the attack on the

miracle of revelation from the quarter of the principle of causality will no longer be successfully sustained.

4. "The assertion of the deity of Jesus Christ contradicts the results of critical historical research." We have before us a question partly historical and partly dogmatical. Lest we open the door to misunderstandings let me say that I myself am an adherent of a rather radical school of Biblical criticism, which, for example, does not accept the Gospel of John as an historical source and which finds legends in many parts of the synoptic gospels. But the most radical criticism will never succeed in proving that Jesus did not consider himself to be the Messiah, i.e., that he did not make a claim for himself which goes far beyond his humanity. Furthermore, no historical criticism can deny, with any reasonable hope of success, that the first church already revered Jesus as the risen Lord. Be that, however, as it may; the contenders against the deity of Jesus as well as its defenders constantly overlook the fact that the revelation of God means that God became really man, that is, he veiled himself so completely that faith only can recognize in the man Jesus the Son of God. This the word of the Lord himself clearly indicates, when he says: "Verily, flesh and blood hath not revealed it unto thee."

The question then is not to be decided by history. It is a question of faith. It ought not to read: "Was Jesus such an one as the historians say or as the believers assert?" It ought to read: "This Jesus, whom the historians try to portray with some degree of accuracy, is he the Christ or is he not?" We accept the historians' portraits of him, well knowing that a generally accepted portrait does not yet exist. But we claim that the historian can see only what St. Paul calls "Christ according to the flesh," the human *incognito* of the Christ. The real Christ is not visible to the historian's eye. To see the revelation of God in Christ is a gracious privilege of faith, of the believer and not of the historian; or metaphysically speaking, the organ with which Christ is apprehended is not the historian's scientific eye but the spiritual eye of the believer.

HOW SHALL WE THINK OF GOD?

Rufus M. Jones

THERE IS NO FUTURE for religion, no permanence to its inspiration and lifting power, unless men and women—and the children who share their outlook and ideals—can continue genuinely and sincerely to believe in God as the ground and reality of that which is good, the spring and basis of a real moral and spiritual universe, the life and inspiration of all our aims at righteousness and truth, the Great Companion who shares with us in the travail and tragedy of the world and who is working through us to "bring things up to better."

I am convinced that the spiritual basis beneath our feet is solid. I have no fear that religion will turn out to be a slowly waning and gradually vanishing subjective dream. I am confident that the testimony of the soul is at least as reliable as a guide to the eternal nature of things as is the witness which mathematics bears. Assertions of confidence, however, are not the same thing as facts, and optimistic statements of individual faith are not demonstrations which carry inevitable conviction to others. We must endeavor to search out the rational foundations of our faith in God, and we must then try to express as clearly and concretely as possible how a modern man thinks of Him. The rational foundations must of course be found revealed, if at all, in the nature of our own experience. Reason, mind, thought, as it appears in our consciousness, is the only clue there is to that deeper fundamental Reason that holds as from one Center all the threads of reality and purpose in the mighty frame and congeries of things. The way of approach is like that to a great mountain peak such as Mount Everest. At first there are many paths which gradually converge, and up to a certain point there are many ways of traveling, but at the very last for the final climb there is only one way up.

In the first place, knowledge of truth, truth which we discover and verify in our human experience, always presupposes something more than finite. Knowledge is something more than the formation of subjective ideas. It implies *a foundational reality* underlying and uniting the knower and objects known in a wider inclusive whole. Sense experience furnishes no adequate basis for *knowledge*. The so-called "items" presented by sense—color, sounds, tastes, odors, roughness and smoothness, weight and hardness—are no more knowlege than chaotic masses of stone, brick, and lumber are a house. Knowledge involves organization, synthesis, unity, consciousness of meaning, interpretation, feeling of significance, a conviction of certainty, a sense of reality, aspects of universality and necessity. None of these features *comes in* through the senses. They belong to the nature of mind

From *Religious Foundations*, New York, 1933, pp. 5-14. Reprinted by permission of the publishers, The Macmillan Company.

and are fundamental to mind. "To know," as a distinguished thinker of our time has said, "means more than to look out through a window at some reality of a different character." Knowledge is not something which originates within. Nor is it something received from without. It is an indivisible experience with an inner and an outer—a subjective and objective—factor, neither of which can be sundered from the other nor ever reduced to the other. Our finite minds, through the process of knowledge, reveal the fact that they belong to a larger whole, a foundational reality, which underlies self and object, inner and outer, and which is the source and ground of the fundamental laws of reason through which we organize our experience, by which we get a world in common, and by which we transcend the limits of now and here, the fragmentary character of what is given to sense, and rise to something universal, necessary, and infinite in its implications, for knowledge with its element of "must be" always reveals the fact that the knower partakes in some degree of the infinite, at least he transcends the finite. We are always *out beyond ourselves* when we are dealing with truth. . . . .

It is not easy to discover the nature of conscience nor to account for its august authority, but one point always stands out clearly whenever the diagnosis is made, and that is the fact that man in his moral capacity is not only more than a bare individual self, but more, too, than a finite cell in a social organism. The full significance of "I ought, I must," carries us beyond the empirical order of things and events, and involves a spiritual reality of which we partake and in which we share. Kant is right when he finds God, Freedom, and Immortality inherently bound up with the moral will of man. He is hampered by his abstract method and by his tendency to divide the mind as well as the universe into compartments, but he is sure that he has found the real trail, and so he has.

Beauty is another revelation of a spiritual reality in the universe which links us up with something beyond ourselves. Beauty is not *there* in any external object taken by itself. It is not, any more, projected out by our minds as a subjective veil of glory which we as artistic creators throw over the iron facts and circumstances of a dull exterior world. Beauty is an experience in which we find ourselves joyously absorbed in something beyond ourselves, in such a way that the outer and inner, the beyond and the within, seem fused into a unity that transcends division. "Two distincts, division none." And the whole universe, from "the bands of Orion" down to the infinitesimal scenery which the microscope reveals when, for example, we examine a piece of mold, is crammed with beauty. All we need to do is to bring a sensitive soul, with its seeing eye, its unifying, synoptic capacity, to any point of observation, and the beauty breaks upon us. It is as though a Spirit like ours, only infinite in scope and range, were breaking through the world to meet us at our best and to raise us into union and to thrill us with joy. . . . .

Values are not tangible things, like Monadnock or a coal mine, but they are certainly as real as anything we ever see or feel. The world of values which includes pure unselfish love of friend for friend, dedication to what

ought to be but is not yet, loyalty to causes which concern unborn generations, appreciation of beauty, truth and goodness, is a world that must be
accounted for somehow. It did not just "happen." It is always in the making. It is revealed through us and is being created through our strivings.
But values are not capricious, subjective things. They are not will-o'-the-
wisps that gleam and vanish in freakish ways. They are the deepest realities
of our human lives. They make us what we are and they shape our destinies at least as much as sunlight and oxygen do. They rest upon some vast
underlying, foundational Reality without which we should lack all spiritual
aim and purpose. Whether God is necessary or not to explain the world
of nature, He is surely necessary to explain our world of values—our Kingdom of Ends.

These are some of the *implications* of human experience which furnish
the ground and basis of a solid rational conviction of faith in God's existence.
The only surer ground is direct experience of God, which many persons
claim to have. Arguments lead to the base of the mountain, experience
alone scales it. He who has climbed the peak gets an evidence—and a
thrill—of summit-vision which the dwellers in the valley-hotels can never
have. My figure of the peak is not meant to refer to the solitary aspect of
the man who climbs, nor to the laborious feature of the enterprise, though
the experience of God is sometimes solitary and does always involve severe
preparation and effort. I am only bringing out the fact that one cannot
know the scenery and circumstance of the top unless he has been there
himself. The mystic has been there, and he comes to tell us that beyond
all conjectures and inferences about the reality of God is the consciousness
of enjoying His presence.

Religion in its first and deepest intention is as solidly based on experience
as is art or friendship. It is at bottom a direct way of vital intercourse between man and God. There would have been no real religion in the
world if God in actual fact had not broken in on the consciousness of men,
producing a feeling of reality no less convincing than that which characterizes our observations of sense. . . . . In short, our spirits touch close upon the
Spirit and there is no fixed "boundary" between spirit and Spirit, any more
than there is where the sea and sky seem to meet. We do not need to go
"somewhere" to find God, any more than the fish needs to soar to find the
ocean or the eagle to plunge to find the air. We only need to be prepared
to see and feel and find what fringes the inner margins of ourselves.

Spirit seems to many persons a vague and unrevealing word. It meant
"breath" originally and it played a lowly rôle in the long childhood stage
of the race. Then and since, it has often been the bearer of occult phenomena and it has been loaded with cargoes of superstition. But, even so,
it is the best word there is to express the essential nature of God. It signifies that He is not to be confused with matter nor to be found in a framework of space. He is like that highest, purest inner nature in ourselves which
we call "spirit." He is intelligent, He is purposeful. He is devoted to the
realization of the good. He *is* what we are trying to be. And wherever in
the universe the good is being achieved, wherever truth is triumphing,

wherever holiness is making its power known—*there* is Spirit, there is God. When we think of God we do not mean vague force, not some dim, vapory abstract reality, not a mere "power making for righteousness." We mean all that can be expressed by the word Person and vastly more, since our word Person carries with it limitations which cannot be applied to God.

We know spirit best as it works through persons in their incarnate, i.e., embodied, form. There is much mystery wrapped up in this junction of spirit and matter in ourselves. We do not know how the chasm is bridged. We have no way of explaining how spirit can move matter nor how matter can report itself to spirit. There never was, and never will be, a greater mystery. We do not allow it to disturb us overmuch. We go ahead and act as though we had a right to do so, and we leave the solution of the immense mystery to some possible metaphysician of a remote age. Meantime, spirit and body work together as though they belonged together, which means that spirit can work through what we call matter.

Our own connection with a body raises the wonder whether God as Spirit uses any medium or works through any secondary substance which is to Him what our bodies are to us. It may be that what we call ether, that curious super-matter which fills the universe, is the medium through which His purposes go forth and are revealed as energy, as law, as mathematical order, as power, as beauty, as ever evolving life. Ether would be, then, the medium of His presence as the visible and tangible body is the medium of our presence. It would not be He any more than the corporeal bulk which the scales weigh is I, but it might be thought of as the garment through which He expresses Himself, the hand of His power, the foot of His swiftness, the transmitter of His will and thought.

On a higher level life, with its upward push, its tendency to differentiate into unique forms, and its endless potency for inaugurating novelty and surprise might also be a medium. On a still higher level consciousness would be a medium through which He could express Himself, a living gossamer robe. There are, again, all levels of consciousness from the nearest sensitiveness up to the most inclusive self-consciousness. Human personality, with its immense submerged reaches of sub-consciousness and its higher ranges of ideal vision, might be regarded as the best type of medium yet known to us for revealing His nature. . . . .

Supremely is He revealed in that one Person who is most like Him and the nearest like us, i.e., in Jesus Christ.

SOME BLIND SPOTS REMOVED

Henry Nelson Wieman

I

Symbols. I use traditional Christian symbols much more than I did ten years ago. I do not think that this indicates any access of orthodoxy. But I find that when the ambiguities and superstitions and superficialities have been cleared away from these ancient forms of expression, they carry a depth and scope of meaning which no other words can convey, because the same history which has made them has made us also. There are deeps in us, generated by past centuries, which can be quickened to life only by these words which likewise reach back into the past.

Also the religious mind today seems to be modified so that these old words no longer carry so many irrelevant meanings as once they did. By irrelevant I mean, of course, irrelevant to what I hold them most profoundly to mean. Then, too, I myself had to get certain meanings clarified by intellectual tools before I could use the symbols which are not clear in their meaning, however potent to move the deeps of devotion. So today I can use old symbols with a freedom, clarity and sincerity not possible to me ten years ago.

II

Sin. As I see it now, sin is not the disparity between our conduct and our highest ideals. It is the disparity between our highest ideals and the concrete goodness in the immediate situation which is the offering of God and his demand. The *sense* of sin in this deepest meaning is not the feeling that comes from doing specific things which we know are wrong. It is the feeling that what we do is against God even when we do not know specifically what it is that is wrong. Sin is not the impossibility of attaining our highest ideals. The assumption that our own ideals, no matter how far beyond our attainment, can be identified with the infinite riches of God, is itself a sinful and arrogant presumption.

I would go so far as to say that ideals by reason of being abstractions, always, even at their highest (and then most of all abstract) can never cover the riches of value to be found in each concrete situation. Therefore he who makes ideals supreme over his life, no matter how lofty and no matter how perfectly he may live up to them, is sinning. Even when these ideals are impossible possibilities, it is sin to set them up as supreme.

Life under the absolute control of highest ideals might be perfectly moral, if you define moral living as such idealistic conduct. But from the Christian standpoint it is a life of sin because it is missing and excluding the unpredictable exigencies and riches of the concrete situation wherein the liv-

Reprinted by permission from *The Christian Century*, June 25, 1939.

ing God operates. We must have ideals, and they should be as lofty and perfect as possible. But they should never be sovereign. They should always be held subject to something richer, more imperative, more divine. This something is not an ideal. It is the actual fullness of good in the immediate concrete situation.

III

Grace. This is the third object of new sight. The grace of God is the good which God puts into each concrete situation over and above all that man can do or plan or even imagine. Every situation contains a plethora of unpredictable riches, along with all the evil which is not the work of God. The most utopian dream is a mere abstraction compared to the fullness of the concrete. I do not mean that we consciously experience any such fullness of value in concrete situations. That is just the point. We do not. We are blind to it. We do not respond. God gives but we are unable to receive. The sovereignty of our own ideals and purposes, set up in place of the good in each concrete situation, is the chief source of our blindness, our hardness of heart, our imperviousness to God's grace. I am pushing to the limit, as I never did before, the instrumentalism of all ideas and all ideals.

IV

The living Christ. The grace of God is in Christ Jesus. Here is the fourth area of new vision. Certain strands of history are powerfully creative of value. The concrete situation is full with an infinite fullness of connections of value, potential meanings, a network of organic relations with all manner of things, *because of the working of a long historic sequence of upbuilding.* This is the importance of creative tradition in general and of the Christian tradition in particular. We are nested and nourished, and could be vastly enriched beyond our powers to describe, if we could be aware of all the bonds which connect our activities, thoughts and feelings into an organic whole with the deeds and propulsions of people around us and before us, together with a great complexity of subhuman nature so organized as to sustain and enrich. All this has come about through the working of a long process of history.

Not all history does this. History tears down as truly as it builds up. But there are strands running through it which weave the connections that yield infinite depth and pathos—which yield humor and sublimity, which would yield meaning and value to us if we could appreciate them for what they are. We live encompassed with glory. But our eyes are holden.

There is one strand of history most important of all. Christianity originated in a seminal situation of a most peculiar sort. Up to the time it emerged, the bonds of mutual support, enrichment and meaning had been forming within the confines of distinct natural groups, clans, families, cultures, races, nations, classes. But in the Greco-Roman world these were mixed together into a welter of confusion. In this conglomerate mixture a catalytic agent appeared which started a process of forming connections of mutual support and enrichment between persons regardless of class, race, nation, family or culture. It was the growth of community in little groups between Jew and gentile, bond and free, Greek and barbarian. It was the beginning of the early church.

This growth of connections of mutual support and enrichment, this growth of the bonds of potential meaning which fills each concrete situation with infinite fullness of value to be appreciated, is the living Christ because it issues from that historic situation in which Jesus Christ, regardless of our theological interpretation of his personality and teachings, was used by a process of history to initiate and promote such growth.

Hence the grace of which we speak is the grace of God in Christ Jesus. Notice it is not the grace of Jesus. It is not the personality of a Nazarene which is so important. It is not his bare teachings. It is the working of a process of history which used that human personality. Not alone the man, but God incarnate in the historical situation, operating as the growth of a community which broke through all barriers of race, nation, culture, law, pattern, custom, idealism, breaking these down and building them anew only to break through them again for the unlimited enrichment of life.

This is the grace of God in Christ Jesus. This is the living Christ. This is the creative tradition. It is growth of connections of value which fill the world with depth and height of meaning if we could see and feel and grasp them in each concrete situation as they unpredictably emerge. It is not the work of man. It is not the achievement of conscious purpose. It is the grace of God in Christ Jesus, found of Paul with a shout that rings down the centuries.

V

The church. I have listed the living Christ and the church under two heads. But they are really the same thing.

The Christian church, I hold, is an association of people which transmits a way of living that is controlled supremely by the grace of God. Living by the grace of God in Christ Jesus began with Paul and the first century Christians. Like any other way of living which continues through successive generations, it must be sustained, fostered and transmitted by a group having historic continuity. This continuity is preserved by means of certain symbols which take the form of ceremonies and doctrines. However, it is the way of life that is important. If the ceremonies and doctrines do not engender and impart this manner of living to participants in the group, there is no church even when the symbols are most ardently upheld.

This way of living is not defined by any set of moral principles. That was one of the main contentions of Paul. It may take on one set of morals and then another, adapted to different cultures. Of course it must always have moral principles, but they change from age to age and from culture to culture. Hence the ideals which it happens to cherish at any one time are not the definitive and distinctive feature of it. What makes it distinctive, clearly different from everything else which has ever appeared upon the planet, is that every moral principle, every plan, purpose, hope, ideal, habit and conviction is crucified with Christ.

This means that the whole personality down to its basic structure (and that carries with it the social order down to its basic structure), all likes and dislikes, plans, purposes and habits, are held ready to be transformed in whatsoever way may be required to enter into the richest values that emerge in each situation. Not my will but thine be done; and God's will is always the greatest possible good for each situation, a good that always transcends the scope of our plans, habits, expectations, hopes. Hence the absolute commitment of the Christian is not to any set of ideals, whether possible or impossible. It is to the riches of God's grace which overflows and breaks through the narrow bounds of all conceivable ideals and doctrines in the concrete fullness of actual situations. He who claims to have enclosed God's grace in any cherished set of formulas is anathema to the true church.

The church is the historic process which engenders such commitment in individuals. It can be viewed either as a local group or as a creative historic power working through the ages from culture to culture. As a local group it is any two or three or more so associated as to transmit and conserve this way of living, namely, the grace of God in control of human life. The two or three so functioning may be in a rowboat in a stormy sea, or in a coal mine or an airplane, and there may be no steepled real estate in sight. But no local group could live in this very strange manner—under supreme control of nothing else save the grace of God—had they not received it from others. Hence they must have had access to a group which used the symbols expressing the grace-controlled life.

Without distinctive symbols man cannot maintain any distinctive way of living from year to year and age to age and culture to culture. So the church uses, and must use, symbols to foster and propagate a life which is freed from every coercive bond save only the riches of God's grace.

VI

The otherness of God. God, I have come to see with increasing clarity, is not merely man lifted to the nth dimension of perfection, any more than he is horse or any other animal so glorified. God is different from man. God works concretely. Man cannot possibly do that. Man must work abstractly. (See Dewey's new book on *Logic*.) That is to say, man's plans, his ideals, his purposes, are necessarily abstractions by reason of the very nature of the human mind. God alone is concrete in his working. God is creator. Man cannot be a creator. The production of unpredictable consequences through the forming of "internal relations" is creation. A common word for it is growth. It is God's working, not man's. Hence mind and personality would cramp God's style, if I may be allowed the expression. He cannot be so limited. The abstractions of mind, no matter how vast, would take from God his greatness and his creative power.

Recognition of the otherness of God, I hold, is the next step which man must take in his climb up from the idolatry which makes a god in man's image. (See *I, Yahweh*.) God in his otherness is always breaking through to man and man to God, but the clouds are always forming anew to obscure the vision. How long, O Lord, how long!

All these six changes which I have mentioned may be only different angles of vision by which one views the same thing. Just what this one thing is, however, I am scarcely able to say. It may be my vision of sin. But I am not sure. It may be the unveiling to my sight of God's grace, the glorious richness of each concrete situation to which we are largely blind. But these two, sin and grace, are obverse sides of the same fact about human life. My awakening to the profound depth of sin and grace may be the key to all the other changes I have undergone in the past ten years.

Finally, I must add that I have been using the writings of Paul almost exclusively in my private devotions. I am stirred and astounded when I contemplate that man as revealed in his own words. Ever tearing him to pieces and lifting him up again was the living Christ.

A glance at anything I wrote eight or ten years ago compared to this writing, will make plain that a very great change has come over me. The crisis and the turning point I cannot describe because of its intimate nature.

MY ALL-GOD

Brown Landone

FROM SPIRITUAL malaria I suffered long and intensely. Its periods of re-frigerated goodness alternated with bursts of flaming youth; its recurring chilly Thou-shalt-not's alternated with heart-hot desires for joy. And so, for a generation, I knew not from one year to the next in what terms I did or could think of God. No sooner did I place my feet flat-footedly on what seemed for the moment to be a solid idea of God than it began to disintegrate beneath me, and I was compelled by spiritual necessity to grasshopper to some other idea, suggested by priest or parson or poet, or born of my own prayer and dreams. Each of these ideas was a part-God concept; each was a reactive concept.

Once a God of punishment to be feared, then reaction—and a God of love too sentimentally kind to enforce justice.

Once a God capriciously blessing or cursing, then reaction—and a God of law, fixed and absolute, and hence unmindful of any appeal of any human heart.

Once a concept of all-dependence upon matter, then reaction—and a concept of all-dependence upon Mind, with its denial of matter and its creation of a thousand little devils of suppositional error, a thousand devils with which to cope in the darkness of mortal mind instead of one well-known Satan to be met in open battle.

Once a personal God in a physical heaven, with angels (if the account be brought up to date) tuning-in Tiffany radio sets and flying airplanes with motors of gold and wings of pearl, then reaction—and a God of Principle only, lacking in personal love, and forever unchanging as the code of the Medes.

Each was a part-God idea, conceived to complement some other part-God idea. More, each was a reactive concept, opposing and balancing some idea previously held. And worse, each was a pendulum swing to one side, necessitating a return to the other, which made me so spiritually dizzy that I visioned a new hell of innumerable dangling pendulums, each pendulum a human soul.

Sick in spirit, I stopped soul-still, resolved that a no-god was better than swinging forever from one part-God to another. So, longing with my whole soul for the stability of an All-God, I found Him!

My All-God is All! He is infinite in fact as well as in phraseology, including not only essence, presence, existence, and attributes, but also all processes, means, conditions, and things. The truth of His infinite presence was

From *My Idea of God*, edited by Joseph Fort Newton, Boston, 1926, pp. 279-286. Published by Little, Brown & Company. Reprinted by permission of Joseph Fort Newton.

at first only an idea. It is now, however, the existence in which I live. He surrounds me; I am in Him and cannot get out of Him; He extends out from me, from star to star and trillions of miles beyond. Within me, He permeates me; He penetrates to every cell and atom of my body. I am saturated with Him; and literally in Him I live and move and have my being.

So also, my All-God surrounds, permeates, penetrates, and saturates the frog and the blade of grass, the bluebird and the cherry blossom, the mountain and the universe.

My All-God is within me. As I know that there is electricity in my study to give me light, so I know that God is in me. As I know that not all the electricity of the universe is in my study, so I know that not all of God is in me. I am a son of God, made in His image; Christ is The Son of God. I am one ray of light, perhaps this color, perhaps that; Christ is the pure Light of all.

My All-God is faith, and I no longer shy even at the term "blind faith," for that at least is freedom—freedom from the petty habit of crabbily doubting all things which my own little eyes have not seen or my own hands made. I have not yet straddled a radio message and ridden it from New York to London, yet I have faith that such messages are sent. So I do not doubt those truths of God which my reason has not yet lassoed and galloped to the end of time. What is reason, anyway, that it should always try to blackball faith and forever fail to do so? Every process of reasoning begins with an assumption; and no man ever reasons about anything except to try to prove to himself that he knows something which he knows he does not know.

With youthful faith, I accepted the doctrines of the Church. With smart learning, I later rejected all of them. Now, with some wisdom sired by humble pride and conceived in suffering, I know that they are true. Since Loeb has whip-whapped soap bubbles into living substance, why doubt that pure Divinity can conceive a Son?

My All-God makes His creation good. Once I assigned to myself the duties of the Super-God-Supreme-Court-Justice, to pass on the reliability of God's statements and the nature of His creation. I divided His works into good things and evil things, commending spiritual means as born of God and condemning material means as born of error.

I was learned then in truth. Now, with less conceit, I know that God knew what He was talking about when He declared that everything He had made was very good. He had all the evidence before Him; I had not a thousandth part of it. First, He had made all things, out of Himself; second, He had consecrated all things to man's use and specifically stated that He did so; third, after His creation was finished, He carefully reviewed all things He had made; and fourth, only when He had done so, did He pass Judgment that all was very good.

I now accept His statement and see God in every substance. Salt for example, is a crystallization of a God thought, radiated to create a certain substance to perform its function after its kind; and consequently the use of a substance, idealized thus to effect a result after its kind, is as spiritual as the use of Mind to work change after its kind.

As to the goodness of man and the trial in Eden, I deem the opinions of theologians of three or five thousand years after the event of little value. I accept only the testimony of eyewitnesses. Other than the woman who was accused as the evildoer, there were but two such witnesses—Adam and God Himself. When the trial was over, Adam declared that the accused should be called "Eve, because she was the mother of all living," in which I find no censure. The conclusion of God was, "Behold, the man is become as one of us," in which I find no "fall."

The nature of the goodness of God Himself is revealed by *tob, tab,* and *tub,* which in the Bible are the only Hebrew words frequently translated by the English words, "good" and "goodness." They are also translated by "prosperity, pleasure, gladness"; or "joyful, cheerful, merry."

My All-God concept condemns nothing, idealizes all things, accepts God's statement that everything is very good, and makes use of all things!

But I wanted something more: I wanted to pray again. I studied the Hebrew words translated in the English Bible by the words, "pray," "prayer," and "praying." I found that the only important Hebrew word frequently translated "pray" in the Bible is *palal* and that the only Hebrew word frequently translated "prayer" is *tephillah.*

All words derived from the root of *palal* prove its meaning. *Pala* means to "be wonderfully made"; *pali* means "wonderful"; *pili* means "wonderful"; *peli* means "secret and marvelous wonders"; and *palal,* which is the word translated "pray," means "to judge oneself to be marvelously made"; "to recognize wondrous things within the self, and to do so habitually and continually."

Tephillah is formed of two basic roots: one means "singing and dancing with timbrels"; the other, the occasion for doing so.

Praying as God asks me to pray, I habitually and continuously recognize the miracle of man being wondrously made in the image of God, and sing and dance with joy because of it.

Learning the mirth of His goodness, my night passed and my sun dawned. The God of mirth and laughter and dancing merriment is my God, this hour and forever. Christ tells me definitely what His aim here was: to give me life and to make His joy complete in me. I accept. Too long I delved in thought; now I dance in sunshine. In Him, the God of cheer and joy and dancing mirth, I live and move and have my being; and all things are well with me.

All-God is a Personal God. God as absolute principle and as personal love is not a contradiction. My soul manifests one minute as mind, working out algebraic problems according to absolute principle, in which operation there is no consciousness of personal love; yet with the touch of her lips to my cheek, or the pat of a little hand on my knee, or even the look of faith in the brown eyes of my Irish terrier, my soul manifests as personal love. One manifestation does not exclude the other. All-God is principle and also personal love.

In what terms I think of God, changes not at all the nature of Him or Them or It; but what I think and feel integrates or disintegrates life for me.

All-God is truly all-inclusive. The harmony of a humming bird's wings, the concert of whizzing electrons, the tam-tam jazz of the dance, the symphony written in the Milky Way with stars for notes and rays of light for bars—all are of God.

The Power that twirls a mist to a star and grinds a sun to star dust, I term God. The Energy that shoots through quintillions of years of space, I term God. The Activity that forever moves the sea and turns a billion suns; the Mind that calls forth a Betelgeuse and creates an electron; the Love that makes brothers of stars and stores up sweets for the bee; the Life that makes man produce man, fern produce fern, and atom atom; the Joy of stars eternally on the wing, of birds at dawn, of running waters, of singing leaves, of all laughter and mirth and cheer and dancing merriment, the joy of knowing that God *is* Joy—I term God.

Power, Energy, Activity, Mind, Love, Life, and Joy!

JESUS CHRIST AS GOD AND SAVIOR

Charles Clayton Morrison

WESTERN PROTESTANTISM has become thoroughly pervaded with the moralistic and humanitarian conception of Jesus. Its most intriguing and absorbing interest for a full half century has been that of reconstructing his earthly life and recovering his moral teaching and spiritual insights. "Lives" of Jesus have been the most characteristic literary output of this period. Underlying this activity there has been the assumption that Christianity *is* essentially the moral outlook of Jesus, and that to be a Christian is to possess his ethical outlook and to devote one's powers to the spread of his spirit. A dominant note in the preaching of this period has been the exultant claim that we have again "discovered" the historical Jesus. It is generally held that his human figure had been eclipsed by the doctrinal, liturgical and ecclesiastical system which the church had developed "about" Jesus, and that this system must be radically overhauled in the light of the new knowledge of his human person. The direction of thought has therefore moved from the human figure of Jesus to what Henry van Dyke called the "humanity of God," rather than from a metaphysical conception of God to the deity of Jesus.

Of the wholesome elements in this movement we shall not be able to speak at this time. The preoccupation of Protestantism with the moral and spiritual insights of Jesus led easily to the assumption that initial Christianity, the Christianity of what we may call the Pentecostal period, was itself essentially an ethical phenomenon answering to this ethical content of the mind of Christ. It was held that, as the church grew, and problems of organization and worship and apologetic became increasingly urgent, the original purity of the simple gospel of God's righteousness and love—the alleged religion "of" Jesus—became overlaid with ecclesiasticism, ceremonialism and doctrinalism. The prime task of modern Christians was, therefore, to dig below all this historic corruption and apostasy, and to recover original Christianity and make it the norm of the Christian enterprise. This "restoration" movement began with the Lutheran reformation and has been the consistent methodology of all Protestant churches ever since. The movement was greatly accelerated in the last half century by the rise of historical criticism whose results tended strongly to create the belief that modern Christians now have a more objective acquaintance with the actual human figure of Jesus than had been enjoyed by the church in any period since the last Apostle died.

Thus a large section of the church of today is, naturally, loath to admit that a metaphysical doctrine of Jesus' deity is a proper emphasis for its

---

Reprinted by permission from *Christendom*, Autumn, 1938.

own understanding of the faith, to say nothing of making it the basis of union or of fellowship. It seems like betraying the very genius of Protestantism which has tended more and more away from the refinements of theology to an emphasis upon the ethical aspects of the faith, under the simpler and more practical concept of "personal loyalty to the personal Christ." To this fairly conservative Protestantism, hardly less than to dissenting liberalism, the proposal to base a World Council of Churches upon the acceptance of the deity of Jesus Christ comes, to put it mildly, with considerable surprise.

The doctrinal problem which the ecumenical movement, therefore, faces in wide areas of Protestant church life is to invest this basic formula with meaning. I do not think this can be done by a revival of the historic controversy over the metaphysics of the nature of Christ or of the Godhead. Nothing could be more sterile and hopeless than such a controversy. Surely the distance we have traveled from the historic battlefields of Nicaea and Chalcedon, of Poland and Hungary and Bohemia, of Holland, and of New England, has brought us to an open place where we can view this whole subject in a new perspective and a new spirit. Unless our liberalism (in the generic sense of the word) has brought us to such a place, the outlook for understanding among Christians is dark indeed.

II

It is my purpose to explore a little bit of the way leading to such an open place. And the first step which I believe we must take is one which leads us definitely away from the moralistic conception of initial Christianity and from the popular moralistic conception of the figure of Jesus. It is clear that this interpretation of primitive Christianity and its Founder presents insurmountable resistance to the serious acceptance of any such formula as that Jesus Christ is God. It is rightly felt, from this moralistic point of view, that the ancient formula is irrelevant and superfluous, laying a burden upon faith which the modern mind is unable to bear; and not only unable to bear but unwilling to consider. How shall this resistance be overcome? As I see it, it can be overcome only by a thorough correcting and revision of the prevailing conception that the moral teachings of Jesus were his decisively significant teachings, and that initial Christianity was the reflection and effect of his moral teachings as such.

The correction of this error can be made only by a general diffusion of the later results of historical criticism. Many so-called liberals do not seem to be aware that New Testament scholarship is now virtually unanimous in declaring that the conclusions drawn from its earlier findings were premature and superficial, and that the popular Protestant picture of the early ministry of Jesus, based upon these findings, is not warranted. The claim, to which I referred above, that criticism had given the modern Christian a clearer picture of the earthly life of Jesus than any generation had possessed since the lifetime of the Apostles, is now seen to be an exaggeration. Allowing for a substantial body of authentic memorabilia in the records, it is the maturer judgment of critical scholarship that the early church itself had a considerable colorative part and a substantial creative part in projecting the Figure that we see moving through the Gospels. Into this aspect of the matter we need not go in the present connection, but intelligent Christian people cannot long be kept in ignorance of the fact that critical scholarship is reversing itself radically as to the predominant element in the teaching and preaching of Jesus.

Whereas scholarship formerly seemed to encourage us to regard the ethical element as the essential and determinative content of his teaching, and to regard the eschatological element as an incidental reflection of the forms of thought prevalent in the Judaism of Jesus' time, this same scholarship has now generally reached the conclusion that it was not the ethical but the eschatological element which gave decisive significance to his brief career. Ethically, Jesus stood in the line of prophetic Judaism. Few, if any, of his moral insights can be claimed as surely original with him. And while we are justified in claiming that he carried the moral insights of the prophets to a final embodiment in word and action, it was not his ethical teaching (in our sense of ethics) upon which the church was founded, but his proclamation of the Kingdom of God.

In the mind of Jesus this concept of the Kingdom cannot be defined in moralistic terms. It was an eschatological concept. This does not mean that the ethical was something apart from the eschatological, for it was folded within it, so to speak. But the ethical teaching of Jesus, taken by itself, would not have produced the tremendous effect in history which actually followed upon his earthly ministry. It was the eschatological element which contained the dynamic of historical Christianity. It was his eschatology which was decisive in carrying Jesus beyond the span of his natural life to the post-resurrection company of his disciples, resulting in their giving him a unique status as a veritable message of God, the fulfilment of Israel's hope, the true Messiah.

III

Pristine Christianity was, thus, not primarily an ethical enthusiasm, but a communal faith that God had himself appeared through the person of Jesus Christ in the Christian community, and that the Kingdom long promised was now here. This enthusiastic faith could not long remain naïve. Upon it, and upon the communal experience in which it was carried, the inquiring and creative intelligence of the church set to work. The faith had to be explained as well as enjoyed. It had to be explained to the Christians themselves. And it had to be explained and interpreted to non-Christians to whom its missioners and apologists offered it as the definitive revelation of God. A long course of inquiry and controversy ensued, characterized by the emergence of theories in bewildering proliferation (including, let us remind ourselves, virtually every type of theory that likes to think of itself in our day as "modern"), and finally reaching a fairly stable equilibrium in the so-called Nicaean formula that Jesus Christ was true God of true God.

Christianity began as an actual and closely knit community that had emerged it knew not how; it only knew that it had emerged in the companionship of a small group around the personality of Jesus of Nazareth. It could explain itself only by explaining him. The so-called "theology" of the church was thus not a system of truth, abstractly constructed. It was the church's explanation of its own existence. It was not the kind of truth which is dealt with in the schools; it was the kind of truth required for an adequate explanation of the existence of this particular community and for the conservation of the treasures of faith and experience which the community carried.

The great problem which the early church faced was itself. This was the datum which underlay all its theorizing and speculation. The church was not an association of persons who first believed certain things about God or about Jesus or about the "good life," and afterward were bound together by these beliefs. When the church first *found* itself it was already bound together. It was bound together not by its beliefs, but by something that had *happened* to it, something that had been *given* to it. They called it salvation. It was an eschatological gift of God, not a discovery or a work of man. What they *discovered* was that they already were in possession of this ineffable communal treasure. They were already a community, and their whole intellectual activity was directed toward explaining how this community had come into being. One thing the community knew: it did not create itself. Its emergence was not a voluntaristic association, on the basis of likemindedness, but an eschatological event. It was God's marvelous doing, and it had all come about through companionship with the person of Jesus.

This priority of the community as against the priority of certain beliefs, whether theological or ethical, is, I maintain, the most important deduction to be made from the findings of historical research in the field of early Christianity. Its importance lies in the fact that it throws the whole system of Christian beliefs into a true perspective. Indeed it lifts them to a higher plane. These beliefs cannot be considered one by one as so many propositions whose truth is to be independently determined by objective criteria, as a scientific proposition is validated, or by reference to a metaphysical system within which the principle of logical consistency must be maintained. Christian beliefs are not to be held true or false in either of these senses. Their reference is not to an observed natural process, nor to a philosophical structure, but to the living community of the faith, a community which was thrust into history by an unseen Hand. Such a community must give some account of itself, and such an account as will preserve the ineffable treasures which it has received.

No moralistic account will suffice. The categories of morality, no less than those of science and philosophy, are incommensurable with the datum to be explained. The only explanation which meets the requirements of a community oriented from its birth toward ineffable values, is an explanation that employs ineffable categories. Such are the categories used throughout the New Testament. They were further defined and developed by the Fathers and Apologists of the early church, crystallized and standardized by the early councils, preserved and enriched—and often, alas, perverted—by the church's tradition through the centuries, and brought down to us as witnesses in our time to the timeless working of God in the living community of the faith.

IV

When, therefore, we are confronted with a particular theological proposition such as that which affirms the deity of Jesus Christ, it is unfair to the Christian faith ruthlessly to detach the proposition from its context and subject it to the scientific test, or the philosophic test, or thrust it aside as ethically irrelevant, or apologize for it because forsooth the modern secular mind can see nothing but nonsense in it—as if the secular mind ever did or ever could see anything but nonsense in the Christian faith! Taken by itself, as an independent proposition, apart from its context in the whole pattern of Christian ideology, and apart from the communal motivation which produced it, the doctrine of the deity of Christ is incredible, it is, indeed, without meaning. It gets its meaning within the community in which it arose as the endeavor of the community to provide its eschatological existence with a conceptual orientation; and it stands in the context of the total ideology by which the community witnesses to its faith.

When a modern man approaches a specific Christian doctrine there is, therefore, a prior question which he must face before he pronounces the doctrine true or false. That question, broken into fragments, is this: Do I belong to the historic Christian community? Do I share in the treasures which it carries? Do I participate in its orientation toward ineffable values? Do these ineffable values mean so much to me that I am bound to inquire how it came about that they entered history and finally came to me? One does not fairly answer this question by first detaching the doctrine from its ideological context and subjecting it to a philosophical examination upon whose results his membership in the Christian community will be determined. Nor does he fairly answer it by detaching himself from the Christian community in the hope of finding a disinterested answer—that is, an answer philosophically valid. The doctrine will not submit to either form of abstraction. It is only in the community that the meaning of any specific doctrine will appear. For it is bound up with the full Christian ideology, and the whole ideology is bound up with the living faith of the community.

If the questions asked above are answered in the affirmative, then follows a question which radically tests how deep this affirmative goes. That question, also broken into fragments, is this: Will my denial of the doctrine (in this case, the doctrine of the deity of Jesus Christ) cause me to isolate or alienate myself from the intimate life of the Christian community? Withholding my assent to an ineffable explanation of a historical event which is itself ineffable, will I be able to "communicate" spiritually and naturally with the members of the Christian community? Can I worship with them in the intimacies of the common faith? Can I share with them in the oblation of the eucharist? Will the sacrament of baptism mean the same to me as to the Christian community? Can I join unqualifiedly with the community in the cultivation of the life of the spirit? To *belong* to the Christian community in the full sense is to share without reservation in such activities as these, for these are the corporate acts of the community, and it is by means of them that the intimate life of the community is communicated to all its members.

When, therefore, one says that he accepts Jesus Christ as God and Savior, he does not affirm a bare intellectual proposition, validated by philosophical reasoning; he is affirming his identification with the historic Christian community which came into existence not by the will or the wisdom of man but by the superhuman working of God. To deny this doctrine is, in that degree, to alienate oneself from this community. It alienates, because it tends to close the channels of free spiritual communication within the community. Such a denial, made in the interest of consistency with a scientific or a philosophical system, introduces an alien criterion into the Christian ideology. The attempt to substitute a scientific or philosophical, or a moralistic, ideology for an ideology that points toward the ineffable, tends to reduce the community to the rationalistic or humanistic level and thus negates the very genius of the faith by which the community lives. . . . .

V

All distinctively Christian concepts reflect the pristine and persistent eschatological faith that the Christian community owes its existence in history to the working of God, and that God dwells within it reconciling the world to himself. Though statable in many other ways, this is the essence of the church's faith, and the church's ideology is a reflection of the ineffable character of its faith. To isolate the deity of Christ, and to attack it on philosophical grounds, while accepting the remainder of the Christian ideology without similar criticism, is a fallacious procedure. The Christian ideology stands or falls as a whole, because it is all of one kind. Philosophical arguments brought against the deity of Christ apply to the entire pattern of conceptual Christianity. If their cogency renders this doctrine incredible, it also renders incredible the whole ideology by which the church testifies to its faith. And conversely, if the main body of Christianity's conceptual system is acceptable, the reason given for making an exception of the doctrine of Christ's deity is unwarranted.

VI

What do we mean by the main body of the church's conceptual system? We mean to include, of course, those structural ideas which form the subject matter of conventional theological interest—such concepts as Divine Fatherhood, Incarnation, Atonement, Trinity, Pre-existence of Christ, Divine Providence, Judgment, Inspiration, Holy Spirit, Messiah, Son of God, Lord, Redemption—these are a random enumeration, but they suggest the entire class of ideas to which I refer. Concerning them all, I am affirming that, as a part of the ideology of the Christian community, they spring from the faith of the community and have their distinctively Christian meaning in this particular community's experience. As such, they all reflect the eschatological and ineffable character of the faith, and their validation cannot be philosophically or scientifically determined, because each refers to an order of reality which, being ineffable, is beyond the reach of purely disinterested human reason.

Their validity is in each case to be determined *within* the Christian community by asking such questions as these: Does this doctrine rightly interpret our Christian faith which is the *given* datum to which it refers? Does this doctrine protect and conserve our Christian faith? Does this doctrine lend itself to the inter-communication of the members of the Christian community in a way that strengthens the bond that unites us, promotes mutuality and corporate action among us, and still further deepens the communal experience which began and, as we believe, continues, in the companionship of Jesus Christ? In a word, does this doctrine—do all these doctrines—fit into an ideological framework or canopy under which our Christian community can maintain its orientation toward the ineffable God who, through Jesus Christ, has revealed himself in its midst for the reconciling of the world to himself?

To this class of ideas the deity of Christ belongs. There is not one of these concepts that is "easier" to accept than the doctrine of his deity. Those who have no philosophical difficulty in accepting any one of these doctrines, not to say all of them, should have no philosophical difficulty in accepting the deity of Christ. And conversely, those who reject the deity of Christ on philosophical grounds should, in consistency, also reject every one of these doctrines. They all belong to the same order—they are the ideology of a living communal faith and have no meaning apart from the community in which they arose.

But this class of concepts by no means exhausts the Christian ideology. Those we have named constitute what might be called the loftier expression of the historic Christian faith. There is, however, another class of ideas, far more intimate and numerous, which are the immediate carriers of the life of the spirit. It is impossible to enumerate them all, and I hardly know how to select samples that will stand for all the rest. They have to do with "faith" and "repentance" and "obedience," with a "burial with Christ," a "resurrection" with him, a "justification" by a "grace" which only he can offer, with a life "hid with Christ in God." Man is a "sinner." The Christian's sins are "forgiven." He is a "new creation." His sins were nailed to a "cross." He stands "justified before God." He is "reconciled" to God. He looks and works for the coming of the "Kingdom of God," yet that Kingdom is already here, and he belongs to it. His citizenship is "in heaven." He is "in Christ," and Christ is "in us." The Christian community, that is, the church, is the "body of Christ," he is its "head," and all its members are "joined together in him." The talents and virtues of each member are "gifts of the Spirit." Christ is a living presence who joins himself to every "two or three" who gather together in his name. To "know" him is "life eternal."

Part IV

THE PROBLEM OF EVIL

THE NATURE OF EVIL

A. Eustace Haydon

WHEN THE AUTHOR of Revelation saw in vision the Holy City of the redeemed he was especially interested to tell us that it is free from all the old
familiar enemies of human happiness. His picture of the ideal is unexpectedly illuminated by the words, "I saw no Temple there." With the passing
of evil, the trappings of religion are needed no more. Religion is, because
life is thwarted and denied. If the world had been made good, religion
would never have emerged. The heroic quest of the ages may be read as
man's persistent refusal to yield to the forces of evil or to accept anything
less than the perfect life. And always the world of cruel fact has mocked
at the dream.

The odds of the primitive centuries were heavily against the new, restless, questing form of being, "troubled by a spark." In the midst of the lush
life of that early world, man must have seemed a sorry candidate for lordship of the planet. Yet the fire of life-hunger burned within him so steadily
that he found the way through toil and tragedy, to triumph. But ever,
evil hung upon his heels and haunted his days and nights. Always he was
perplexed, torn between the ought-to-be of his hopes and the actuality of
his unsatisfying attainment. The shadow of frustration, the presence of
active hostility to the aims of man are deeply etched into the picture of the
age of dawn.

Did fear then rule the human spirit? From Lucretius to Hume this was a
favorite theory to account for the origin of religion and the gods. The
theory falsified the facts. Danger there was enough, and terror at times,
but long before the developed form of religions as we know them, groups
of men had come to terms with their world in tested custom and safe habits.
Their ways of winning the needful satisfactions of life made up the body
of their religions, while near to them, ready at call, were the gods as kindly
and beneficent friends. One phase of all early religions was directed specifically against the active forces of evil—the protective and apotropaic devices of spell, curse, charm, and exorcism. In the presence of visible dangers our primeval ancestors were probably no more fearful than we.
Against the unseen evils, creations of their imagination, they had a perfect
protection in the magic spells—an imaginary cure of imaginary ills. For
surer psychic peace there were always available the friendly heavenly powers of light. Dark was real danger. There is probably a deep significance
in the fact that for practically every religion light is synonymous with
goodness, while darkness is the symbol for evil. Certainly there was fear
and it played its part in shaping the cults, but religion, as the mastery of evil

---

From *The Quest of the Ages*, New York, 1929, pp. 125-148. Reprinted by permission
of the publishers, Harper & Brothers.

and the quest of the goods of life, was not nearly so much fear-ridden at the beginning as in some later centuries of culture.

When man had sufficient security and leisure to brood about his world, the presence of evil perplexed him. He had tasted the happiness of life; but sorrow, pain, defeat, and death monotonously marred the flowing rhythm of the days. Not until the coming of the theologians, however, did evil stare at him with the inscrutable eyes of the Sphinx. . . . .

The rudiments of our modern classification of evils as physical or natural, and moral were already apparent in primitive societies. The organizing concepts were spirits or demons, magical power, and taboo. All kinds of unfortunate and unhappy experiences could be attributed to the activity of malicious, invisible powers. They could produce disease, pain, misfortune, or death. Even the souls of the thwarted, unburied, or unhappy dead might torment the living with physical suffering and affliction. This power was also available to the sorcerer who could sing a charm or pronounce an incantation. Many mishaps, bodily pains, and accidents might flow from the malicious use of magic power. Taboo was primarily the sign of evil flowing from violation of the safe habits and customs of the group. It was the "thou shalt not" of the early world. Great danger to the food supply, to the safety of the group, might flow from the contagion involved in thus venturing into the unknown and untried mode of behavior. In this lies the primitive concept of "sin." It involved a dangerous contagion which required magical methods of removal. The commonest forms were washing with water, or blood, or mixtures of mana-filled fluids; passing through fire; the use of the scape-goat to carry away the contagion; exile, and in extreme cases death. In general the evils which have registered their presence in earlier religions were of these three types—physical suffering, the dread of the uncanny, mysterious, unseen forces of the environment, and the social evil resulting from breaking of the group code. Against each of them there was a psychically reassuring technique of protection. . . . .

In whatever way the evils of the world may be classified they present a problem for the religious philosopher, since his task is to give this tragic phase of existence some rational status in an orderly universe. The religions of the world all refuse to accept evil as ultimate. They are compelled to read the deeper meaning of reality in terms of the realization of joy and perfection of life. A final optimism, or at least meliorism, dominates them all. For man, evil is a sad and somber actuality. For man's hopes, it must be overcome in the victory of the good. The interpretation of evil, therefore, varies according to the understanding of the final goal and the nature of cosmic control. There are three great types—theistic religions, nontheistic, and religions with impersonal or superpersonal Absolutes.

For theistic religions, when one supreme and all powerful God ruled the world, evil was not only a problem but an insoluble problem. There was always the necessity of a theodice to justify the ways of God to man; for evil was a part of God's world. The end was usually a confession of agnosticism, acceptance of the inability of the human mind to penetrate the mystery, and assertion of faith in the goodness of God and in immortality.

Positing a finite God only complicated the problem, for a Deity limited in power might be finite also in wisdom and goodness. Moreover, there was little relief for man in allowing God to escape responsibility for the world's ills, if it could be done only on the intolerable condition of his lacking sufficient power and wisdom to guarantee the final fulfillment of his plan. The central difficulty in all theisms lay in making God the creator of the world and interpreting the process of time as the working out of his purpose to a perfect goal. Evil then became part of the plan. Logical thinkers grasped the nettle firmly, and accepted evil as a means to larger good. Thought thus came to rest in resigned faith, but the problem remained. . . . .

Christian theology has been forced to put evil within the plan of God in creation. The implications of that ultimate responsibility were covered by the doctrines of Satan, man's free will, disobedience, fall, corruption of nature and sin, which involved the whole salvation program. In the classical theological systems the question was handled fearlessly in terms of the absolute will of God. All was included in the eternal plan of the Creator, even before the beginning of the world. The moral evil of men who were created to be eternally damned was a dark, dread mystery, without meaning. It was mellowed somewhat by saying that not even those redeemed had any claim on God; and in regard to the lost souls, God did no more than withhold from them the necessary redeeming grace. This was heroic treatment of the problem, but logical on the premise of an absolute Creator. For modern Christianity it has proved too strong a doctrine. The day of absolute monarchs is past. There is a constant effort to relieve God of responsibility for evil, even at the great risk of making him finite. The necessity of free will, which was the source of moral evil according to theology, is another method of alleviation. But this fails, because its only purpose can be the production of persons who are so perfect as to will only the good, and they might have been made so at the beginning. If, otherwise, they still possess free will in the sense of being able to will good or evil, then moral evil may continue forever and God's plan end in futility. Even against God, men are now daring enough to assert that human beings cannot be used as mere means; that God may not will evil as a means to his revelation or for his own glory. Thus the beautifully logical systems of historic Christian theism face shipwreck on the dark rock of evil. . . . .

Zoroastrianism escaped the problem of evil by positing two eternal beings—one good and one evil. All forms of evil over the whole area of space and time could then be treated as the creations of Ahriman. Unfortunately, this simple interpretation by the classical orthodoxy of Iran is being spoiled by contact with other religions and their solitary supreme gods. Like the devils of all the world, Ahriman has now been denied. One school interprets evil as the result of an unworthy thought in the mind of the good God; another prefers to preserve the eternal goodness of God by making man altogether responsible for evil. Thus Zoroastrianism is drawn into the snare of the theistic dilemma.

Beyond the personal gods is the Absolute. When the religious philosophies reach this high level, both good and evil, as men experience them, vanish in one harmonious perfection.   In Hinduism and Mahāyāna Buddhism real Reality, as Paramatman, or Dharmakāya, is beyond all relativities and distinctions.   From that eternal standpoint evil is unreal.   As in the absolute idealisms of all the world, there is a dual viewpoint, that of the changeless and eternal Absolute and the view of phenomenal beings in the whirl of temporal events.   The ocean of reality is static; its waves of human generations may be sunlit or tortured in the agony of storms.   Evil for man must ever be something different from the same evil fact seen from the standpoint of the eternal.   Logically, then, existence in the illusory world of time is itself evil, and religion a quest for escape to the blissful Real.   Nevertheless, the analysis of the specific ills of life is clear enough in Hinduism. Greatest of all, however, is bondage to the wheel of endless rebirth.   Karma dominates the time cycle, but each individual determines his own fate.   Both moral and physical evil are woven into the pattern of a cord that winds through the centuries; yet in perfect justice, the fruit of deeds is eaten in sorrow or joy by the doer.   Only beyond the puppet play of time is real being and peace.   Ignorance of the way of release is the ultimate evil. Religion shows the way.   It is noteworthy that in these systems of uncreated and beginningless universes, no God is responsible.   There is no need for a theodice.   There is no sin in the Western sense.   Karma belongs to the individual and is his lonely sadness and responsibility.   Fortunately, great personal gods who are themselves far advanced on the way of release from the wheel, reach out, in Buddhism at least, to help their fellow-pilgrims of the quest. . . . . .

Though evil is as real as the beneficent phases of the world with which man deals, religions have always weighted the scales with faith on the side of the good.   During all ages they have viewed reality through the colored glasses of their hopes.   In spite of their disillusionment, even the Charvakas and Epicureans could say, "Evil may be endured, good may be attained."   The struggle of thinkers to find a place for this element of irrationality, in a world assumed to be orderly, may be seen by setting side by side a few of the characteristic interpretations: evil as embodied in a personal, spiritual power; as a necessary phase of existence overcome in the good; as a stimulating and disciplinary element necessary to the realization of virtuous, free wills; as an intractable quality in the material stuff of creation; as lack of harmonious adjustment to the cosmic order; as illusion and unreal; as existence in the bodily world; as negation or absence of the good; as simply unhappy experience to be endured. . . . .

There was no adequate means of mastery over environment available for early religions.   Man was only one of many forms of life striving for existence in a conflicting welter of purposes.   He had no effective knowledge either of the world about him or of his own nature.   His religious ideas and groping methods of control tell that story plainly. . . . . The recurrent wastage of civilization produced some of the great prophets of world denial, as well as many compensatory dreams of super-earthly realms beyond the ravages of time.   Sobering memories speak to modern man amid the wreckage of these long-lost splendors.   But there is a new light in his eyes.   He walks in the worn highways of the world with new hope, for today, evil, both natural and social, faces the challenge of a new instrument—the method of science.

There is also a new understanding of the nature of evil. It is no longer a metaphysical problem. Religion "coming of age" faces the world neither with blind optimism nor with blank despair. When even the gods are challenged by the fact of evil, it is a sign that the many modes of theological interpretation of the past no longer act as psychic anaesthesia nor even help to patient resignation. . . . . On a planet which has produced the various forms of life revealed by its geologic and historic record, evil, for any one of them, is relative to the nature of the environment and its capacity for adjustment or control. The test of adjustment is satisfaction of the desires of the life pattern of the organism. For one form of life satisfaction was won only at the cost of some other form. Many types met the ultimate evil—extinction. There is more than poetic truth in Tennyson's "Nature, red in tooth and claw with ravine." Blood stains the record, in the ancient past and now, but mutual aid was there, too. Life early learned to overcome many threatening dangers by alliances, by protective devices, by co-operation. More effectively than his intelligence, man's group unity lifted him to the van of triumphant life. His religions were co-operative quests for values to be shared by every member of the group. It was religion, compensatory, world-denying, drunk with faith, that through the centuries of defeat kept burning for men the torch of hope that ultimately wrong and evil might be overpassed. It is religion now, a self-conscious revival of the quest of the ages, that turns once more to the ancient task of mastering evil in the name of the higher life of man. In social idealism, it is a return from heaven to earth, from dreams of golden ages to prosaic actuality. Evil is a fact of protean form to be met by understanding through analysis and, in the light of the ideal adjustment, if possible, overcome.

Evil falls into two great classes—natural, and social or moral. The first comprises all those elements of the natural environment dangerous or hostile to the form of life activity which man represents. The second is created by maladjustments in human relationships. And the second is the source of most of the unhappiness that modern man endures.

In natural evil, so far as we can now foresee, there are elements which are irreducible. Man has no power to guide our solar system among the stars. But the Phoenix-like death and rebirth of suns a million million years in the future is not an acute anguish for the average mortal man. Nearer to him is the fact of his own mortality. There seems to be no escape from this ruthlessness of nature in sweeping the generations into the silence of death. Though philosophized as a boon for mankind, it nevertheless remains for the individual a sinister fact, in a world which has not yet learned how to give to every man a full life of creative joy and a mellow age of memory. . . . .

Less universal in their incidence for the masses of men are the destructive forces of a still restless planet—earthquake, volcanic eruptions, tidal waves, the violence of storms. They do not constitute a very large percentage of the evils for a generation of mankind. All these are old familiar phases of the world. None of them, not even glacial eras, could daunt the conquering life of man. The effect of drought, the dread of cold and storms, the fear of lightning bolt, are registered in religious cults. But these more spectacular threats of the Earth Mother are in reality the lesser evils. Other forms of natural evils are nearer to us, more stealthy, and a greater threat. Treated in the old religions as the work of spirits or demons, they are now classed as diseases, effects of the malignancy of various forms of living organisms, defective bodily structure, especially defective nerve or brain structure. Against them now, in place of charm, exorcism, and prayer, there is arrayed the increasingly effective understanding and technique of the sciences. If natural evil were his only menace, modern man might fare forward toward the future, lifting a confident song of triumph.

Unfortunately, the great group of social evils is the larger, comprising almost all the elements that make life unsatisfying. Maladjustment in social relations is responsible even for much of the purely physical suffering of the world. It is in happy, human relationships that the ideal of the good life is always visualized in religions of culture. All the heavens are places of joyous, harmonious comradeship. With the passing of primitivity, the spiritual values of the higher life received always the supreme place in the human quest. But moral evil baffled every age.

On this level, history reveals a discouraging paradox. With greater ability to satisfy his wishes, with higher culture, man found himself entangled in a more complex social web with an increase in the evils of personal maladjustment. Some of the wisest seers of the Orient gaze, skeptical and aghast, upon the endless complexity of the civilization created by the instruments of Western industrialism and its threatening train of evils—the cheapening of man, the exploitation of weaker peoples, poverty, hovels, strife and war. "The test of a civilization," says Tagore, "is, how much has it evolved and given expression to the love of humanity by its laws and institutions" (Sadhana, p. 111). The paradox is easily explained. It was not that the religious ideal of the good life had altogether vanished. The difficulty was rather that man's material mastery outran his social science and powers of social control—a difficulty accentuated wherever religion escaped responsibility for making a good world here, by postponing the good life to another world or to a future age. . . . .

The larger meaning of moral evil is maladjustment, and an individual who could be branded by none of the old terms might still be a victim of moral evil. Situations which deny satisfaction and thwart the creative potentialities of the individuals spell evil. The higher the culture, the more sensitive may persons be to suffering. Satisfying adjustment of personal beings in social structure is still an ideal. Farther removed is the society co-operatively self-selected for self-fulfillment, with a conscious method of adjustment of conflicts in the light of a shared quest of recognized values. Complete adjustment must ever be a flying goal.

Our complex, modern civilization has multiplied the number and the seriousness of social ills resulting from the conflict of desires. The rivalry of man with man, group with group, nation with nation, and race with race grows more menacing because of the parochial aspect of the earth and the amazing development of instruments of power. Titanic forces toy with the lives of men. Selfish groups strive to their objectives over the broken hopes of their unknown victims. More brutal than the struggle of primeval monsters is the clash of imperialisms in modern war and equally devoid of control by any intelligent idealism. This is "man's inhumanity to man." The major evil confronting modern religions is the conflict of purposes of organized groups, extending from the village community to the arena of international affairs. No single individual can visualize its manifold ramifications. It presents the supreme challenge to the human quest. . . . .

The one heartening thing is that we now recognize that evil has nothing ultimate about it. Taken naturalistically, the world and human nature are in the making. Both may be changed. Evil is a contingent and separable element, and therefore subject to removal by intelligent adjustment of personal relations. Escape from the shadow of an unknown cosmic force of evil, from the idea of an inherent taint in human nature, from a resigned acceptance of evil as a necessary moment in a universal harmony, has removed the most sinister characteristics of any specific evil for modern man. When its true nature is brought home to the minds and consciences of men, the quietistic, *laissez-faire* attitude toward it may give way to an acceptance of common responsibility for its removal. It will then become, for religion, "a challenge and a task."

Both natural and moral evil promise to yield to larger knowledge directed by good will. The same instruments of science that have made a chaos of the simple civilizations of the past, may also serve to build the better world. The failure is in religious idealism. There has been no unified social vision to set the stakes for the use of the new mechanical and natural sciences. The vision of the quest of the ages grows clearer now. To the social sciences we are turning for clarification and for knowledge—knowledge of human nature, of methods of analysis of social situations, methods of control and organization which will obviate or remove the recognized maladjustments of our social relations. Idealism is sobered by knowledge. Utopias are outmoded. There is no longer a search for panaceas. In a growing and changing world there will always be problems and new forms of evil. But there is no threat in this prospect since we have the hope of achieving a scientific method of adjustment of crisis situations as they arise. A method of meeting and overcoming maladjustments is more important than any specific cure.

Religions are entering upon a new phase of their history. Fatalism and blind faith, resignation and blind optimism, belong to the older order of the world. Instead of escape and compensation, there is now courageous and confident acceptance of human responsibility. The age has become too dangerous for drifting. Instead of flight modern religions prepare for battle. To the skeptical and disillusioned spectator of the human scene this is not the least of the wonders of the new age. When evil is faced realistically as removable, a method may be found for the actualizing of social ideals.

HOW CAN MODERN MAN BE RELIGIOUS?

Harry F. Ward

THUS THE BASIC FACT which should determine the program of organized religion is that American society is on the way, all unaware, to repeat the sins of past civilizations whose manifest wages are death. Unless these evils are recognized when they first appear as the symptoms of a disease which unchecked always proves fatal, their development cannot be prevented. If they are to be stopped, it can only be done, as in the case of tuberculosis, in the incipient stages.

Does this demand of current life upon the resources of religion appear any different if the situation is viewed from the standpoint of the traditional concern of Christianity with the individual, if we ask on what terms the modern man—that is the man bred and born in the intellectual climate produced by science—can be religious? First of all, and last of all this question means on what terms can he pursue holiness—that is wholeness—both within himself and in his relations to the universe. How can he overcome the evil that mutilates and destroys? In the order of business for religion this issue always takes precedence over the cosmic problem and imperatively so in times of moral crisis like these. True the riddle of the universe also has its imperative, but in moments of peril intellectual curiosity is out of place.

What the modern man needs to know about the universe is whether it is hostile, indifferent, or friendly to his moral aspirations and struggle. That he discovers by uniting faith and action, not by intellectualizing. The intellectual need is negative rather than positive, that religion should not contradict what science demonstrates concerning the nature and behavior of the universe. The quicker religion is content to leave to science and philosophy those aspects of the nature of man and the universe concerning which it formerly spoke with authoritative ignorance, the sooner it will be able to co-ordinate its work with theirs, prevent them from being unmoral or becoming immoral, and so help modern man to such wholeness of life and outlook as is now possible. Also by making ethical development its first concern organized religion will be able the more rapidly to aid the modern spirit to recovery from that paralysis of the moral will whose chief cause is its refusal to attack the moral problem because it cannot now read all mystery.

When he seeks after righteousness the modern man finds that all the sins that beset him are tied in with the evils that threaten civilization, which corrupt him even as he strengthens them; he discovers that he can move toward holiness only as he becomes intelligently aware of their causes and strives to eliminate them. He finds his salvation not in running away from the city

From *Which Way Religion?* New York, 1931, pp. 71-80. Reprinted by permission of the publishers, The Macmillan Company.

of destruction but in helping to prevent the evils that are destroying it. Failing this, he is indeed lost, because he has eaten of the fruit of the tree of knowledge. Knowing what he knows, facing possibilities that have come to no other generations, if he neglects to use his knowledge to make a new world, he is of all men the most miserable. He has fallen not from any original state of innocence but from the high estate of intelligence and capacity. He has missed the opportunity to live creatively, and descended into the company of the destroyers.

As for the masses whose destiny it has ever been to suffer and die unaware of what life may be, they can only live religiously if they are awakened to the possibilities of human existence and become willing to pay the price of their development. This is the vital germ of good in the great Russian upheaval, that human beings who have been little more than beasts of burden are now becoming conscious makers of a new society. Salvation for the crowd in this country means transforming its members from mere consumers of standardized comforts, ideas, and amusements into creators of personality and a social order. If our present institutional religion cannot function in this manner then a new form will arise to that end and it may not call itself religion at all.

If then organized Christianity is to help man to live creatively, it is not sufficient that it aid him to escape the forces of evil that oppose his every constructive effort, it must lead him to conquer them. The Barthians are right enough about the fatal pride and self-sufficiency of scientific intellectualism. They are just as wrong in proclaiming the utter helplessness of man, his absolute dependence upon a transcendent power—who is also a conception of the intellect made and proclaimed not entirely without pride. The facts continue to show, and moral development requires, interdependence between the person and the cosmos, between man and God, neither one being only the creation of the other, nor without the other capable of realization. Immanence and transcendence are not after all mutually exclusive.

The religion that brings salvation to modern man will help him to understand and develop the moral aspect of the universe even as science aids him to do that with its physical aspect. Then he will be able to direct life creatively instead of toward destruction, no matter how many times he stands baffled and ignorant, acknowledging his limitations and confessing his failure. At present most of our intellectuals perceive as little as the masses the nature and course of the forces that are undermining industrial society and piling up the chances of disaster for their children.

The preliminary condition of cure for the sickness of the acquisitive society —of which the United States is the climactic development just as Rome was the culmination of the great military empires—is that the prevailing pride and self-righteousness give way to an awareness of the premonitory symptoms and to some co-operative action against them. The efficacy of any program depends upon identification of the dominant causes of the disease, upon recognition of the fact that the acquisitive society is sick because it is acquisitive, because its attitude toward the cosmos is possessive rather than creative. To be effective this must be accompanied by a perception of the necessity of achieving a harmonized economic life, both between the classes and the nations. As Reinhold Niebuhr has emphasized, modern man is not whole in his own life because there is no solidarity in the common life; he cannot achieve the organic unity which the machine presupposes because while it unites him mechanically with a larger world, it sunders him spiritually from his fellows. Because its bonds are impersonal and being used primarily for money-making, it sets the interests of one section against those of another.

Equally necessary to spiritual health and vigor is the recovery of some sense of the organic unity of life and culture. Now its various aspects are warring against each other—the practical needs against the intellectual, aesthetic, and spiritual—because commercialism has divided them. Such unity of life as belonged to simpler societies has been lost because economic pursuits have been put under the domain of the acquisitive spirit, subject to a morality different from that of art, science, or religion. The impetus of the machine added to the prestige and power of money-making has given the immediate and practical necessities of life a double ascendancy over its long-time imponderable values, and the house of civilization is thus divided against itself.

If it can be led to realize such organic unity as is possible to human life, the machine age will get some sense of direction to replace its present confusion and its distrust of purpose and ideals. Our generation has achieved its loss of direction largely through its inherited reliance upon the automatically beneficent outworkings of self-interest. Much of the contradiction in our political policies, for instance the increasing collectivism in behalf of profit seekers alongside the vociferous demand that the government refrain from interfering with business, is due to the survival of this eighteenth century belief. It is undoubtedly partly responsible for the naïve confidence of many preachers that our political and economic life will be saved merely by putting good men into executive positions. In the long run self-interest can never work out an intelligent social policy, no matter how much it is shown inevitable consequences, because it is inhibited from taking the risks involved in necessary change.

The other factor in keeping this generation without any conscious goal is the influence of the laboratory method and the philosophy that has developed around it. Under these influences we go from situation to situation, learning from each but with no sense of continuity or direction. What more then are we than opportunists? It is a curious turn of our intellectual life which deprives the generation that knows most of history and the rest of the world of any sense of social creativity. Here the Communists clearly have the advantage for they know what kind of world they want. Whereas our American liberals, religious and otherwise, seem to know only that they want to learn from the next experience, and some of them are as afraid of a purpose as medievalists were of the devil. Yet history shows that even a mistaken purpose may move the common life further forward than can those who know not where they are going. It is significant, however, that Dewey himself has said in the matter of war that next steps which are only refinements of the war making process are worse than nothing, because they are next steps in the wrong direction. This means that at least we must have enough sense of direction to know that we want to get away from war. And if war, then also some other equally menacing evils.

Thus the unconscious demand made upon the religion by the modern man, all unaware of his need, is that it should help this wandering generation to fashion a goal for itself, should lead it to a creative consciousness of its organic possibilities, a dynamic awareness of present deficiencies. Religion has a twofold function for society as for the individual—to produce repentance accompanied by the power to forsake and overcome evil; to develop ideals along with the capacity to pursue and achieve them. In this twofold task it uses jointly the factual method of science and the imaginative insight of poetry. Concrete situations show the consequences of war, economic inequality and class division, along with the necessity of moving away from them. The vision of the ideal reveals the faint form of a warless world, a just and fraternal commonwealth, whose outline becomes clearer as man moves toward it by experimentation based on an increased understanding of past experience. It is by the power of the ideal that religion can encourage him to that creative effort in remaking his own life and fashioning the Great Society in which alone the modern man can harmonize the various aspects of his being and culture and find some organic relationship to the universe.

A religion that does this will be something more than a *Preface to Morals* that unwittingly ends ethical development by leaving the good man a disinterested spectator of the drama of life. It will sustain him as a creative participant in the common struggle, renewing his hope and courage in times of defeat and increasing his enjoyment of its lighter interludes, because it gives him the consciousness of being allied with all that is timeless in continually diminishing its tragic catastrophes.

If Protestant Christianity is to become such a religion it must needs escape from the bonds of its traditional individualism and become conscious of its social value and mission. It must, as Freemantle urged a generation ago, take "the world as the subject of redemption" and understand what Ross a little later tried to teach it, the social nature of sin. Then it may be able to keep the growing awareness of his habitat by the modern man from becoming sterile sophistication and help it to become the creative intelligence that he needs. Early Protestantism helped to make it inevitable that the democratic individualism which supplanted the centralized and graded authority of the medieval world should in its turn gather Dead Sea fruit, by reinforcing the economic virtues without recognizing that they had been grafted on to the root of all evil. If modern Protestantism should likewise by its social service strengthen the collectivism of the machine age without perceiving where and how it is class dominated and mechanistic, without striving to transform it into a spiritual unity of co-operative effort for the development of all, its last state will indeed be much worse than its first. To avoid such an ending it must acquire on a larger and truer scale that sense of the civic nature of religion which possessed Greece in the days of her glory and distinguishes the faith of the Hebrews. But this must now be cast in the form of a continuous, humble, and repenting search for corporate salvation. The saving of civilization must be as prominent in the consciousness of modern religion as the saving of the soul was in the days when the world of the individual was replacing that of an interlocking feudal structure.

This means that it is the business of the churches today to know and to teach in what such a salvation consists. How can religion prevent the United States from developing into another parasitic empire, perishing in due time from the corruption of its luxury and power, unless it understands the nature of the forces that are making for decay, unless it knows the road that leads away from destruction, and the goal toward which man must strive? How can it help this broken, chaotic world and the mutilated, maladjusted personalities who inhabit it toward wholeness unless it realizes that human nature is more than the individual. American Protestantism is imperatively summoned to free itself from the absorption in the individual which has misled our psychology, and from the delusion that the common welfare is developed by the enlargement of personal self-interest which has deceived our classical economics. The ecclesiastical corollary is a doctrine of personal redemption in terms of self-gratification, followed by an assurance of salvation for society by the aura emanating from men who are good according to the standards of conventional religion. There are as few results to support this belief in the one field as in the other. In the easy calculation the overpowering effect of social institutions has been ignored. It is remarkable to see how liberals are confused by this hangover from the philosophic individualism of the eighteenth century. Why for example should the climax of Lippmann's *Preface to Morals*, after a diagnosis of a social situation and a glimpse at the Great Society in the making, be the disinterested individual? Why should liberal preachers keep repeating that we are to save modern society according to the method of Jesus by changing individual lives, regardless of the fact that Jesus never conceived of the individual apart from the community as moderns do, and of the fact that he was not facing a responsibility for the organization of society as we are?

In the kind of world in which we find ourselves a religion that is to help man into creative living must perceive and aid the increasingly organic relationship between the individual and society, must be aware of the social nature of the self, and all of its teaching and program must root in this knowledge. Society and the individual being inseparably bound together, religion cannot save either without the other, nor will the salvation of either follow automatically upon that of the other. What religion can do for the world is determined by what it can do for the person, and what it can do for the person is likewise limited by what it is able to do for society.

Unless it can progressively redeem the corporate life from its sins, religion cannot even keep the individual from the evil that is in the world. How much of holiness has it gained by keeping him from the carnal sins if the graces of the spirit are prevented by the conditions of associated living? How can it keep him pure in heart if the acquisitive society continually incites him to the love of riches and to covetousness? How can it enable him to enjoy the peaceable fruits of righteousness if his country orders him to bomb villages or cities? How can it inspire him to love his enemy if those in authority are determined that he shall hate him? How can he love his neighbor as himself if business causes him to use that neighbor—here or across the seas—as a serf laboring to supply his creature comforts? It is too late in the day for religion to proclaim an ethic of abstract personal virtues. To be anything more than an escape from surrounding iniquity these virtues must be translated into terms of current situations. The conscientious objector is justified against the society from which he rebels only when he cares more about the saving of mankind than his own soul. The modern man can find healing and wholeness, can become at home in the universe, only as he is conscious of working out an ethical salvation in cooperation with his community and with the rest of mankind.

COSMIC AND ETHICAL ATHEISM

Max C. Otto

Now to ATHEISM. We remind ourselves that it is one of the ideas most certain to stir up feelings of repulsion and to stir them up profoundly. Few people have tried to decide what atheism means, yet most of them have learned that hardly anyone cares to be known as an atheist even though he is without any positive belief in God. One reason for this is the disrepute associated with the very name. To be thought an atheist is to be the object of a suspicion that one is all manner of things which are strongly disapproved of by decent people.

Theism, on the other hand, is very appealing. The inferences drawn as to consequent beliefs and practices are of the socially approved kind. The feeling tone of the word is therefore very agreeable. Belief in God may be so weak, indefinite, or abstract that it can only be called theistic by courtesy, or it may refer to nothing more divine than the noblest qualities of human nature, nevertheless the "believer" will hold to the term theism because it makes him feel more comfortable to do so. A Chicago taxicab driver phrased the common feeling very nicely: "I don't know anything about it, but I'll be damned if I'll call myself an atheist."

Matters grow worse the farther we look. The slightest acquaintance with God-ideas is disconcerting, if we really desire to know what people mean when they speak of belief or disbelief in God. Socrates, one of the most God-conscious of human beings, was condemned as an atheist; Jesus, whose every thought would seem to have been God-centered, was crucified because his theism was atheism to others; Spinoza, later to be spoken of as "God-intoxicated," was persecuted and reviled for atheistical teachings. What enormous quantities of human blood the earth has been made to drink by theists who slaughtered men and women as atheists because their theism was of a different kind! Rabbi Solomon Goldman, without aiming to be exhaustive, has enumerated some forty-five conceptions of God in Hebrew literature alone. How many kinds of atheists does that make? William Blake went so far as to call anyone an atheist who believed in the real existence of a physical world.

For us just now the thing of importance is that atheism, like materialism, has a metaphysical or cosmic and a moral or social denotation. It may refer to the universe at large or to the human scene. It may be primarily a denial that "there is a divinity that shapes our ends, rough-hew them how we will," or an assertion that nothing in the experienced world is of value; that intelligence, human affection, character, good will, social idealism are amiable delusions. Atheism may be disbelief in a Divine Purpose at work

From *The Human Enterprise*, New York, 1940, pp. 292-312. Reprinted by permission of the publishers, F. S. Crofts & Company.

behind or within the whole of things, or it may be disbelief in greatness of purpose in man's life; disbelief in truth, love, justice, beauty, any of the great ends which, for innumerable persons, are sublimated in the concept of God. Joseph Wood Krutch, speaking of the cynical devaluation of love by certain contemporary writers, is profoundly right: "We have grown used . . . . to a Godless universe, but we are not yet accustomed to one which is loveless as well, and only when we have so become shall we realize what atheism really means."

We must therefore make a distinction between what we may term *cosmic* and *ethical* atheism, and try to decide which of them is the more destructive of the highest human potentialities. . . . .

The wide difference between cosmic and ethical atheism is evident in this curious fact. Well-known men who are far apart in their beliefs about God may be almost indistinguishable when it comes to enlightened interest in the ethical advancement of mankind. Bishop McConnell is a theist; H. S. Jennings is at best an agnostic; Julian Huxley is an outspoken atheist; John Dewey prefers to be neither a theist, an agnostic, nor an atheist. Yet each of them—bishop, biologist, or philosopher—is committed to very similar ideals of social progress. Each is opposed to *ethical* atheism. A slight examination will show this to be true.

It is a fundamental mistake, writes Bishop McConnell in *The Christian Century*, to regard the commandments, "Thou shalt love thy God with all thy heart" and "Thou shalt love thy neighbor as thyself" as two commandments. "They are not two, but one." We have come to a pass in human affairs, Bishop McConnell believes, where "mystical unity with God, God remaining undefined or a God of social passivity, amounts to nothing." So too of God conceived as an Absolute above all human striving, "the source of all beauty," "the fount of reason," "the center of all power in the universe." If this is all that theological or philosophical thinking can make of God, Bishop McConnell is not sure "that it is especially worth while for men to think overmuch of God, *just now*." His position is amplified in the following paragraphs:

Just now the main question concerning God is as to whether we can think of him as morally responsible in the use of his power in dealing with the billion and a half persons supposed to be living at any one time on the face of the earth. Let us withdraw for contemplation—withdraw into desert solitude, if need be, for the sake of fashioning a nobler idea of God, if we do so for the sake of coming out of the desert with the nobler idea taking the form of a deeper responsibility on the part of the divine for the right outcome of human affairs.

The actual process followed in humanity's moralization of the idea of God is the seizure, usually by a prophet or seer, of some larger or finer ideal of human life as binding upon God as well as upon men. Then the adjustment of this moral insight to the conception of the divine gives that divine itself new force for human life.

These are brave words for a religious leader to print. Only an exceptional interest in humanity and an integrity equally exceptional would make them public. And they hit the mark. They indicate what the issue turns upon. They help to make clear which meaning of atheism is the one that has serious consequences for our time.

Mr. Jennings would prefer not to use the term God.   Gods and goddesses he speaks of as reflecting the highest characteristics in men, as devils represent the worst in men, animals, and insects.   He declines to believe in any power supposed to have existed before biological life began its progressive course to which the direction of that course can be ascribed.   Of belief in God, taken in this sense, he has written frankly in his book, *The Universe and Life:*

In part, it is a reflection of wishes, the outgrowth of a desire for an all-wise, all-powerful protector and father.   In the practice of science, the tendency to base convictions upon wishes is one of the chief errors to be avoided: it does not lead to verifiable truth; on the contrary, it leads to demonstrable errors.

As this biologist sees the situation, the thing of superlative value is not life in conformity with the supposed commands of the wished-for protector and father, but a life of "fullness, variety, and adequacy."   The highest aim of morality is to spread forbearance, generosity, good will, and love of truth, virtues which he believes have not kept pace with advances in practical efficiency.   And for the furtherance of these aims men are dependent upon themselves and the resources at their disposal:

It is only experience, it is only living itself, that discovers what things in life are of value.   What life, in direct experience, finds satisfactory, is satisfactory; what life finds valuable, is valuable.   The worth while includes all those satisfactions and experiences of life that are discovered to be good, as food is discovered to be good by a hungry creature; and that do not yield later consequences of evil that overbalance the good.

Mr. Huxley puts it in this way:

I do not believe in the existence of a god or gods.   The conception of a divinity seems to me, though built up out of a number of real elements in experience, to be a false one, based on the quite unjustifiable postulate that there must be some more or less personal power in control of the world.

What does he say as to the consequent value of life?   Does his disbelief in "the existence of a god or gods" carry with it what we have called ethical atheism?   Not at all.   Without belief in cosmic theism, "men and women may yet possess the mainspring of full and purposive living, and just as great a sense that existence can be worth while as is possible to the most devout believers."   He could not very well say this more emphatically:

I believe that life can be worth living.   I believe this in spite of pain, squalor, cruelty, unhappiness, and death.   I do not believe that it is necessarily worth living, but only that for most people it can be.
I also believe that man, as individual, as group, and collectively as mankind, can achieve a satisfying purpose in existence.   I believe this in spite of frustration, aimlessness, frivolity, boredom, sloth, and failure.   Again I do not believe that a purpose inevitably inheres in the universe or in our own existence, or that mankind is bound to achieve a satisfying purpose, but only that such a purpose can be found.

Mr. Dewey, as I have said, rejects theism, agnosticism and atheism.   He finds the evidence insufficient for the belief in a particular supernatural or superhuman Being.   Nor does he think such a Being morally or religiously indispensable.   But while we can get on, indeed get on better without such a Being, we do need, he thinks, what he terms "natural piety," or "the sense of a connection of man, in the way of both dependence and support, with the enveloping world that the imagination feels is a universe." And we need, especially in a distracted age, a clear and intense conception of "the natural forces and conditions—including man and human association—that promote the growth of the ideal and that further its realization." Atheism and agnosticism, this philosopher believes, lead men to regard the natural environment as indifferent or even hostile to them. Ideals are then "mere rootless ideals, fantasies, utopias," to be realized, if at all, only in defiance of nature and of natural human desires. "Use of the words 'God' or 'divine' to convey the union of the actual and ideal," he hopes, "may protect man from a sense of isolation and from consequent despair or defiance."

Obviously, Mr. Dewey's objection is to ethical atheism. He is well aware that his refusal to give up the word God is likely to be interpreted as endorsing the belief in a divine cosmic Being. His book, *A Common Faith*, although explicit in its denial of theism, has been interpreted as a defense of it. He takes the chance of being thus misunderstood rather than the other chance of being misunderstood to hold that man's ideal endeavors are not sustained by the world in which we live. The word God stands for "those factors in existence that generate and support our idea of good as an end to be striven for." It "denotes the unity of all our ideal ends arousing us to desire and actions." It stands for "the ties binding man to nature that poets have always celebrated."

Here then we have four eminent men who differ as regards the theistic interpretation of the cosmos, but are in essential accord in their conduct allegiance. Theist, atheist, agnostic, and adherent of none of these cosmic views, each is intent upon encouraging active co-operation of man with man, and men with processes of physical nature and the social order, to the end that, individually and collectively, we may attain to a fuller realization of the good life.

A tantalizing phase of the problem grows out of the fact that a person whose chief objection is to ethical atheism may insist that what he is against is cosmic atheism. The most clean-cut example I know of is Upton Sinclair. It was the report that Mr. Sinclair is an atheist, widely circulated during the closing days of his political battle for Governor of California, which is believed by competent observers to have turned the tide against him. Some were honest in spreading the report; but some, I am reliably informed, did it to hold well-paying jobs on venal newspapers. The lie could not have succeeded had the two kinds of atheism been clear in the public mind.

In his book, *What God Means to Me*, published after the campaign was over, Mr. Sinclair declares himself to have been a believer in God since boyhood. But his theism is primarily ethical or social. Had the book been available during the campaign, many would still have voted against its author on theological grounds. To them he could only be a nonbeliever or atheist because he does not believe in their kind of cosmic God.

The impression must not be left that Mr. Sinclair disbelieves in a God of the cosmos, for he expressly states the contrary:

So it is that I believe in a *personal* God: a power operating at the center of this universe, which creates, maintains, and comprehends my personality, and all other personalities, those which were, and those which are, and those which have yet to be; a power which causes my being—otherwise it would not be; which sustains my being —otherwise it would cease; which understands my being—otherwise I should not conform to my pattern, but would become a chaos.

He believes in this personal cosmic God, and he promises to give a scientific proof of his existence. If he does this anywhere I have missed the place. So far as I can discover he never seriously undertakes it. Why should he? For the thing that matters to him is not something outside in the universe, but something inside at the core of his own being. It is a "still small voice in the heart," as he says, "a sense of the worth-whileness of what I am doing," an "impulse to develop our faculties," a freedom from the pessimistic, self-refuting doubt which to give way to "is to be mentally sick, and part of a mentally sick age."

These attitudes are his evidence for God. That is why he can honestly say, "I believe those things about God which make it possible for me to develop my own powers, and thus to serve God better." He can believe that it makes no difference whether you say you *discover* God or *make* God, for the two phrases mean the same thing. The cosmic interpretation given to this inner psychical process or experience seems to him relatively unimportant. "If my materialist friends," he declares, "prefer to say Nature, or Universe; if my philosophical friends prefer Elan Vital with Bergson, or Life Force with Bernard Shaw, or Cosmic Consciousness with Bucke, or Oversoul with Emerson, or First Cause with Plato, or Noumenon with Kant— that is all right with me."

It is all right with him, but it would not be if he took cosmic theism seriously enough. Mr. Sinclair is not that kind of a theist. His theism, as I have said, is primarily ethical and social, and it is from this ethical theism that his cosmical theism, such as it is, derives. How else is one to read what must be a final quotation from his book?

This God whom I preach is in the hearts of human beings, fighting for justice, inside the churches and out—even the rebel groups, many of which reject His name. A world in which men exploit the labor of their fellows, and pile up fortunes which serve no use but the display of material power—such a world presents itself to truly religious people as a world which must be changed. Those who serve God truly in this age serve the ideal of brotherhood; of helping our fellow beings, instead of exploiting their labor, and beating them down and degrading them in order to exploit them more easily.

A good many people are inclined to dismiss this subject as a purely academic one. They are not the people who care what the deeper motives are that move men to action. For it is not a purely academic question. Let us make one more comparison with special reference to practical attitudes. James Weldon Johnson was frankly nontheistic. What was the conduct aspect of his nontheism as set forth in his extraordinary book, *Along This Way?* Arthur Brisbane was theistic in his newspaper column. What did his theism mean when applied to international relations? His Eminence

William Cardinal O'Connell is an ambassador of God on earth. What side did he take in a crucial struggle for child welfare in Massachusetts?

Toward the end of Mr. Johnson's autobiography he makes this statement:

I do not know if there is a personal God; I do not see how I can know and I do not see how my knowing can matter. What does matter, I believe, is how I deal with myself and how I deal with my fellows. I feel that I can practice a conduct toward myself and toward my fellows that will constitute a basis for an adequate religion, a religion that may comprehend spirituality and beauty and serene happiness.

As far as I am able to peer into the inscrutable, I do not see that there is any evidence to refute those scientists and philosophers who hold that the universe is purposeless; that man, instead of being the special care of Divine Providence, is a dependent upon fortuity and his own wits for survival in the midst of blind and insensate forces. But to stop there is to stop short of the vital truth. For mankind and for the individual this state, what though it be accidental and ephemeral, is charged wih meaning. Man's sufferings, his joys, his aspirations, his defeats, are just as real and of as great moment to him as they would be if they were part of a mighty and definite cosmic plan. . . . .

Perhaps it is desirable, even if not strictly necessary, to conclude the chapter with a summarizing statement of its main theme. Viewed with respect to resulting conduct, atheism may have reference to the superhuman or to the supremely human. It may be disbelief in a Cosmic Being at work in the universe and in history, seeing to it that mankind shall not suffer ultimate defeat; or it may be an unconscious or a deliberate disregard of the aspirational side of the human struggle. Harry Emerson Fosdick's doctrine that disbelief in God is a rationalization of the evil in human nature is one of those errors which thrive in language but cannot stand exposure to fact. Truer words than Dr. Fosdick's were spoken by Judge Holley at the funeral service for Clarence Darrow, the most widely known atheist in America:

The heartless call has come, and we must stagger on the best we can alone. In the darkest hours we will look in vain for your loved form, we will listen hopelessly for your devoted, fearless voice. But, though we lay you in the grave and hide you from the sight of man, your brave words will speak for the poor, the oppressed, the captive, and the weak; and your devoted life inspire countless souls to do and dare in the holy cause for which you lived and died.

Are we to say, then, that cosmic atheism has no effect on behavior? No. not that. *All* beliefs have *some* effect on behavior; they make some difference in the conduct of the believer. Beliefs about the cosmos have consequences and they may be very profound. But the point is that only by making sure of the conduct meaning of theism or atheism in a given case is it possible to determine what these consequences are. "Vanity of vanities, all is vanity," we read in Ecclesiastes. This is surely the quintessence of atheism, if there is such a thing; but throughout the poem in which it appears a cosmic God is constantly assumed to exist.

The reason why many people refuse to think of themselves as atheists is not that they are theists, but that they understand atheism to commit men to a way of life of which they strongly disapprove. Their cosmic outlook, if frankly stated, would be atheistical. But this seems to them of purely academic interest compared with a correct appreciation of their ethical and social convictions.

We have found a most striking illustration of this mood in Mr. Dewey. He defends the use of the word God to designate "the natural forces and conditions—including man and human association—that promote the growth of the ideal and that further its realization." Whether we agree with him or not on the desirability of this usage—personally, I do not—we can all join him, all of us but those whose attitude has been described as *ethical* atheism, in aiming to keep alive the temper of mind which he seeks to encourage. We need a sense of community with the environing world and with our fellows. We need to recognize continuity between ideals and actuality. In no other way can we keep idealism healthy and realism sane.

THE PROBLEM OF EVIL

John Laird

Haslett. It has been represented to me, ladies and gentlemen, that our discussions have tended to lack perspective owing to the absence of an initial thesis to be debated *pro* and *con.* I therefore ventured to suggest to some of our symposiasts that today, when we consider the problem of evil, it might be advantageous if I put before you a statement regarding the locus and nature of evil, and I am glad to say that the suggestion found immediate favor. The statement itself is from the pen of my former teacher the late Professor Dixon who was accustomed to use it as the basis of discussion in his seminar, and I have often wondered how it would fare in a more exacting atmosphere. As some of you may know, ladies and gentlemen, Professor Dixon came to this country from Owen's College, Manchester, as a very young man, and found the exigencies of teaching so onerous that he never contributed to the literature of philosophy in a way commensurate with his knowledge and abilities. Since I have been unable to mimeograph sufficient copies, I shall be compelled to read the statement to you.

Miss Gotto. Do be an angel and read it in full. The only problem of evil for me at present is the problem of getting back my breath after all this climbing. This lovely canyon is perfection—all except the approach to it. How you contrive to be so fit I'm sure I don't know. I suppose you take one easy stride to our two. Anyway, the rest of us seem pretty well wilted. There wasn't even a fog to cool us.

Haslett. Dixon's statement is not very short. But perhaps I had better begin. It runs as follows:

"Leibniz divided evils into three classes or kinds, physical, moral, and metaphysical. This threefold classification is probably the best of the simpler divisions of this subject. It divides evil into (1) pain, (2) sin, and (3) finitude. But it tends to be incurably superficial.

(1) "Physical evil cannot be restricted to simple pain. On the contrary, on any ordinary interpretation, it should be understood to include weakness and impotence, the brevity and futility of human life, as well as disease and ill-health. Regarding the last of these, it is clear that the correlation between disease, even grave disease, and actual physical pain, need not be very close. Regarding the former, it is obviously questionable whether the *sense* of evil should properly be reckoned as physical even when it may be said to be due to physical causes. For man's physical littleness and transitoriness seem to be evils, not in themselves, but in comparison with man's aspiration after something greater and more enduring. If men suffer on this account they

From *Morals and Western Religion*, London, 1931, pp. 133-148. Reprinted by permission of the publishers, Edward Arnold & Company.

suffer from oppression of spirit, not of body, and the cause of the oppression would seem to be rather metaphysical (i.e. due to finitude) than, in strictness, physical.

"Again, confusion is almost certain to arise when pain is equated with what is physical. The truth may well be that *all* pain is mental, but even if, in the common-sense way, we reckon as physical all pains that are localized to some region of the body, it seems clear that the worst and most poignant suffering is not physical discomfort or even short-lived physical agony but spiritual wretchedness, over-whelming anxiety, despair, or brooding melancholia. Some of this suffering may be 'moral' and some may not. But it is not, for the most part, 'physical.'

"Indeed, looking to the history of this subject, we might say that physical evil has seldom been regarded as simple animal pain. For the Manicheans, *matter* was evil, because it was physical darkness warring with the light which alone was good and pure. According to the Neo-Platonists, evil was non-being, and our present universe a sort of half-being compounded of reality and of nothingness. Since nothingness, on this theory, was probably regarded as the 'void' which actively prevented completeness and perfection, it is apparent that the void, in this sense, was at least quasi-physical. (Alternatively, it was the principle of finitude and very thoroughly metaphysical). A third view was that evil is the indeterminate, the chaotic, the unlimited, these terms also being interpreted at least quasi-physically. If so, finitude is not an evil; for the finite is precisely what is limited, determinate, and proportionate. There cannot, however, be any equation, or even any profound relation, between the indeterminate and the painful. According to many philosophers, indeed, the *pleasure*-principle was one of the best illustrations of indeterminateness. Pleasures, they thought, were as insatiable as a leaking bucket.

"We might, perhaps, improve the accuracy of Leibniz's division if we distinguished between *sensitive* and moral evil, instead of between *physical* and moral; but we should still find a great many difficulties in his equation of *sin* with moral evil.

(2) "For the Greeks, the overwhelming evil was ignorance—'the lie in the soul'—and this evil seems to be intellectual rather than 'moral'. Manifestly, if the possession of knowledge is one of the greatest of human goods, the absence of such knowledge must, in some sense, be a very great evil. And this view was strongly upheld, though in a way that was held to be 'above' the intellect, in the Christian as well as the Greek tradition, especially among the contemplative orders. For when the characteristics of the blessed life were set in review, and the sensuous trivialities were banished from the idea of heaven, union with God was held to imply the possession and contemplation of true being, while aloofness or separation from God were regarded as alienation from the truth.

"It might be maintained, no doubt, that although possession of the truth is a very great good, the lack of such knowledge is only the *absence* of a good, not the *presence* of a positive evil. If so, our problem is really a problem in the logic of privative terms. We should not say that a stone or a tree suffers from the evil of not being able to see; but if a *man* is blind, or regarded as *deprived* of his birthright, we might well be disposed to regard this deprivation as a real and positive evil. In this case, however, we should have to meet the objection that the evil in the blind man's lot is not, strictly speaking, positive, but instead is comparative. He is distressed at his awkwardness and impotence in comparison with what is normal for mankind. And similarly with other examples. A man who fears he is going mad, or who suspects he is certifiably insane, is, in general, filled with misery and horror. An idiot who is too foolish to appreciate the fact of his foolishness may be perfectly cheerful and contented. . . . .

"In the modern tradition, sin is usually regarded as pertaining, not to ignorance, but to those other departments of the soul that are technically called Feeling and Will. In the former case, sin is regarded as a pollution of the soul, and is opposed to purity. The conception, if it is not frankly magical and superstitious, seems to be fundamentally aesthetic, although the foulness of sin is regarded as much more serious than any mere blot with an ugly look. This aesthetic theory shows a very clear parallelism with what has been already noted concerning ignorance. 'Conviction of sin,' for example, is the sense of pollution or shame, perhaps pathologically oppressive like Lady Macbeth's horror at the stain of blood; but we have always to reckon with the circumstance that the man who is foul in his mind and not at all abashed at his foulness, is a *worse* creature than the man who is ashamed of the pollution within him, just as a cheerful vulgarian is the artist's supreme despair.

"It is not easy to reconcile this aesthetic doctrine of the shamefulness of sin with the current moralistic doctrine that sin is wholly a matter of evil willing, and identical with wicked, selfish or rebellious volition. In this Protestant-Puritan, or, going further back, in this semi-Pelagian tradition, it is assumed that we have a sufficient knowledge of good and evil, and that our wills are 'free'. If, then, we commit a moral wrong, this is a wittingly chosen or 'willed' action, and as such is positive. On this view, therefore, moral evil is always a positive evil. Sin is disobedience to the law of God or of our 'nature' in regard to right and wrong. There may, of course, be all sorts of motives or occasions for such rebelliousness—selfishness, pride, ambition, the deliberate choice of sensuality in preference to what is nobler if more austere. But it is needless, here, to recount those motives and occasions.

"It should be noted, however, that this voluntaristic doctrine of sin is not easy to reconcile with the aesthetic-emotional. No doubt the natural man may do something, by his will, to purge himself of impurity, and he may conceal his impurity from others by abstaining from overt lasciviousness. In the main, however, it seems to be held that we cannot voluntarily alter such conditions. Our sins must be washed by the blood of the Lamb. The taint of sin must be destroyed by divine grace and healing just as our bodies are strengthened and purified, not by taking thought, but by fresh air, the mountains and the sea. The best we can do voluntarily is to put ourselves in the way of receiving these benefits, and to avoid a vitiated or pernicious atmosphere.

(3) "The third type of evil in the Leibnizian classification, i.e. the meta-

physical evil of finitude, obviously states, rather than solves, problems. For it is not self-evident that finitude *as such* is evil at all, and even if it were, further argument would be necessary in order to show that finitude is a *positive* evil.

"Anything that is less than the whole universe is, in some respects, finite, or limited. Therefore, if the universe has parts, or even if it has discernibly different features, each of these parts or features is finite. The 'problem' of evil in the universe, we suspect, must be something much more profound than the simple consideration that there is differentiation within the universe. . . . .

"The answer that is usually given is that there is positive evil in man's finitude because of the contrast between man's *de facto* condition and the heights towards which his spirit aspires. By a necessity of his being, man aspires to something much less paltry and insignificant than his physical forces, and the short fever of his life, permit. His recognition of this contrast is said to be a great and positive evil. Even so, however, it would seem peculiar to aver that man should aspire after the total abolition of his finitude. Even the mystics have seldom been so extreme, although the mantle of 'union' hides much in their thought. It seems better to conclude that what man should aspire after would not be evil and would still be finitude, although such ideals would be immensely greater and more powerful than the obvious ends suggested by his physical insignificance.

"Man's finitude is an evil, if it is an evil at all, only because there is so great a contrast between his little life and the greatness at which he aims. Ultimately the problem is that of the place and potency of man's spirit in the cosmos. If the Christian religion is true, man could and can strive after a condition which, while it is still a condition of finitude, is immeasurably less insignificant than his present state, physically and superficially regarded. Helplessness, aimlessness, perhaps even temporal finitude should be swallowed up and blotted out."

Fixby. This *précis* of Dixon's supplies an excellent map of the whereabouts of evil, and has considerable cartographical merits, but I have scanned it in vain for any adequate explanation of the *problem* of evil.

What *is* the alleged "problem"? Take suffering, for instance. Is the "problem" that there should be *any* suffering at all? Or *so much* suffering? Or certain *kinds* of suffering, such as the agonies of child-birth or of malignant cancer? Or is it the problem of *purposeless* suffering, suffering that leads to nothing good? Again, is it *so much* purposeless sufferings? Or such and such a *kind* of purposeless suffering? . . . .

I submit with some confidence that there is, properly speaking, no problem for the *moralist*. There is simply the plain recognition of a plain task. Evil exists and we should try to overcome it so far as we may. That is the duty of our situation, and it is not in any respect a problematic duty. It is a perfectly definite imperative. If the evil is suffering, we have to try to alleviate the suffering, and, where possible, destroy the roots of it—unless such suffering is good (like the suffering of a tender conscience); or unless certain kinds of suffering, although not positive goods, are also not positive evils (for example, the sharp short pains of certain physical combats and of many games); or unless it is clear that the suffering is a means to a greater good without which the greater good would not be what it is. In all this there is no problem. There is only a duty.

The conception of sin, I am told, is full of problems. I admit it; but I do not see that these problems (which are, for the most part, problems of analysis) entitle us to speak of *the* problem of evil. Spiritual pride, vulgar Philistinism, selfish grabbing ought (I am told) to be fought. I shall let it go at that. The conclusion is simply that the moral man ought to guard against these temptations.

I agree that there is a relevant difference between suffering and sin. Sin is more complicated than suffering. The existence of suffering is just a fact—as much a fact as that grass is green. And even when the suffering is intentionally inflicted, the ethics of the matter is comparatively simple. Cruelty is bad, and pain should not be intentionally inflicted except when it is reasonably considered a means to a good end. The existence of sin, on the other hand, is something more than a simple fact. It is a moral fact, and the vileness of leading others into temptation is also more complicated than the mere hurting of them. We usually hold that it is never a duty to incite and encourage anyone to *sin* in order that a greater good may arise—and this although some men tell us that if they had not sinned deeply they would never have loved greatly.

I might have to admit also that heredity predispositions to certain vices (if such hereditary predispositions exist) and, generally speaking, "original sin" in the sense of some proneness to evil on the part of a nature not inherently and irremediably corrupt, raises difficult and characteristically moral problems concerning personal responsibility. But I deny that these intricate analytical problems have any good title to be called *the* problem of evil.

Similarly of "metaphysical" evil. Here Dixon himself was plainly uneasy but not uneasy enough. He saw that the fact of finitude is not a problem, and that if it were a problem it would not be an evil. He also saw that the "problem" of non-being is only a pseudo-problem. It is manufactured *ex nihilo*, and is simply a problem about *nothing*. And nothing is not an evil. Man's littleness and impotence, again, stand confessed. But why this grouch about a problem? And if man feels he has something great and deathless within him—well, I think we all find it hard to consider this opinion either, on the one hand, nonsensical, or, on the other hand, wholly accurate.

In short, there are ever so many problems *about* evil, and there are several problems connected with the analysis of evil, but there is not, in any significant sense, a "problem of evil."

Miss Gotto. A! la, la! I do admire Mr. Fixby's ingenuous moralism, when all the time he is trailing his coat with a flourish. It is really Dr. Bowie he is going for. For we all know perfectly well that evil is a theological problem and not an ethical problem at all.

Munro. Would Miss Gotto be good enough to explain why she is so certain on the point?

Miss Gotto. Of course, my dear Watson. The "problem" of evil concerns the moral government of the universe. Moral creatures have to struggle against suffering, temptation, and galling limitation. As Mr. Fixby has told us, playing to perfection his rôle of the apostle of the obvious, there is nothing problematical here for the moralist. The problem of evil is why the struggle should be required. Why should there be this waste and misery and failure if the universe is righteously ordered? Would it not be a better universe if all human spirits were as the angels in heaven—and a little more secure, since some of the angels fell? In short, why does a good God cause, or even permit, evil to occur? And by this I mean *any* evil, even the least.

Munro. So the smallest twinge of rheumatism lets loose an insoluble problem?

Miss Gotto. Why shouldn't it? You are trying to say that the matter can't be quite so simple as that. I'm telling you that it has precisely that utter simplicity. The existence of *any* evil does reveal an insoluble problem for theism, neatly, fully, and with the utmost precision.

Munro. And why is this "obvious" problem obviously insoluble?

Miss Gotto. As if you didn't know! There is no problem at all unless the universe is righteous altogether, or, in theological language, unless God is omnipotent. If the universe is partly righteous and partly not, the "problem" disappears. There are then two or more opposed forces—surely nothing so very out of the way. But how can the universe be righteous *altogether*, and also contain the least scintilla of genuine evil? Otherwise put, how, said she, if God be perfect and also omnipotent, can He allow any evil to occur and still retain any vestiges of a moral character? Being omniscient, He also is perfectly foreseeing. He knows each future event as he counts the sands of the sea—a process tedious to us, but mere play to Him. Therefore He can't plead that he meant well, but that things somehow came unstuck. In the alternative, if He is a "limited" deity, either in respect of knowledge, or power, or any other attribute, the alleged problem disappears. He has to struggle, like any other finite and moral creature, with obstacles that hamper Him and over which He has but partial control.

Munro. Why, then, speak of an *insoluble* problem? You seem to be saying that evil is not a theological problem, but a theological *impossibility*. You should therefore infer that it is as little of a theological problem as of a moral problem. There is no problem about an impossibility.

THE SICK SOUL

William James

THERE ARE PEOPLE FOR whom evil means only a maladjustment with *things*, a wrong correspondence of one's life with the environment. Such evil as this is curable, in principle at least, upon the natural plane, for merely by modifying either the self or the things, or both at once, the two terms may be made to fit, and all go merry as a marriage bell again. But there are others for whom evil is no mere relation of the subject to particular outer things, but something more radical and general, a wrongness or vice in his essential nature, which no alteration of the environment, or any superficial rearrangement of the inner self, can cure, and which requires a supernatural remedy. On the whole, the Latin races have leaned more towards the former way of looking upon evil, as made up of ills and sins in the plural, removable in detail; while the Germanic races have tended rather to think of Sin in the singular, and with a capital S, as of something ineradicably ingrained in our natural subjectivity, and never to be removed by any superficial piecemeal operations. These comparisons of races are always open to exception, but undoubtedly the northern tone in religion has inclined to the more intimately pessimistic persuasion, and this way of feeling, being the more extreme, we shall find by far the more instructive for our study.

Recent psychology has found great use for the word "threshold" as a symbolic designation for the point at which one state of mind passes into another. Thus we speak of the threshold of a man's consciousness in general, to indicate the amount of noise, pressure, or other outer stimulus which it takes to arouse his attention at all. One with a high threshold will doze through an amount of racket by which one with a low threshold would be immediately waked. Similarly, when one is sensitive to small differences in any order of sensation, we say he has a low "difference-threshold"—his mind easily steps over it into the consciousness of the differences in question. And just so we might speak of a "pain-threshold," a "fear-threshold," a "misery-threshold," and find it quickly overpassed by the consciousness of some individuals, but lying too high in others to be often reached by their consciousness. The sanguine and healthy-minded live habitually on the sunny side of their misery-line, the depressed and melancholy live beyond it, in darkness and apprehension. There are men who seem to have started in life with a bottle or two of champagne inscribed to their credit; whilst others seem to have been born close to the pain-threshold, which the slightest irritants fatally send them over.

Does it not appear as if one who lived more habitually on one side of the pain-threshold might need a different sort of religion from one who habit-

From *The Varieties of Religious Experience*, New York, 1917, pp. 131-141. Reprinted by permission of the publishers, Longmans, Green & Company.

ually lived on the other? This question, of the relativity of the different types of religion to different types of need, arises naturally at this point, and will become a serious problem ere we have done. But before we confront it in general terms, we must address ourselves to the unpleasant task of hearing what the sick souls, as we may call them in contrast to the healthy-minded, have to say of the secrets of their prison-house, their own peculiar form of consciousness. Let us then resolutely turn our backs on the once-born and their sky-blue optimistic gospel; let us not simply cry out, in spite of all appearances, "Hurrah for the Universe!—God's in his Heaven, all's right with the world." Let us see rather whether pity, pain, and fear, and the sentiment of human helplessness may not open a profounder view and put into our hands a more complicated key to the meaning of the situation.

To begin with, how *can* things so insecure as the successful experiences of this world afford a stable anchorage? A chain is no stronger than its weakest link, and life is after all a chain. In the healthiest and most prosperous existence, how many links of illness, danger, and disaster are always interposed? Unsuspectedly from the bottom of every fountain of pleasure, as the old poet said, something bitter rises up: a touch of nausea, a falling dead of the delight, a whiff of melancholy, things that sound a knell, for fugitive as they may be, they bring a feeling of coming from a deeper region and often have an appalling convincingness. The buzz of life ceases at their touch as a piano-string stops sounding when the damper falls upon it.

Of course the music can commence again; and again and again, at intervals. But with this the healthy-minded consciousness is left with in irremediable sense of precariousness. It is a bell with a crack; it draws its breath on sufferance and by an accident.

Even if we suppose a man so packed with healthy-mindedness as never to have experienced in his own person any of these sobering intervals, still, if he is a reflecting being, he must generalize and class his own lot with that of others; and, doing so, he must see that his escape is just a lucky chance and no essential difference. He might just as well have been born to an entirely different fortune. And then indeed the hollow security! What kind of a frame of things is it of which the best you can say is, "Thank God, it has let me off clear this time!" Is not its blessedness a fragile fiction? Is not your joy in it a very vulgar glee, not much unlike the snicker of any rogue at his success? If indeed it were all success, even on such terms as that! But take the happiest man, the one most envied by the world, and in nine cases out of ten his inmost consciousness is one of failure. Either his ideals in the line of his achievements are pitched far higher than the achievements themselves, or else he has secret ideals of which the world knows nothing, and in regard to which he inwardly knows himself to be found wanting.

When such a conquering optimist as Goethe can express himself in this wise, how must it be with less successful men?

I will say nothing, writes Goethe in 1824, against the course of my existence. But at bottom it has been nothing but pain and burden, and I can affirm that during the whole of my 75 years, I have not had four weeks of genuine well-being. It is but the perpetual rolling of a rock that must be raised up again forever.

What single-handed man was ever on the whole as successful as Luther? yet when he had grown old, he looked back on his life as if it were an absolute failure.

I am utterly weary of life. I pray the Lord will come forthwith and carry me hence. Let him come, above all, with his last Judgment: I will stretch out my neck, the thunder will burst forth, and I shall be at rest. . . . .

The Electress Dowager, one day when Luther was dining with her, said to him: "Doctor, I wish you may live forty years to come." "Madam," replied he, "rather than live forty years more, I would give up my chance of Paradise."

Failure, then, failure! so the world stamps us at every turn. We strew it with our blunders, our misdeeds, our lost opportunities, with all the memorials of our inadequacy to our vocation. And with what a damning emphasis does it then blot us out! No easy fine, no mere apology or formal expiation, will satisfy the world's demands, but every pound of flesh exacted is soaked with all its blood. The subtlest forms of suffering known to man are connected with the poisonous humiliations incidental to these results.

And they are pivotal human experiences. A process so ubiquitous and everlasting is evidently an integral part of life. "There is indeed one element in human destiny," Robert Louis Stevenson writes, "that not blindness itself can controvert. Whatever else we are intended to do, we are not intended to succeed; failure is the fate allotted." And our nature being thus rooted in failure, is it any wonder that theologians should have held it to be essential, and thought that only through the personal experience of humiliation which it engenders the deeper sense of life's significance is reached?

But this is only the first stage of the world-sickedness. Make the human being's sensitiveness a little greater, carry him a little farther over the misery-threshold, and the good quality of the successful moments themselves when they occur is spoiled and vitiated. All natural goods perish. Riches take wings; fame is a breath; love is a cheat; youth and health and pleasure vanish. Can things whose end is always dust and disappointment be the real goods which our souls require? Back of everything is the great spectre of universal death, the all-encompassing blackness:

What profit hath a man of all his labour which he taketh under the Sun? I looked on all the works that my hands had wrought, and behold, all was vanity and vexation of spirit. For that which befalleth the sons of men befalleth beasts; as the one dieth, so dieth the other; all are of the dust, and all turn to dust again. . . . . The dead know not anything, neither have they any more a reward; for the memory of them is forgotten. Also their love and their hatred and their envy is now perished; neither have they any more a portion for ever in anything that is done under the Sun. . . . . Truly the light is sweet, and a pleasant thing it is for the eyes to behold the Sun: but if a man live many years and rejoice in them all, yet let him remember the days of darkness; for they shall be many.

In short, life and its negation are beaten up inextricably together. But if the life be good, the negation of it must be bad. Yet the two are equally essential facts of existence; and all natural happiness thus seems infected with a contradiction. The breath of the sepulchre surrounds it.

To a mind attentive to this state of things and rightly subject to the joy-destroying chill which such a contemplation engenders, the only relief that healthy-mindedness can give is by saying: "Stuff and nonsense, get out into the open air!" or "Cheer up, old fellow, you'll be all right ere long, if you will only drop your morbidness!" But in all seriousness, can such bald animal talk as that be treated as a rational answer? To ascribe religious value to mere happy-go-lucky contentment with one's brief chance at natural good is but the very consecration of forgetfulness and superficiality. Our troubles lie indeed too deep for *that* cure. The fact that we *can* die, that we *can* be ill at all, is what perplexes us; the fact that we now for a moment live and are well is irrelevant to that perplexity. We need a life not correlated with death, a health not liable to illness, a kind of good that will not perish, a good in fact that flies beyond the Goods of nature.

It all depends on how sensitive the soul may become to discords. "The trouble with me is that I believe too much in common happiness and goodness," said a friend of mine whose consciousness was of this sort, "and nothing can console me for their transiency. I am appalled and disconcerted at its being possible." And so with most of us: a little cooling down of animal excitability and instinct, a little loss of animal toughness, a little irritable weakness and descent of the pain-threshold, will bring the worm at the core of all our usual springs of delight into full view, and turn us into melancholy metaphysicians. The pride of life and glory of the world will shrivel. It is after all but the standing quarrel of hot youth and hoary eld. Old age has the last word: the purely naturalistic look at life, however enthusiastically it may begin, is sure to end in sadness.

This sadness lies at the heart of every merely positivistic, agnostic, or naturalistic scheme of philosophy. Let sanguine healthy-mindedness do its best with its strange power of living in the moment and ignoring and forgetting, still the evil background is really there to be thought of, and the skull will grin in at the banquet. In the practical life of the individual, we know how this whole gloom or glee about any present fact depends on the remoter schemes and hopes with which it stands related. Its significance and framing give it the chief part of its value. Let it be known to lead nowhere, and however agreeable it may be in its immediacy, its glow and gilding vanish. The old man, sick with an insidious internal disease, may laugh and quaff his wine at first as well as ever, but he knows his fate now, for the doctors have revealed it; and the knowledge knocks the satisfaction out of all these functions. They are partners of death and the worm is their brother, and they turn to a mere flatness.

The lustre of the present hour is always borrowed from the background of possibilities it goes with. Let our common experiences be enveloped in an eternal moral order; let our suffering have an immortal significance;

let Heaven smile upon the earth, and deities pay their visits; let faith and hope be the atmosphere which man breathes in; and his days pass by with zest; they stir with prospects, they thrill with remoter values. Place round them on the contrary the curdling cold and gloom and absence of all permanent meaning which for pure naturalism and the popular science evolutionism of our time are all that is visible ultimately, and the thrill stops short, or turns rather to an anxious trembling.

For naturalism, fed on recent cosmological speculations, mankind is in a position similar to that of a set of people living on a frozen lake, surrounded by cliffs over which there is no escape, yet knowing that little by little the ice is melting, and the inevitable day drawing near when the last film of it will disappear, and to be drowned ignominiously will be the human creature's portion. The merrier the skating, the warmer and more sparkling the sun by day, and the ruddier the bonfires at night, the more poignant the sadness with which one must take in the meaning of the total situation.

The early Greeks are continually held up to us in literary works as models of the healthy-minded joyousness which the religion of nature may engender. There was indeed much joyousness among the Greeks—Homer's flow of enthusiasm for most things that the sun shines upon is steady. But even in Homer the reflective passages are cheerless, and the moment the Greeks grew systematically pensive and thought of ultimates, they became unmitigated pessimists. The jealousy of the gods, the nemesis that follows too much happiness, the all-encompassing death, fate's dark opacity, the ultimate and unintelligible cruelty, were the fixed background of their imagination. The beautiful joyousness of their polytheism is only a poetic modern fiction. They knew no joys comparable in quality of preciousness to those which we shall erelong see that Brahmans, Buddhists, Christians, Mohammedans, twice-born people whose religion is non-naturalistic, get from their several creeds of mysticism and renunciation.

Stoic insensibility and Epicurean resignation were the farthest advance which the Greek mind made in that direction. The Epicurean said: "Seek not to be happy, but rather to escape unhappiness; strong happiness is always linked with pain; therefore hug the safe shore, and do not tempt the deeper raptures. Avoid disappointment by expecting little, and by aiming low; and above all do not fret." The Stoic said: "The only genuine good that life can yield a man is the free possession of his own soul; all other goods are lies." Each of these philosophies is in its degree a philosophy of despair in nature's boons. Trustful self-abandonment to the joys that freely offer has entirely departed from both Epicurean and Stoic; and what each proposes is a way of rescue from the resultant dust-and-ashes state of mind. The Epicurean still awaits results from economy of indulgence and damping of desire. The Stoic hopes for no results, and gives up natural good altogether. There is dignity in both these forms of resignation. They represent distinct stages in the sobering process which man's primitive intoxication with sense-happiness is sure to undergo. In the one the hot blood has grown cool, in the other it has become quite cold; and although I have spoken of them in the past tense, as if they were merely historic, yet Stoicism and Epicureanism will probably be to all time typical attitudes, marking a certain definite stage accomplished in the evolution of the world-sick soul. They mark the conclusion of what we call the once-born period, and represent the highest flights of what twice-born religion would call the purely natural man—Epicureanism, which can only by great courtesy be called a religion, showing his refinement, and Stoicism exhibiting his moral will. They leave the world in the shape of an unreconciled contradiction, and seek no higher unity. Compared with the complex ecstasies which the supernaturally regenerated Christian may enjoy, or the oriental pantheist indulge in, their receipts for equanimity are expedients which seem almost crude in their simplicity.

THE RESULTANT IDEA OF GOD

Edgar Sheffield Brightman

GOD IS A CONSCIOUS Person of perfect good will. He is the source of all value and so is worthy of worship and devotion. He is the creator of all other persons and gives them the power of free choice. Therefore his purpose controls the outcome of the universe. His purpose and his nature must be inferred from the way in which experience reveals them, namely, as being gradually attained through effort, difficulty, and suffering. Hence there is in God's very nature something which makes the effort and pain of life necessary. There is within him, in addition to his reason and his active creative will, a passive element which enters into every one of his conscious states, as sensation, instinct, and impulse enter into ours, and constitutes a problem for him. This element we call The Given. The evils of life and the delays in the attainment of value, in so far as they come from God and not from human freedom, are thus due to his nature, yet not wholly to his deliberate choice. His will and reason acting on The Given produce the world and achieve value in it. . . . .

GOD AND HUMAN SUFFERING

The Given is to be regarded as of the nature of consciousness. The arguments for idealism make the supposition of a nonmental or extramental content or matter unreasonable. Qualitative dualism raises more problems than it solves. Furthermore, The Given must be within the divine consciousness and not external to it; for otherwise it does not explain why God has so much genuine difficulty in expressing his ideal purposes, combined with so much control and achievement. If The Given is external to God, then either he created it or he did not. If he created it, one needs something within the divine nature to explain why he should create that sort of thing. If he did not create it, the presence of two ultimate powers in the universe —God and The Given—raises the problem of their interrelation and engenders many of the difficulties to which other forms of dualism are subject. This Given, then, is a limitation within the divine nature, a problem for the divine will and reason additional to that which is constituted by the existence of finite selves who are other than God. It may be conceived as a conscious datum or perception, analogous to human sense experience, yet not produced by any stimulus or cause external to God. Just as human sense data create for men an *unendliche Aufgabe*, so The Given is the source of an eternal problem and task for God. It is irrational, not in the sense of containing logical contradictions or immoral purposes, but in the sense of being given to reason as a datum and not derived from rational premises or

---

From *The Problem of God*, New York, 1930, pp. 113, 182-189. Reprinted by permission of the publishers, Abingdon-Cokesbury Press.

purposes. In itself it cannot be understood; yet an understanding use may be made of it, and through the conquest and shaping of it meaning may be achieved. Our hypothesis is that God can make an increasingly better conquest of it throughout eternity without ever wholly eliminating it. The divine perfection, then, is an infinite series of perfectings. Perfection means perfectibility. . . . .

If there is such a Given within God, it would not only explain why the ineffably dignified Person should be moved to activity, but it would also explain, or at least be a step toward the explanation of the slow and painful methods of evolution and the miseries and accidents of human life. The Given would take over many of the functions of matter, potentiality, the devil, and what the Germans call "the irrational." Yet there would be no dualism either of stuff or of ultimate principle in the universe; there would be only a dualism of process within the Supreme Person. There would be no sacrifice of the unity of divine personality and so no division of purpose within the divine will. The creation of the world would be no more than certain phases of the divine activity in controlling and shaping The Given by rational law. The so-called "mistakes" of evolution would be due to its recalcitrance. There would be a definite surrender of the omnipotence of the divine will and probably of omniscience, at least as far as foreknowledge is concerned. God would remain personal, ethical, and rational, but the temporal process would be more significant for him than it was on the older view. God would not dwell in an eternal separateness from the world, but would enter more intimately into the ongoing of things. . . . .

It may be urged that our hypothesis renders the goal of the universe precarious and irrational, and it must be granted that The Given introduces a factor of hazard and uncertainty about details. Yet it would in no way imperil the divine ideals and purposes; it would cause tactical difficulties, not difficulties in major strategy. God will always know every possible contingency and nothing could catch him unprepared. If God be James' cosmic chess-player, he can always make the move in any given situation which will lead to the victory of his cause. But any view of the experienced world must take full account of the disturbing empirical facts; our hypothesis suggests the real possibility of the achievement of divine meaning and purpose through just the kind of empirical order that we have, although it does assert that that order is the best imaginable. The degree of irrationality which is inevitable if The Given be admitted is no fundamental incoherence in the cosmic purpose but is simply the acknowledgment that that purpose must deal with brute facts which it has no choice but to accept and use. . . . .

Again, it may be asked whether this finite God has not suffered so great a loss in dignity as no longer to be worthy of worship. If a being is to be worshiped, he must be of transcendent value and so must be capable of eliciting the deepest feelings of loyalty and reverence. A feeble or helpless being might be loved or pitied but could not be worshiped. Does the attempt to bring the idea of God nearer to experience really eventuate in removing it from an adequate relation to the experience of worship? I do not see why this should occur. It is not at all evident that the worshipful attitude is contingent on any belief in omnipotence whatever. If the worshiper confronts a being who is at once the supreme good and the supreme power in the universe, and if that being in the long run can find a meaning in every situation, a good beyond every evil, a value for every phase of The Given, then the worshiper has all that his experience could justify him in hoping for, even if he has to grant that his God is not omnipotent. In no case can the worshiper demand a God according to his heart's desire.....

It may further be urged that this hypothesis is an evasion rather than a solution. It may be said that the problem occasioned by the presence of Given factors in human experience receives only a mock solution from the hypothesis of the Given in God. The problem is simply repeated in God, the objector may urge. But it may be replied that the status of The Given in man is that of an indefinite plurality of partially solved or unsolved problems which must remain thus incoherent unless there is in the universe a being capable in principle of facing and coping with every Given moment and of creating value out of all material, however unpromising it may be. Otherwise there is no reasonable object of worship. . . . .

As we have said, any empirical philosophy of religion must recognize both the divine dignity and human suffering. It must conserve the divine dignity, for if the object of worship were on a level with the suffering worshiper, so that God shared but did not solve the problems of human suffering, such a God would be neither worthy of worship nor capable of saving the worshiper. On the other hand, human suffering must be genuinely shared and explained by the divine life. If God transcended but did not share human suffering, his relation to human experience would be so remote as to be in question. His function as present comforter can be fulfilled only if he both confronts and controls the conditions which engender the need of comfort. The conception of a God limited by The Given within his own nature, yet wresting meaning from it by the achievements of his rational will, seems to account more adequately than other ideas of God for the paradoxical assertion of religious experience that its object is both a Mighty God and a Suffering Servant. It places the Cross in the eternal nature of God. . . . .

THE TRAGIC FALLACY

Joseph Wood Krutch

TRAGEDY, SAID ARISTOTLE, is the "imitation of noble actions," and though it is some twenty-five hundred years since the dictum was uttered there is only one respect in which we are inclined to modify it. To us "imitation" seems a rather naïve word to apply to that process by which observation is turned into art, and we seek one which would define or at least imply the nature of that interposition of the personality of the artist between the object and the beholder which constitutes his function and by means of which he transmits a modified version, rather than a mere imitation, of the thing which he has contemplated. . . . .

Tragedy is not, then, as Aristotle said, the *imitation* of noble actions, for, indeed, no one knows what a *noble* action is or whether or not such a thing as nobility exists in nature apart from the mind of man. Certainly the action of Achilles in dragging the dead body of Hector around the walls of Troy and under the eyes of Andromache, who had begged to be allowed to give it decent burial, is not to us a noble action, though it was such to Homer, who made it the subject of a noble passage in a noble poem. Certainly, too, the same action might conceivably be made the subject of a tragedy and the subject of a farce, depending upon the way in which it was treated; so that to say that tragedy is the *imitation* of a *noble* action is to be guilty of assuming, first, that art and photography are the same, and, second, that there may be something inherently noble in an act as distinguished from the motives which prompted it or from the point of view from which it is regarded.

And yet, nevertheless, the idea of nobility is inseparable from the idea of tragedy, which cannot exist without it. If tragedy is not the imitation or even the modified representation of noble actions it is certainly a representation of actions *considered* as noble, and herein lies its essential nature, since no man can conceive it unless he is capable of believing in the greatness and importance of man. Its action is usually, if not always, calamitous, because it is only in calamity that the human spirit has the opportunity to reveal itself triumphant over the outward universe which fails to conquer it; but this calamity in tragedy is only a means to an end and the essential thing which distinguishes real tragedy from those distressing modern works sometimes called by its name is the fact that it is in the former alone that the artist has found himself capable of considering and of making us consider that his people and his actions have that amplitude and importance which make them noble. Tragedy arises then when, as in Periclean Greece or Elizabethan England, a people fully aware of the calamities of life is never-

From *The Modern Temper*, New York, 1929, pp. 120-136. Copyright, 1929, by Harcourt, Brace & Company, Inc. Reprinted by permission of the publishers.

theless serenely confident of the greatness of man, whose mighty passions and supreme fortitude are revealed when one of these calamities overtakes him.

To those who mistakenly think of it as something gloomy or depressing, who are incapable of recognizing the elation which its celebration of human greatness inspires, and who, therefore, confuse it with things merely miserable or pathetic, it must be a paradox that the happiest, most vigorous, and most confident ages which the world has ever known—the Periclean and the Elizabethan—should be exactly those which created and which most relished the mightiest tragedies; but the paradox is, of course, resolved by the fact that tragedy is essentially an expression, not of despair, but of the triumph over despair and of confidence in the value of human life. . . . .

Comedy laughs the minor mishaps of its characters away; drama solves all the difficulties which it allows to arise; and melodrama, separating good from evil by simple lines, distributes its rewards and punishments in accordance with the principles of a naïve justice which satisfies the simple souls of its audience, which are neither philosophical enough to question its primitive ethics nor critical enough to object to the way in which its neat events violate the laws of probability. Tragedy, the greatest and the most difficult of the arts, can adopt none of these methods; and yet it must reach its own happy end in its own way. Though its conclusion must be, by its premise, outwardly calamitous, though it must speak to those who know that the good man is cut off and that the fairest things are the first to perish, yet it must leave them, as *Othello* does, content that this is so. We must be and we are glad that Juliet dies and glad that Lear is turned out into the storm.

Milton set out, he said, to justify the ways of God to man, and his phrase, if it be interpreted broadly enough, may be taken as describing the function of all art, which must, in some way or other, make the life which it seems to represent satisfactory to those who see its reflection in the magic mirror, and it must gratify or at least reconcile the desires of the beholder, not necessarily, as the naïver exponents of Freudian psychology maintain, by gratifying individual and often eccentric wishes, but at least by satisfying the universally human desire to find in the world some justice, some meaning, or, at the very least, some recognizable order. Hence it is that every real tragedy, however tremendous it may be, is an affirmation of faith in life, a declaration that even if God is not in his Heaven, then at least Man is in his world.

We accept gladly the outward defeats which it describes for the sake of the inward victories which it reveals. Juliet died, but not before she had shown how great and resplendent a thing love could be; Othello plunged the dagger into his own breast, but not before he had revealed that greatness of soul which makes his death seem unimportant. Had he died in the instant when he struck the blow, had he perished still believing that the world was as completely black as he saw it before the innocence of Desdemona was revealed to him, then, for him at least, the world would have been merely damnable, but Shakespeare kept him alive long enough to allow him to learn his error and hence to die, not in despair, but in the full acceptance of the tragic reconciliation to life. Perhaps it would be pleasanter if men could believe what the child is taught—that the good are happy and that things turn out as they should—but it is far more important to be able to believe, as Shakespeare did, that however much things in the outward world may go awry, man has, nevertheless, splendors of his own and that, in a word, Love and Honor and Glory are not words but realities.

Thus for the great ages tragedy is not an expression of despair but the means by which they saved themselves from it. It is a profession of faith, and a sort of religion; a way of looking at life by virtue of which it is robbed of its pain. The sturdy soul of the tragic author seizes upon suffering and uses it only as a means by which joy may be wrung out of existence, but it is not to be forgotten that he is enabled to do so only because of his belief in the greatness of human nature and because, though he has lost the child's faith in life, he has not lost his far more important faith in human nature. A tragic writer does not have to believe in God, but he must believe in man. . . . .

Let us compare a modern "tragedy" with one of the great works of a happy age, not in order to judge of their relative technical merits but in order to determine to what extent the former deserves its name by achieving a tragic solution capable of purging the soul or of reconciling the emotions to the life which it pictures. And in order to make the comparison as fruitful as possible let us choose *Hamlet* on the one hand and on the other a play like *Ghosts* which was not only written by perhaps the most powerful as well as the most typical of modern writers but which is, in addition, the one of his works which seems most nearly to escape that triviality which cannot be entirely escaped by anyone who feels, as all contemporary minds do, that man is relatively trivial.

In *Hamlet* a prince ("in understanding, how like a god!") has thrust upon him from the unseen world a duty to redress a wrong which concerns not merely him, his mother, and his uncle, but the moral order of the universe. Erasing all trivial fond records from his mind, abandoning at once both his studies and his romance because it has been his good fortune to be called upon to take part in an action of cosmic importance, he plunges (at first) not into action but into thought, weighing the claims which are made upon him and contemplating the grandiose complexities of the universe. And when the time comes at last for him to die he dies, not as a failure, but as a success. Not only has the universe regained the balance which had been upset by what *seemed* the monstrous crime of the guilty pair ("there is nothing either good nor ill but thinking makes it so,") but in the process by which that readjustment is made a mighty mind has been given the opportunity, first to contemplate the magnificent scheme of which it is a part, and then to demonstrate the greatness of its spirit by playing a rôle in the grand style which it called for. We do not need to despair in *such* a world if it has *such* creatures in it.

Turn now to *Ghosts*—look upon this picture and upon that. A young man has inherited syphilis from his father. Struck by a to him mysterious malady he returns to his northern village, learns the hopeless truth about himself, and persuades his mother to poison him. The incidents prove, perhaps, that pastors should not endeavor to keep a husband and wife together unless they know what they are doing. But what a world is this in which a great writer can deduce nothing more than that from his greatest work and how are we to be purged or reconciled when we see it acted? Not only is the failure utter, but it is trivial and meaningless as well.

Yet the journey from Elsinore to Skien is precisely the journey which the human spirit has made, exchanging in the process princes for invalids and gods for disease. We say, as Ibsen would say, that the problems of Oswald Alving are more "relevant" to our life than the problems of Hamlet, that the play in which he appears is more "real" than the other more glamorous one, but it is exactly because we find it so that we are condemned. We can believe in Oswald but we cannot believe in Hamlet, and a light has gone out in the universe. Shakespeare justifies the ways of God to man, but in Ibsen there is no such happy end and with him tragedy, so called, has become merely an expression of our despair at finding that such justification is no longer possible. . . . .

True tragedy capable of performing its function and of purging the soul by reconciling man to his woes can exist only by virtue of a certain pathetic fallacy far more inclusive than that to which the name is commonly given. The romantics, feeble descendants of the tragic writers to whom they are linked by their effort to see life and nature in grandiose terms, loved to imagine that the sea or the sky had a way of according itself with their moods, of storming when they stormed and smiling when they smiled. But the tragic spirit sustains itself by an assumption much more far-reaching and no more justified. Man as it sees him lives in a world which he may not dominate but which is always aware of him. Occupying the exact center of a universe which would have no meaning except for him and being so little below the angels that, if he believes in God, he has no hesitation in imagining Him formed as he is formed and crowned with a crown like that which he or one of his fellows wears, he assumes that each of his acts reverberates through the universe. His passions are important to him because he believes them important throughout all times and all space; the very fact that he can sin (no modern can) means that this universe is watching his acts; and though he may perish, a God leans out from infinity to strike him down. And it is exactly because an Ibsen cannot think of man in any such terms as these that his persons have so shrunk and that his "tragedy" has lost that power which real tragedy always has of making that infinitely ambitious creature called man content to accept his misery if only he can be made to feel great enough and important enough. An Oswald is not a Hamlet chiefly because he has lost that tie with the natural and supernatural world which the latter had. No ghost will leave the other world to warn or encourage him, there is no virtue and no vice which he can possibly have which can be really important, and when he dies neither his death nor the manner of it will be, outside the circle of two or three people as unnecessary as himself, any more important than that of a rat behind the arras.

Perhaps we may dub the illusion upon which the tragic spirit is nourished the Tragic, as opposed to the Pathetic, Fallacy, but fallacy though it is, upon its existence depends not merely the writing of tragedy but the existence of that religious feeling of which tragedy is an expression and by means of which a people aware of the dissonances of life manages nevertheless to hear them as harmony. Without it neither man nor his passions can seem great enough or important enough to justify the sufferings which they entail, and literature, expressing the mood of a people, begins to despair where once it had exulted. Like the belief in love and like most of the other mighty illusions by means of which human life has been given a value, the Tragic Fallacy depends ultimately upon the assumption which man so readily makes that something outside his own being, some "spirit not himself"—be it God, Nature, or that still vaguer thing called a Moral Order—joins him in the emphasis which he places upon this or that and confirms him in his feeling that his passions and his opinions are important. When his instinctive faith in that correspondence between the outer and the inner world fades, his grasp upon the faith that sustained him fades also, and Love or Tragedy or what not ceases to be the reality which it was because he is never strong enough in his own insignificant self to stand alone in a universe which snubs him with its indifference.

BEYOND TRAGEDY

James McBride Dabbs

I SHALL ATTEMPT in this essay to compare, especially as to emotional effect, the biography of Jesus with literary tragedy, and to indicate the significance of such a reading of the story. Why did I not write it before? There are several reasons. Though I approached the story of Jesus as I was accustomed to approach all stories, all poetry, as the possible expression of my own experience, I found it at that time less expressive than I had previously found, each in his turn, Wordsworth, Homer, and the great tragic writers, Aeschylus, Sophocles, Euripides, and Shakespeare. I seemed to find more of my life in poetry than in the life of Jesus. This was because I brought to the poets a sufficient experience—to Wordsworth, of nature, to Homer, of heroic man in general, to the tragic poets, of heroic man against nature; whereas I brought to the story of Jesus an unsufficient experience. His story was for me at that time more prophetic than poetic, more suggestive of my future than expressive of my past. Through the poets I had become conscious of the meaning then underlying my life; through further life I was to become conscious of a meaning not then apprehended in the story of Jesus.

At the time of this reading of the story I had reached in actual life an attitude which found its best expression in tragedy; as I shall explain later, this seems to me now the pagan attitude. The subsequent deepening of my imaginative insight through actual experience occurred naturally, perhaps inevitably, for there seems to be but one step from tragedy to Christianity, or from the pagan to the Christian view of life as tragic. It is the purpose of this paper to describe that step. As Nicholas Berdyaev says, "It is through tragedy that man finds his way to Christianity in which tragedy is finally resolved." The curtain that falls on the last, awe-inspiring scene of tragedy rises, if at all, on the first scene of Christianity. Jesus begins where the tragic hero leaves off.

For the life of Jesus impresses me now as the final dream, or ideal, of human life. Reading that story, conscious of that abiding peace, we feel, if we have come to him through actual tragedy, that his life was from the beginning, and is, what our life would be but cannot become until it has been purified in the fires of tragic experience. But was his life actually this from the beginning? Or did he too come to peace through suffering? I do not know, but I am inclined to think that he too fought his battles and won his peace; that he too found life tragic. If this is true, his battles were fought behind the scenes; fought perhaps fiercely and for the most part won soon. There is an account of a temptation overcome. But there is also that last great cry, "My God, my God, why hast Thou forsaken me?" . . . .

Reprinted by permission from *Christendom*, Spring, 1936.

I

This large, gracious carelessness, especially noticeable during the early months of Jesus' ministry, stands in sharp contrast to the limited, intense world of tragedy. All the events of tragedy hint of coming doom; many of the events of the life of Jesus do not. The most important reason for this lies in the difference of purpose of the two narratives: tragedy would show the individual destroyed by universal forces but heroic in disaster; the Gospels, whatever their conscious intention, tend to show Jesus befriended by the universe but destroyed by human selfishness. In their pervasive sense of a friendly universe, the Gospels are in strong contrast to tragedy.

The large, gracious carelessness of the life of Jesus is a proof of his faith in the friendliness of the universe. The tragic hero has faith, but in himself and, to a degree, in a cold world of ideals to which he stoically adheres. Jesus had faith in the universe within him: "I and my Father." There is an incident in his life which stands in striking contrast to two incidents in the tragedy of Othello. Although Othello can lightly command his friends and enemies to keep up their bright swords, or can tell them more sternly, "Were it my cue to fight I should have known it without a prompter," in a really desperate situation he seeks that "sword of Spain, the ice-brook's temper" with which to enforce his will. Jesus, taken for his life, says calmly to Peter, "Put up again thy sword into his place. . . . . Thinkest thou that I cannot now pray to my Father, and He shall presently give me more than twelve legions of angels?" Othello at strongest trusted himself, at weakest his sword; Jesus trusted God.

We may consider this large, gracious carelessness from still another point of view. It is an evidence of freedom, and, as Berdyaev would probably say, a mark of the spiritual life, as the inevitability of tragedy is an evidence of bondage and a mark of the unspiritual life: the freedom of the spirit, the bondage of matter. In spite of the fact that the Gospels here and there foretell the death of Jesus, they do not create the impression of the inevitability of that death, as tragedy creates the impression of the inevitability of its denouement. Living in the world, Jesus was not of the world. By accepting its laws, he was made free of them; and, though he yielded his life at last to the world, we feel throughout that he could, if he would, have transcended at any moment the limitations of the world. . . . .

The tragic hero, on the contrary, in spite of the fight he makes against it, is of the world. Indeed, it is his involvement in the world that causes the struggle. The fierceness of this struggle is proof of the inwardness of the foe; it is civil war. He is fighting indeed against his own worldliness. The tragic conflict, therefore, in spite of its overarching ideality, takes place in the air of this world, of cause and effect, of inevitability, very different from the air of freedom that surrounds the life of Jesus.

It is paradoxical that the tragic hero lives in this narrow world as though under a universal doom, while Jesus lives in the universe in an air of freedom. The explanation, perhaps, is that those who cannot live in the universe, will die in the universe, that freedom belongs only to those who can take the universe into their confidence. The tragic hero lives to die; this is the whole bent of his action. Jesus died to live—died for life; his death was a means not an end. . . . . .

But, though there is no truly tragic fear of the universe in the story of Jesus, there is something akin to it, something that serves a similar purpose in our experience of that story. This is our awe of his universal nature, our sense of infinite strength and meaning existent in him. He is awful in his transfiguration and in many of his miracles, as when he commands the waves, "Peace, be still," and they obey him. (I am reading the story, you remember, with the "willing suspension of disbelief." The miracles *as told* seem true.) We are awed when he asks his disciples if they are able to drink of the cup of which he shall drink. Most of all we are awed by the closing events of his life. There is the moment when Judas, dining with Jesus, asks, "Master, is it I?" and Jesus replies, "Thou hast said." There is no moral fear here, fear that goodness will be destroyed, though there is awe at the realization that evil causes goodness to suffer. Here is the mystery, not of evil, which is clear, but of sacrificial goodness, of God.

There is the moment when Judas betrays him with a kiss. In tragedy this would be a moment of utmost fear, fear of the universe that permitted such betrayals. Here it is a moment of awe, of fear too perhaps, but simple fear, not moral, and not for Jesus and goodness but for Judas and evil. Judas is tempting the lightning, the fire from heaven will fall and consume him. In a moment the fire does fall, and we are reading how, in remorse for having betrayed innocence, he goes out and hangs himself, and the universe is avenged. The indignities of the trial and crucifixion of Jesus move us to the same awe: the crown of thorns, the reviling, the petty persecutions. And then the sympathy of nature at the end. Contrast the coming on of night before the murder of Banquo in *Macbeth:*

> "Light thickens, and the crow
> Makes wing to the rocky wood;
> Good things of day begin to droop and drowse,
> While night's black agents to their preys do rouse. . . . ."

with the coming of darkness when Jesus died. *Macbeth* is fearful; *Matthew* is awful. Earth quivers in sympathy with stricken goodness, and if not held in check by the will of God might shake itself and bury mankind in oblivion. And then there is the awe, the joyful awe, of Easter. "He is not here; he is risen."

Awe, then, instead of tragic fear; the fear of the Lord instead of the fear of evil. What becomes of tragic pity in the story of Jesus? Pity, that is for innocence or worth swept aside by a careless or heartless universe; the obverse of tragic fear. The pity that the story of Jesus arouses in the unprejudiced reader is, I think, in most of its manifestations, a simple human pity for the disappointments of life. It is the pity we feel for man's universal failure to actualize his dreams; pity for dreams unrealized, **not** tragic pity for dreams perhaps unreal. We pity Jesus because the refractory nature of man made so difficult the attainment of his goal. We never doubt the reality of the goal nor its final attainability, never doubt that goodness and God are one. . . . .

In general, the events of his trial and crucifixion are not separately awful or pitiful, but at the same time both awful and pitiful. I have spoken already of some that move us most to awe and of others that move us most to pity. There is one moment that seems the essence of combined awe and pity: the moment of that despairing cry, "My God, my God, why hast Thou forsaken me?" It is possible that he himself, isolated at last in the fearful loneliness of the tragic hero, felt the universe against him in that moment. But I do not think we feel it so; it is not necessary that we feel it so. We are too filled with the sense of his gracious strength, too conscious of the friendly relation he has always borne to the universe, to feel that he is now forsaken. His gentle humanity, however, fills us with pity for him; he thinks he has failed. But our pity is shot through and through with awe of him, and with awe of the universe of which he is a part, whose very heart, indeed, he is, in spite of his momentary despair. We behold in a man the tortured heart of God. We do not know why it is tortured, but there it is, the tragic mystery of goodness. Jesus is at the same moment our brother, and pitiful; and the Son of God, and awful. The seasoned Roman centurion speaks for us when he says, "Truly this was the Son of God. . . . ." But in the last despairing cry of Jesus, we pity him as a man and stand in awe of him as God. Mankind has been lifted up to heaven, God has been brought down to earth.

II

Thus I became in imagination and during my reading a kind of Christian. Jesus became the God-Man. My conversion was not, however, complete, for I was not as yet deeply convinced that I must be saved through him, even in the sense of being saved through a life like his. Sufficiently sympathetic to his life to realize it in some measure in imagination, I still found the tragic attitude nearer to the reality of my life at that time. The tragic hero had to live in this world alone, had to face it at its worst and conquer through trust in himself. The Christian could depend upon something beyond himself and had another life to fall back upon. It took more courage, I thought, to be tragic than to be Christian, and being in the tragic mood I felt that courage was the final virtue. . . . .

Yet the imaginative pity I felt for Jesus, and with him for men, was, as I see it now, a postlude to tragedy and a prelude to the actual pity I was to feel later. One does not go from Christianity to tragedy. I do not see now, nor think I shall ever see, how one who has really come to Christianity ever goes beyond it. One goes from tragedy to Christianity, and it is but a step; but it is not an easy step. Let us consider in some detail its nature.

In the first place, I do not mean that one necessarily goes from the reading of tragedy to Christianity; one may, of course, if tragedy is a sufficiently accurate expression of one's life at that time, and if a certain kind of life follows the reading. I mean, first, that the life that finds expression in tragedy is only a step from Christianity; I mean, second, that the tragic hero himself is only a step from Christianity. . . . .

Whether the tragic hero dies in defiance of the universe or not, the tragedy leaves in the mind of the reader a mood not of defiance but of awe. The tragic hero has courage, and courage is basic as well in Christianity as anywhere else. He may lack tenderness, he may lack humility, but his sufferings arouse our tenderness, and the awful complexity of life as revealed in his career moves us to humility. These emotions, combined with our awe of and respect for life as revealed in him, take us definitely toward the Christian attitude. To see a great individual as a symbol of mankind is to see mankind greatly, and to see mankind greatly is finally to see it at home in the universe. A high respect for man is inconsistent with a belief in his final insignificance.

Yet, though it is only a step from tragedy to Christianity, it is a difficult step because it is a step from pride to humility. The tragic hero is self-relying; too self-relying; proud in his self-reliance. This is his strength and, as the Greeks were aware, this is his weakness. The step is possible, however, because of the common mood of pity. Life is pitiful in both the tragic and the Christian view, but in different ways: it is more purely pitiful in Christianity; in tragedy pity is balanced by fear. . . . .

But what will force a man to take this step from pride to humility, from the fearful, defensive pity of tragedy to the pure and positive pity of Christianity? Only a catastrophe so great that pride begins to seem absurd and our chief defense a weakness. It is through necessity that we feel our deepest kinship with our fellows, through suffering that we are forced to prove the essential goodness of the universe. When we have been left defenseless we can see how defenseless all men are. Our pity for ourselves then is at the same time pity for mankind; and our pity is love. If we have not seen life through tragic eyes, we cannot see it through Christian; if we have not feared its loss, we cannot be assured of its abidingness. Because of fear we pass beyond fear, beyond tragedy, into the personal world of Christianity.

THE PROBLEM OF EVIL

Eugene William Lyman

.... THEISM FINDS THE GROUND of both nature and man to be Active Purposeful Spirit working creatively to achieve the highest values, and to bring into being a spiritual universe. For theism man's freedom and creative action are metaphysically real, and necessary for the attainment of a universe which is genuinely spiritual. And for theism the sub-structure for man's creative living in the pursuit of the highest values appears in nature as a whole by reason of its orderly processes, and by reason of its age-long upward trend. But at the same time theism, in consequence of its loyalty to the highest values, cannot take the world-accepting attitude which characterizes pantheism. Nor can it acquiesce in the relativity of values which results from naturalism. Instead, it recognizes in values of intrinsic and ultimate worth the clue to the nature of God and the destiny of man.

Thus theism affords a solution of what Professor Montague has significantly called "the Problem of the Good." He states the problem in the following terms: "How can the amount of goodness and purposefulness in the world be compatible with the non-existence of a God?" And he insists that the Problem of Evil and the Problem of the Good need to be considered together. We have seen how theism makes intelligible the presence of goodness and purposefulness on a cosmic scale, and at the same time opens to man a life of transcending and transforming the world, by the conception of God as a Cosmic Purposeful Spirit who is creating and conserving value. And at the same time we have pointed out, as we concluded our discussions of evolution, of history, and of ultimate values, how this very solution of the problem of the good opens the way to a constructive treatment of the problem of evil. But as the problem of evil is the characteristic difficulty for theism, just as the problem of the good is for naturalism and pantheism, we should now go on to a fuller examination of it.

Let us undertake to face the problem comprehensively in its most salient aspects. It may be considered under the three aspects of suffering, frustration, and sin. We must be sure, however, that these aspects are viewed in their full range of meaning and in their inter-relatedness.

The problem of suffering is the problem of Job.

> "Wherefore is light given to him that is in misery,
> And life unto the bitter in soul?"

In contrast to moral evil, suffering may be called physical evil, but it is an evil none the less. Suffering is something that we cannot directly will. At the most we can accept it if it is found to be accessory to the attainment

From *The Meaning and Truth of Religion*, New York, 1933, pp. 399-413. Reprinted by permission of the publishers, Charles Scribner's Sons.

of a good—as when one undergoes a surgical operation for the sake of fuller health. But the suffering of the world appears to be far in excess of what can be understood as means to the end of good. Moreover, it is one of the highest objectives of man to relieve suffering and to eliminate its causes. Why then, we must ask with Job, should there be so much suffering in a world which owes its existence to a good God?

But the drama of the book of Job includes also the problem of frustration.

> "Why is light given to a man whose way is hid,
> And whom God hath hedged in?"

The defeat of our purposes, if they are themselves intrinsically worthy, is an evil even though no physical suffering be involved. Calamities which frustrate high enterprises bring mental suffering. Bereavement brings the pain of sorrow and brings the added evil of frustration. Thus the interrelatedness of suffering and frustration must be appreciated if we would realize some of the more grievous forms of the problem of evil.

On the other hand, as the problem is presented in the book of Job, the absence of sin on the part of Job determines the acuteness of the problem. Suffering which is the plain consequence of sin, as when one falls into the pit that one has digged for another, or suffering which is a brief chastisement for transgression in order that one may learn the way of righteousness —these are not the forms of suffering which baffle the understanding and create moral confusion. The integrity of Job is real—else his accusers have solved the problem of the book. It is the absence of sin in Job, and the positive presence of moral integrity instead, which makes the problem of his suffering and frustration so acute. Sin, however, enters in to aggravate the problem in the form of the sins of others on whom no calamities fall. Hence Job complains accusingly of God:

> "The earth is given into the hands of the wicked;
> He covereth the face of the judges thereof:
> If it be not he, who then is it?"

Injustice goes unpunished while calamity falls upon the righteous. So far as this is true, are we not driven to say that God is unjust? Or else, that aimless forces are in control?

The problem of frustration, however, is peculiarly the problem of the prophet, and is illustrated most clearly in the experience of other characters than Job. Jeremiah, like Job, curses the day of his birth:

Cursed be the day wherein I was born: let not the day wherein my mother bare me be blessed. Cursed be the man who brought tidings to my father, saying, A man-child is born unto thee, making him very glad.

The frustrations of the prophet come to him because he is more sensitive than others to the social injustices of the world and more determined to "make righteousness and the will of God prevail." The prophet is keenly aware of the cruelty, ruthlessness, and oppression which result from man's greed and wanton use of power, and he cannot but pronounce woe upon them. He seeks to win men from devotion to power and privilege and to bring in the reign of justice and love, but the devotees of power and privilege overwhelm him. The frustration of the prophet finds its ultimate expression in the cry of Jesus on the cross, "My God, my God, why hast thou forsaken me?"

Thus we see that the evil of frustration in its most tragic form springs from the third aspect of the problem of evil—the problem of sin. The core of this problem consists of moral evil. There are tendencies within us, in the realm where personal insight and control are possible, which defeat the higher good and work injury to our fellows. Objective wrong springs out of dispositions and sentiments which might have been controlled for objective good and which therefore must be judged to be morally evil. Not that any natural disposition taken by itself is evil. On the contrary all natural dispositions are potencies for good as well as for evil. But when natural dispositions become waywardness, willfulness, callousness, when these qualities get expressed in overt action and become parts of our "second nature," the moral factor is unmistakably present and the result is moral evil, deeply rooted in the self. Here we face evil in its gravest form —moral evil in men's hearts and wills. For this form of evil corrupts that which has intrinsic worth—personality—and is the chief source of the defeat of the highest good—a universal community of creative personalities.

We have called moral evil the core of the problem of sin. But we must use the term sin as the most far-reaching and searching designation of moral evil. Sin is moral evil viewed in the relationships which religious faith apprehends. From the standpoint of religious faith on its highest levels man is not only a denizen of earth and a citizen of society, but a being possessing kinship with the Unseen and Eternal. The individual man and all his fellowmen possess the capacity to become co-workers with God in achieving a spiritual universe. Moreover, in ethical religion there is an interpenetration between the religious relationships and those which are specifically ethical. Sin is moral evil seen as transgression against the total system of spiritual relationships to which man belongs or into which he may enter—against men as sons of God and against God as the Eternal Good Will. Hence it is that, while moral evil is most characteristically defined in terms of the doer's responsibility and his knowledge of what his action will involve, sin denotes the rupture of moral and spiritual relationships even when it is largely unwitting. Doctor Adler has pointed out this aspect of sin by saying: "It is characteristic of sin that the fuller knowledge that the harmful deed is sinful *comes after the act.*" And Royce was expressing the same thought with another shade of meaning when he said that in sinning "we consciously choose to forget."

If, then, we would face the problem of evil in its acute forms and in its comprehensive meaning, we must have in view the problem of Job, or the problem of suffering; the problem of the prophets and of the creative spirits in any realm—the problem of frustration; and the problem of sin, that is, of moral evil and of the injury which it works, far beyond the doer's ken, in the doer's soul, in society, and in the entire realm of man's religious relationships.

And again we must emphasize that these forms of evil are intricately interrelated. The frustration of the prophets is chiefly due to the sinfulness of those who are ready to stone them. The worst and most widespread human suffering springs from causes which lie in the human realm, and which are controllable or which may be brought under control by sufficient coöperative endeavor. And the sin of one inevitably means some measure of suffering and frustration for others. On the other hand, suffering, or physical and social handicaps, often enfeeble the moral resources of men. Thus physical evil, and the external evil of practical situations, often condition individuals heavily in the direction of moral evil.

The most serious form of this interrelatedness of the different aspects of evil appears when the causes of suffering, frustration, and sin become established in the institutions of society. War, economic injustice, governmental corruption, oppressive social customs, racial antipathies, senseless methods of education, persist and work their havoc very largely because of the sheer momentum of institutions. It is here that "the sins of good people" can be most clearly discerned. For we acquiesce in injustices and cruelties done by institutions which we would not tolerate for a moment if done by individuals, although we are implicated in varying degrees in those same institutions; and personal goodness in those who guide these institutions, plus amiable intentions on our own part, assist us to this acquiescence. At least partly through the sins of good people, as well as through sheer human greed and the ruthless use of power, injustices and oppressions may become so entrenched in social institutions as to constitute something like what Rauschenbusch called "a kingdom of evil"—the very opposite of the kingdom of God.

Having thus sought to face fully the problem of evil in its most salient aspects, we must now go on to consider what contributions toward the solution of the problem reason and faith may afford. In so doing we must maintain the position already adopted that the Problem of Evil and the Problem of the Good must be taken together. And since theism alone can reach a solution of the Problem of the Good, we must ask, to what attitude toward the Problem of Evil the type of ethical theism developed by our previous thought leads, and whether this attitude can be accepted as a working solution of the problem. If ethical theism does not make possible such a working solution, it is seriously challenged, if not invalidated. But if ethical theism be found to contain a working solution of this supreme problem, its meaning will be further unfolded.

We have spoken of the solution to be sought as "a working solution." It would be contrary to the spirit of ethical theism if we sought for a full intellectual solution of the problem of evil. We have been concerned already in this chapter to face the reality of evil and not to tone it down in the interests of a theological or metaphysical view. Evil is inherently irrational. How then can a reason be given for all the evils of the world? It is the most serious defect of thorough-going monism that it has to make evil a permanent constituent of the Whole. Hence idealistic monism tends to treat evil as simply imperfection or incompleteness. Or if an idealistic monist is bent, like Royce, upon not minimizing the gravity of evil, he still must treat it, because of his doctrine of the Absolute, as something that, though bad in itself, is indispensable to the good—like the bad characters in a good play. Thus when one persists in solving the problem of evil solely by interpretation, an aesthetic view of evil tends to take the place of a fully moral view.

But the possibility of evil may be recognized as inevitable along with the denial of the inevitableness of the actual evils of the world. The possibility of evil is inevitable because of the limitations inherent in the process of the creating of good. A spiritual order which is to have love as its supreme principle cannot be established by coercion; hence from the process of achieving such an order evil cannot be simply banished. An order in which man's initiative and freedom are to bear a part cannot be pre-determined against all evil. An order that is to be achieved through voluntary co-operation of its members cannot be made immune from all injustice.

Evil, then, springs from the reality of freedom in the human realm, and from the reality of contingency in the orders of existence below man. And this contingency we see to be present, not only by reason of the spontaneity evident in the realms of life, but also by reason of the principle of indeterminacy with respect to the ultimate units of nature, which as we have seen has become a part of the new physics. Contingency and freedom cannot be looked upon as themselves evil, for they are conditions of growth and of the achievement of the good. But they are also inevitably the source of the possibility of evil.

The problem of evil, accordingly, is susceptible of this much of intellectual interpretation: if evil is due to the presence of contingency and freedom in the world, then the actual evils of the world spring from finite centres of origination and not from God. The God in whom we find it rational to believe is a God who by his very nature grounds the enterprise of achieving the good and the endeavor for the conquest of evil.

But the good, so far as we empirically see, must be achieved by a growing process. This means that earlier and more primitive stages tend to hold the field against more ideal stages, which can be reached only by persistent effort. The phenomenon of inertia thus becomes a condition from which evils springs. Sins of sloth will be in large measure responsible for the final judgment, "Inasmuch as ye did it not."

More specifically, the realization of the purpose of God, according to all our experience, involves an educational process. This means that the presence of ignorance in the human realm becomes a source of evil, which can be overcome only by the growth of knowledge and its application to life. How great are the evils which mankind suffers today through ignorance of what those who have had the benefits of scientific medicine have already learned!

Furthermore, it is inherent in the purpose of God that it must be achieved through a social process. This means that the interaction of lives which are only partially socialized and ethicized will be a source of evil. The founder of a school may have a wholly good purpose, and may work wisely and persistently for its accomplishment; but he can eliminate wrongs done by members of the school to each other only as he evokes in the members appreciation of the values he has in view and co-operation toward their attainment.

Too often men have assumed that God creates by fiat, and then have said: "Why have we not a universal harmony now?" Or they have assumed that God really moves his creatures about as the chess-player moves his chessmen, and they have said: "Why the mistakes in the way in which the game is being played?" This is the conception which produces the pessimism of Omar Khayyam:

> "Impotent pieces of the Game He plays
> Upon this Checker-board of Nights and Days;
> Hither and thither moves, and checks, and slays,
> And one by one back in the Closet lays."

But the Cosmic Creative Spirit is not a chess player, moving impotent pieces about. He is building a Cosmos, but the Cosmos is not complete, for there is much that is chaotic still, at least in human life. He brings into being organic life abounding in centres of spontaneous growth; and through this process there come to pass forms of loveliness such as the universe could not otherwise show. But there remain other forms of beauty to be realized which no eye has yet seen and no ear has yet heard. He achieves finite spirits to whom he can impart a creativity in some degree, however slight, like his own; and then he summons them to work with him in building a social order in which force and selfish competition shall be replaced by reason and love.

In such a universe there will be collisions between the finite spirits and the basic cosmic order already established. There will be error and pain. These could be prevented only by fiat. But God does not work by fiat; he works, rather, by the silent forces which spring from impartial love. "He maketh his sun to rise on the evil and the good, and sendeth rain on the just and the unjust." God works not by the method of fiat but by the method of growth. And the method of growth, which for us means stimulating the creative within us, can achieve what the method of fiat cannot. The whole meaning of our existence is that we are called upon to be sharers with God in creative work. We cannot rightly relate theism either to the problem of evil or to the problem of the good unless we replace the conception of a cosmic chess-player, which has underlain too much of our theology and has lingered on in our popular-science philosophy, by the conception of a God of creative love who makes possible for men

> "The glory of eternal partnership."

We thus far have been taking the point of view of interpretive reason, although recognizing that interpretation alone cannot suffice for dealing with the problem of evil, since what is inherently irrational and evil cannot be made into good by interpretation. But when interpretive reason brings us to the conception of eternal partnership, it directs us beyond itself to the point of view of active faith. And we must go on to this point of view, because only through active faith can many of the gravest evils be dealt with.

Among the gravest evils are those of human oppression. It is such evils which often evoke the darkest pessimism. The Jewish sage from whom came the book, Ecclesiastes, was facing realities when he wrote:

> Then I returned and saw all the oppressions that are done under the sun: and, behold, the tears of such as were oppressed, and they had no comforter; and on the side of the oppressors there was power; but they had no comforter. Wherefore I praise the dead that have been long dead more than the living that are yet alive.

Here is a sensitiveness to injustice which condemns us if we do not respond to it. But we are still more condemned if we are callous to the oppressions of our own day—oppressions such as force so many textile workers and coal miners into revolt; oppressions such as leave their stamp upon the anemic faces of so many thousands of children in our large cities; oppressions such as are always before us in the lot of the Negro race.

But a sensitiveness to injustice which ends in disillusionment and pessimism, as was the case with the sage of Ecclesiastes, serves simply the purpose of repudiating those interpretations of evil which subtly aggravate the evil. Only as moral sensitiveness issues in active faith can our fuller resources for solving the problem of evil be known. In other words, there must be no solution of the problem of evil which does not include the fight with evil. Faith in God is no less vital in this aspect of the solution of the problem of evil than in any other; but it is the faith in God that strengthens for the conquest of evil and for its elimination which is called for, instead of a faith which acquiesces in evil as being inscrutably a part of God's will.

Active faith is always the attitude of the prophets toward evil. A prophetic spirit of modern times may be cited as an example. The Earl of Shaftesbury, England's greatest social reformer in the last century, was a man of intense religious faith, and his faith was the mainspring of his work for reform. What his fight against injustice and oppression cost him may be seen from an entry in his journal at a time when the outcome of his efforts for factory legislation looked dark:

> Twelve years of labor, anxiety, and responsibility! I have borrowed and spent in reference to my income enormous sums of money, and am shut out from every hope of emolument and path of honorable ambition. My own kinsfolk dislike my opinions and persecute me. I am excluded from my father's house because I have maintained the cause of the laborer. It has been toil by day and by night, fears and disappointments, prayers and tears, long journeys and unceasing letters.

But Shaftesbury's pain and struggle bore their fruit, and at the time of his death it could be said that all the great social reforms of his generation were due more to his influence, character and perseverance than to any other single cause. There could be no clearer demonstration that active faith is an indispensable part of the solution of the problem of evil.

It is thus a source of the strength of ethical theism that it does not offer an interpretation of the actual evils of the world by finding them to be necessary as a part of the good, but that instead it summons men to the fight with evil, in the faith that such a fight will be victorious. The will of an ethical God must be understood to be directed toward the conquest of evil; and men are co-workers with God, consciously or unconsciously, wherever they are striving courageously and intelligently for the elimination of evils and are changing the processes which produce evil into processes which produce good.

In this fight with evil, science may bear a most indispensable part through its mastery of physical and social conditions. But for this very reason the enlistment of science in the service of the highest ends is of the utmost importance. For science may be used to entrench evils in society still more strongly, and to reinforce destructive agencies. Hence the conquest of evil is in the last analysis the responsibility of ethics and religion. The fight with evil becomes a matter of building a moral world and of evoking the fullest responsiveness to God in the depths of the human heart.

The final contribution to a working solution of the problem of evil springs from direct religious insight. It is the discovery, made by the supreme prophets of religion and capable of being made anew by each religious soul, that in the secret processes of the inner life evil may be transmuted into good, and that thereby active faith may be nourished and the vision of God rendered more profound. Beyond the interpretation of evil which carries us to the recognition that the possibility of evil cannot be precluded from a universe in which finite spirits must bear their part, and beyond the fight with evil which aims at its conquest and elimination, comes the principle of the transmutation of evil through the life with God.

The need of the principle of the transmutation of evil arises from the fact that life must be lived in the midst of many evils not yet eliminated. The fight with evil, in fact, brings with it added evils of frustration. These evils we must not think of as sent from God, since the will of God is directed toward eradicating them from the world. But they may be met nobly instead of ignobly. Through strength from God we may transcend them instead of being overwhelmed by them. And a spiritual victory on our part may help others to their own spiritual victory. Thus experiences, which in and of themselves could be only experiences of evil, may become transmuted into experiences of good having a unique and lofty quality.

The author of the seventy-third Psalm examplifies one form of the experience of which we are thinking when, in the midst of his own sufferings and of the prosperity of the wicked, he finds that the inward presence of God suffices for him:

"Whom have I in heaven but thee?
And there is none upon earth that I desire besides thee.
My flesh and my heart faileth:
But God is the strength of my heart and my portion for ever."

The principle of the transmutation of evil in its application to physical suffering is impressively illustrated in the following instance. Katherine Mansfield, the gifted author who died in 1922 at the age of 34, after a long struggle with disease, wrote thus in her *Journal:*

> I should like this to be accepted as my confession. There is no limit to human suffering. When one thinks: "Now I have touched the bottom of the sea—now I can go no deeper," one goes deeper. . . . . I do not want to die without leaving a record of my belief that suffering can be overcome. For I do believe it. What must one do? . . . . Do not resist. Take it. Be overwhelmed. Accept it fully. Make it *part of life.* Everything in life that we really accept undergoes a change. So suffering must become Love. This is the mystery. This is what I must do. I must pass from personal love to greater love.

And a little later, pressing on through suffering to her work, she wrote: "May I be found worthy to do it! Lord, make me crystal clear for thy light to shine through."

The principle of transmutation of evil is expressed in its profoundest meaning in the portrait of the Suffering Servant. "The chastisement of our peace was upon him; and with his stripes we are healed." This is the principle which Jesus found to be inseparable from sonship to God and which he incarnated when he accepted his Cross. His ultimate interpretation of his mission was that he came "to give his life a ransom for many." The conquest of evil involves the expression of self-sacrificing love on the part of those who have learned the meaning and power of love. It was Jesus' insight that such love is the outcome of the experience of sonship to God. Hence sonship to God means sharing in saviorhood. The deepest implication of this insight is that God himself is eternally expressing himself in redemptive work as well as in creative work, and that the evil of the world means suffering for Him. The suffering, self-giving love which we see in Jesus we may also discern at the heart of the universe.

LIGHT SPRINGING UP IN THE DARKNESS

Neville S. Talbot

LIGHT DEEPER THAN DARKNESS

LIGHT WILL spring up in the darkness. That is, I think, what we must look for. We must abandon all effort to explain away the black facts which confront us—all effort to wave over them some theory which shall make them to be other than they are, or to arrive at some satisfying explanation of their origin. And, instead, we should, so to say, let the facts speak for themselves, while we watch and listen to see whether they disclose some deeper meaning than was apparent at first sight. A welling-up of light within the darkness is to be looked for, a coming of relief from the same source as the affliction. It is as though we have to be healed by a hair of the same dog that has bitten us.

Life is full of this experience. The very phenomena which perplex and distress are found to have within them a testimony which, while it does not explain, reassures and encourages. Thus our very sense of the fleeting transience of this mortal life points to and implies the reality of that which is eternal and abiding. It has within it the evidence that we are more than creatures of time. So with sorrow—the sorrow of bereavement, the pain of the sundering of lovers by death. Nothing, no matter how one pretends, can mitigate the sorrow. Consolation cannot still it, indeed, cannot reach it. But within sorrow is love. Out of love it springs. Were it not for love it would not be. Its very strength testifies to a reality deeper than itself. . . . .

So it seems justifiable in face of the dark facts of life's riddle to expect that the facts will themselves prove to be luminous—to have light within them deeper than the darkness.

And so it is. It is the reality of goodness which gives force to the realization of what is evil. The blackness of what is evil is splashed against the whiteness of what is good—else it would not be known. Black upon black is invisible. The dark things of life are indeed mysterious, they affront and perplex the believer in God and in goodness. They are a problem to him. But the good things in life—they are also mysterious, the more mysterious in face of the presence of the evil things. They are a problem to the disbeliever and the pessimist. There is, in short, a problem of good as well as a problem of evil. The facts of life are not all of one color. They have in them the force of contrast. We know this, of course. Nature declares it. Day succeeds to night, spring to winter. There is "clear shining after rain."

From *The Riddle of Life*, London, 1929, chap. iii. Reprinted by permission of the publishers, Longmans, Green & Company.

LIGHT UPON HEROIC BROWS

But a further bright light is to be seen glowing at the heart of the dread scene of suffering and calamity. Such things happen to men; and the light is the way in which they meet, use, and overcome them. We may speak (and truly) of a darkness environing man, but it cannot smother the blazing light of human heroism. In fact, it seems to be of life's very savour that it should abound in difficulty, risk, danger, calamity, just because of the tremendous glories of character which spring from the brave encountering of them. "Our highest admiration is always reserved for men who master difficult circumstances. If the story of Joseph, begun beside Bedouin campfires centuries ago, can easily be naturalized beside modern radiators; if Robinson Crusoe, translated into every tongue, is understood by all, the reason lies in the depth of man's heart, where to make the most out of untoward situations is a daily problem. Not everyone can grasp the argument or perceive the beauty of 'Paradise Lost' and 'Paradise Regained,' but one thing about them every man appreciates—the blind Milton, sitting down to write them:

> 'I argue not
> Against Heaven's hand or will, nor bate a jot
> Of heart or hope; but still bear up and steer
> Right onward.'

The full understanding of Ole Bull's playing on the violin was necessarily restricted to the musical, but no restriction bounds the admiration of men, learned or simple, when in a Munich concert, his A string snaps and he finishes the composition on three strings. That is the human problem in epitome. Getting music out of life's remainders after the break has come; winning the battle with what is left from a defeat; going blind, like Milton, and writing sublimest poetry, or deaf, like Beethoven, and composing superb sonatas; being reared in an almshouse and buried from Westminster Abbey, like Henry M. Stanley; or, like Kavanagh, born without arms or legs, and yet sitting at last in the British Parliament—all such hardihood and undiscourageable pluck reach back in a man's bosom beyond the strings that ease and luxury can touch, and strike there a reverberating chord. Nothing in human life is so impressive as pluck, 'fighting with the scabbard after the sword is gone.' . . . . If adversity, rightly used, so develops and reveals character, we may expect to find trouble as a background to the most admirable men of the race. We read the luminous histories of Francis Parkman and do not perceive, behind the printed page, the original manuscript, covered with a screen of parallel wires, along which the blind author ran his pencil that he might write legibly. We think of James Watt as a genius at invention, and perhaps recall that Wordsworth said of him, 'I look upon him, considering both the magnitude and the universality of his genius, as perhaps the most extraordinary man that this country ever produced.' But Watt himself we forget—sickly of body, starving on eight shillings a week, and saying, 'Of all things in life there is nothing more foolish than inventing.' Kant's philosophy was a turning point in human thought, but lauding Kant, how few recall his struggle with a broken body!

Said he, speaking of his incurable illness, 'I have become master of its influence in my thoughts and actions by turning my attention away from this feeling altogether, just as if it did not at all concern me.' Wilberforce, the liberator of British slaves, we know, and beside his grave in Westminster Abbey we recall the superb title that he earned, 'the attorney general of the unprotected and of the friendless,' but the Wilberforce who for twenty years was compelled to use opium to keep himself alive, and had the resolution never to increase the dose—who knows of him? One of the chief rewards of reading biography is this introduction that it gives to handicapped men; the knowledge it imparts of the world's great saints and scripture makers, conquerors and reformers, who, in the words of Thucydides, 'dared beyond their strength, hazarded against their judgment, and in extremities were of excellent hope.' " [1]

So it is that against the dark background of the stage on which mankind plays its part, the light that shines upon the brows of heroic men and women is thrown into sharp relief. Here is that which is a real counterweight to misery and adversity. A change comes over the tremendous scene of human existence when character rather than happiness is made paramount in our judgment upon it. "We may well inquire, when we complain of this world's misery, what sort of world we are seeking in its place. Are we asking for a perfectly happy world? But happiness, at its deepest and its best, is not the portion of a cushioned life which never struggled, overpassed obstacles, bore hardships, or adventured in sacrifice for costly aims. A heart of joy is never found in luxuriously coddled lives, but in man and woman who achieve and dare, who have tried their powers against antagonisms, who have met even sickness and bereavement and have tempered their souls in fire. Joy is begotten not chiefly from the impression of happy circumstance, but from the expression of overcoming power. Were we set upon making a happy world, therefore, we could not leave struggle out nor make adversity impossible. The unhappiest world conceivable by man would be a world with nothing hard to do, no conflicts to wage for ends worth while; a world where courage was not needed, and sacrifice was a superfluity. Beside such an inane lotos-land of tranquil ease this present world with all its suffering is a paradise. Men in fact find joy where in philosophy we might not look for it. Said MacMillan, after a terrific twelve-month on the Arctic continent: 'This has been the greatest year of my life.' . . . . That we should be merely happy is not an adequate end of the creative purpose for us, or of our purpose for ourselves. In our best hours we acknowledge this in the way we handle trouble. *However much in doubt a man may be about the theory of suffering, he knows infallibly how suffering practically should be met.* To be rebellious, cursing fate and hating life; to pity oneself, nursing one's hurts in morbid self-commiseration—the ignobility of such dealing with calamity we indubitably know. Even where we fall feebly short of the ideal, we have no question what the

---

[1] From *The Meaning of Faith*, by Harry Emerson Fosdick, New York, 1917, pp. 130-133. Reprinted by permission of the publishers, Association Press.

ideal is. When in biography or among our friends we see folk face crushing trouble, not embittered by it, made cynical, or thrust into despair, but hallowed, sweetened, illumined, and empowered, we are aware that noble characters do not alone *bear* trouble; they *use* it. . . . . They make it the minister of character; they set it to build in them what nothing save adversity can ever build—patience, courage, sympathy, and power. They even choose it in vicarious sacrifice for the good of others, and by it save the world from evils that nothing save some one's suffering could cure. They act as though *character*, not happiness, were the end of life. And when they are at their best they do this not with stoic intrepidity, as though trouble's usefulness were but their fancy, but joyfully, as though a good purpose in the world included trouble, even though not intending it. . . . . If now, we really want a world in which character is the end and aim—and no other world is worth God's making—we obviously may not demand the abolition of adversity. If one imagines a life from its beginning lapped in ease and utterly ignorant of what words like hardship, sorrow, and calamity imply, he must imagine a life lacking every virtue that makes human nature admirable. Character grows on struggle; without the overcoming of obstacles great quality in character is unthinkable. Whoever has handled well any calamitous event possesses resources, insights, wise attitudes, qualities of sympathy and power that by no other road could have come to him. For all our complaints against life's misery, therefore, and for all our inability to understand it in detail, who would not hesitate, foreseeing the consequences, to take adversity away from men? He who banishes hardship banishes hardihood; and out of the same door with Calamity walk Courage, Fortitude, Triumphant Faith, and Sacrificial Love. . . . ." [2]

In the midst of the darkness then light springs up. The facts of life, for all their terrific character, reveal and communicate that which stimulates and reassures.

THE TESTIMONY OF ISRAEL

At this point the voices of the people whose experience is recorded in the Old Testament ask to be heard. To pass on to them is natural after the eye of the mind has rested on the procession of heroic souls, illuminating the darkest pages of history by their victory over evil circumstance. The Jews never solved the riddle of life, though they were in persistent travail to do so. But, at any rate, they found inspiration in the great roll of the heroes and martyrs of their race. They kept a tenacious hold upon the glories of their past. So the converted Jew, the author of the Epistle to the Hebrews, writing to his fellow Jewish Christians, bade them cast their eyes back on the past, and see it lit up by those who in the past had been the successive embodiments of faith—"who through faith subdued kingdoms, wrought righteousness, obtained promises . . . . they were tortured, not accepting their deliverance . . . . others had trials of mockings and scourgings, yea, moreover, of bonds and imprisonment: they were stoned, they were

[2] From *The Meaning of Faith*, by Harry Emerson Fosdick, New York, 1917, pp. 148-151. Reprinted by permission of the publishers, Association Press.

sawn asunder, they were slain with the sword . . . . of whom the world was not worthy."

Here, indeed, are the mysteries of suffering, here are the circumstances which prompt pessimism and despair, yet they ring with victory and hope. From this great chapter valiant souls will ever draw encouragement as water from a spring.

But for further reasons the pressure of the riddle of life upon the soul sends us back to the Old Testament, over which the writer to the Hebrews casts his eyes in survey. We return not just to the book, but to the people behind the printed page. For once the basic and elemental questions of life are alive, they too spring forward to life again. Before they may have seemed buried in the past—people of an antiquity remote from the present. But once anyone is in real travail with life's riddle, lo! at his side he finds Jewish companions, who have stepped forth, as it were, from their graves, and are found to have in their hearts the very same pain as he has, and on their lips the cries which perfectly express it. For by no other people in history was the pain of life more acutely felt, to no other people did it befall to be so nakedly exposed—as it seemed—to the cruel bludgeonings of fate. The prolonged experience of this little people is an epitome of the spiritual strivings and sorrows of mankind.

It would take long to expound this. Two salient facts are to be apprehended about the people of the Old Book. First, they were the people, who, as they emerge into the light of historical times, are found to be charged with a passion of concern for the righteousness of God. For they were a people who—so they repeatedly testified—had been laid hold of by Another. And out of an infancy of savage, tribal conceptions of Him, He had led them up to a maturity of faith in him as the One, the Only, the Righteous and Holy God. More and more it had come home to them that, despite their ever-recurrent infidelity, they were a people of destiny: that they were in the hands of Him who had a purpose for them and through them for the world.

Secondly, this conviction, painfully enwrought into their souls and written on their hearts, was intimately connected with history. Out of history their destiny had come to them. God to them was He who had taken action in history in the past, and who would fulfil His action in the past by action in the future. Such is the burden of their great prophetic teachers, who were the instruments in God's hands of their religious education and purification.

Hence it was to history, to the actual facts of life, that they looked for the trace of the divine footsteps. Hence again and again the agony of dismay which filled their hearts. For history again and again was a wild scene of confusion and calamity. It was the scene where God—despite all "their fathers had told them" of His presence and His power—was, to all appearances, absent. As they went to the facts of history for reassurance it seemed to be not forthcoming. . . . .

The Jew "was always asking—Why is the earth allowed to be what it is? Why is it left alone by God, to suffer such dire injustice: to bow under such unremedied **wrong**: to lie stricken by so much undeserved pain: to be the pitiable prey of plague and violence and cruelty and slaughter? Why is God so little in evidence? Why does He not rend the Heavens and come down? Why is He a God who hides himself? How can He patiently tolerate this welter of evil? Why should the earth, if it be His earth, nevertheless be so full of darkness and cruel habitations? These were the questions that haunted pious Jews day and night, as they tossed through the weary hours on sleepless beds, under the stress of their perplexed broodings. We still rehearse their bitter cries every month, though with little result, so far as we can judge. . . . .

"And there are two points to note in their passionate protests. First, the passion, the anguish, in this appeal, draws all its intensity from the ardour of their belief in the God whom they adjure. As an historical fact it is only the Jew who has been seriously sensitive to the acuteness of the problem —for it is only he who looked to God to verify Himself as a God of Righteousness. That was the very heart of his Faith. And this Divine Righteousness was to be exhibited on the earth in human affairs, under the category of history. God had been apprehended by the Jew in this special character—as a God of action, engaged on this very historical scene in which man played his part, pledged to achieve, for all men, a consummating blessing, here and now, in tangible fact, working through the men chosen specially to co-operate in the task. God acts and works before our eyes. That is the manner of His manifestation. So the Jew signalized himself by believing. And this then is the secret of his clamorous outcry at God's failure to vindicate His purpose on the very ground and under the very conditions to which He stood pledged by His Holy Covenant. It was a collapse at the center. So the question, which our boys lightly asked, had burned itself into the very soul of the Jew. No one ever knew its force as he did. And the height of his indignation at the divine defect, at the hiding of God's Face, is a measure, therefore, of his loyalty to the Divine Name. . . . . It is the fact that these heroes of the Old Testament have rooted in us their conviction that God must be just, and God must be good, which alone accounts for the anxiety of our boys today as they ask, 'Why does God allow the earth to be what it is?—to go on as it does—to be disgraced by such outrages as this wild war of ours?'

"The trouble then sprang out of the Faith. It bore witness to the sincerity of the Faith. And this explains the second characteristic of it, in its Old Testament form. This characteristic is that those who feel the trouble go straight to God with it. They let loose their protest in His presence. This is so remarkable, both in Job and in the Psalms. The vehement indignation, the extraordinary cries of complaint, are all addressed to God. That is why the very vehemence does not signalize a revolt against God, but an appeal to Him. To whom else should they appeal? Their confidence in His justice is the motive which drives them wild. He and He alone must reassure them. There must be reasons why He does what He does. He is Lord of all; He can do what He will. Let Him then open His mind and His counsel to those who desire so passionately to vindicate His Name before the heathen. . . . ." [3]

Thus these spiritual leaders of mankind go ahead, with an unquenchable ardour. They press on into the darkness, never satisfied, never possessed of a final answer, yet never despairing. And all the while they nourish a great heart-held hope, which they guard as a flame against extinction, feeding it with the oil of faithful expectation. It is the hope that the day of God will arrive, bringing His vindication, the day of His Kingdom and victory.

---

[3] From *So as by Fire*, by H. S. Holland, pp. 51-54. Published by Wells Gardner, Darton & Company. Reprinted by permission.

Part V

THE MEANING OF WORSHIP

WORSHIP AND THE ROOTS OF LIVING

Robert Lowry Calhoun

A. THE MOST POIGNANT occasion of worship is a time of human extremity, when man's work clogs or crashes about him, and he is acutely aware of the presence of powers mightier than he. It may be individual frustration, failure, or loss. It may be social disaster. In any case, human prowess is brought to a halt. If now, out of such an *impasse* a person or a group find unsuspected ways opening, and fresh access of endurance, insight, and tranquility emerging in the midst of the ruin, each participant may come thus to his first living apprehension of such Reality as grown men can worship. Of peculiar power and significance among such experiences of release, for individuals and groups, are those involved in repentance and moral regeneration. Then, not merely is one thwarted, but one recognizes that "the source of dislocation" is in oneself, and that the thwarting is not only deserved but is to be welcomed. One acknowledges a good violated by oneself, alone or with others, and one reacts, it may be with profound disturbance of habitual thought and behavior patterns, against such violation. One welcomes being brought to a halt; and in the struggle for better orientation, sometimes there will come new perspective, power, and conviction of the reality and mercy of God, who can requite repentance of sin with enlargement of life. The consequences of sin cannot be annulled, but they can be worked into new life patterns, in the midst of the complex interworking of natural, social, and divers other factors that make up man and his total environment, in such fashion that the outcome is positively though never perfectly good. And one who becomes acutely aware that this is so not by merit nor prowess of his own, but by grace of powers beyond his own, may find himself irresistibly persuaded of the living presence of God.

Other occasions correlative to these may come as what have been called "experiences of consummation." Not failure transcended but success achieved, or joy discovered, is here the vehicle of revelation. To the complete egoist, naturally, no revelation will come. For him the achievement, the joy, is his doing and his alone. But for one able to look beyond the confines of his privacy, it will be plain that his success is won, his joy attained in co-relation with a world whose ultimate order is not of his devising; yet which it appears can welcome his best effort, and which offers him freely such beauties and wonders as he is able to receive. This demands openness on his part, of the sort we have been calling sagacity: alertness to present stimuli which an obtuse or preoccupied observer would miss. It demands also venturesomeness that breaks beyond the bounds of what is given.

From *God and the Common Life*, New York, 1935, pp. 237-250. Reprinted by permission of the publishers, Charles Scribner's Sons.

Appreciation of an instance of beauty as given is good; but worship is more than appreciation. It is venture and self-commitment also. Worship can be, only for one who is able to worship; and not seldom the shock of failure and loss is needed before one is able.

B. The character of such experience defies analysis and record, but words may suggest something of it to one who already knows by acquaintance what it is. In adoration one stands face to face with that which moves him to the "noble fear," *Ehrfurcht*, which we call awe. It is like one's response to the sublime, but more inclusive and profound. . . . . Mountain peaks, the desert, the interstellar spaces are sublime, some would say; a twisted pine high up, above the timberline; a wild thing dead in defending its young; a coast guard crew going out through icy breakers; the still face of one whom death did not frighten; a man nailed to a cross between thieves; a man saying, "Why callest thou *me* good?" If we are sensitive or timid, we shrink from the pain of these things, and may never learn to face them with eyes fully open.

But if they take hold on us until we cannot turn aside, it may come that beyond them all we discern "as in a mirror, dimly," a Ground that is greater than they, from which we also have our being. It may come that we welcome being alive in such a world; not because it is all good, but because through it, good and bad together, we discern the presence of God, and into His hands commit our living. That I take to be worship.

But such commitment does not stop with contemplation. It seeks issue in work. For the God discovered thus is a God at work, reconciling the world to Himself. And those who worship in spirit and truth find themselves called to a ministry of reconciliation. A world unfinished and broken is to be made whole. Ultimately it is God, not we, who must heal it, but in our small measure, we may be co-laborers with God. That is our calling. Worship sends us out to work. But work in turn, through frustration or consummation, may continually tend again toward worship, wherein illumination and renewal are to be found. Such, in part, is man's way toward God. . . . .

THE WAY OF GOD WITH MAN

We need continually to reiterate to ourselves and one another: that words may point toward God, but cannot make Him known. He must make Himself known; and only to one who has come to believe himself confronted by God, in the concrete rise and fall of his own living, can such words be more than counters in a mental exercise.

We have said we believe in God as Mind, Spirit, Holy Will at work within and beyond our half-made actual world; a Creator-Redeemer God bringing order out of chaos. Not mere chaos and not perfect order; but concrete stuff (matter, energy, flux, whatever it be) in process of being shaped into more complex and meaningful parts and wholes. God, we have said, is transcendent beyond the actual world of any specified epoch, even while operative within it as effective organizing power; effecting change in the current world-situation, while extending beyond it in time-span, in cognitive range, and in mode of being.

Men are not parts of God, nor one with God, nor gods in their own right. They are creatures, in the sense that for their existence they are utterly dependent upon powers beyond themselves; and in the further sense that their goodness and their powers to achieve good are likewise derived, and when compared with even such good as men themselves can clearly envisage, and far more when compared with what one may dimly suppose God to be, must seem humiliatingly small. Yet men, for Christian faith, are likewise, such that they may become "sons of God" and "co-laborers with God. . . . ."

But the initiative is first and forever from God's side.

I

"God speaks." Aye, and with what voice? (1) Ordinarily we men communicate, one with another, by perceptible signals—gestures, sounds, written symbols, and the like—which need to be interpreted by the observer, if the intent of the sender is to be revealed. Something comparable to this is, perhaps, to be seen as Berkeley thought in the order of nature and human life, so far as these appear significant and intelligible. . . . .

Not all of such data, needless to say, stand on the same level of meaningfulness and value as revelation; and not one kind of skill alone, on the observer's side, will help to find their meanings. A man is of more value than a sheep, for the seeker after God's will; and some among human lives —a prophet's life, a martyr's, a saviour's—will shine with peculiar clarity as luminous foci through which immense ranges of meaning are made plain. Through "the starry heavens and the moral law within" comes general revelation; through illuminating crises, apparently slashing across but in fact carrying forward eruptively the stream of events, come special revelations. Scientists, men of affairs, poets, plain folk look out upon all these signs. To some, keen and powerful grasp of facts and logic is given; to some, sensitive feeling and subtle imagination; to some, inarticulate steadfastness and patient desire. Men and women of all these groups will add their special contributions to our understanding of ourselves, the world, and God.

Jesus' life and death has brought us into focus, for many, what otherwise would be blurred and disheartening turmoil. Among "special revelations" it has a central place. But the meaning of it, too, needs to be discovered and apprehended through patient, penetrating study. It is not self-explanatory. For many besides the Jews and the Greeks of St. Paul's day, the cross has been a stumbling block and an absurdity. Only to those who by faith, insight, devotion, have penetrated beyond the obvious, brutal denial of human decency and human hope in such a tragedy can it serve to reveal "the power of God and the wisdom of God."

By such communication as this, one may surmise, must come detailed divine "guidance" for men; which needs to be deciphered, year after year, generation after generation, by individuals employing all their powers of sensitive observation and appreciation, and critical judgment, always at the risk of error but not without hope of increasing insight.

(2) Besides this more usual mode of communication through detailed,

intentional signals, there is a rarer sort of communication between human persons, especially between those who know each other well through long life together. . . . . There are clairvoyant moments when, without a word spoken or a conscious gesture made, the presence of another self comes home to one with vivid reality. One's friend, one's child, one's mate emerges from the fragmentary and often perfunctory contacts of routine association into galvanic aliveness and "immediacy." With such experiences, I venture to think, the visions of the mystics are to be compared; not the hallucinatory phenomena of sights and sounds which the great mystics have themselves disparaged as mere adjuncts or even distractions, but the central conviction of the overwhelming presence of God.

Such experiences are not everyday occurrences as between human friends, even the most intimate; and I doubt that they should be expected as routine happenings in man's quest for communion with God. Doubtless one may become more sensitive, and in some sense more fit for such experience, through discipline. But I suspect it must be a much more inclusive discipline than simple devotional exercise; and I suspect too that seeking the experience directly and frequently, as an everyday guide to living, is not without danger that one may mistake a less significant but more readily exploitable sort of experience for the greater and rarer vision, and cultivate the less instead of seeking the greater. . . . .

In sum, if this way of conceiving the matter have any validity, one may hope by patient deciphering of the laws of nature and of human life to discover what details may be discernible of God's will as revealed through the media of actual events. To such interpretation both the acumen of scientists, the vision of poets, the vigor of men of action, and the patient fortitude of plain folk must all contribute. To this end we read our Scriptures and our newspapers, we search the stars and the shop and street-corner, with what wisdom we may. And as we search, the air may brighten and the heart lift from time to time, and we go on, still groping but of good cheer.

II

Of God as co-working with men, little more need be said. The phrase must not, of course, be taken to suggest anything like parity of man with God, nor the substitution of human for divine ends. But it does quite frankly affirm, against extreme doctrines of the discontinuity of God and the world, that so far as men wittingly or unwittingly align themselves with the divine order, God himself sustains and furthers what they do. . . . .

To think of God as co-working with man seems to me to involve two affirmations. . . . . First, the environing conditions of human life result continuously from God's creative ordering of the extra-human world. The world-order which thus continuously issues into being is not God, nor wholly the work of God, but at every point is the resultant of God's working *and* other factors, material, formal, and dynamic. Of no single event can one say, "This is God's doing alone," nor of another, "From this God's hand is wholly absent." Rather, every event showeth His handiwork, yet in every event rigid forms, continuous flux, and the stresses and strains exerted by other agents and actual events are involved also. . . . . There is dependable order, as we have tediously insisted, present wherever our minds have probed; and in establishing and maintaining the particular ordering that obtains in actuality, God assures man of a fit environment for life, growth, and creative struggle. But also there is process, change, surprise, and one may suspect "real indeterminacy"; not concentrated into certain gaps, as it were—certain vacua from which order is absent—but present everywhere in all actual events as correlate to order, so that every resultant case of actual orderedness comes to be as it is contingently, rather than necessarily, as an event which up to the moment of its occurrence might not have come about as it does. . . . . Nature as man's environment is in process of being brought into accord with the demands of "what ought to be"—in process of being "reconciled"—rather than already exemplifying perfectly the will of God. In its progressive ordering God, men, and other agents may work together.

Secondly, the same correlation of order and contingent process appears also in the lives of men and women, and that in all their details. For this reason, human persons can sin, in real rebellion against God, and be saved through God's persuasive grace. If God works with men in that He effects within their environment such ordering as fits it for human life, growth, and learning through meaningful work, He works with men also in that He calls them to work and to communion with one another and with Himself. Man in waywardness and folly is able, since his conduct shares the indeterminacy of all actual events, to act in conflict rather than in harmony with God's will to bring about what ought to be. He may act thus in ignorance of God and of his own obliquity; or he may act thus in deliberate rebellion. In either event God is with him—"the Hound of Heaven"—patiently, silently turning him back from satisfaction craved but wrongly sought; silently urging upon him, by signs within him and without, the need to repent, to orient himself anew. By the suffering he brings upon others and upon himself; by the failures and the unnourishing successes he achieves; by the love of those who love him, and the pain of those he may love; by the inward gnawings of whatever repugnance he may have for cowardice, cruelty, sham, and by the outward and upward pull of whatever may be his measure of response to beauty, truth, and right: by all these ways, epitomized in confrontation with Christ crucified, God works with him to his own salvation. . . . .

III

A final word concerning God as sovereign Ground and Goal, and the need for what has often been called negative theology. . . . . He is Ground of being, we say sometimes, and Goal of the world-stream. Mind in a sense is both. It is a medium by which possibilities become actualized; and it is a concrete culmination of simpler stages of growth. But other factors than mind must be looked for both at the beginning and at the end. Some of them we know or suspect: some we cannot now even conceive. . . . . We tell our stories of Him as best we can, and know when we have done that silence is better.

AT HOME IN THE UNIVERSE

Bernard Eugene Meland

CAN MAN BE AT HOME in the universe? Here is a question of first importance to our modern world. In fact, it is so important that until we answer it decisively, life and religion will continue to be ambiguous, both in meaning and in worth. Our generation would do well to ponder the question that is so frequently raised, *Why are convictions so rare in our day?* The common reply, "Relativity and its implications," is a good conversational comeback, but it does not penetrate the problem. Convictions are dependent upon theories, to be sure; but they are not wholly an intellectual matter. They are not even *mostly* a matter of the intellect. Convictions are essentially emotional attitudes that issue from deep orientation in a situation. We have convictions when we feel a matter to the core. Convictions are so rare among us today because we have lost track of the centers of life. Today we are searching for those centers as few generations before us have searched. The controversy between Humanists and Theists, and the widespread "conversations about God," are clear indications that the modern mind is troubled about basic matters. . . . . .

Now the empirical direction of this searching is worth noting. Fifty years ago, theologians and philosophers would probably not have identified the theistic question with the problem of man's place in nature, for theism in those days related to a realm beyond the natural order; and man's essential nature likewise belonged more to that other world than to the natural world. Thus, man's place in nature in no way complicated the doctrine of God or belief in the integrity of man. That matter has changed today. Whatever else the scientific outlook has done to our thinking, it has so amplified the scope and activity of the natural world as to shift the direction of the average person's thinking from the supernatural to the natural scene. The world of nature has become so significant to our day that thoughtful laymen as well as metaphysicians are saying that God apart from nature is unthinkable. If He is not apiece with nature, then He does not exist. And on the other hand, the reality of God's existence increases in proportion as his activity becomes relevant to the natural process. Abstract reasoning in defense of a modified supernaturalism will not change this mental set. For like all mental sets, it is rooted in a total orientation of human thought and emotions. . . . .

Now the whole basis for the Humanist's thesis is that the universe, as he sees it, does not reveal any evidence for such an affirmation of God. Rather, he insists, it gives evidence for an "affirmative *disbelief* in God." The problem then shifts back upon a prior question, What do you see in the

From *Modern Man's Worship*, New York, 1934, pp. 144-159. Reprinted by permission of the publishers, Harper & Brothers.

universe? and that question in turn often hinges upon a corresponding one, How do you look at the universe?

Actually, then, faith in God and confidence in the worth of human aspirations have come to rest with full weight upon the basic inquiry, Can man be at home in the universe without cultivating illusions? Can he establish his affinities with its life on a basis genuine enough to warrant the mood of at-homeness? Emersonian or Wordsworthian idealism is hardly convincing enough to satisfy the realistic temper of modern thinkers. We seek not merely a metaphysical, but a religious at-homeness, rooted in a biological and psyhcological at-oneness with its life. Ultimately, then, this comes to be a question of man's organic relations with the life of earth.

The extent of man's intimacy with the life of earth has only recently come to be fully realized. Wherever supernaturalism has influenced human thought, man has conceived his life on earth as only a temporary residence in a vale of tears. His real home was in the skies. The tragedy of supernaturalism has been that it has lured man away from the universe. It has left him hostile, fearsome, or indifferent to the great life that surges through him and through his fellow creatures.

Liberal religion has not succeeded in saving the modern man from this dilemma. The reason is that, fundamentally, it too is moored to supernaturalism. As a matter of fact, religious liberals seem to be straddling two world views. Influenced by their ethical ideal, they have recognized the importance of present-day living and have turned with zeal to its tasks; but on the other hand, many of their religious concepts are still cast in a prescientific framework, and their religious emotions still seem to respond most readily to that other-worldly temper. To be sure, their other-worldiness has not completely alienated them from the natural world, for they have sought to correlate the present world with the transcendent "far-off divine event" in their program of the Kingdom of God. Nevertheless, the direction of their religious outlook ultimately tends away from the natural world.

Humanism has brought men to the halfway station. The Humanist has sloughed off his supernatural garb, but has not yet mustered up confidence enough to jump all the way into the cosmic sea. Hence he stands upon the shore unclothed, shivering from the "cosmic chill." To put the matter less figuratively, Humanism is a truncated supernaturalism. The super-structure has gone, but the age-old human hopes linger, either as haunting memories or as tenuous ideals, heroically defying truculent forces that threaten their undoing. The same attitude of distrust toward the natural world persists. The crucial fact is that neither the Theist nor the Humanist is at home in his universe. . . . . .

Just here is where the crux of the dilemma seems to lie. Two matters demand clarification: what actually is man's place in the world of nature, and what can one mean by blending human life with earthways?

The place of man in the world of nature is a problem of grave concern today. Our knowledge of the universe, particularly with reference to those aspects which most concern human life, is as yet so inadequate that one hardly feels warranted making confident assertions. Humanists, eager to stay within the bounds of factual observance, have concluded that whatever place man is to have in nature, he must achieve for himself. Nature, so far as they intererpret her life, is quite indifferent to the human scene. Others, sympathetic in the main with the tenets and aims of the Humanistic movement, find evidence, they believe, which assures them that man is not alone in his venture. Much depends, of course, upon what one means by the world of nature. And what one means by nature will depend greatly upon what he includes in his data as evidence. I think it is important to recognize that the universe, as the modern sciences describe it, is not the same kind of universe which the physical sciences of the nineteenth century portrayed. Naturalism of the contemporary sort is significantly modified by data which have come from the social sciences. The dictum that issues from this standpoint is that any legitimate picture of the universe, as science sees it, must include man as well as society, for human life, as it appears both in the individual and in group association, is a genuine product of the natural forces.

As a starting basis, that assumption seems valid. To what extent, then, may we reason from that basis that Earth is *for* man? To what extent do cosmic forces actually sustain human life and help men fulfill their ventures? It is all too easy to become over-optimistic and fantastic at this point when one has a *will* to *believe*, so we need to guard against speaking over-confidently. But let us approach the problem from its basic level, holding persistently to the biological foundations. Man as an organism lives by virtue of direct relations with his environment. Certain conditions in that environment make it possible for him to exist. The presence of atmosphere is one very important condition. Scientists are unanimously agreed that without the blanket of atmosphere that enevelops our planet no such creature as man, or any other form of organic life, could exist. And further, when man's finely constructed instruments for interacting with that atmosphere, his respiratory system, cease to operate, that interaction, which we call breathing, stops, and death ensues. Obviously, then, interaction with this wealth of atmosphere that environs us is one of the essential conditions for human life. Or, to put the matter positively, man is sustained as an organism when he is properly adjusted to his atmospheric environment.

Another condition revealing man's intimacy with the life of earth is his dependence upon organic food and water. This as a phenomenon is not very different from the interaction of his organism with atmosphere. It is true that in the matter of food and water, man is *put to it* to procure these elements and to imbibe them by consciously directed effort. And in this sense he provides himself with food and water. But there is something to the fact that the kind of food, congenial to man's needs, and of a character that contributes toward sustaining his organism and toward building it up during his growing years, is available in his surroundings. Or, to put the matter less teleologically, there is significance to the fact that man is so adaptable in his organic functions that he can establish the necessary congenial relations with such elements as are available in his environment as to be nourished by them. . . . .

This organic at-homeness extends beyond the physical level. For man is more than physical; he is a psycho-physical organism. Here again, this psychical behavior is a condition which has emerged out of the natural order that has produced all organic life. It is, in fact, as has been pointed out in studies by Lloyd Morgan, Smuts, Sellars, and others, part of an order or structure that has existed with varying degrees of clearness, sometimes only in incipient form, throughout all levels of the natural order. The psychically sensitive human is still natural man acting in accord with his universe; for his psychic life and his physical life are rooted in a common structure.

Out of this capacity to respond feelingly to environing things and events have issued the many actions and reactions that have added the emotional overtones to existence. Out of this sensitivity have come all the emotions, base and noble, ranging from jungle ruthlessness, motivated by elemental fear and rage, to the rare and deep love of the pure in heart.

Mind, too, is earthborn. The story of man groping his way through un-trammeled forests during the infancy days of the race; emerging from jungle environs to try his hand at a systematic search for food; domesticating animals and turning them to his support; lumberly experimenting with crudely made implements until finally their usefulness was established; applying his instruments to till the soil so as to increase his produce and thereby strengthening his security against starvation; organizing his group life into complex units, inventing methods of economic exchange; cultivating his arts, his speech, his literature—all this, and much more, is the romantic story of mind in the making. It is also the story of culture and civilization in the making, for they are the by-products in the growth of mind. Mind was no free gift of the gods; it was the hard-earned achievement of struggling humans, painfully, yet heroically, adapting themselves to their world. . . . .

We proceed a step farther. Not only is man physical, psychical, and mental; he is a social organism. That is, he projects himself co-operatively in relation with other organisms. Here again man is perpetuating and developing a pattern of behavior that is prevalent to some extent among the lower forms of organic life. This social form of behavior, in fact, appears at the very lowest level of conscious life. Creatures among almost every known species—ants, bees, fish, wolves, cattle, human tribes, society—behave according to organizational patterns. To be sure, sociologists are no longer of the opinion that society is merely an outgrowth of animal gregariousness, yet society and the pack are parallel phenomena, and doubtless have certain origins in common. Their bases are identical. Their objectives are similar. The qualitative difference between them has arisen because of the increase in symbols among humans, which has enabled them to enter into a progress-ively enriching experience of interaction. The story of civilization in its simplest terms is the story of man's symbols increasing in number and com-plexity, thus enabling him to participate in increasingly complex social interaction. At the base is primitive group life; at the peak, the city commonwealth.

What is this social interaction, seen in its cosmic context? A complete answer is not possible. Sociologists may describe it, and may provide us with a set of concepts and principles that will enable us to account for, or to predict, social behavior; but neither factor answers the question "What?" in cosmic terms. Beyond the area of observable behaviors there are cosmic workings which are too widespread in implication, too deeply involved in the environing structure, and too subtle in operation to appear visibly intact in the abstracted and isolated data upon which the social scientist must base conclusions. The wealth of organic process, everywhere operative in the surroundings, environing man and society, escapes our analysis. . . . .

There is still a further aspect. Social interaction is not merely a quantitative process; it is also qualitative. There is social interaction that is conflict, and a social interaction that is co-operation. The one tends toward the disintegration of group relations; the other leads toward higher degrees of mutuality among individuals and groups. Civilizations have pursued both courses, although the story to date seems to be weighted on the side of conflict. But we are beginning to strike out boldly in the direction of co-operative interaction. We are talking more about interdependence and co-operation than almost any generation prior to our time. This, in fact, is one of the hopeful signs of our time. . . . .

Now the point that we have been aiming to make clear is that man as a phenomenon is not epiphenomenal, but that he is a genuine portion of cosmic life, earthborn and earthsustained. Whether he has been aware of it or not, every phase of his development from his pre-human stage to his present state of culture has been achieved through his asserting his power in co-ordination with sustaining earth forces. The universe *has* supported him in basic ways of which he has been hardly aware. Here on this earth, where thousands of life forms have failed, as Haydon has reminded us, man has been allowed to live. He belongs to the universe, body and spirit. "On this earth alone, could we be at home!"

If men could only become awakened to this sense of belonging to the age-old cosmic process, thoroughly at home in the universe that has produced them and at present sustains them, we should have the psychological basis for common devotion to reality. . . . .

The datum of that wealth of experience which emerges in men's organic interaction with cosmic environment is far too complex to be treated scientifically with any methods or instruments thus far devised. But we are working in that direction. The fact that we have come to think of ourselves as being organically related to the environing universe brings us nearer to that objective. The fact that we are discerning our dependence upon that environment more fully makes that objective more urgent. And the fact that we are coming to envisage our destiny, our fulfillment of life, in terms of adjustment to those sustaining factors in our environment, places us on the road toward understanding that all-important interaction between organism and environment. In a word, can we not say that the biological pattern of thought has brought our thinking about these realities more genuinely into accord with the facts of experience than was ever possible in the legal or forensic mode of thinking? It is my conviction that we shall continue to increase our insight into man's relations with the universe by steadily pursuing this biological and psychological path toward reality, working from our point of dependence, out toward the reality upon which we depend. That there may be other means of establishing insight here is certainly a reasonable thesis. And no fruitful line of inquiry or experience may be ignored which will help us to penetrate this fundamental matter.

PRIVATE WORSHIP

Henry Nelson Wieman

1. Preconditions of Worship

THERE ARE THREE PRECONDITIONS which must be met before effective worship is possible. The first is that one must go out into deep water. He must take life seriously. He must not shirk the heavy responsibilities. He must venture out to depths where wading is difficult. No one ever worshiped profoundly and with largest results who was not struggling. That does not mean that he must do something conspicious before the world; much less does it mean that he must seek trouble. It merely means that he assume the tremendous responsibilities that inevitably fall upon every one who lives earnestly and has sufficient insight to discern the tragedies in the lives of men. It means, for example, if one is a parent, that he treat his child not as a plaything only, but shall assume the enormous responsibility of that child's highest development. If he has any direct access to the industrial process, it means that he be not indifferent to the lives that are thwarted and perverted by industry. If he has friends, it means that he be not unaware of that profounder community with them which he has missed because of his mistaken attitudes. If he lives in a world addicted to war, he will not wash his hands of the problem.

The second precondition is sincerity. That means that he will not take into his worship any beliefs which he doubts. If, for example, he doubts there is a God, then in worship he will earnestly seek the best adjustment to whatever in all the universe he believes to be that which can help him most, even though it be nothing more, in his belief, than his own subconscious self, or his fellow associates in the group to which he belongs.

We are very sure that a man who thinks will not limit himself in worship to such objects as we have mentioned. There is something we call God which is vastly more than these. But the point we want to make is that in worship one must be absolutely honest with himself. Worship is the time when a man deliberately undertakes to make the best possible adjustment to that which he believes in all sincerity to be the matter of greatest concern. God is the matter of greatest concern.

A man who thinks he doubts the existence of God still believes that something is most important. When he denies God he is merely asserting that what others hold to be most important and call God is not supreme or does not exist. But in his belief something else is supreme and does exist or has objective being of some sort. This something else is for all practical purpose what he believes God to be, although he may be mistaken in holding it to be so important. He probably is mistaken in at least some of his ideas

From *Methods of Private Religious Living*, New York, 1929, chap. i. Reprinted by permission of the publishers, The Macmillan Company.

about it. None of us has the whole truth; all of us are subject to error in our beliefs about God. But all of us can and should worship, whether we use the word God or not. Thereby we shall attain a more adequate idea of God.

A man in worship must not try to make himself believe that which he doubts, for if he does he will ruin his worship. Whenever any belief or word puts him under a sense of constraint, or gives him a sense of unreality, he must set it aside. Worship is pre-eminently probing down beneath all the sham and pose which inevitably accumulate in every man's life with the daily routine. Worship is struggling to cast off all this unconscious and unintended but inevitable hypocrisy and getting down to reality about himself and his world, as he is able to experience it. Absolute sincerity, completest honesty, is indispensable to helpful worship, and ultimately it will lead to more adequate and well-established beliefs.

A man does not need to believe in God in order to worship. Let us state that in other words. A man must believe in God in order to worship; but he may be so constituted mentally that doubts arise in his mind whenever he uses the word God, and therefore in his worship he will not apply the word God to that upon which he feels he is dependent for the preservation and increase of values. But one thing is certain. Every man needs to worship, whether or not he uses the word God.

Private worship is doing two things: finding out what is wrong with oneself; and establishing that personal attitude through which one can receive from sources outside himself those influences which will correct the wrong which is in him. This is why every man needs to worship and why complete sincerity is indispensable, requiring the exclusion of every belief which is doubted. The hardest thing for a human being to do, and the thing most critically important for himself and all affected by him is to discover what is wrong with him and so be able to expose himself to those influences which can work in him the needed transformations. Worship helps one accomplish this. Without worship one is likely to fall into that most hopeless and wretched state wherein he thinks he has no need of transformation; or, discovering that he needs it, cannot find that which will accomplish it. To discover one's need but not know how to meet it, is not quite so hopeless a condition as to be completely ignorant of the need. Through worship we are delivered from both these wretched conditions; but without worship we cannot be.

The third precondition has to do with time and place and surroundings. The time may be any hour of the twenty-four; but the best time, we are very sure, is just before retiring at night and soon after rising in the morning. The ideal place, we think, would be a mountain top at night. That is the place Jesus seemed to prefer for his private worship. But for the most of us most of the time that is impossible. Some room will serve, especially if it can be shut so that one need not fear others will hear even when he speaks aloud, and where his mind will not be distracted by any sights, sounds or apprehensions. The purpose of worship is to turn the mind away from lesser things and give the whole attention to the supreme thing. But these lesser things from which we want to escape are almost invariably suggested to the mind by immediate physical stimuli; hence these latter should be shut out so far as possible.

In private worship we seclude ourselves from physical association with others. Does this imply that private worship is unsocial or anti-social? Not at all. Community of heart and mind is not identical with physical contact. As we have just indicated, immediate physical stimuli tend to distract the mind to lesser things. One will never discover the largest import of all the physical stimuli that come to him from the bodies of his fellow men if he does not occasionally isolate himself from their bodies and take time to meditate in solitude. He does not thereby isolate himself from their minds. On the contrary it is only in this way that he can reach the profounder levels of fellowship. When one goes into seclusion he does not suddenly cut himself off from all the experiences he has ever had with his fellows. On the contrary all those experiences, and all the problems they involve, are with him still. But in the seclusion of worship he is seeking to catch those deeper currents of life which open up the larger meaning of all our little words and deeds. Above all he is seeknig to join most fully with that integrating process which works through all the world not only to bring human lives into organic fellowship with one another but also to maintain and develop organic interdependence and mutual support between all parts and aspects of the cosmos. This integrating process is God. We must have private solitary worship, as well as public worship, if we would join ourselves with this working of God.

Thus far we have been considering the preconditions of worship—earnestness of living, sincerity of belief, seclusion from distracting stimuli. Let us now turn to the act of worship itself.

2. The Act of Worship

The first step in the act of worship is to relax and to become aware of that upon which we are dependent, that which sustains us in every breath we breathe, that which shapes the cells of our bodies and the impulses of our hearts according as we adjust to it in this way or that. One can think of this all-encompassing reality as atoms, if he wishes, or electric tension, or use some other such imagery. The imagery adapted to one mind will not be adapted to another. To talk about all our lives being sustained and shaped by atoms or electric tension, is, of course, pure mythology. But some minds may be of such a twist as to find such a myth helpful. The point is that we are sustained; and in so far as we rise to higher levels of living we do so by adaptation to that which lifts us. In this first act of worship we fill and suffuse our minds with the sense of this encompassing presence that sustains and lifts and works toward the organic community of each with all. . . . .

The second step in worship is to call to mind the vast and unimaginable possibilities for good which are inherent in this integrating process called God. These possibilities are actualized in us and in others and in all the world round about us in so far as we and others find and establish the required adjustment between ourselves and this cosmic process which is

God. In the meantime, however, these possibilities are genuine constituents of our world by virtue of the pervasive working of that which we call God. . . . .

The third step is to face the chief problem with which we are struggling. If we are living earnestly we are always struggling with a problem which taxes our powers. We shall frequently have the sense of being baffled because we do not see the way to its solution. But most of the time, unless we take opportunity for the kind of worship we are here describing, we shall not face the problem in its entirety and get it in its true perspective. We are too busy dealing with some pressing detail to face it in all its fullness. But in this third stage of worship, after we have become aware of God (called by another name if we must) and of the total maximum of possibility for good which inheres in God and our relations to him, we face our problem. We survey it as comprehensively and acutely as possible to find what most needs to be done.

The fourth step is self-analysis to find what change must be made in our own mental attitudes and personal habits. No problem was ever solved, no desired result ever attained, by worship or in any other way, which did not require some personal readjustment on the part of the person through whom it was attained. Worship has practical value and is a way of doing things only because it enables us (1) to discover what personal readjustment is required of us and (2) to establish that readjustment in ourselves. . . . .

What, then, has worship to do with God? It has everything to do with God. God is the integrating process at work in the universe. Worship is the way we press the button, that is, establish the mental attitude and consequent behavior, and so make those connections through which this work of God can fulfill itself to the end of maximum good. That is the rôle of worship in the practical work of the world and it is a rôle of exceeding great importance. To neglect worship is disastrous. We cannot make right connections with the integrating work of God without it. . . . . It is not so much that we press a button but rather we ourselves are pressed into place and so through us the circuit is closed and the wider and richer integration which God achieves is brought to pass. In worship we are thus finding the way to join ourselves with God in his work of integration. Worship has everything to do with God.

The fifth step in worship is to formulate in words as clearly and comprehensively as possible the readjustment of personality and behavior which I have discovered is required of me if I am to close the circuit between certain disconnected factors in the world round about me. This verbal statement of the needed readjustment is very important. It should be accurate, comprehensive, concise. Above all it must be affirmative; not negative. For in worship we are not primarliy trying to break a connection but to establish a connection. We are trying to do something constructive, not destructive. We must be positive, not negative. No good thing was ever done by merely a negative attitude. No problem was every solved in that way. The overcoming of a fault is always a positive, constructive operation. . . . .

3. Worship and Auto-suggestion

The last step in the complete act of worship is a kind of auto-suggestion. There is so much misunderstanding and difference of opinion concerning this matter of auto-suggestion, especially in its application to worship, that we must examine it briefly in this context.

The words repeated for purpose of auto-suggestion are not necessarily prayers to God, although one may so apply them if he chooses. But the communion with God has already been accomplished in the earlier stages of the worship as previously described. What one is now doing by this repetition is to reap the benefits of that worship and enter into realization of the possibilities which it has opened up. Through this repetition of words you are simply establishing as an enduring habitual attitude of the total personality that adjustment to God which you have attained through worship. You are sealing, conserving, "nailing down" the benefits of that worship. Anyone who will try this method of worship, ending with this practice of auto-suggestion, and continue it for several weeks, performing it each night just before retiring, will note some remarkable results of great benefit to himself and his associates.

But why, one may ask, should you tack any worship on to this auto-suggestion? Why not practice it by itself? Anyone who raises such a question will have missed the whole point of our discussion. Of course one can practice auto-suggestion without the help of worship and can thereby establish in himself the attitude which he suggests. But will the attitude thus established help him? It will not if it is the wrong attitude. But how can he ever discover what right attitude to establish by means of auto-suggestion? He can never discover it unless he does three things: (1) Attains some sense of what the sustaining process is through which he must work to attain the good he seeks; (2) clearly comprehends the specific problem which he faces at the time; (3) knows his own attitudes and needed reconstruction of attitude in relation to this sustaining process and specific problem. But the worship we have described is precisely the doing of these three things. Therefore, while one can practice auto-suggestion without worship, he is not likely to accomplish much good by it; and he may work fearful evil through auto-suggestion without worship by establishing the wrong attitudes.

The benefits that result from worship are not merely the benefits of auto-suggestion. To make this plain let us again resort to analogy. Suppose I want to experience an electric shock. I sit down far removed from any electric charge and with all the best technique of auto-suggestion say to myself: I am experiencing an electric shock. By this method I may make myself think that I have received a shock, but it will not have occurred and its objective consequences will never take place. I might practice auto-suggestion in this way all my life and the shock and its consequences will never occur, however completely I might succeed in producing in myself an illusion to that effect.

To get a shock I must put myself in contact with an electric charge. But I am psychologically incapable of holding my finger in contact with the source of an electric shock which has any marked strength. Right here is where auto-suggestion may be used. It cannot be used to produce a shock; but it can and must be used by me to establish in me the mental attitude in which alone I am able to keep my finger in contact with that which can produce the shock. That is precisely the work of auto-suggestion in worship. It cannot itself do the work of that process called God; but it can enable me to make the required adjustment to this process. When this adjustment on my part is made the process does the work. The process, at the level of its widest scope and greatest power for good, is God.

The beneficial results of worship, then, are not merely the results of auto-suggestion any more than an electric shock or a growing crop is merely the work of auto-suggestion. But in all of these auto-suggestion has *its* part to play.

CREATIVE WORSHIP

Edgar Sheffield Brightman

WHAT WORSHIP CREATES: PERSPECTIVE

IF RELIGION BE RIGHT in its faith that the true worship of God is one of the highest points of the universal creative process, there arises the problem, What is it that worship creates? What qualities of life are produced? What sort of persons are made? . . . .

First, worship gives man perspective. The natural man starts with his body and its needs, what his senses experience and his desires demand, and with the conventions of his group. A certain perspective is given in the very conditions of existence; but it is not the ultimate perspective that man needs. The accidents of life soon force him to acknowledge that he and his are not all that exists. There are powers beyond his domain. He tries to explore their ways of acting, and to understand and control them for his own ends. But in worship he comes to his most intimate relations with those powers, relations of a quite different order from those of his natural life. Worship enables him to look at his life not alone from his own point of view, or from any human standpoint, but, in some measure, from the point of view of his God. If creative prayer be, as Mrs. Herman calls it, "the soul's pilgrimage from self to God," when one finds God, one finds a new perspective, which is not only new but unique.

This perspective is not identical with the emotional glow of a conversion experience or a mystical ecstasy. It is, rather, the insight that comes to man when his life and the whole world are set into relation to his God and when he thus recognizes himself as member of the whole in which God is supreme. For many mystical souls this experience of perspective and its attendant emotions are the whole of religion. For all who truly worship it is most precious. He who said, "Unless a man say in his heart, I and God are alone in the world, he will never find peace" was expressing the common faith of most deeply religious natures. The vitality of pantheism among mystics is probably due largely to its interpretation of this perspective. We are the branches; he is the vine. We are thus one with God. The intellectual defects of pantheism are, in the eyes of the mystic, atoned for by its religious genius. . . . . Thus it is evident that religious worship connects man's inmost life with a realm that is more-than-human, more-than-social —the realm of what is eternally real.

Such a perspective is no mere barren theory, if, indeed, theories are barren; it is a force in life. It gives man what he most needs, namely, the combination of a sense of his personal worth with a sense of personal subordination. Either of these alone is easily achieved. A sense of personal

From *Religious Values*, New York, 1925, pp. 212-223. Reprinted by permission of the publishers, Abingdon-Cokesbury Press.

worth is the native element of the natural man. A sense of personal subordination is the ready attitude of the fawning politician, the self-seeker, or any man who is in a mood of depression. But how easily each of these changes into something less valuable than itself! It takes but little to transform the sense of personal worth into intolerable self-conceit and the sense of subordination into false humility. But every true value creates the union of the two to some extent. Loyalty to the true or the good or the beautiful nourishes the worth of the individual and yet subjects him to the law of the ideal which he is seeking to attain. Yet no experience in life deepens and intensifies both of these aspects in such perfect balance as does the worship of God. "The practice of the presence of God," says Jeremy Taylor, "is the cause of great modesty and decency in our actions . . . . when we see ourselves placed in the eye of God."

To be truly and inseparably a member of the whole of which God is the Supreme Power creates the sense of personal worth. Man communes with God! The Infinite God condescends to man, and seeks him as a shepherd seeks his lost sheep! Yet the sense of the value of one's own soul, while preserved, is set at once into violent contrast with an idea that serves as its check and balance. To be truly a member of the whole exalts my self-esteem; but to be member of such a whole! A whole of which God is center and source! Overwhelming power, blinding beauty, ineffable wisdom, stainless goodness, all reveal to me my dependence and my subordination. . . . .

Personal worth and personal subordination thus fuse in the worshiper's experience. Out of this tension of opposites is born religious personality with its peculiar qualities—a poise that, while worship lives, can never become apathy, a peace that cannot become mere passivity, a joy that cannot become frivolity, a confidence that cannot become overconfidence. True religious worship, therefore, will feed the springs of inner life with a secret calm that supplants the fears which paralyze humanity. A popular writer has well said that "if hope and courage go out of the lives of common men, it is all up with social and political civilization." The rebirth of worship is an urgent need of civilization. . . . .

WHAT WORSHIP CREATES: A SPIRITUAL IDEAL

Wherever true worship has created perspective the current of spiritual life begins to flow deeper. Worship has a fashion of intensifying and enriching itself as it proceeds from contemplation to revelation, from revelation to communion, and from communion to fruition. . . . .

The fact that man is an ideal-forming being is one of the most significant facts about him. How he comes to form ideals is a subject for psychological investigation. But let psychology describe that process in any way it please, for the worshiper two things will be true: he will see the law of that process as his God's way of working in the mind of man, and he will know that his ideal assumes its actual form precisely because he worships. When true worship creates perspective, it brings in its train an ideal of what spiritual life ought to be. The infinite perspective generates an infinite ideal of perfection. . . . .

God is perfect goodness, perfect value. The worshiper of such a God has had revealed to him an ideal of his own personality as completely devoted to the perfect values of his God. In the nature of this spiritual ideal lies its peculiar creativity. It is an unattainable, an inexhaustible ideal; one the pursuit of which is self-justifying and utterly satisfying, yet one which requires eternity for its realization. No infinitely repeated cycle of world history, of which the ancients dreamed, could express or exhaust this ideal. . . . .

The nature of the spiritual ideal gives rise to problems, one of which we may now examine. Just how is the worshiper to think of the realization of this ideal? He believes that it has been revealed to him by God; in God, then, is its home, its guarantee, its eternal realization. Yet there is a peril in dwelling too exclusively on the realization of the ideal in God. If the universe be already perfected, there is ground for faith, but there is also ground for inaction. . . . . The Divine Sovereign, divinely perfect, has made his universe the home of value. What has the religious soul to do but to accept and contemplate the divine perfection? Quietism is the natural conclusion from this premise. The logic of certain forms of absolutism, of pantheism, and of Calvinism all points in the same direction. Worship, then, is in peril of causing a barren and passive inaction. To "fold the hands and calmly wait" is the highest achievement of which this phase is capable. Calm faith is assuredly a blessing when it engenders loyalty, a curse when it creates indifference to the duties of life.

In order to avoid this peril of indifferentism some fly to the opposite extreme of holding that the ideal is to be made real, if at all, by man's own efforts. This is the typical attitude of the entirely nonreligious person; within the religious camp it develops the purely humanistic religion (if it may properly be called religion) which identifies the whole of religion with the Golden Rule, makes service its motto, and regards worship and inner spirituality as superfluities, or at best luxuries. . . . .

If these opposed perils are both to be avoided, the spiritual ideal of religion should constantly be viewed in the perspective of which we spoke earlier. When thus regarded, the realization of the ideal is seen to be an infinite co-operative process in the whole to which man belongs; yet man's part in that process, however small, is seen to be essential to the whole. The ideal that is born into the worshiping soul cannot then lead to mere blessed contemplation of a perfect universe when it is fully grasped in its total meaning; nor can it lead to mere feverish, despairing activity. What religion offers is the high adventure of co-operation with God.

What Worship Creates: Power

If religion created no more than the perspective and the ideal of which we have been speaking, it would have justified itself. Yet perspective and ideals seem to the average man feeble and futile. He craves something that makes it possible for him to live in accordance with the ideal. That something is the creation of communion, the third stage of worship. The fruit of communion at its highest levels is power. From its most primitive forms to its most developed, religion has been a search for power, a faith that there were untapped reservoirs of spiritual energy in the unseen. He who in worship becomes conscious of communing with the Eternal God is able to report that he is endued with power from on high. . . . .

Religious power has certain striking traits. In common with all power, it makes a new future possible for the person. That new future may not be a control of environment or of bodily disease, but perhaps something more valuable—the control of inner attitude. But religious power has an additional aspect that is more characteristic. Not only can it, within limits, control the future; it can also transform the past. The common idea that the past is a record that has been written once for all and can never be altered in the slightest iota is true enough so far as the content of the past is concerned; but it is not true of the meaning of the past. One never knows what a picture means until one has seen the whole picture. One cannot understand a poem from the first few lines; one must read the entire poem. Likewise one cannot read off the meaning of one's past experiences without considering their relation to the present and future. This fact is of great moment to religion. The worshiper, believing that present and future may be given new power by his communion with God, has faith that his whole life, including his past, is also transformed by that same power. He who worships will always know that his past has been what it was, with all its weaknesses, sins, and shames. But before he communed with God that past was sin; after meeting God his past is still the same sin, but that sin forgiven, the sinner redeemed. The same facts are there; but religion has power to give them a different meaning. As the final stroke of the artist's brush changes the whole effect of a painting, so the experience of the forgiving mercy of God changes the whole effect of a soul. . . . .

WHAT WORSHIP CREATES: A COMMUNITY OF LOVE

No account of the fruit of worship in personality would be complete if it omitted what is the supreme consummation of worship, and, if the experiences of religion foreshadow truth, the very goal and purpose of the universe: I mean, the Community of Love, or, as Royce called it, the Beloved Community. So far we have been considering the creative power of worship in the experiences of the individual worshiper. But, however true it may be that in the act of worship there is always a "flight of the alone to the alone," and that the moment of worship is a temporary forgetting of one's fellowmen, the experience of finding God is also a rediscovery of every other human soul. Worship needs and finds God who is a God of all. . . . .

Individual worship in the secret places of the heart is indeed essential to all true religion; but experience shows that when individuals come together and become a worshiping community, new spiritual levels are reached, new values created, new powers released. No function of consciousness remains precisely the same when others are present as when the individual is alone. Social worship adds new depth and meaning to the experience of God. It is not a substitute for private devotion, any more than opinions of one's social group are a substitute for one's conscience or intelligence. But through social worship love is made more sacred, the feeling of unity with our fellow creatures (for which John Stuart Mill yearned) becomes more vivid and binding, and the fact that God is God of all is more adequately expressed than through any private worship. Hence, he who seeks to be religious apart from the worshiping congregation of the church is surrendering more than he can well afford to lose.

Worship, then, is necessarily social at its highest point. . . . . The wellspring of social unity and spiritual love in the mystical worship of the God of love should never be forgotten. Religious worship, alone of all the forces known to man, is able to perform that miracle of pity and of hope which enables him who has seen God to see not his fellow worshipers only, but all mankind, as a potential Community of Love. That miracle, I say; for the natural man lacks this vision; and the presence of traces of such a feeling toward the human race is almost universally regarded as a token of the presence and work of God in the life of man.

WORSHIP AND PERSONALITY

Clarence Seidenspinner

MEN AND WOMEN may engage in the forms of worship without actually experiencing the act of worship itself, that complete relaxation in the presence of God during which insights are deepened and emotion is released for the reorganization of life. Every parish minister knows that this auto-delusion happens repeatedly to his laymen, but sometimes he needs to face the fact that often it happens to himself.

By auto-delusion in regard to worship I do not mean those dry periods when we are well aware that we are simply repeating forms and are getting no benefit from them. I mean rather those periods during which we react aesthetically to the beauty of worship forms or sentimentally to associations in the content of worship. When the service consists for us of aesthetic joy in the rich timbre of organ diapasons, in the structural perfection of an anthem, in the lyrical quality of a poem or in the sonorous reading of the service, we are limiting our response to only one facet of God's nature, His presence in beauty. When the service consists for us of gregarious joy, of that pleasant sense of well being in the presence of friends, of feeling's gush over some touching story or of the rapid movement of associations in either dolorous or happy paths, we are limiting our response to reality to the superficial emotions resident in the occasion.

This is using worship as a means of escape from God. It has within it nothing of that fine relaxation in the presence of God during which insights are deepened and significant emotion is released, as we face with Him the major tensions of life.

Such delusive worship is not merely harmless; it is positively dangerous to the development of personality. Because our feelings have been touched we think that we have been in the presence of God when merely a complex system of reflexes has been put into operation. There has been no integration of personality around some new insight into reality; there has been no significant emotion released that will sustain us through the weeks in our new relation to reality; there has been no genuine fellowship with God, that factor in this universe who is forever relating men to reality when they do have fellowship with Him. Undirected and insignificant emotion not only fails to aid the process of personality building; it is actually disintegrating in its influence. The victim of persistent auto-delusion in worship is bound to get farther and farther away from God; the umbilical channels which allow the divine energy to flow into body and mind are dammed up by foolishness and selfishness, and in him there is no health.

On the other hand, worship can be a very definite aid in the process of building personality. It may take the ragged ends of a man's days and

Reprinted by permission from *Religion in Life*, Spring, 1938.

integrate them around all that is true and beautiful and good. That this process of integration may be clear, I want to describe in some detail the worship experience which underlies it. I want to reduce the worship experience to essential form, to that basic psychological pattern through which the soul is bound to move in its approach to God, whether it be alone in some private oratory or with the congregation in the nave of the church.

The adoring soul ought at once to place itself before God. As the Divine Presence is reaffirmed and rediscovered the human spirit goes forth to meet God in adoration. This is the first step in private worship and is the basic act of liturgy. It corresponds in the other arts to the portal of a building, to the overture of an opera, to the opening movement of a symphony, to the first act of a play.

This mood of adoration presently changes to one of contemplation as God's will is revealed. In Protestant worship the chief instruments accomplishing this are the scripture lessons and their interpretation in the sermon. Prayer is also used in this connection as an instrument by means of which one responds to the word of God in terms of need, failure, desire, and thanksgiving. This second phase of worship will take considerable time as private prayer or public liturgy proceeds. This is right psychologically, for the eagerness of adoration has passed into the leisurely experience of contemplation.

Finally and swiftly, though never thoughtlessly, the soul moves to dedication. The emotions of adoration and the insights of contemplation are fused into the desire to live on behalf of God, to obey His imperative will, to build His kingdom upon the earth, in order that His nature and will may be concretely, materially set forth. These specific dedications are why the offering in the liturgy should follow the sermon, because it is really a symbolic act, the final summary of the total experience of worship. It affords a few quiet moments of recollection during which the worshiper may summarize the service and sermon in relation to his own life and may silently and personally make his own dedications. All of these individual dedications are then wrought into a magnificent corporate dedication as the entire congregation rises to present its offering to God.

From this discussion of the movement in worship it is apparent that there are three basic steps: 1. The Adoration of God. 2. The Contemplation of God's will. 3. The Dedication. An analysis of typical accounts of the worship experience recorded in scripture and poetry reveals the frequent presence of this devotional pattern. The story of the religious experience of Moses as set forth in Exodus 3 and 4 suggests the adoring worshiper in the presence of God; the long period during which God's will is clarified, and finally the act of dedication, the journey to Egypt. The conversion of Paul follows the same general trend: vision, contemplation, action. Many of the psalms which are complete devotional units reveal this pattern, among them psalms 19, 27, 46, and 90. Shelley's poem "Hymn to Intellectual Beauty" is the record of an essentially devotional experience as the poet apprehends God in beauty and dedicates his life to the increase of beauty upon the earth.

In private worship, one sits down in a quiet place and allows his mind to rest for a few minutes. This is for purposes of orientation and transition. Then he consciously makes an act of the will, placing himself in the presence of God. As an aid to this he may repeat the profoundly numinous Sanctus or some other hymn of adoration. Imaginatively he tries to sense the sublime meaning of that supreme miracle! God, alive and radiant in the world; God, eagerly going forth to meet man in worship; no, not man, but me; O marvelous thought, something utterly impossible but undeniably true, God going forth to meet me in worship.

Adoration then moves into contemplation. It is wise to have a preliminary period of contemplation during which one reads to himself some prayers, some devotional poetry or some passages of fine prose. Then one reads from the gospel, for in the life and teachings of Jesus, God is unmistakably present. One must read those accounts of the supreme experience of mutual interaction between God and man, of desperate discovery and perfect revelation which occurred in Christ Jesus. In reading this gospel one summons every energy he possesses in order that he may transcend the effects of earthly Time upon his consciousness and enter that space-time manifold where the Here and Now is eternally present, where Jesus is just as alive as ever He was, where His clear, compelling voice still speaks of the Fatherhood of God and its manifold implications, where God and Christ and all the blessed realities of the Spirit become the great "I AM." By this act of transcendence one is enabled to be part of that apostolic company who walked about the Galilean country with Jesus and heard from His own lips concerning the deepest revelations of the nature and will of God. In this way the gospel becomes unutterably compelling as Time is foreshortened to the eternal Here and Now.

The gospel is then immediately related to some area of life. If this is not done, the emotions and insights generated by contemplation dissipate themselves into sentimentalism. The gospel says something about a man's work, his character, his health, his fellowship with other persons, his church, his world. These manifold implications must sincerely and eagerly be considered in order that worship may become a fruitful experience for life in the kingdom of God, and personality be immeasurably enriched thereby.

Mingling with this latter andante movement of contemplation are the first notes of the allegro of dedication. Down on your knees in colloquy with God. Now is the time to share with God every fear, every aspiration, every shortcoming and every desire. Speak freely to Him. Then in humility and yet in joy clearly phrase at least one proposition which you intend to express in character and conduct, and which has grown out of your period of contemplation. Unify your aspirations around some aspect of the divine will which you honestly mean to express by your life from now on. This is the allegro movement of the soul and is suggestive of the energy now available for the expression of your purposes.

Perhaps you will not want to spend the amount of time each day that this devotional pattern will consume. In that case it is better to have two or three complete unhurried devotional experiences each week than seven hurried and unsatisfactory ones. You cannot go forth to meet God when you have an eye on the clock.

When worship is thus sincerely experienced, the effect upon personality is profound. At least four important results occur.

1. The personality is related to reality in all its forms: eternal truth, redemptive love, supernatural beauty. The soul confronts the one, solid, dependable fact in the universe, the aliveness of God in all of His radiant and manifold expression. Upon this fact a man can base his life. It gives his life significant content; it expands his margin of joy; it sustains him in times of grief. At any given moment he knows that his life is undergirded by reality, or as the psalmist has so beautifully said,

> "The eternal God is thy refuge,
> And underneath are the everlasting arms."

This gives the personality a toughness of fiber, a richness of overtone and a fundamental confidence in life itself which otherwise it would not have.

2. Worship unifies the personality around the divine will. Day after day insights become deeper and deeper as the will of God revealed in Christ Jesus is explored. Gradually the loose ends of expression are gathered together by the centripetal force of the gospel. The worshiping soul discovers that nothing matters except the content and will of God; that only the truth and beauty and love of eternity can satisfy the heart of man. The soul resolves with Saint Paul to know nothing except the mind of Christ, who reveals the infinite mystery of God by giving it meaningful symbols. This saves the soul from disaster because it leads to an integration around the most significant content in the world.

3. Worship brings the whole integrated personality to brilliant concentration in the act of dedication. It forces the soul into creative expression. This is salvation, of course, for otherwise the personality would rest in harmless passivity or spend its precious days in a mild, diffusive activity. Worhip fastens the attention upon a particular aspect of God's will and summons all the energies a man possesses to the dedicatory act, to the significant and creative deed. This socially useful expression not only raises the level of human life in the community, but also saves the soul from a sense of impotence by giving meaning and verve and splendor to its days.

4. For the personality, this act of relaxation and unification means that the tensions of life become resolved into rational and beautiful patterns of thought and activity. Emotion is no longer dissipated, but now is harnessed to a significant design for living. When tension is thus intelligently and devotionally resolved, poise results, and serenity, together with courage, confidence, great driving power and even peace. It results in all the gifts of the Spirit: in joy and peace in believing and that abounding in hope through the power of the Holy Spirit of which Saint Paul speaks in his letter to Rome. It makes of human life a beautiful happening upon this earth and conserves its every good for eternal life with God.

MYSTICAL ECSTASY AS PRODUCED BY PHYSICAL MEANS

James H. Leuba

AMONG MOST UNCIVILIZED populations, as among civilized peoples, certain ecstatic conditions are regarded as divine possession or as union with the Divine. These states are induced by means of drugs, by physical excitement, or by physical means. But, however produced and whatever level of culture they may be found, they possess certain common features which suggest even to the superficial observer some profound connection. Always described as deligtful beyond expression, these ecstatic experiences end commonly in mental quiescence or even in total unconsciousness. Common features should not, however, lead to a disregard of dissemblances. The presence, for instance, of an ethical purpose places some of these states in a separate and higher class.

In this chapter we shall confine ourselves to mystical experiences induced by physical means, and chiefly by drugs. Our main task is to discover their forms, their motives, and the gratification they yield. Why their fascination and why the religious significance ascribed to them? . . . .

I. THE USE OF DRUGS AND OTHER PHYSICAL MEANS

We have already had occasion to remark that in nearly every savage tribe is found a knowledge of narcotic plants employed to induce strange and vivid dreams or hallucinations. And we have quoted Brinton who writes that "in many parts of the United States the natives smoked stramonium, the Mexican tribes swallowed the *peyotl* and the snake plant, the tribes of California and the Samoyeds of Siberia had found a poisonous toad-stool— all to bring about communication with the Divine and to induce ecstatic visions." The priest among certain Indian tribes had apparently learned to snuff a "certain powder called *cohoba* (perhaps tobacco) up his nose which makes him drunk, so that he knows not what he does." The Indians of New Mexico are "unacquainted with intoxicating liquors, ... yet find drunkenness in the fumes of a certain herb smoked through a stone tube and used chiefly during their festivals."

Of the New Mexicans, Bancroft says, "drunkenness prevails to a great extent among most of the tribes; their liquors are prepared from the fruit of the ptahaya, mezquite-beans, agave, honey, and wheat. In common with all savages, they are immoderately fond of dancing, and have numerous feasts, where, with obscene carousals and unseemly masks, the revels continue until the dancers, from sheer exhaustion or intoxication, are forced to rest." These feasts have nearly always a religious character.

From *The Psychology of Religious Mysticism*, New York, 1925, chap. ii. Reprinted by permission of the publishers, Harcourt, Brace & Company.

Taken in moderation, mescal enables a man to face the greatest fatigues and to bear hunger and thirst for several days. A sort of pilgrimage is organized to gather the plant for festivals and for private consumption. As the Indians approach the plants, they uncover their heads and display every sign of veneration. Before gathering them they sprinkle themselves with copal incense. In some tribes mescal is consumed only by medicine men and certain selected Indians who sing invocations to it to grant a "beautiful intoxication." A rasping noise is made with sticks while men and women dance before those who are under the influence of the god. The remarkably beautiful coloured hallucinations produced by mescal have been described by several experimenters.

In the Indic and Iranian cult there was a direct worship of deified liquor analogous to Dionysiac rites. It has even been maintained that the whole Rig Veda is but a collection of hymns for Soma worship. It contains, in any case, a large number of such hymns. Soma, an intoxicating liquor, was prepared from a plant unknown to us. It became identified with the moon, and hence was called moon plant. The brahmanic priest crushed in a small mortar the stalk of the plant and poured into the fire a libation, usually to Indra; but he himself drank the greater part of what he had prepared, until he became inebriated, or at least until he felt the stimulating effect of the beverage. The drinking ceremony was accompanied by magical incantations and invocations. The officiating priest offered the liquor with these words: "O, Indra, accept (our offering), ... drink of the soma, thou the friend of prayer and of the liquor, well disposed God, drink in order to intoxicate thyself." Here is one of the numerous invocations made during the sacrifice: "Come to us who have pressed out the soma, come; to our good praises drink, O helmeted hero, of the juice of the plant, I pour it out, into the double cavity of thy belly; may it spread through thy members; may it be sweet to thy taste; may it steal upon thee, veiled, as women seeking a *rendez-vous*. Hero with the strong neck, full-bellied, strong of arms, ... O Indra, hurl thyself forward upon them triumphing by thy strength. . . . . O Indra, praised by many, accept the pressed out soma, father of divine energy: drink, make the assuaging sap rain in upon thee. . . . . Let those who desire the inexhaustible celestial glories attach themselves to Indra." The desire for sexual vigor is one of the dominant notes of the soma hymns.

In Greece also, intoxication was customary in connection with established cults. The Pythia at Delphi after a fast of three days, chewed laurel leaves, and in a state of intoxication stood upon a tripod placed over an opening from which issued noxious vapors. Her body shook, her hair stood on end. and out of her convulsed and frothing mouth came the answers to the questions addressed to her. Wine drunkenness was prominent in the worship of Dionysus. To the effect of the wine was added that of dancing, music, shouting, and the expectation of divine ecstasy. Rhode makes a vivid picture of the worship of the Thracian Dionysus: "The celebration took place in the dead of night on the mountain tops by the flickering light of torches. Noisy music resounded: the pealing tones of the cymbals, the hollow thunder of kettle-drums, mingled with the 'frenzy-summoning harmony' of the deep-voiced flutes. Stirred by this wild music, the crowd of worshippers danced and shouted in exultation. We have no mention of songs; for these, the vigorous dancing left no breath. This was not the rhythmic dance with which, perhaps, the Greeks of Homer's age accompanied their paeans, but a frenzied, whirling, plunging sort of round in which the crowd inspired devotees rushed about over the mountain slopes. For the most part it was women, oddly clad, who whirled about to the point of exhaustion. They wore 'Bassaren,' long flowing garments, apparently made of fox-skins; over these they wore besides, deer-skins with the horns sometimes remaining on the head. . . . . Thus they raved, until they reached the utmost excitement. In this 'holy madness' they rushed upon the animals chosen for the sacrifice, and tore off with their teeth the bloody flesh, which they devoured raw."

But drugs are not the only physical means of producing the ecstacy to men of every degree of culture. Deprivations of food and sleep, isolation, even active tortures are well-known and frequent means of religious ecstasy. Rhythmic bodily movements and shouting or singing, when long continued, yield results similar in several respects to that of alcohol, stramonium, mescal, and other drugs. . . . .

III. SUMMARY OF THE EFFECTS OF NARCOTICS AND INTERPRETATION OF THEIR RELIGIOUS SIGNIFICANCE

We are now prepared to formulate with some precision the main effects to which narcotic drugs owe a favoured place in the religious life of the non-civilized. These effects vary widely as to kind, frequency, and intensity, not only according to the drug but also with the same drug, according to the person; and different doses of a drug may induce not only different but antagonistic effects. . . . .

(a) Alteration of sensation and feeling; illusion and hallucination

The mind does not perform its perceptual functions with improved accuracy; on the contrary, it exhibits an activity which is to an abnormal degree independent of external stimuli. The type of these perturbations vary with the drug. We have seen, for instance, that mescal induces delightful, coloured hallucinations of a somewhat definite pattern. Hallucinations of other types may convince the ecstatic that he sees and hears, unhampered by opaque obstacles and distances, or that he travels bodily through space, now here, now there, according to his good pleasure.

The sensations and feelings arising from the moving limbs and from the internal organs are also modified. Some of these are dulled or even disappear altogether. Frequently, particularly in the more interesting period of intoxication, the dominant result seems to be a multiplication, intensification and qualitative alteration of these feelings.

Now these kinaesthetic and visceral feelings, obscure though they are ordinarily, constitute nevertheless a substantial background of the consciousness of self. Let them be changed or removed, and the feeling of self is altered. This may give rise to remarkable delusions. One of the subjects we have quoted felt separated from his own body. In more ordinary instances, a sense of the unreality of the body and of the outside world is reported or the outside world and body seem altered in particulars difficult to formulate. . . . .

The intensification and perhaps also the qualitative alteration of certain organic feelings account for one of the most enticing characteristics of ecstatic consciousness. It is as if usually dormant parts of the organism had awakened; feelings well up from unknown depths and raise their multitudinous voices in a paeon of life. Horizons open up as warm and unlimited as the work-a-day world is cold and circumscribed. . . . .

(b) Alterations of intellectual functions and of emotional attitude

The intellectual functions—retentiveness, recall, observation, classification, judgment, etc.—stand, as everyone knows, in a relation of close dependence upon each other and upon the activity of the senses. In narcotic intoxication an impairment of these functions goes hand in hand with that of the senses. It is one of the main causes of the impression of self-exaltation, of power, and of freedom.

But drugs seem to act otherwise than as inhibitors of mental activity, some of them appear to exercise a direct stimulating effect upon certain tendencies and emotions. Alcohol increases self-confidence, optimism, and courage. A man never appears or thinks himself braver than after a bottle of wine, and never is his mouth so full of arrogant self-praise. Opium, on the other hand, exaggerates diffidence, apprehension and fear. It makes of its victim a shrinking and self-deprecating object. It may, however, be maintained that the change in the emotional tone following upon the use of alcohol is due entirely to the general reduction of the activity of higher nervous organizations, and not to a stimulation of those parts of the nervous system that are correlated with instinct and emotion. We must remember in this connection that even when motor activity is temporarily enhanced, the action of alcohol is regarded by the most competent students as a paralyzing one. . . . .

We have seen that in the case of alcohol, scientific measurements demonstrate a deficiency in acuity of perception, in recall, discrimination, and, therefore, in every mental function dependent upon these. But this fact is not realized by the intoxicated; on the contrary he delights in a directly opposite conviction; never is he so sure of himself, and so ready to undertake the impossible. A limitation of mental activity would suffice to account for this delusion. If, in any particular situation, I do not recall all the essentials that bear upon it; or if I do not discriminate correctly and analyze completely, I shall necessarily conclude wrongly. . . . .

Excessive motor activity is one of the obvious characteristics of a phase of alcohol intoxication. This might be due altogether to decreased self-control, itself the result of the inhibition of the higher nervous centres. For, the quietness of the well-mannered person, his moderation in gesture and in facial expression are not signs of inertness, but the result of a self-control established under social tuition. Remove this control and the organism will behave like a machine without a fly-wheel. When, as in the case of hasheesh intoxication, motor activity is not increased, and there is less inclination to physical arrogance, the higher mental functions are found not to be so unfavourably affected as in the case of alcohol; i.e., self-control is not so markedly decreased. The action of hasheesh is exerted first of all upon the external senses and the organic feelings.

To the intoxicated, the way seems clear; the required virtues, the knowledge, and the ability seem present. What there is to be done can be done; done with ease, with exuberance, with joyous laughter or crushing scorn. Imagination is no longer restricted to rational channels or checked by the sense of the irrelevant, the improper, or the grotesque. Its quality, judged objectively, may not be high, but what matters so long as the subject thinks differently and is proudly happy? The mind seems to have broken its earthly shackles, taken wings, and soared, unrestricted, in a world of infinite possibility. If to be human means to be hemmed in at every turn by physical and moral infirmity, then intoxication must in truth seem divine.

Here and there, a poet is said to have found "inspiration" in wine, opium, or other drug. But when those of his works that have been written with the assistance of narcotics are examined, they turn out to be inferior *in point of intellectual and ethical* content to his other productions. It is only in the rhythmic and phonetic expression of a peculiarly amorphous mood that they may possess distinction and superiority. But superior word-music should probably be regarded as a consequence of an abnormally complete surrender to the enjoyment of feeling at the expense of purposive, rational thinking. Helmholtz is reported to have declared that when trying to give form and being to some dimly apprehended conception, the smallest quantity of alcohol sufficed to dispel from his mind every idea of the creative order.

REALITY IN WORSHIP

Willard L. Sperry

EVERY MAN of scrupulous conscience shrinks from using forms of worship which he thinks do not correspond to truth, or which he is unable to make real to himself. There is something absolutely intolerable about the suggestion of dishonesty or insincerity in the presence of God. And yet no problem in connection with churches is more familiar than this. Every man who habitually goes to church finds himself again and again provided with vehicles for his worship which he has the greatest reluctance to use, either because he doubts their truth or because they have no correspondence with his own experience. The world has a single brutal word by which it defines and dismisses a man who tacitly consents to forms of worship which are thus problematical for him; he is a hypocrite.

There are not, however, many downright hypocrites in the world. Hypocrisy is the deliberate and persistent practice of insincerity. The cynic says that all of us are hypocrites, every day of our lives, and that society lives upon the lie. This may or may not be so. . . . .

There is, then, no more cruel judgment passed by one man upon another than this verdict of hypocrisy. It has been fairly used and can be so used. Jesus used it pitilessly. Apologists for the scribe and the Pharisee have accused him of using it unfairly. Christians, perhaps, have been over-careful in their imitation of this particular gospel precedent, when they could have been more profitably employed in seeing that they stood clear themselves of the imputation of hypocrisy. We know so little about one another. We understand so little the other man's struggle. We see so clearly the difference between what he is in immediate fact and what Christianity expects him to be, that it is easy to account for the contradictions in him on this facile ground of hypocrisy. We forget that sincerity implies in the first instance a self that has been integrated, and that such integration is very rare and comes only after long discipline. There are so many factors in the case that we should be very slow to pronounce the verdict of hypocrisy.

This remains, however, the world's most common judgment upon a congregation of people at worship. How little their lives conform to the words which they are saying and the attitudes which they are taking. This humility, this self-abasement, these protestations of piety, these reckless affirmations as to God and these revolutionary affirmations as to man, do they spring out of the daily life of these people? It is incredible. We know them too well.

The average church-goer will admit the grounds for the caricature. But

From *Reality in Worship*, New York, 1925, pp. 203-222. Reprinted by permission of the publishers, The Macmillan Company.

he cannot admit its final truth because he is not wholly sure of himself yet. If he were sure he was the kind of man the cynic says every human being is, he would have to admit the truth of the indictment. Because he suspects himself of something better, and because in church he gives that something better in him a fair chance, he cannot admit that he is a fraud pure and simple.

There are probably very few church-goers who are constantly conscious of insincerity in intention and hypocrisy in practice as they participate in the familiar forms of public worship. What perplexes them is the depressed vitality of these forms. They are supposed to mediate life more abundant and yet they seem strangely unreal, lacking in the salty tang of indubitable reality. Here and there the issues of sincerity and insincerity are plainly present. But a far more common and a far subtler problem is that raised by the suspicion that when we go to church we leave "the real world" behind, and enter some ghostly realm of auras, ectoplasms, disembodied spirits, and unattainable ideals.

It may be laid down as a sound canon for the ordering and conduct of public worship that the service should give to the worshipper a strong impression of truthfulness and sincerity in its total transaction. No ingenuity or factitious interest which may be aroused can do permanent and equivalent duty for this basic intimation of reality. To say that the natural man cannot discern spiritual things may be the ultimate wisdom. But it is the last resort, to be invoked only when we are sure that everything we do and say in church represents our devotion to truth and is the best we can do to open the way to reality.

The reality required in worship is double in its nature. There will be first of all the objective truthfulness of the propositions and transactions of the act of worship. Then there will be our sincere subjective response to this truth. Every church is under bonds to be as real as it can in both these ways. Without claiming infallibility or finality for the objective account of truth a church must be sincere in its profession of the truth as it believes it. Plainly, religion has gone on and can go on, though at a cost to man, when their ideas as to the order of the universe, the nature of man, and the being of God are inadequate or in error. St. Francis' Christianity was not true in so far as he believed the Ptolemaic astronomy. Nevertheless he knew more, religiously, about the sun and the stars than many Copernicans. We should all agree that, despite the discrepancy between his ideas and the astronomical facts, he was a far more religious man than Galileo, who, knowing the truth about the starry world, recanted. Galileo sacrificed the initial sincerity of religion, the agreement of his ideas with one another and their correspondence to facts, to a quiet life. There were, as this world goes, many extenuating circumstances for his recantation of the Copernican astronomy. But he gave the case for his religion away when he said, "It moves for all that."

Religion may have to get along without the full measure of objective truth, because our knowledge of the universe is forever short of the total fact and often in error as to detail, but it cannot dispense with the other kind of truth, namely that agreement between our convictions as to reality and the words and deeds used to express those convictions, which we call sincerity.

That is what we mean when we say that a church service must be real. Not that it is an exhaustive and accurate account of the universe, but that it has an interior truthfulness, its forms and practices faithfully expressing what the worshipers believe about God and man.

The most subtle and powerful enemy of such reality in public worship is tradition. The poignancy and tragedy of the struggle for reality in the life and offices of the church have their origin in the power of tradition. That which the tradition celebrates, or at least the forms which the tradition uses, may no longer be real to us. But the tradition itself is real, usually one of the most real facts in the religious life. Those who find themselves relentlessly forced out of step and line with Christian history in the service of a fresh sincerity always make the parting reluctantly because the marching generations are true, even if the route of march no longer seems plain and possible. Changes in the usages and manners of the church are not so simple and easy as they may appear. . . . .

In the present divided condition of the church we cannot hope for a single service of worship conveying final truthfulness in any one order of public worship. But we have the right to expect of others, as we have the duty to require of ourselves, sincerity in the application of science and art to our own experience and to the body of our belief. One does not have to be a Romanist to get the suggestion of reality conveyed by the high altar. And one does not have to be a Quaker to get the suggestion of reality conveyed by silence. We know that for the good Catholic the Mass is real. And we know that for the good Quaker the silence is real. What would wreck the whole affair would be the suspicion that the Mass was merely a pageant to the Catholic, and that the silence was simply inertia with the Quaker. In either case we require faith in "The Real Presence."

So long as a form of public worship is substantially real to those who worship through its help, it is for them a valid form. The moment it raises questions that will not down, kindles suspicions that refuse to die out, and leaves the worshiper in doubt as to its objective truth or his sincerity in participating in it, it has become a defenceless form of worship, unprofitable to those in whom it wakens such reactions and even dangerous to the whole cause of religion. . . . . What is in question is rather the suggestion of something only half real, a playing at religion, the suspicion that here life has not come to terms with itself, let alone its universe.

The implications of this major premise are many and by no means clear. The minor premise will be the actual order of worship to which a man finds himself committed. No single individual will find a service of worship equally real to him in all parts. But every individual has a right to require of his church that in a service of public worship it shall provide him with a vehicle for communion with God and man which imparts a strong suggestion of reality from the transaction as a whole. If his church cannot provide such a service, because as artist or scientist he is at loggerheads with the science and art of his own communion, he is probably under the necessity of seeking another church, or of gathering persons like-minded with himself and founding a new church. . . . .

A man must be clear when he passes adverse criticism upon a service of worship that he understands the true intention and implication of the service and that in his own spirit he measures up to that which the service may rightly require of him. There is no service of worship in existence which would not profit by the thoroughgoing attempt of those who habitually use it to come nearer to exhausting its possibilities. Such an effort to measure up to the service should certainly precede all hasty and careless revision. Only personal religion can give sure instinct and insight into the strength or weakness of a particular order of worship. Liturgical knowledge and theological learning do not suffice. A sentimental feeling for aesthetic values is a very fallible guide. What every service asks of us is an honest effort to test its form by its inspiring idea.

The first thing to be discovered regarding the setting and substance of an act of worship is its history. If a treatment of building stone, a symbol, a ceremony, a prayer or creed has its roots deep in church history there was originally a religious idea behind it. Our first task is to recover that idea which was the inspiration of the usage. If it still stands for credible truth the usage has significance and is valid. If the idea is at variance with our conception of the truth the usage is misleading and perplexing. We do not question the central place of the altar in a Catholic church. We have a right to question the implication of a similar piece of furniture, similarly placed, in a church which is frankly non-sacramentarian.

But only a fraction of our present difficulties can be defined and solved by this historical inquiry. By far the larger number of our difficulties arise from another source. The half-real character of the average church and its transactions is due in a far greater measure to the prevalence of patterns which plainly have no religious ideas behind them and represent the vagaries of some decorator who had a blank wall space to cover with designs, a window space to fill with colored glass, or forty minutes to fill with words and music. Two-thirds of the patterns which have crept into the church art in the last half century have no precedent in Christian history and no occasion in any contemporary religious idea. The serpent swallowing its own tail, which winds all through early Celtic design, meant something once—eternal life—and still has interest for us as a symbol of that idea. The formal tree which appears in Jesse windows meant something once, and may still mean something. The symbols of the four evangelists never cease to stir the imagination. All these patterns are intelligible.

But the chill and numbing sense of unreality which we get when we enter so many churches springs from the riot of meaningless patterns which have neither historic warrant nor symbolic worth. Few of us who have ever spent idle hours during interminable church services studying the monotonous vagaries of dull mechanical patterns stenciled on a wall or set in glass will assert that here is beauty authentic and altogether lovely and here is a religious idea adequately intimated in art. Polygons of red and blue glass seem to say, "I believe in Euclid," and a wearisome stencil along the border of a wall seems to say, "I believe in the plenary inspiration of the local decorator." The plain truth is that half the decoration in American churches means nothing and never can mean anything. . . . .

Once you become conscious of the utter meaninglessness of most of these patterns which you find in the ecclesiastical decoration of the last fifty years, your life is made miserable for you as you go from church to church. Even if you are not conscious of a lack of meaning, the total suggestion must often be uncertain, confusing, and distracting. We may be grateful that the best church architects today will have nothing to do with the adventitious decoration which has no warrant either in history or symbolism.

On the contrary, symbols which plainly have a religious idea behind them are powerfully effective, even though they may be poorly executed as works of art. There is, for example, painted on the wall behind the pulpit in a little Baptist church in a fishing village down on the coast of Maine, a ship's anchor. It is the only attempt at religious symbolism in an otherwise bare meeting house. The anchor itself is not perfect as a work of art. The painter has wrestled rather ineffectually with the problem of perspective and the three dimensions. But for all its queer flat angularity it is one of the best pieces of chancel art I know, simply because it suggests what the Christian religion means to those who go down to the sea in ships. . . . .

But what is far more important, as one of my friends once pointed out in talking of these things, there is an element of illusion in the drama which is not compatible with the conception of worship. A service of worship is a deliberate and disciplined adventure in reality. In church if anywhere, we are under moral bonds to be real. Assuming the rôle of Esther, David, an angel, Charity, the League of Nations, is one thing. All these may be useful parts to play in the inculcation of historical and ethical lessons. But worshiping God is a more intimate and first hand transaction. In the worship of God you may if you choose deck yourself out in vestments, surround yourself with light and color, and express yourself in the ceremony. But you remain yourself, you do not play at being some one you are not. Drama demands that the actor play many rôles, and depends upon the convention of an illusion, accepted by both player and spectator. Things are not what they seem. Worship requires us to put off the playing of rôles and to be ourselves. It has no interest in creating illusions. It requires authentic sincerity. . . . .

I have only hinted at a problem, which is a capable of statement in a hundred ways other than those immediately cited. A church service must have reality. It must not compare unfavorably in its setting and transactions with the "real world" of every day. . . . . Most of us in our effort to "beautify" our services only complicate a problem already very serious, because we add decorative features to our fabric and our procedure which have no history behind them and no clear religious idea sustaining them. We do not need "beautiful" services, in this decorative sense of the word, half as much as we need real services. And real services have no place for decorative pattern apart from Christian conviction.

RITUAL AND SYMBOL

Evelyn Underhill

HERE THEN is Man, the half-animal, half-spiritual creature; living under the conditions of space and time, yet capable of the conscious worship of a Reality which transcends space and time. He has certain means at his disposal for the expression of this worship, this response to besetting Spirit; and again and again he tends, at every level of development, to use these means—which indeed are forced on him by his situation, and by his own psychological characteristics. Of these, the chief are (1) Ritual, or liturgic pattern; (2) Symbol of significant image; (3) Sacrament, in the general sense of the use of visible things and deeds, not merely to signify, but also to convey invisible realities; and (4) Sacrifice, or voluntary offering—a practice too far-reaching in its importance, and too profound in its significance for brief definition here.

All these sensible signs of supra-sensible action appear, in a rudimentary form, wherever man begins to respond in adoration to God. Combined in various ways and degrees, they are the chief elements of Cultus, or the agreed embodiment of his worship. As such both their character and their origin are of great importance to us. For in the first place, the object of Cultus being real communion between Man and God, its formal constituents must be of a kind which further, support, and express this communion. It is set "between the Unseen and the Seen." On the one hand it must be adapted to the psychological nature of the worshipping subject, making the fullest possible contact with his imaginative and sensitive life. But on the other hand, it must embody and express the substance of that Divine revelation which invites man's adoring response. It is conditioned at one and the same time by psychological and metaphysical necessities: and is to be judged by the perfection with which its twofold function is performed—opening a door through which Mystery approaches the creature, and the creature moves out in response. . . . .

When we take together the four chief elements of Cultus—that is to say, the deliberate activity in which man expresses his worship—at once we see that Ritual, Symbol, Sacrament, and Sacrifice have certain common characteristics. First, they possess a marked social quality. They all make it possible for men to do things together. Hence their almost world-wide diffusion does not support Dr. Whitehead's definition of religion, as "what the individual does with his own solitariness." On the contrary, the most characteristic means of human worship are precisely those which the solitary does not require: namely the agreed symbols, and the established formulas and rites, which make concerted religious action and even concerted re-

From *Worship*, New York, 1937, pp. 20-41. Reprinted by permission of the publishers, Harper & Brothers.

ligious emotion possible, and so create the worshipping group. Certainly the religious vitality of this group and its proceedings must depend in the last resort on the spiritual sincerity and action of the individuals composing it: personal and social action must co-operate all the time. It is only too easy for the best and most significant cultus to lose spiritual content when it is not a vehicle for the worship of spiritual men. Then it declines from religion to magic, and from a living worship to a ceremonial routine, in which the exact recitation of the accepted formula or the correct performance of the ordained act is held to satisfy the full obligations of religion. But this tendency, so perpetually attacked by the Hebrew prophets, and Christian reformers, is inseparable from a method of expression which is forced upon man by his own social and psychological characteristics.

Next, Ritual, Symbol, Sacrament, and Sacrifice all have a twofold quality, which closely parallels our human situation. In their living state they have an outside and an inside; a visible action and an invisible action, both real, both needed, and so closely interdependent that each loses its true quality if torn apart; for indeed an idolatry which pins religion to abstract thoughts and notions alone is not much better than an idolatry which pins it to concrete stocks and stones alone. Either of these extremes are impoverishments, which destroy the true quality of a full and living cultus; wherein spirit and sense must constantly collaborate, as they do in all the significant acts and experiences of men. Man, incited by God, dimly or sharply conscious of the obscure pressure of God, responds to Him best not only by a simple movement of the mind; but by a rich and complex action, in which his whole nature is concerned, and which has at its full development the characters of a work of art. He is framed for an existence which includes not only thought and speech, but gesture and manual action; and when he turns Godward, his life here will not be fully representative of his nature, nor will his act of worship be complete, unless all these forms of expression find a place in it. His religious action must be social, as well as personal; rhythmic and ceremonial, as well as interior and free. It must link every sense with that element of his being which transcends and co-ordinates sense, so that the whole of his nature plays its part in his total response to the Unseen. Therefore those artistic creations, those musical sounds and rhythmic movements which so deeply satisfy the human need for expressive action, must all come in; and the most ancient and primitive levels of our mental life be allowed to co-operate in our acts of adoration, no less than those more recent achievements of the race on which we prefer to dwell.

Indeed as ritual worship develops in depth and beauty it is seen more and more that its rhythmic phrases and ceremonies, its expressive movement, dialogues, concerted outbursts of praise, are all carrying something else: the hidden supernatural action of the group or church by which the ritual is being used.

Ritual, Symbol, Sacrament, and Sacrifice are therefore more, not less valid expressions of the Spirit of Worship, because they belong at one and the same time to the world of sense and the world of spirit: for this is the actual situation of the amphibious creature by whom these means have been

devised and used.   Taking from that sensible world which surrounds us—
and of which alone we have direct experience—finite realities, to which
they attach religious significance, and which can therefore be used for the
conveyance of infinite truths, all these perform the essential office of weld-
ing the world of things into human worship.   The obvious dangers of
materialism and aestheticism, and the constant invitation to a relapse into
more primitive religious conceptions and practices, which wait on all external and stylized expressions of worship, must never be allowed to obscure
this truth.   These dangers, it is true, are perpetually asserting themselves,
and provoking a reaction towards Puritan ideals.   The inconoclast, the
Cistercian, the Protestant reformer, the Quaker, stand each in their different
ways for that ever renewed revolt from external elaboration towards aus-
terity and "inwardness"—that constant re-discovery of the inadequacy of all
images and all means—which corrects the excesses of ritual worship and is a
necessary constituent of the Mind of the Church.   There is a deep religious
truth in that awed sense of the "otherness" and utter transcendence of the
spiritual, and horrified perception of the hopelessness—even profanity—of all
attempts to represent it, which underlies this trend to an imageless and
unembodied worship.   It finds its supreme expression in the *Via Negative*
of the mystic; where every affirmation, every imaginative embodiment is
rejected in favour of that which "can be loved but not thought."

In spite of all this, however, it is not really possible for human creatures
to set up a watertight compartment between visible and invisible, outward
and inward worship.   The distinction which we commonly make is arbitrary, and merely means that which is or is not visible from the human point
of view.   Indeed, since we can only think, will, and feel in and with a
physical body, and it is always in close connection with sense-impressions
received through that body that our religious consciousness is stirred and
sustained, it follows that we can hardly dispense with some ritual act, some
sensible image, some material offering, as an element in the total act of
worship, if that act of worship is to turn our humanity in its wholeness
towards God.   The mysterious feeding of spirit upon Spirit is made more
not less real by the ritual meal which drives home the practical truth of
our creaturely dependence.   The self-oblation in which adoring love culminates, must find some costly act, however inadequate, by which it can be
expressed; as human love is truly—however inadequately—expressed in spontaneous gifts and gestures, which would seem absurd enough to those who
had no clue to their meaning.   Here those who look with either horror or
contempt on physical austerities miss the point, and set up an un-Christian
contrast between body and soul.   Thus it is that for millions of Christians
the ritual service and the symbolic gesture—even the amulet and the food-
taboo—are essential constituents of the cultus; vehicles by means of which
genuine worship is expressed.   The pilgrimage, the healing spring, and the
votive shrine still play their part.   Nor should we dismiss all this too breezily
as "mere superstition."   It is rather naïve expression of the deep conviction
that God acts, in particular ways, and asks of man a particular response.

Further, cultus has its subjective and reflex importance; in that it tends to evoke and stabilize the mental and emotional state which it is meant to express. Here at least the James-Lange law has a direct application to facts. As those who deliberately smile are rewarded by an increase of cheerfulness, so those who deliberately kneel are rewarded by an increase in worshipping love. Hence symbolic gestures, verbal formulas, and sacramental acts, in spite of the soul-deadening quality which may so easily invade them once they are accepted as substitutes for the movement of the heart, are—when used and valued rightly—impressive as well as expressive in effect. It is an important function of cultus to educate and support the developing spirit of worship, by presenting to the senses of the worshipper objects intimately connected with his faith, or carrying strong devotional suggestion, and leading him out along these paths towards the invisible Reality. It is true that in its highest reaches worship becomes an act of pure love; but never for man an act stripped of all contingency. Because of the unity of our being, sensible stimulation of eye and ear, or even of taste, touch, and smell, can give supra-sensible suggestions to us and awaken, nourish, and deepen the worshipping sense; and the exclusive spirituality which rejects these homely aids merely defeats its own ends. So, too, the faithful repetition of appropriate acts can deepen our understanding of the realities they are intended to convey. Moreover, such repetition creates appropriate paths of discharge; and sets up those habits of worship within which the attention can concentrate on the deeper realities of our spiritual situation.

Habit and attention must therefore co-operate in the life of worship; and it is a function of cultus to maintain this vital partnership. Habit alone easily deteriorates into mechanical repetition, the besetting sin of the liturgical mind. Attention alone means, in the end, intolerable strain. Each partner has his weak point. Habit tends to routine and spiritual red-tape; the vice of the institutionalist. Attention is apt to care for nothing but the experience of the moment, and ignore the need of a stable practice, independent of personal fluctuations; the vice of the individualist. Habit is a ritualist. Attention is a pietist. But it is the beautiful combination of order and spontaneity, docility and freedom, living humbly—and therefore fully and freely—within the agreed pattern of the cultus and not in defiance of it, which is the mark of a genuine spiritual maturity and indeed the fine flower of a worshipping life. Thus it is that the Litany and Rosary have an enduring value which their critics will never understand. The liturgical use of the psalter has fed the inner life of many a saint: and the Jews' daily repetition of the *Shema*, the Christians' ritual use of the Lord's Prayer, and the Moslems' use of the First *Sura*, are all justified by psychology no less than by religion. They evoke, deepen, and maintain that obscure sense of God which is the raw material of worship; and because of their inexhaustible meaning, serve the devotional needs of worshippers of every type. This depth of devotional significance is indeed the distinctive characteristic of genuine liturgical material; so that souls at every level and stage of development can find in it a disclosure of the supernatural, a stimulus to adoration, and a carrying-meduim for their prayer.

When man enters the world of worship, he enters a world which has many of the characteristics of an artistic creation. Much crude and un-edifying controversy would die away, were this fact commonly admitted: and the poetry and music which enter so largely into expressive worship were recognized as indications of its essential character. The true Object of our worship cannot be directly apprehended by us. "No man hath seen God at any time." The representative pattern, the suggestive symbol, the imaginative projection too—all these must be called into play and their limitations humbly accepted if the limited creature is to enter into communion with the Holy and so develop his capacity for adoring love. But the difficulty of our situation is this: none of these devices will be effective unless the worshipper takes them seriously, far more seriously indeed than in their naked factualness they deserve. This is the element in expressive worship which is so puzzling to those who stand outside it. Why, for instance, this devout contemplation of a rather bad picture, or punctual recitation of a rather silly prayer? Why this wholesale and unexamined use of a metaphorical language which reveals under analysis so many irrational references; or this acceptance of the obvious and charming creations of religious fancy—the crib, the crowned Madonna, the guardian angel—as representative of religious fact? Why, too, this discipline, this ceremonial care over the distribution of the simple Eucharistic elements? The answer is that in each case a sensible sign has been accepted as the representative of a supra-sensible Reality, in order that it may bridge the gap between the sensible and spiritual worlds: and it will only do this, in so far as the worshipper is willing to give it royal or at least vice-regal rank. The necessity is one which presses hardly upon intellectuals. For they see, with more or less clearness, the symbolic or phantasmic character, the doubtful origin of that "carrying medium" which the less sophisticated mind easily accepts as a literal reality. They are aware of the temptation to regression involved in its uncritical use; and so, cannot employ it in the same whole-hearted way. Thus they are brought up against the paradox, that whereas it is here, in these most deep and solemn of all his actions, that man in proportion to his greatness of soul will struggle for truth; yet it is precisely here, that truth in the direct sense eludes him. He is compelled by his own limitations to accept symbol, phantasy, and the workings of the creative imagination, as vehicles of his communion with God.

II

We can now go on to consider the chief elements of expressive worship: and first the nature of ritual. A religious ritual is an agreed pattern of ceremonial movements, sounds, and verbal formulas, creating a framework within which corporate religious action can take place. If human worship is to be other than a series of solitary undertakings, some such device is plainly essential to it. We cannot do things together without some general agreement as to what is going to be done; and some willing subordination to accepted routine.

Ritual, like drill, is therefore primarily justified by necessity. But there is much more involved in it than this. It utilizes, as Dr. Whitehead has

pointed out, that general tendency of living creatures to repeat their actions
and thereby re-experience the accompanying emotion, which also lies at the
origin of the drama and the dance. Indeed, it is hardly necessary to insist
on the dramatic character of great religious ceremonies, Christian and non-
Christian alike; or the powerful influence of rhythmic speech and movement, as a stimulant of corporate emotion. David dancing before the Ark
"with all his might" represents an important and enduring form of religious
expression. Psychologically, therefore, ritual tends by means of appropriate
sounds and gestures to provoke the repetition of a given religious attitude
which can be shared by all taking part in the rite. Its greatest creations—
e.g., the Eucharistic liturgy—are sacred dramas, in which the mystery of
salvation is re-enacted and re-experienced by the worshipping group. So,
too, the congregational litany or hymn, the procession, the corporate
act of penitence or praise, acts as a powerful stimulant to the religious
feeling of the worshippers. It gives them something to do, and also
incites them to do it: again exhibiting its kinship with the dance. For,
as we must abandon ourselves to the dance, lose ourselves in it, in order to
dance well and "learn by dancing that which is done"; so with the religious
rite. We can never understand it without taking part in it; moving with
its movement and yielding to its suggestions. In genuine ritual, as Dr.
Marett says, the tune counts for a great deal more than the words. Moving
and speaking to a measure and rhythm, the more deeply impressive because
familiar and loved, we not only catch enthusiasm, but are able to carry on
when enthusiasm fails. Social action reinforces our unstable fervour. Giving ourselves with humility to the common worship, we find that this common worship can rouse our sluggish instinct for holiness, support and en-
lighten our souls. Nor must we be too quick in assuming that improvement
in the ritual of worship always consists in the triumph of words over tune;
for we are concerned with an action and an experience which transcend
the logical levels of the mind, and demand an artistic rather than an intellectual form of expression. Even the great liturgic value of the psalter
does not entirely depend on the spiritual truths which the psalmists convey: but at least to some extent on that peculiar quality in poetry, which
tends to arouse and liberate the transcendental sense.

In its first emergence, ritual appears as a stylized religious emotion. Spontaneous cries of joy, outbursts of praise, entreaty, self-abasement, seem to
represent the earliest response of man to the incitement of God: and these
by repetition gradually acquire the sanctions of a rite. The constant "Hear
my ringing cry!" of the Hebrew psalmist, and the "Alleluia!" of the Christian, have a long ancestry of which they need not be ashamed: reaching
back indeed to the inarticulate sounds by which the most primitive peoples
are found to express the emerging spirit of worship. The transition from
the common cry to the common utterance and movement is almost inevitable. Thence it is but a step to the conviction that this agreed routine
of sense, sounds, and action alone is truly valid, and carries its own guar-
antees.

At this point the rite assumes, for good or evil, a life and authority of its own; and with it that propensity to become the master instead of the servant of devotion, which is the vice of ceremonial worship. For the immense poser of custom and habit—in other words, of tradition—is nowhere more strongly felt than in religious ritual. Here that tendency for any ordered series of acts to crystallize and assume a fixed character, to which even in daily life our whole psychological make-up inclines us, is seen in an extreme form. Departure from the ordained routine always produces a feeling of discomfort, and usually arouses hostility; as anyone well knows who has tried to introduce "desirable changes" into the worship of an English village church. Hence the two outstanding and opposing dangers, of ritualism and of formalism, which dog the history of ceremonial religion; both arising from the same source—a failure to look through and beyond worship to its end.

Ritualism represents the constant tendency of the human creature to attach absolute value to his own activities, whether personal or corporate: to assume that the precise way in which things are done is of supreme importance, and that the traditional formula has an inherent authority extending to its smallest details, from which it is blasphemy to depart. For ritual always acts as a conservative force. It is the very home of tradition; one of the chief means by which the historical character of worship is preserved and carried forward, and permanence given to the devotional discoveries of men. But this irreplaceable function carries with it its own perils of exaggeration and over-emphasis, leading straight to the absurdities of the ritualist and the "folly of the sacristy." The right form of the vestment, the right number and placing of lights, the correct performance of manual acts or genuflections—or even by inversion, the determined rejection of these things—may then assume such importance that attention is transferred from the meaning of worship to the means, from the total adoring action of the creature to the detail through which it is expressed; and Martha takes the place of Mary as the pattern of the worshipping soul. Ritual worship only retains sanity and spirituality where there is a clear and constant realization that it is a form taken by the creature's homage and love. "It is not for the purpose of pleasing ourselves. It is the offering of wealth in form, art, or substance to God for His Glory, since all creation belongs to Him." . . . .

At the opposite pole from the unbalanced enthusiasm of the ritualist and religious aesthete, so busy with the particular that he forgets the universal which that particular is intended to incorporate, there is the tendency of the formalist to allow the ceremony to degenerate into a mechanical substitute for genuine religious action. The exact but uninterested routine performance of the prescribed movements, attendance at services, or punctual repetition of traditional words, is then regarded as a full satisfaction of the duty of worship. The Buddhists' prayer wheel is the extreme example of this perversion. But instances can be found much nearer home; whether in those Christians who attach an almost magical efficacy to the reading of the "daily portion" or those who put their trust in the obedient recitation of "indulgenced prayers." If the extreme ritualist is an artist so interested in the acting that he loses sight of the total movement and intention of the play, the extreme formalist is a practical man, who acknowledges his religious obligations and fulfils them in the cheapest and easiest way. Such formal worship may at its worst lose all contact with reality; and justify Dr. Heiler's wholesale condemnation of ritual as "a fixed formula which people recite without feeling or mood of devotion, untouched both in heart and mind." In practice, of course, these aberrations are constantly found together; and most congregations contain examples of both. Every ritualist has his "bad days," on which he becomes a formalist; and on the other hand even the most bored and conventional of church-goers may have his moment of fervour, in which the over-familiar phrases of the liturgy are suddenly lit from within, revealing to him the beauty and power of that ordered and historic worship in which man expresses his humble adoration of God.

Ritual weaves speech, gesture, rhythm and agreed ceremonial into the worshipping action of man; and thus at its best can unite his physical, mental, and emotional being in a single response to the Unseen. The use of symbols and images—which is, in some form or degree, a feature of every cultus—is again forced on him by his own psychological peculiarities; the fact that all his thinking and feeling is intimately related to that world of things in which he lives. It is to the apprehension of these that his mind and senses are trained: it is by the responses they wake up in him that he becomes aware of an external world, independent of himself and imposing its conditions upon him. So, the attempt to respond to God without some acknowledgment of the order within which He has placed us, and reveals Himself to us, is hardly likely to be either a spiritual or a psychological success. It is only by recourse to our image-making faculty, or by some reference—direct or oblique—to the things that are seen, that we can ever give concrete form to our intuition of that which is unseen. . . . .

Whether the symbols which man uses for the purposes of worship be drawn from religious tradition or from his own rich phantasy-life, or whether he frankly accepts and gives symbolic rank to certain things which the sensible world presents to him, the principle involved is the same. Particular things and images are accepted and used, as in some way representative of that which lies beyond all things and images; as carriers of a spiritual reality. By this association of sensible object and idea, a new entity is created of which the reality is guaranteed by the fusion of sign and significance: even though the symbol is never truly adequate to the fact conveyed. Once the group or the individual worshipper has given this rank to any image or act—for the symbol may be, often is, a bodily action, e.g., the sign of the Cross, the kiss of peace, the prostration, the laying on of hands—it is henceforth placed in a special class, as carrying a spiritual reference. In a general, not a technical sense, it has become a "sensible means of grace"; and the first step has been taken on the road to sacramental worship. For the symbol, or significant image, is not, as its unfriendly critics suppose, a substitute for spiritual truth. It is rather the point where physical and metaphysical meet—a half-way house, where the world of things and world of spirit unite, and produce a new thing possessed of sensible and supra-sensible reality. And man, who partakes himself of this double character, finds in it the natural means of access to God. . . . .

In practice, ritual and symbol perpetually reinforce and enrich one another in all developed cultus. The symbolic act or object comes to the rescue, where words and ordered movements fail. The smoke of incense, the lighted taper, the solemn exhibition of the sacred sign—all this is found to say something, to add something deeply satisfying to the worship, which cannot otherwise find sensible expression. Here all the great religions, even those which most sternly repudiate everything which savours of idolatry, seem to be agreed. For the Jew, the Eternal God, though He had no image, yet "dwelt between the Cherubims" upon the mercy-seat within the veil; and was worshipped, not only with sacrifice and the ritual use of the psalter, but with incense, lights, and sacred dance. Even the intense transcendentalism of Mohammed recognized "the consolidating effect of fixing a central spot round which through all time should gather the religious feelings of his followers"; and gave symbolic rank to the Kaaba at Mecca, as the sacred shrine of the true faith and focal point of the believer's prayers. So, too, Buddhism and Jainism, beginning as ethical and largely unembodied faiths, have produced under pressure of human necessity an organized cultus, rich in concrete symbols, images, sacred objects, and other sensible aids to worship: and those Christian sects in which the use of visible symbols is at a minimum, and the cultus has been deliberately stripped of sensuous appeal, seem to tend instinctively to hymns rich in concrete images and emotional suggestion—thus giving to the primitive layers of the worshipping mind the sensuous food that they need, by means of the ear instead of the eye.

SYMBOLS AND SACRAMENTS

Von Ogden Vogt

THE ARTIST HAS usually used one of two methods. He has begun with an idea and then selected some specific object to represent his idea; or he has looked upon an object in such a way as to see its ideal significance. In the one case we see his idea objectified, in the other the object idealized. These methods are Classicism and Romanticism in the history of the arts. In religion, they are Symbolism and Sacramentalism.

Almost everyone will readily think of examples of this fact. A mural decoration in a courthouse, for instance, begins with a conception of the majesty of the law and portrays the theme by a series of figures intended to symbolize it. Statues, paintings, tableaux, certain novels, certain music, or other works of art definitely represent "Justice," "Autumn," "War," "History." Such works are Scopas' "Demeter," the most of the early Italian Madonnas, Breton's "Gleaner," Puvis de Chavannes' "Physics." Other works seem not to have been conceived in this generic manner. They, rather, picture some specific object, call our notice to the object that we may look upon it until we see that it is infinitely significant. Such objects are "The Dying Gaul," a bowl of "Roses," "Gleaners," as Millet sees them, "Burghers of Calais," persons in the "Spoon River Anthology." . . . .

Religion has always used and must always use both of these methods. Symbolism in religion is of the nature and of the perennial need of the classic method in art. The person who claims to have no interest in symbolism talks nonsense. He cannot read the morning paper—for every word is a symbol. He could not sing "The Star-Spangled Banner." Some sort of symbolism is necessary to communication of any kind. The theater, the army, the government, the commercial world, all make constant and varied use of symbols to remind people of their existence and character. Religion also must communicate itself by powerful and beautiful symbols. Even those who do not take kindly to the use of an actual wooden cross upon an altar or gable of a church readily sing "In the cross of Christ I glory," and "O make thy church a lamp of burnished gold." Christianity is represented to the consciousness of millions of people by the sign of the cross. Should Constantinople again fall under the governance of Christian powers, it will be symbolized in the East by the taking down of the Crescent from the ancient church of Haggia Sophia and the raising of the Cross upon the noble dome. Symbolism is not, of course, confined to the instrumentality of physical objects, but includes also the use of great symbolic conceptions. A creed is not the faith itself, but a symbol of the faith. In his religious teaching, in his attempt to make God conceivable and real and near to ordi-

From *Art and Religion*, New Haven, 1921, pp. 97-106. Reprinted by permission of the publishers, Yale University Press.

nary people, Jesus was constantly using the symbol of Fatherhood. The inventor of new and true symbols of the truth is a great benefactor.

If symbols are powerful, they are also weak and inadequate. No symbol can present the fulness of the reality. No particular can contain all the nature of the universal it seeks to represent. It is useful, however, and true, if it leads in the right direction, if its partial and pale reflection is correct so far as it goes.

And if symbols are powerful they are dangerous. They tend to take the place of reality. They tend to become idols. They are likely to attract the devotee to themselves, failing to lead him on to the larger realities they stand for. No one denies this danger, but no strong man or no vitalized community has ever been disposed to reject powerful and useful instruments because they were dangerous. The surgeon's knife may be used for murder, but it must still be kept sharp as an instrument of good. Human passions are dangerous, human liberties are dangerous, but for their several possibilities of good we value them all. If you want an instrument of power, you must risk an instrument of danger, understand it, master it, and use it aright. . . . .

If the symbol is at times likely to take the place of the reality, there is also a sense in which the reality does reside in the symbol. A soldier on patrol duty, guarding whatever he is set to guard, might well say, "Strike me and you strike the United States." Christians have always conceived of Christ as the great symbol of God, but also have always conceived of God as being in some profound sense in Christ. To reject him is to reject the Father, to see him is to see the Father. With this suggestion, we turn to the other side of the artistic and religious method.

As the artist portrays a particular object, lifting it into its universal import, so the religionist performs a specific act which he calls a sacrament.

Protestants in general do not have a very clear conception of what a sacrament is. We do not understand the meaning of the word and we are suspicious of it. Certainly it is used oftentimes to mean something entirely foreign to our whole conception of religion. Possibly the word should be entirely discarded, as being obscure and misleading. Possibly, also, there are more important meanings in it which we have forgotten or undervalued.

To begin with, the word is derived from the same root as the word sacred, itself only slightly less obscure in our thought. Yet we do recognize the necessity of making some distinction as between the sacred and secular. If in some sense all things are sacred, the result of attention to this side of the truth is really to conceive of all things as merely secular. There are many conceptions and the words which represent them that merge into each other or that are simply the opposite sides of the same shield. Nevertheless, the shield has two sides. A sacred thing is a thing dedicated, belonging to God, partaking of the nature of Divinity. . . . . If the dedication is to God it becomes a definite sacrament.

It is a religious view to hold that God is literally present in the sacrament. A human being in the act of consecration, putting forth the spiritual effort of self-offering, is then and there godlike, then and there partakes of the nature of Divinity, then and there has God in him, and is seen to be God possessed. As the artist portrays a particular object to help us see that it is more than it seems to be, so the priest draws his people to the performance of an act in which they are seen to be not only human but divine. In the sacrament of Baptism the child is dedicated to God; his life is seen to be divine as well as of human origin; his life is recognized as belonging to God as well as to his parents, the state, or to himself. His parents dedicate themselves to the task of bringing him up in the "nurture and admonition of the Lord." They are seen to be not merely and physically father and mother, but priests of God entrusted with a holy office.

In view of the paucity of ritual material amongst the Protestant churches, and of the difficulties in the invention of new exercises instinct with deep and moving meaning, it may be well to consider increasing the number of sacraments. Perhaps one or more others of the early seven could be re-established. Perhaps two sacraments should be developed out of the present usages connected with the sacrament of Baptism. It would simply involve our all becoming Baptists in the matter of the restriction of that sacrament to believers only. It would constitute a more notable form to mark the matured acceptance of the Christian life and thus go far, as the Baptists have always held, to safeguard the purity of the church and its regenerate life. In this case, we should stand greatly in need of a sacrament of Christening to take the place of infant Baptism. Such an act, to mark the Christianizing or the inclusion of the child in the Christian community, the recognition that it belongs to God, and the vow of responsibility for its Christian nurture, would constitute, as at present, a beautiful and holy presentation.

In the formal sense, a sacrament has an outward as well as an inward side: it includes physical elements. There is nothing especially mysterious about the nature of the elements, except in so far as the nature of matter in general is mysterious. Nor is there anything exceptionally mysterious about the nature of the influence or purpose of the material elements, except as the nature of all sensational influence is mysterious. The formulas that are spoken, the water that is poured, both physical act and material element, these call for, signify, and express the inner effort and act of the spirit. And if they do so successfully, then God is in the sacrament. If the outward acts, elements, or symbols do not serve to produce any motion of the spirit, either in the heart of the priest or of the people, then no sacrament has occurred, and no grace of God has been imparted.

It is only by long association that many have come to regard the material element as sacred. To the Protestant experience, the material element is essentially only a matter of artistry, a symbol, an idealization. The use made of the material element is not a matter of artistry, but a sacrament in which Divinity is present. In other words, the view of many Protestants that God is not in the sacrament is not the view here expressed. The conception here set forth is that Divinity is actually in the sacrament, as being in the spirits of persons performing the religious act which we call the sacrament. On the other hand, the view excludes the conception of any sense in which Divinity is extraordinarily resident in the material elements. Of course our conclusion comes from our definition. Otherwise define a sacrament and you must otherwise conceive the elements. Or begin with another conception of the outward form and it would be difficult to define the sacrament, in our manner, as a dedicatory religious act of persons.

The sacrament of the Eucharist is more complicated and so more mysterious than any other. Just as with some works of art it is difficult to decide whether we have the idea objectified or the object idealized, so here we halt between the symbolic and mystic conceptions. Both are involved. If even in Protestant feeling the strictly symbolical is minimized and merged into the sacramental or mystical, it is not difficult to see how the Romanist has confused the self-offering of the devotee with the formal offering of the elements, taking the elements out of the realm of symbolism into that of idealization and transubstantiation.

It is essentially the same point of view, often expressed by Protestants when they refer to the actual bread and wine as "the sacrament." In our view these elements are not the sacrament, but the symbols idealized to call forth and assist the inner and profound sacramental act. In whatever sense sanctity may be said to attach to the elements, according to the practice of some after they are set apart and thus consecrated, in actual usage amongst the reformed churches, the prayer of "consecration" expresses only a slight interest in the setting apart of the elements and deep interest in the consecration of persons.

The abundant danger of this view is the danger of subjectivity and informality; the danger of placing a too slight value upon the external and formal administration, and the danger of a merely humanized experience. We do not sufficiently believe in or expect an actual visitation of Divinity in the sacrament, thinking rather of the experience as our own. And so, thinking of the experience as our own production, we have too little considered the powers of the church and of the formal administration.

There is an objective value in the historic sacraments. The nature of the spiritual life in a material world is ever a profound mystery. The nature of human salvation and sanctification is mysterious. . . . . The sacrament bears the burden of initiation. It is not complete without the actual presence of God to give power to carry out the dedication that has occurred. But the power to make the dedication is lacking without the divine presence, and this visitation cannot come without humility. But even your humility you cannot produce of yourself. It is induced in you by your appreciation of something outside that makes you humble. This is the function of the material elements and the formal administration of the sacrament. They are symbols which bring near to you and represent the sacrifice of Christ. Through them you are helped to "be in contact with the real and living Christ." That contact begins in you a process of divinization which is partly your act of consecration and partly the action of the divine grace toward you and within you. "What we consecrate, God will sanctify." The transubstantiation which occurs is not that of the material elements, but a real transubstantiation of persons, a real change of human nature into divine nature. This is the essential miracle. . . . .

Religion always offers more than ideas, and more than moral precepts; it supplies the energy to live by. It cannot be described in terms of truth or in programs of right conduct, but rather and chiefly in manifestations of power. . . . . The world of the unknown is larger than the known. Known forces we can begin to understand and to manipulate; it is the vast unknown with which we must come to terms. . . . .

Two things, therefore, I am trying to suggest: that religion must use symbols, definitive, concrete representations, to set forth what it knows or definitely believes; and that it must use sacraments as exercises of personal consecration to the highest reality, whatever that reality is, however much unknown, that the presence and power of Divinity may become more fully operative in human life. The first usage is merely artistic, the embodiment of ideas in objects, after the fashion of all Classic artists. Such embodiments may be in the form of pictures, or creeds, or more familiar concepts, or statues, or classic music, or the elements of a sacrament. By all these forms, fairly clear ideas are objectified and symbolized. The second usage quickly becomes more than artistry, more than the idealization of particular objects. The Romantic artist portrays objects so that we can see them in all the reaches of their relations, idealizing them. Religion takes hold on a man by a sacrament and not merely idealizes him but transforms him into the ideal. The process is carried out of the realm of artistic idealization into that of religious transubstantiation.

THE PRACTICE OF CORPORATE WORSHIP

Douglas V. Steere

THE NEED FOR CORPORATE WORSHIP

REMEDY IT AS YOU WILL, it is a great misfortune to be brought up as an only child. The family constellation is too close, too concentrated, for either parent or child to receive a full appreciation of the other, or for the child to discover what it means to be at home, literally at home, with his fellows. At best, an only child has to learn outside the family, and outside its close circle of affection and common life, what it means to be one among others and to be a beloved one among others who are no less beloved, to learn how a mother's or father's love is not divided when it is shared. And an only child seldom comes to know the parent's love as a child does who has seen it shared with his brothers and sisters and knows how dear each is to them. There are times in a large family of children when a child can and should be alone with the parent. But even these times are enhanced by the occasions when the child is with the parents in the midst of the family and as a member of the family.

Nowhere is this psychological truth better revealed than in the relation between private and corporate worship. For central as is the relationship between the separate individual and God, each man needs an experience of life in the great family of God if he is to grow to understand the real nature of that love and the real character of his response to that love, to say nothing of growing to understand and to live creatively with his fellows.

For the past fifteen years I have lived among students and intellectual people both in this country and abroad. And I have seen the pain and the blocking of inner growth that has come to people who have known the religious life, for the want of fellowship and of active participation in the corporate worship and family life of some religious group. The "only child" often turns into a kind of migratory religious tramp who floats from one church to another and only rarely stays long enough to become established in its form of corporate worship. It is not unusual for him to become disgusted with all forms of corporate worship and to take refuge in Professor Whitehead's well-known remark that religion is what a man does with his solitariness. Even this surface contempt, however, does not always conceal the lingering wistfulness in such a person for a religious fellowship.

Critical as this generation is, and may be justified in being, of the existing forms of religious fellowship, it can no longer be content with the emphasis of men such as William James, who interpreted religion as an individual affair that had little to do with its group expressions, or even with Henri Bergson, for whom the corporate side of religion can never be other than a

From *Prayer and Worship*, New York, 1938, pp. 36-45. Reprinted by permission of the publishers, Association Press.

static element. This Olympian aloofness of "sitting like God, holding no form of creed but contemplating all" and feeling above active participation in corporate worship has flatly failed to help its defenders to grow in the religious life. And no matter what form these religious associations may be destined to take in the future, they cannot be abolished entirely if religion is to live.

I know of a dozen young religious leaders in the East between the ages of twenty-five and forty who constantly express to one another that they run down in the vital personal religion which they have at times discovered. With their connection with corporate worship for the most part very loose, and a certain sense of spiritual poverty about some of these institutional contacts, they are finding it ever so hard to get beyond that stage where they commenced their growth. As for the contagious communication of this spiritual life to others, it has changed from being central to being incidental with them. I think of a South American friend who has been alienated from his native church by a long-standing enmity and has been kept out of Protestantism by what he regards as its sectarian divisiveness and social apostasy. I think of a Danish friend who has given up the Danish Lutheran Church but can find fellowship in no other corporate worship. They are seeking to live the religious life alone. I see here the agony, the tragic loneliness, the cramping sense of martyred superiority, the hardening process of doubt about the validity of the whole spiritual life, and the temptation to be content with rational presentations of it which they would be the first to admit. In all of this I seem to see the sterilizing effect of religious individualism, of being God's "only child."

Lawrence Hyde, a young English critic of culture, has equally sensed this in his generation in England. "I suggest that the modern cultivated person is *over-estimating* his power of maintaining contact with the realm of the spiritual in his present condition. . . . . He imagines in his self-sufficiency that he can get along satisfactorily without rites and ceremonies, without private disciplines, without associating himself on a religious basis with a group of his fellowmen. But the plain fact is that he cannot—unless he is a very exceptional person indeed. The great mass of more highly educated men and women today—those anyway of a more spiritual type—are psychologically unstable, restless, unfulfilled, and morbidly self-conscious."

Religious Behaviorism

There is, in many, an aversion to entering into corporate worship because they do not feel worthy of all that it stands for or because they do not yet feel sure of their beliefs. I know how many go through struggles about partaking of communion because of their sense of unworthiness and want of complete conviction. They seem often enough to have forgotten Jesus' words, "They that are whole need not a physician, but they that are sick." A friend of mine went to a teacher in a religious seminary and told him that he had considered entering the seminary and training to be a minister but that he felt that he was unworthy to become a representative of Jesus Christ. He rather expected to be rallied. But to his secret dismay, the teacher agreed with him about his unworthiness and quietly suggested that if he felt otherwise, then he might seriously doubt his place in the church either as minister or parishioner.

Vida Scudder, the lifelong champion of so many radical social causes, tells in her recent autobiography, *On Journey*, of her entrance into a lay Episcopal society: "The act did not mean that my religious vision had cleared; my faith was still provisional. But I was increasingly aware that, for me, rejection of what the Church offered would involve more falsity than acceptance. . . . . Many thinking moderns who would like to be Christians spend their lives in a state of religious incertitude; we fall into two groups. Some, remaining poised in hesitation, including well-known minds I will not name, pause with imaginative and perhaps intellectual sympathy toward Christianity; others, passing beyond theory, made the definite venture of faith, and seek less to know the doctrine than to live the life. Through the years of which I am now writing, I came, deliberately and with finality, to range myself on their side of the barrier."

The rôle that actual participation in corporate religious worship plays in nurturing the life of us halting ones has too long been obscured. Augustine's regular attendance on the church celebrations and the sermons of Bishop Ambrose in Milan played no small part in preparing him for that scene in the garden where he consciously yielded to the Christian way. Only in vital action, whether it be symbolic or direct, does thought ripen into truth, and the modern mind would do well not to confuse religion with a state of consciousness. "Thou art man," *The Imitation of Christ* gently reminds us, "and not God; Thou art flesh and no angel." And Pascal saw that this flesh must be disciplined not alone by thoughts but by acts of love and by corporate acts of worship. "For we must not misunderstand ourselves; we are as much automatic as intellectual; and hence it comes that the instrument by which conviction is attained is not (rationally) demonstarted alone." We become what we do. A great religious interpreter of our times once said that he kissed his child because he loved her and that he kissed his child in order to love her more. Regular participation in corporate worship is a school and a workshop in which those who would grow in the religious life, no matter how tenuous may be their present connections, should be in attendance.

CREATURELINESS AND SOCIAL RESPONSIBILITY

It is almost impossible to avoid a self-centered religion when one has no active regular share in the corporate worship of a larger religious fellowship. This is particularly true of those who are not engaged in manual work. There is the subtle temptation to become one of those who mistake being "agin'" the group, being otherwise-minded, for following the dictates of conscience. Eccentricity, the sense of martyrdom, and an almost total absence of that precious element of "creatureliness," of humility in one's religious life as one of the great family of fellow creatures offering up their lives before the great Father—these frequently accompany this reluctance to share in corporate worship. Friedrich von Hügel used to tell of the sense of common need and of common love that came to him as he prayed through his rosary or listened to the mass while kneeling next to some Irish washerwoman. For this woman and millions of others, whatever their place in man's petty order of rank, would that very day perform the same act of love and devotion before a Father in whose loving regard each was of equal worth.

It is this vivid sense of creatureliness and the felt attitude of the creature towards the creator that many have declared to be the central experience of worship or devotion and the very secret source of the religious refreshment at the base of their lives. For in this sense of creatureliness, the springs of the only enduring center of equality between men are forever being renewed. Here is the heart of a social gospel that is eternal. Here each is visited with a sense that he, in his need, is one and only one among other needy ones; that he is one among the many who have come to offer up their adoration and aspiration; that he is responsible for all and can never wrench loose from that responsibility. Howard Brinton has expressed the effect of this approach to the center in the fellowship of worship by the figure of the spokes of a wheel. The nearer the spokes of the wheel are to the center, the nearer they are to each other. If the worship is real this new sense of nearness to others will invade the rest of life and be brought to work on the barriers which retard it there. Dean Sperry, in his *Reality in Worship*, has suggested that, if men were to cease to worship God, the greatest single incentive to fraternal ways among men would be withdrawn. For in such offices or worship addressed to God "the imagination is kindled, the heart is made catholic in sympathy and the good-will is fortified. . . . . Sincere and true thoughts of God are the strongest known nexus between man and man."

FELLOWSHIP AND NURTURE

Corporate worship, however, does much more than to induce creatureliness and to strengthen the bonds of the divine family. The regular participation in corporate worship nurtures the tender insight of private prayer and helps to give it a stalk, a stem, a root, and soil in which to grow. Without its strengthening power of believing in your conviction, you may be overcome by the general attitude of the world in which you live or by the same attitude that is being pressed upon you from within by the vast residue of fear-carcasses that the mind and habits are still laden with and that have not yet been cleared away. How many such personal "openings" have become mere pressed flowers in your book of memories for the want of a sensitive fellowship in which you might have recast your life and seen the next steps that were to be taken. In this fellowship you might have found others more mature in this life, from whom you could get counsel, and you might have found an association in which you could quicken some by your own discoveries. Not only in the tender beginning, but at every point in the life, we need this fellowship of corporate worship. For again and again, dry times and doubt and conflict level the fragile house of our faith and compel us to rebuild it on deeper foundations. At times the fellowship seems to be the only cord that holds us.

It is well not to ignore the fact that we are creatures of short memories. Corporate worship, regularly practised, calls us back again and again to the divine background and to our life that springs from it. We need a supernatural witness, a great sheet anchor for our souls. We need corporate encouragement to recall and be rededicated to that deep citizenship to which our lives stand pledged. To scorn such reminders and to claim all days as sabbaths and all places as equally holy may mean that one has reached a high sense of spiritual freedom. But it may also mean that one is approaching indifference. This corporate ceremonial communion in any Christian group that is more than occasional in its character carries a sense of historical continuity with a great spiritual tradition. You do not begin this quest nor will it end with you. It has been lived in the world of space and time by others who have gone before. Their lives have irrefutably proved and tested it and lifted it above the realm of speculative ideals and theories. It is no mean asset to have and to be regularly reminded of what T. S. Eliot calls "the backing of the dead." In such corporate worship you become a working member of that great community and you enter the vast company of souls whose lives are opened Godward. Your life takes on a new perspective in this great communion of the church invisible. This is not confined to the members of the historic churches but to any group that draws its life from the Christian stream, that possesses the biblical record, and that is sensitive to the witness of the saints.

Worship and Adoration

But the deepest need in man which corporate worship ministers to has yet to be mentioned. If man is ever to rise to his full humanity, he must praise and adore that which is the highest that he knows and freely offer up to it the best that he has. The impulse in man to sacrifice to deity is primary in his nature. Even the great baboon solemnly bows again and again to the rising moon. Primitive man tremblingly prostrates himself before the sacred grove. The shepherd brings the most perfect lamb of his flock to be sacrificed on a rude heap of stones. The farmer brings to the priest his best sheaf of grain or a cruse of the finest oil from his grove of olives. The widow brings her mite. The Massachusetts pilgrim family tramps through the forest to the rude log church to kneel and sing and pray. The Pennsylvania Quaker family gathers with others in the plain stone meetinghouse to sit in silent prayer and fellowship. The Maryland Catholic family enter the little chapel to share in the celebration of the mass and to donate themselves, as there is dramatized before them the sacred pageant of a self-donating God. Here is the operativeness of the same magnetic field on all of these differently sensitized dials. Here is what Hans Denck and after him Pascal sought to make explicit by their "you would not have sought Him if you had not already found Him."

No one can deny that in primitive man (and in that considerable substratum of the primitive that dwells in all of us) this longing to offer up the best that he has, to the highest that he knows, is often overlaid with fear and with the desire to propitiate or gain favors from the power or powers beyond his control. Yet even this cannot blind us to this basic longing in men to praise and to adore and to pour out their best gifts. For this longing persists after these fears or cravings for favors have been almost wholly stripped away. It is this longing in man that makes him God-man. It is this restlessness with the most secure self-sufficiency he can devise; it is this urge within himself to put himself in second place, to prostrate himself before the holiest of all, that is the hope in him. Deny man the right to offer himself to this as the saints have done; destroy his monuments of devotion, his cathedrals, his paintings, his carvings, his organizations for good works; ridicule his aspiration as infantile; try, in short, to roof over his sundial; try to choke out this longing to yield to Deity or to divert it to exclusively social aims—and man ceases to be man and something of his essence goes dead in him. Man is a praising and adoring being. He longs to celebrate all of his common experiences and to lift them up to a higher love by dedicating them. God bless my tools. It is because he spoke authoritatively to this center in men that they recognized the authenticity of Jesus and his message. It was because Jesus, too, praised and adored and fell down before his Father that they knew him to be flesh of their flesh and bone of their bone.

From the beginning of recorded history, religious institutions and the priesthood in nurturing and ministering to this basic human need have all too frequently preyed upon, perverted, prostituted, and misled this impulse in man. It is not insignificant that, with all of their betrayals, this longing in man to praise and to adore has persisted. And again and again it has purified itself.

Part VI

IMMORTALITY

THE PROBLEM OF IMMORTALITY

Charles Francis Potter

IF IMMORTALITY MEANS surviving after death as an influence in the lives of those who live after us, or if it means surviving biologically in our children, then of course Humanists believe in immortality. There is inspiration for right living in both these conceptions and many noble souls have looked forward to no other immortality.

But immortality has usually meant the continuance of human personality after death in an ideal society apart from the earth.

This concept contains two elements, the idea of an ideal society and the idea of personal survival. The two have been so blended in the Christian tradition that it is difficult to separate them in our thinking, but in some religions the two are not so equally present. Sometimes one is emphasized and sometimes the other. They rise from different sources.

The idea of an ideal society in the future naturally rises when men are hindered from building the society here. The oppressed classes see no hope of justice in this life and they look for it in the next. A blissful heaven is a compensatory hope in a world of misery. Men have looked forward to many mansions in their heavenly Father's land when their hearts were troubled and afraid here. Happy hunting grounds, the islands of the blest, the golden age to come, the Mohammedan paradise—many have been the forms that man's imagination has chosen as the ideal place of final abode for man. All that weary mankind has failed to find on this earth it has hoped to find after death in some fairer clime.

Humanists sympathize with such a desire for a perfect home for man, but hold that the ideal society is to be achieved on this earth if anywhere.

They maintain, moreover, that the expectation of finding the perfect society in heaven is a distinct hindrance to the achievement of a better society on this earth.

The real heaven-hunters have no interest in improving the conditions here. To a Humanist the beliefs of the Fundamentalists who hope for a speedy return of Jesus on the clouds of heaven seem positively immoral. In their frenzy the millennialists hail with joy the news of famine, pestilence, "wars and rumors of wars," for such catastrophes are portents that the end is near. The worse things get, the better, for the sooner Jesus will come! These are the "latter days" and "millions now living will never die." So why do anything to make the earth better: it will only delay the millennium.

Two leading preachers of New York City who continually featured in their sermons the imminent return of the Lord, refused to co-operate in a child welfare program, saying frankly that they had no time to waste on the fads of social reformers as they were too busy saving souls from the wrath to come.

Even in those Protestant circles where adventism is not so strongly emphasized, the stress has too frequently been laid on preparing for the next world. Christians have sung lustily, "I'm a pilgrim and I'm a stranger," "I'm but a stranger here: heaven is my home," "Sometime we'll understand," "When the roll is called up yonder," "Jerusalem the golden," "Safe in the arms of Jesus," "Beulah Land," and a hundred other similar hymns. Meanwhile unscrupulous men have taken advantage of the absorption of the righteous in the next world and have exploited them and their children. And a world war that could have been prevented loomed nearer and nearer while the Christian nations who were to wage it sat in their churches and heard sermons about the coming glories of heaven.

Dr. A. Eustace Haydon, in *The Quest of the Ages* (p. 156), recently wrote:

> With the coming of modern science and the new age of industry, the result of the projection of the religious ideal to another world was tragic. It allowed the whole mechanism of modern civilization to develop without the control of religious idealism.

So, inasmuch as the existence of heaven is at least debatable and its location problematical since we have studied astronomy, Humanists make the suggestion that we assume the agnostic position in regard to heaven and devote our energies to improving our imperfect planet.

The second element in the concept of immortality, the idea of personal survival, is popularly, but not necessarily, connected with the first element, the idea of an ideal society into which the individual may be inducted after his decease. A person might conceivably survive after death without going to a heaven. It might be a neutral sort of place, like the Hebrew Sheol or the Greek Hades. It might be a bad place, like hell. Or the immortal soul might wander alone as a ghost in far spaces, or even return unseen to his former haunts.

The origin of the idea of personal survival has had several explanations, but the ghost theory seems as plausible as any. It seems likely that very early in human history men must have developed the idea of immortality, because primitive graves contain food and weapons for the departed warrior to use in the next life.

When a man visited a place where he had often walked with a friend recently dead, he naturally recalled their companionship there. It seemed as if the friend were still with him. Perhaps he was still there, but invisible, a ghost. In other words, a person who survived in memory was supposed to have survived in some non-corporeal form, invisible but really present.

If that were so, early man argued, then all the dead must be around their old haunts. It gave the living a sense of awe and fear to think that their old friends and relatives might be still around them, possibly influencing their lives in unseen ways. Elaborate methods of pleasing the good ghosts and of placating the evil ones developed and were incorporated into religion.

But Humanists have little belief in spirits, and think that the survival of the individual is based on flimsy foundations if it has no other evidence for it than the suppositions of primitive, fearful, and superstitious folk.

That is not to say that Humanists would dismiss without examination the evidence submitted by societies for psychical research. Cleansed of charlatanry and self-deception, psychical research, scientifically conducted, may afford preliminary observations and experimental data concerning this as yet little understood thing called human personality.

Here again, the Humanist is agnostic, but open-minded. He thinks that evidence of survival, if any such evidence exists, is more likely to be discovered by the developed science of tomorrow when it seriously turns its attention to the study of unusual personality phenomena, psychic and otherwise, than by revealed religion.

Believing as he does, that human personality is of supreme value, and self-perfectible, the Humanist will not assume any dogmatic position against immortality, if immortality is conceived as a state of improved and perfected personality.

There have been three crises in evolution thus far: first, when matter took on the form of life; second, when life developed mind; third, when mind became conscious of itself.

The fourth crisis may be upon us now, and it may be what people mean when they talk about immortality. If the third crisis was when the animal, man, achieved self-recognition, when he became conscious of himself as a self, perhaps the fourth crisis is the recognition by man of his potential immortality.

But the word immortality is so inadequate. It has been used with such time and space connotations, life-everlasting and heaven, that we hesitate to use it for what the Humanist would substitute for the old concepts of immortality.

For when man has asserted his immortality, he has been simply using the best words and thought-concepts he had to express his confidence in the supreme value of his own personality.

When a Humanist is asked if he believes in immortality, he may answer that he doesn't need to, for he has something better. The Theist has sometimes expressed the idea of immortality quantitatively, by saying it means endless life. The Humanist regards the time element as not so important, the quality of life being a higher consideration.

Again, the Theist has defined immortality as living in an ideal society beyond the grave. The Humanist prefers to try to build it on this earth.

Still again, the Theist has defined immortality as living with God. The Humanist replies that God is but the personification of humanity's highest ideals, and that the circumlocution is unnecessary and confusing.

Immortality has too often been considered a state into which a person is suddenly inducted. Now he is mortal and the next minute immortal. Such dualism is not consistent with the Humanist's idea of the unity of life.

The Humanist substitutes for immortality, what? Faith in the supreme value and self-perfectibility of human personality. When mankind comes to that faith, it will be seen that the idea of immortality was an interesting but temporary method of asserting man's supreme worth.

And the recognition by man of the infinite possibilities of human personality, of itself and by itself, is the fourth crisis of evolution. We shall arrive at that period as soon as we dare to believe in ourselves, individually and socially, and when we do we shall be what we used to call immortal, and we shall find a better word for it.

RELIGIOUS BELIEFS OF AMERICAN SCIENTISTS

James H. Leuba

IT WOULD NOT have done to inquire simply: "Do you believe in God?" That would not have been a sufficient designation of the object of the inquiry, for there are different conceptions of God. There is, for instance, that of Robert A. Millikan, Nobel Prize winner for 1923. Science, says he, shows us a "universe that knows no caprice, a universe that can be counted upon; in a word, a God who works through law. . . . . The God of science is the Spirit of rational order and of orderly development." That is substantially what the great philosopher of the 17th century, Spinoza, had said: "By the help of God I mean the fixed and unchanging order of nature." One should, of course, be careful not to confuse the "Spirit of rational order" with the God who demands worship and answers the supplicant. The God of Millikan and of Spinoza cannot be influenced by supplication, adoration, etc.; he is not the God of our Churches. Strange to say, the old philosopher was persecuted for atheism, while the modern scientist is acclaimed as a defender of religion!

I submitted to the American scientists for acceptance or rejection the following three statements: "(A) I believe in a God to whom one may pray in the expectation of receiving an answer. By 'answer' I mean more than the natural, subjective, psychological effect of prayer. (B) I do not believe in a God as defined above. (C) I have no definite belief regarding this question."

I chose to define God as given above because that is the God worshipped in every branch of the Christian religion. In the absence of belief in a God who hears and sympathizes with man, and who, under certain conditions, answers his prayers, traditional worship could not go on. . . . .

Many of the disbelievers in the God defined were annoyed that I had not provided a way for them to say in what other God they placed their faith. They feared that a negative answer to the statement (A) would class them among the materialists—to them a very obnoxious company. For, although these disbelievers reject the God of the religions, they are at one with most contemporary philosophers in placing a spiritual Power at the root of the Universe. A distinguished chemist wrote, for instance, in a note added to his answers: "I cannot subscribe to statement (A), but I, nevertheless, believe in a God. To classify me as one who does not believe in a God as here defined would be misleading to anyone who has not carefully noted how you define God." Very well, let us not call this man an atheist; let us speak more discriminately, and say only that he does not believe in the kind of God worshipped in the religions. Praising God, supplicating him for the good things one may want, returning thanks for his assistance, seem to this

Reprinted by permission from *Harper's Magazine*, August, 1934.

man a futile behavior, because, as many of my correspondents said, "God is not moved to action by my desires or my feelings; he acts according to his laws." For one who holds that conception of God, a conception widely prevalent among scientific men, the way to secure one's desires is to discover the laws of the Universe (psychical, biological, and physical) and then to conform one's behavior to them.

I wish I might say how many of the disbelievers in the God of the Churches are, nevertheless, anti-materialists. Unfortunately, in order to make the task of my correspondents easy, I had to restrain my curiosity.

Regarding immortality three statements, corresponding to those referring to God, were presented. The first read: "I believe in continuation of the person after death in another world." Thus both belief in the survival of the self with a body of some sort, and survival of the self without a body, are included in the affirmation of that statement. Whereas, what is sometimes called "social immortality," *i.e.*, the continuation of the influence of a person after death upon persons still living, is not.

Dr. Cattell's *American Men of Science* provided me with the needed list of scientists. The latest edition (1933) includes about 23,000 names, which means that every person who had the slightest claim to it found a place in that directory. But sending a questionnaire to so many people would have been too arduous an undertaking. Neither was it necessary. . . . . Polling a sufficiently large proportion of the group, while avoiding the "sampling" error, was then the first condition to be realized in order to get vital statistics.

Because of the widely different size of the classes into which I divided them, or for other practical reasons, the proportion of scientists to whom the questionnaire was sent was not the same in every class. It was least in the two largest, designated here as "physicists" and "biologists." In the first I included all the scientists concerned with inanimate matter—physicists proper, chemists, geologists, astronomers, engineers, etc.; in the second, all those concerned with living matter—biologists proper, physiologists, bacteriologists, botanists, horticulturists, etc. One tenth of these two very large classes received the questionnaire. As to the teachers of sociology and of psychology, and those engaged in research in these two fields, about half of them received it. In order to avoid the sampling error, those to be included in the inquiry were chosen in every instance by a rule of chance.

A second condition for trustworthy statistics had to be fulfilled: answers had to be obtained from a sufficiently large proportion of those who got the questionnaire. I succeeded in securing, in each class, answers from at least 75 per cent. Among the sociologists and the psychologists the proportion rose to 83 per cent; and, among the 50 "more distinguished" representatives of the latter class, it reached 90 per cent. . . . .

Several returned the questionnaire with remarks intended to justify their refusal to answer: "Most of those who believe in God will answer an inquiry like this. Most of those who do not believe in God will put it in the waste basket. How are you to draw any conclusion?" It turned out, however, that over half of all the scientific men who answered are disbelievers and, in certain classes, a much larger proportion. Another wrote: "I am refraining from complying with your request because I believe that real harm is done in announcing to the world the opinions of scientists relative to religious matters."

Several refused to answer because, as I had occasion to remark before, by limiting their answers to the statements offered them, they could say only what they did not believe and not what they did believe: "Forgive me if I return your inquiry unanswered. It is not because of indifference, but only because I could not, in answering any of the questions, give any fair expression of my own attitude toward God and immortality." This person and a few others did not answer because they wanted to be asked other questions! It is worth noticing that the instances of refusal to answer, in which a reason was given, came obviously from disbelievers in the God defined.

We come at last to the results of the inquiry. Let it be recalled that the term "physicist" denotes all the scientists concerned with inanimate matter and the term "biologist" all those concerned with living matter. In the following table, as in all the others, the figures are percentages of the total number of those who answered.

| | The Belief in God | | |
	Believers	Disbelievers	Doubters
Physicists	38	47	16
Biologists	27	60	13
Sociologists	24	67	9
Psychologists	10	79	12

If class distinctions are disregarded and all the scientists put together, one gets 30 per cent of believers in a God moved to action by the traditional Christian worship: supplication, thanksgiving, songs of praise, etc.; 56 per cent of disbelievers; and 14 per cent of doubters.

The order in which the four classes of scientists place themselves with regard to the proportion of believers should by no means be disregarded. The scientists concerned with inanimate matter come first with the largest percentage (38 per cent), and those concerned with the mind come last (10 per cent); the biologists and the sociologists occupy intermediary positions. Does a knowledge of animal and plant life make belief in an interventionist God difficult, while psychological learning makes it almost impossible? These figures provide food for serious reflection, but before commenting upon their significance, let us consider the statistics on immortality. . . . .

II

The history of immortality shows that it is extraordinarily difficult to understand how a being can exist in a satisfactory way without a body of some sort. The uncivilized did not think it possible, and so they did their utmost to prevent the body from falling to pieces at death. They embalmed it and, when they could, protected it with massive, indestructible monuments.

The early Christians were not better able than the old Egyptians to understand the continuation of life without a body; its resurrection was set down in the creeds as an article of faith, and present-day theologians continue to struggle with the problem.

Many Fundamentalists accept the view of Tertullian, a Church Father of the second century, who held that the celestial body has the form and appearance of the earthly one. Asked of what use the teeth could be in heaven since the Blessed did not eat, he replied that they served to illumine an eternal smile.

As to the Modernists, they continue, on the whole, in verbal agreement with the creeds. They hold, however, that the celestial body is something utterly different from the earthly one. But how different? Here they get into a bad muddle. "We believe for certain in the resurrection of the body," said the English Bishop Gore. "This does not mean that the particles of our former bodies, which have decayed, will be collected again; but it means that we in our same selves shall be re-clothed in a spiritual body." Unfortunately, the two words "spiritual body" and "body" flatly contradict each other: what is spirit is not body, and what is body is not spirit. Nevertheless, that unintelligible expression, "spiritual body," gives satisfaction to a great many.

Another English theologian, Canon B. H. Streeter, struggling with the same difficulty, throws out this venturesome suggestion: "We may suppose that during our life on earth we are, although we know it not, building up an unseen celestial body, which is a sort of counterpart of our earthly body. Or, again, we may hold that the death of this body is the very act of birth of a new body." Dr. S. D. McConnell, the American Episcopal divine, looks to the wisdom of the East for help. He speaks of an "astral" body. That is a body "material to be sure, but compacted of a kind of matter which behaves quite differently from that which our sense perceptions deal with." Others prefer to "astral" the term "ethereal," for it is a term upon which science has conferred a high degree of respectability.

The difficulty involved in the survival of a soul able to enjoy an active existence without some sort of material body is so great, and the contradiction involved in the expression "spiritual body" is so undeniable, that modernists like Professor William Adams Brown, of Union Theological Seminary, prefer to stop with the bare affirmation of the survival of the personality; thus they get over an insurmountable difficulty by ignoring it. It remains that for these theologians, as the Reverend Dr. Fosdick has remarked, an instrument seems necessary for the "effective execution of our social purposes in the Other Life."

The would-be believer in immortality is beset by another enormous difficulty: not any kind of existence is desirable. Life in heaven could not be mere contemplation, for life means activity; eternal immobility would not be life. And such an occupation as twangling harps at the feet of the Lord during all eternity would be an unbearable pastime—if not immediately, then after the first few hundred years. What might be a worth-while occupation for heavenly souls? Dr. Fosdick, without specifying farther, speaks of the "execution of our social purposes in the Other Life." To what social purposes might efforts be directed in order to make life eternally endurable?

The impossibility of conceiving a kind of celestial life which could last forever and be satisfactory has compelled the keenest among the religious leaders to say, in effect, that the best we can do here, as with the question of the soul's body, is to refuse to think about it. They agree with Dr. Van Dusen: "Concerning the nature of life after death we know practically nothing save one thing—and we want to know only one thing—that it is good." There are, of course, others in high positions who want to know, and think they know, much more. Bishop Manning, of New York, for instance, knows as many details concerning the other life as the uncivilized who picture the ghosts as very much like the individuals on earth. Says the Bishop: "When I enter there (heaven) I shall be myself. This personality, these tempers and tastes, this character that I am forming here will be mine there. I shall be seen as myself, and I shall be judged by what I am, I shall know my dear ones in the other life. I shall see and be seen, I shall speak and be spoken to." (Easter Sermon, 1931). . . . .

In a general way the scientific men who believe in the God of the religions believe also in immortality; the two beliefs usually go together. The proportion of believers is nearly equal: 33 per cent for immortality and 30 per cent for God. But there is a much smaller number of downright disbelievers in immortality: 41 per cent against 56 per cent. This difference is compensated by a markedly larger number of doubters in immortality, so that when disbelievers are added to doubters one gets almost identical figures for immortality and for God: 67 per cent against 70 per cent. Apparently the problem of life after death leaves scientific men more often perplexed than the problem of a God in social communication with man.

The several classes of scientists remain in the same order in the table on immortality as in the one referring to God: the physicists head the list with the largest proportion of believers (41 per cent) and the psychologists close it with the smallest (9 per cent).

| | The Belief in Immortality | | |
| | | | Disbelievers |
	Believers	Disbelievers	and Doubters
Physicists	41	32	60
Biologists	29	44	71
Sociologists	25	48	75
Psychologists	9	70	91
All together	33	41	67

III

It had occurred to me that it might be worth while to find out what differences there are in matters of religious belief between scientists of different degrees of eminence. It would, of course, have been impossible for me to make the separation. Even had I been competent, it would have been inadvisable: I might have been suspected of prejudices in the choices I should have made. Fortunately, a certain proportion of the names listed in

American Men of Science are starred; they are the names of the more distinguished men. How Dr. Cattell made the selection may be found in that book. I might say, however, that it was, in each science, the joint work of a dozen prominent men in that science.

	The Belief in God		
	Believers	Disbelievers	Disbelievers and Doubters
Lesser Physicists	43	43	58
Greater Physicists	17	60	83
Lesser Biologists	31	56	69
Greater Biologists	12	76	88
Lesser Sociologists	30	60	70
Greater Sociologists	20	70	80
Greatest Sociologists	5	95	95
Lesser Psychologists	13	74	87
Greater Psychologists	2	87	98
All Lesser Scientists	35	51	65
All Greater Scientists	13	71	87

In every one of the four classes the more eminent men provide a much smaller percentage of believers. That this is not an accident is made evident by the statistics on immortality and by the investigation of 1914.

Why this unfailing difference in every branch of science between the more and the less eminent men? Why this wholesale rejection of immortality and of the God of the religions by the most distinguished scientific men? Before venturing an answer, let us complete the presentation of the facts at hand. There remains for us to consider the statistics gathered in 1914 and to compare them with those just presented.

	The Belief in Immortality		
	Believers	Disbelievers	Disbelievers and Doubters
Lesser Physicists	46	29	55
Greater Physicists	20	43	80
Lesser Biologists	32	40	68
Greater Biologists	15	62	86
Lesser Sociologists	31	40	69
Greater Sociologists	10	60	90
Greatest Sociologists	10	70	90
Lesser Psychologists	12	65	88
Greater Psychologists	2	79	98
All the Lesser Scientists	37	36	62
All the Greater Scientists	15	56	85

Many have found pleasure in affirming that since the War there has been an increase of religious belief. One may, probably, understand "religious belief" in such a way as to make that statement true. But if one has in mind the two cardinal beliefs with which we are concerned, the data I have gathered tell another tale. . . . . .

Now for the first time we are in possession of a solid, if limited, basis of information regarding the modifications in religious convictions which have taken place in large and influential bodies of men. The importance of that knowledge will not be denied by those who realize that the course of human events not only determines beliefs, but is also determined by them.

In the inquiry of 1914 the believers amounted to 42 per cent, against 30 per cent in 1933; the disbelievers to 42 per cent, against 56 per cent; and the doubters to 17 per cent against 14 per cent. A marked increase in unbelief during the last two decades is thus recorded. That increase does not appear only in an average of all the scientists; it appears also in each of the different classes, and in the more as well as in the less distinguished groups, with the single exception of the Lesser Sociologists, where the figures are almost the same.

	The Believers in God			
	Lesser Scientists		Greater Scientists	
	1914	1933	1914	1933
Physicists	50	43	34	17
Biologists	39	31	17	12
Sociologists	29	30	19	13
Psychologists	32	13	13	12

Corresponding differences appear in the statistics for immortality:

	The Believers in Immortality			
	Lesser Scientists		Greater Scientists	
	1914	1933	1914	1933
Physicists	57	46	40	20
Biologists	45	32	25	15
Sociologists	52	31	27	10
Psychologists	27	12	9	2

In every group, without exception, the figures for 1933 are considerably smaller than those for 1914. It should be noted also, that both with regard to immortality and God, the order in which the four classes arrange themselves with regard to the proportion of believers is the same in the two investigations.

IV

If it may be said that the foregoing statistics represent adequately the prevalence of the belief in the God of the religions and in personal immortality among all the men of science, the same claim may not be made for the statistics of students; for my investigation, in so far as reportable here, was limited to two colleges. One of them, College A, is of high rank and moderate size. Its students come from families divided in their affiliation between all the important Protestant denominations, and its spirit is probably as religious as that of the average American college. College B is, as to religion, much less nearly representative; it is definitely radical in its leanings.

In 1933, 93 per cent of the students of College A and almost as large a proportion of those of College B answered the questions on God. In College A, there were 31 per cent of believers in God, 60 per cent of disbelievers, and 10 per cent of doubters. In College B, the corresponding proportions were 11 per cent, 74 per cent and 15 per cent.

A decrease in the number of believers takes place in both colleges as the students pass from the freshman to the senior class. In the radical College B, believers have almost disappeared by the time the students have reached the senior class:

	The Believers in God, 1933	
	College A	College B
Freshmen	34	20
Sophomores	37	14
Juniors	30	6
Seniors	20	5
All together	31	11

I am unfortunately unable to give an account of an earlier, more extensive investigation of the beliefs in God among students. I can say, however, that the proportion of believers in an interventionists God was considerably larger in College A in 1914 than in 1933. . . . .

In 1914 and again in 1933 I secured expressions of conviction on immortality from over 95 per cent of all the students of College A. As to College B, no inquiry was carried out in 1914, but over 90 per cent registered their convictions in 1933. The percentages obtained are as follows:

	The Belief in Immortality, College A					
	Believers		Disbelievers		Disbelievers and Doubters	
	1914	1933	1914	1933	1914	1933
Freshmen	80	42	15	33	20	58
Sophomores	76	50	19	30	24	50
Juniors	60	37	32	37	40	63
Seniors	70	27	24	47	30	73
All classes together		39		37		61

	The Belief in Immortality, College B, 1933		
	Believers	Disbelievers	Disbelievers and Doubters
Freshmen	29	44	72
Sophomores	20	44	80
Juniors	14	63	86
Seniors	5	68	95
All Classes	18	55	83

In College B the believers constitute a surprisingly small part of the student body, and their number decreases rapidly as the college years pass. But, as I have already remarked, that institution is not typical of the average American college.

If these statistics, referring either to one or to two colleges only, indicate what is taking place among students in general, it would appear that: (1) The students, in considerable numbers, lose their beliefs as they pass from the freshman to the senior year. (2) During the last twenty years a marked decline in belief has taken place, a decline similar to the one revealed by the statistics of scientists. The first of these diminutions measures changes undergone by individual students during the four years spent in college; the second testifies to the change in beliefs which has taken place during the last two decades in the social circles from which the students come. (3) Both in 1914 and in 1933, the number of believers in God is smaller than that in immortality; this, it will be remembered, was also the case among the scientists.

How far religious beliefs are matters of tradition may be gathered from the fact that in the older investigation (the only one in which this was inquired into) 51 per cent of the believing freshmen admitted that they had never assigned any reason for their belief in immortality. That is not very surprising. One may, however, be astonished at the discovery that three years later in the senior year, the proportion of naive believers had been reduced only to 40 per cent. One cannot fairly accuse these mature senior students of being too critical of religious beliefs imbibed in their infancy.

IMMORTALITY OF THE UNFIT

Arthur J. Brown

THE FOLLOWING IS THE substance of a letter that I wrote to each of the authors named. With their permission I append their replies with only the abbreviations required by space limits.

I venture to write you about a phase of the subject of immortality. I have been deeply impressed by several comparatively recent books, particularly by Bishop Charles Gore's *Belief in God*, Harry Emerson Fosdick's *The Assurance of Immortality*, James Y. Simpson's *Man and the Attainment of Immortality*, John Baillie's *And the Life Everlasting*, James H. Snowden's *Christian Belief in Immortality in the Light of Modern Thought*, Frederick C. Spurr's *Death and the Life Beyond*, William Adams Brown's *The Christian Hope*, and A. Seth Pringle-Pattison's *The Idea of Immortality*. These volumes form a remarkably able addition to the literature of this always interesting subject.

All of them, however, discuss immortality with primary reference to those who are spiritually fitted for it. But what about the unfit? This question was serious enough when the population of the earth was believed to be small and of recent origin. Now, however, we are told not only that there are 1,800,000,000 people in the world but that man has been on the earth over 100,000 years; some scientific men assert 1,000,000 years. If even the shorter estimate be true, imagination falters in the effort to estimate the number of human beings who have lived and died on this planet. The most ardent lover of humanity must sadly admit that a startlingly large proportion of them could not, in the judgment of the widest charity, be considered "fit for heaven," as heaven is represented in the Bible and the historic creeds. Even in Europe and America, where moral standards are supposed to be higher than in other lands, every well informed person knows that there are myriads of people who have little thought beyond satisfying the animal appetites and passions of hunger, thirst, sex and selfishness. When we go to other lands and when we probe into the history of former centuries, we find that the proportion of such people is distressingly large, not because they are by nature any worse than we are but because they have not been under as morally invigorating influences. Is it too much to say that since the appearance of man on earth a majority of the human race have not shown those qualities that are supposed to fit men for immortal life? I gladly recognize that it is not for man to judge. I cherish the conviction that multitudes are better than we think. But it is useless to shut one's eyes to plain facts.

What then becomes of the clearly unfit in the future life? The church in all ages has held that the Bible teaches that all souls are immortal and that

Reprinted by permission from *Religion in Life*, Winter, 1934.

reward and punishment are equally so. This is commonly regarded as "a hard saying." Henry Ward Beecher said:

> If now you tell me that this great mass of men, because they had not the knowledge of God, went to heaven, I say that the inroad of such a vast amount of mud swept into heaven would be destructive to its purity; and I cannot accept that view. If, on the other hand, you say that they went to hell, then you make an infidel of me. . . . . If I lose everything else, I will stand on the sovereign idea that God so loved the world that he gave his own Son to die for it rather than it should die. To tell me that back of Christ there is a God who for unnumbered centuries has gone on creating men and sweeping them like dead flies—nay, like living ones—into hell, is to ask me to worship a being as much worse than the conception of any mediaeval devil as can be imagined.

This is shockingly rhetorical. But if what Beecher termed "such a vast amount of mud" can neither enter heaven nor be justly consigned to hell, what is the alternative? Is it a purgatory in which souls are purified till they are fit for heaven? Is it a second probation for those who did not have "a fair chance" on earth? Is it conditional immortality—a blending of the modern scientific theory of the survival of the fittest and the Calvinistic doctrine of election which represents God as selecting some for eternal life and "passing by" the rest? Is it, as John Fiske appeared to think, an elimination of the ideas of heaven and hell and an expectation of the continued evolution of the human spirit in the world to come? Or is it abandonment of the idea of personal immortality, as James H. Leuba, in *The Belief in God and Immortality*, says that so many psychologists advocate? Or is it something else, and if so, what is it?

It is of course easy to solace one's self with the conventional statement that we should leave the unfit to an all wise God. Doubtless we should and must. But there are times when one feels obliged to ask himself whether a teaching regarding the future of humanity which ignores or condemns a large part of the human race does not carry with it responsibility to seek some other answer than one that merely shifts the question to God. Foreign missionaries are compelled to face this question whether they will or no. A missionary, preaching Christ as the only Saviour, is often confronted by a hearer who demands: "What then has become of my parents and my ancestors for centuries past who knew nothing of your Christ?"

Orthodox churches believe in the salvation of children who die before reaching the age of moral accountability. But where does "infancy" end and the age of moral accountability begin? How far does the baby of an Australian bushman differ from his ignorant nad superstitious father who, at the age of thirty, has little if any more sense of moral responsibility than an American or British boy of four? While we cherish hope for children who die in infancy, can we fairly say that such a hope solves the problem for humanity? And what of adults? I am persuaded that the number of those who, having intelligent knowledge of God in Christ, deliberately reject him is so small as to form an infinitesimal fraction of the vast mass of human beings. Not the willfully incorrigible but the "carnally minded" appear to form a large part of the human race. What becomes of them?

Critics outside of the churches who imagine that they rid of the problem by discarding the traditional view of hell surely have not thought the problem through. They must still face the question: What hell could be worse than an eternity in which one is unfitted for that fellowship with God in Christ which alone can make eternity a blessing! I am a lover of my fellow men, but I have no sympathy with a weak sentimentalism that obscures moral values and makes light of sin. No sterner words have ever been uttered on this subject than those spoken by Christ himself. Divine love is compatible with righteousness, else the universe would be a moral chaos. As modern science has taken away ghosts but given us germs, which are worse, so they have dispelled fear of a physical lake of fire but have made more clear the dire consequences of wrongdoing. The word of inspiration still stands: "The wages of sin is death."

Perhaps it is not reasonable to expect any uninspired human being to solve the problem of the future of the obviously unfit but not deliberately wicked. I venture to write to you because your published writings show that you have thought so profoundly on this problem that you may be able to throw more light upon it than I possess. If you can help me, I shall be deeply grateful. Meantime, I can only subscribe myself as one who loves his fellow men and who, as he thinks of the teeming myriads that he has seen not only in America and Europe but in Asia who apparently neither serve nor reject God, can understand something of that which must have been in the heart of Christ when he wept over Jerusalem and had "compassion on the multitude."

Reply of the Rt. Rev. Charles Gore

I have really nothing to add to what you yourself say. I am not surprised that I should be left in ignorance of the ultimate destinies of masses of men. Judge nothing before the time. We know in part. My business is within the limit of what I can be said to *know*. . . . . I do not think the New Testament can be accused of any pretension to expound the secrets of divine justice for the satisfaction of our intellect. It does what is much better. It assures us of the character of God and thus enables us to feel quite confident that he will deal in justice and love with every human soul he has created. Thank God, the New Testament sets no limit to the activity of the divine Spirit. What lies in the secret counsels of God for humanity beyond the area of this message, or where the message has been misunderstood because misdelivered, is not part of the message, though it may be part of the hope of the human heart which has been taught in Christ that God is justice and love, and that there is no limit to his love.

We must note that the deeply impressive voices that have so continuously assured us that God is good, and in face of all their torturing experience of the world as it is have finally assured us also that his love has eternity to work in and is bound in the long issue of things to do the utmost that love can do for every single conscious human soul. Finally lost souls, only so by their own persistence in refusing the known good and choosing the evil, I feel bound to believe there will be. To believe that it may be so is, I think, bound up with accepting the reality of moral freedom. But I conceive that the lost also will recognize that the mind of God toward them was only good. And though their awakening must be awful indeed, and the figures under which it is described are so, I do not think an orthodox Christian is precluded from hoping that the issue of hell, which is the state of the lost, will be extinction of personal consciousness or dissolution of personality. Heaven is nothing else but the home of the godlike; and hell is nothing else but the state of those who have made themselves, by their own faults, radically incompatible with God.

Reply of the Rev. Harry Emerson Fosdick

The question which you raise is a very important one and I do not feel in the least able to give you a satisfactory answer. I suppose that my own thinking begins by eliminating the thought of a twofold division of the future world. I simply cannot believe in that old, bifurcated arrangement whereby you have static bliss on one side and eternal torment on the other, and so far as possible I eliminate even the leftovers of that thoroughly artificial and incredible arrangement. In that sense I believe neither in heaven nor hell, if by hell you mean eternal torment and by heaven static bliss. In fact, with such a picture of heaven as I can remember imagining in my youth, I can readily understand the wish of one man I know of who hoped that he might be allowed to spend weekends in hell.

When I think of the future life, therefore, rewards and punishments do not assume the primary place in my imagination. It seems to me that there must be moral continuity between this life and that, and that without such elements as adventure, growth, and work, no desirable future life can possibly be conceived. What I hope, therefore, is that for those who enter the next life prepared in spirit to meet the test of the change, there will open unimaginable vistas of opportunity alike for a developing mind, a developing spirit and a developing service. As for those who face the test of death utterly unprepared in spirit, the last I see of them is that they go down into an experience whose disaster needs no fanciful hell to make it worse. I can conceive no tragedy within the experience of human life on this earth worse than to face the test of an experience for which one is utterly unprepared. Such a test, in a supreme sense, death must be and the emergence of the spirit into a new world. A man must be indeed "lost" who goes through such a test unprepared for what comes after.

This, however, does not for a moment involve in my thinking anything that could be remotely symbolized by torture chambers or arbitrary punishments or hopeless suffering. I confess that in the background of my mind conditional immortality has always lurked, but I have never been completely contented with it and have never been able to say that I really believe it. Certainly, I think that if ever a soul should prove absolutely hopeless in any future life God would end its existence rather than continue its existence with purposeless suffering that could have no emergence in refined character. In general, my position can be stated very briefly— a profound conviction of the persistence of personality, a profound agnosticism about the circumstances of the life to come, a profound assurance of a great and beautiful adventure for those who are prepared for it, and a certain fearful looking forward to judgment for those who face the great change with spiritual unreadiness.

REPLY OF PROFESSOR JAMES Y. SIMPSON

As one would expect, you go to the very heart of the questions concerned. Frankly, I do not know that I have any answers to give to particular questions. All that I tried to show in that book was that, so far as I understand them, the trends of science and of some philosophy point in the direction of a selective process as the very mainspring of the evolution of life. I have become more and more convinced of this and of the difficulty of setting one's finger upon any point in the evolution of man, after which you could say: "Now we are dealing with an inherently immortal soul." I have also felt increasingly the insufficiency of the old Platonic conception on this point, and re-reading the Old, and more particularly the New Testament, I was struck with the number of passages in which this conditional view of things constituted the main teaching about a future life.

I have never been much impressed by the argument about the "fair chance" in this life. If, after all, the end of the whole business is the formation of character as the result of living most truly to the best one knows, I do not see how it is possible seriously to maintain that there are men and women today who do not get a fair chance. I should never stand for the Calvinistic conception of election which represents "God in his infinite wisdom and power as selecting some for eternal life and 'passing by' the rest?" My disbelief in the Calvinistic conception of election would simply cover that so far as it suggests an arbitrary selection by God of certain individuals and the passing over of others. Construed as a selection of the individual by himself in the light of the purpose and power of God as revealed to men in Jesus Christ, there is no conflict as it seems to me with the evolutionary conception of things. The decision rests in each case with the individual, and the ethical advantage of the point of view that I was trying to support is that it lays a tremendous emphasis on the present and makes men realize, as otherwise they would not on the older point of view, that every day and every hour of each day are fraught with destiny for the individual soul. The whole purpose of the process has been made inexcusably clear to men in Jesus Christ; but from the beginning of human history men, according as they have lived closest to the best they knew, have realized this purpose in some dim way, and I think that this also is the teaching of Scripture.

I cannot, of course, say in any individual life what degree of relationship to God carries with it, as implication, eternal life; but I cannot imagine that any soul that looks to him consciously and deliberately in any measure, however vague of trust, can be cut off, and to the hearer who confronts the missionary with the question: "What then has become of my parents and my ancestors for centuries past?" why should he not reply: "Throughout the ages God has never left men without a witness, and those who looked to him in trust and lived consistently close to the best they knew will have found that in the end underneath them were 'the everlasting arms.' "

REPLY OF THE REV. PROFESSOR JOHN BAILLIE

My reply to your most interesting letter will, I fear, be aimed rather at the further clarification of your questions than at definite answers.

You say that "a startlingly large proportion of these human beings could not, in the judgment of the widest charity, be considered 'fit for heaven.' " This, you say, is true even of the present inhabitants of Europe and America, but when we go to other lands, and to former centuries, its truth becomes distressingly apparent, so that "an overwhelming majority of the human race have not showed those qualities that are supposed to fit men for heaven." But are any of us fit for heaven? Are any of us fit to judge that others are unfit? Must we not take more seriously the word of Christ: "Judge not, that ye be not judged"? And does Christianity really teach that it is those who, by the possession of certain "qualities," are "fit" for heaven that are admitted into it? No doubt the morality of Europe and America is higher than that of Asia and Africa, and the morality of today higher than that of former centuries (though we must here beware of being carried away by Western pride and by our Western conception of progress); but surely the difference must almost shrink into nothingness when placed against the infinite perfection of God. Perhaps Saint Paul did not go too far when he said: "There is no difference; for all have sinned, and come short of the glory of God" (Romans 3:22-23). In God's eyes, then, we are *all* unfit for heaven, and if any of us are to be admitted at all, it is because (as the Apostle goes on to say) "we are justified for nothing by his grace." It is not to the fit nor yet (in the absence of the fit) to those who are slightly less unfit than the others, that God gives his heaven as a reward; rather is it to sinners, and not least to the chief sinners," that he gives it as a free gift.

The teaching of the Westminster Confession (as of the thirty-nine Articles of the Church of England and all other Protestant confessions) is that those in whom the development of the Christian graces has not yet had time to manifest itself (as would be true in the case of death-bed repentances) are not thereby precluded from immediate admission into heaven, since at death they are at once, by the power of God, "made perfect in holiness" (32:1). The Roman Church, as is well known, follows the other view—that souls cannot be admitted into heaven until their justification has borne fruit within them in a certain degree of sanctification, and that therefore many have to pass through a place of purgatory before being admitted into heavenly glory. This is because the Roman Church has never so whole-heartedly (or is it one-sidedly?) followed the doctrine that entrance into the heavenly kingdom depends upon faith *alone*.

I call attention to this teaching (which, if I am right, appears with only slight variation in all the Protestant standards) not by any means because I believe it to express the whole truth of the matter, but because it does seem to me to contain an insight which is not only most important in itself but which goes some way to meet the sort of difficulty you propose. For myself, I do not think we are in a position to settle the issue between the doctrine of purgatory and the doctrine that the souls of the righteous are at death made perfect in holiness and "received into the highest heavens"; nor do I think we are in a position to exclude the doctrine of a future *probation*. I am strongly disposed to think those right who insist that if there are any human souls who are so corrupt that the divine image has been completely effaced from them, so that they no longer have so much as the capacity left to them to respond to the divine election and call or to lay hold by faith upon the grace of God, then such souls must pass into nothingness, instead of being (as our forefathers believed) preserved alive to all eternity in an everlasting chamber of horrors. *But the question is whether we can believe that there are any souls of which this is true.* When we remember in what unlikely places our Lord himself was wont to find, not certainly any fitness of character or good works, but at least the seed and germ of faith, we must surely hesitate to answer this question in the affirmative. And when we remember that (if Saint Matthew is to be trusted) our Lord told "the chief priests and the presbyteroi of the people" that "the publicans and the harlots go into the kingdom of God before you," we must hesitate to say who it is who can *deserve* to be excluded, if we ourselves are to be royally admitted.

REPLY OF THE REV. JAMES H. SNOWDEN

Your letter goes to the heart of the difficulties of the subject. I have always been troubled by the matters you mention and additional study and thinking have not shown me the way out. I lean decidedly and perhaps with increasing tendency toward conditional immortality, and yet I feel the force of Professor Benjamin Jowett's contention, in his Introduction to Plato's *Phaedo*, that when we cast what we consider the unworthy and unfit to the void, we weaken and imperil the whole argument for immortality. I also see more clearly that there is a broad universalism in the Bible that has been obscured. Paul's teaching that "as in Adam all die so in Christ all are made alive," his teaching that "all things shall be put in subjection to Christ and God that God may be all in all," the general teaching that "the earth is the Lord's and the fullness thereof, the world and they that dwell therein," Christ's own great utterance that "God so loved the world," and many more such teachings and implications create a current and impression of universalism that are weighty.

But then there are other equally specific teachings on the other side. The matter of the enormous numbers of what seem to us to be unfit presses heavily upon me. It is true that the infinite God may not be troubled with such numbers, but we are. More and more I find myself falling back in my theology on the question: "Shall not the Judge of all the earth do right?" That is the one thing that I am sure of and perhaps that is enough. We have not got on very much since the days of Abraham in such matters. The continuity of the life in this world with that in the next, due in part to our doctrine of evolution though it is also plainly taught in the Bible, is now generally held and emphasized. This throws considerable light on the whole subject and lends itself to conditional immortality as falling in line with the survival of the fittest. I think evolution has strengthened the case for immortality and is our most important modern contribution to the subject.

REPLY OF THE REV. FREDERICK C. SPURR

Your letter greatly stirs me, as the subject must stir any man who thinks at all. The problem you raise has been raised in my own mind long ago, and settled once for all. I am an Evangelical; but upon the subject of the hereafter I have always held a very open mind for the reason that Scripture is nowhere dogmatic upon the subject. The main thing to hold to is that without holiness no man shall see the Lord, not even the most orthodox person in the world. The whole subject of salvation needs reconsidering in the light of character rather than of creed. Eternal life is correspondence to God (John 17:3, 4), and death is non-correspondence (Romans 6:23). I do not believe in the Roman Catholic purgatory, nor in "conditional immortality," nor with Professor Leuba (who so patently misses his point), nor in automatic salvation. But I do believe for all in the evolution of the human spirit in the world to come. . . . . It is not necessary to postulate a purgatory. It is sufficient to believe that the conditions of progress there are exactly what they are here. The same thing applies to lower grade souls. Whatever kind of soul we take over, we must begin there as we end here. I cannot see that there is anything in the Bible to warrant the dogmatic conclusion that the work of God in the soul ceases at death. Many criminals here are such by virtue of physical infirmity—brain lesion, disease, etc. When the prison in which they have been bound is open, they may for the first time find themselves. Psychology increasingly teaches us that there are unexplored depths in every soul, and that when these are explored they explain much that on the surface is puzzling. More and more I return to the point that God alone is Judge, and that he will do right for he alone knows all. Willful sin in anyone has to be paid for bitterly. Here, we see that pain, remorse, etc., are part of a curative process in the soul. Why should it not be hereafter? I prefer to believe that the moral laws of the world operate in all worlds; and that no salvation is possible without a moral response to Christ. What happens to men who have never heard of the Christ, can only be surmised by the just principle of Acts 10:34, 35 and Romans 1:18-23; 2:12-16.

The abstract question as to what will be the fate of final rejection of Christ, I cannot answer. A hint is supplied by evolution. The flower that does not advance to its proper perfection retrogrades to the condition from which it came. And it may be that any man who deliberately refuses to perfect his personality through Christ will be doomed to lose that boon and to survive in lower form. Or again, there may be a relative annihilation. Conscious, vindicative torment is unthinkable. This is as far as I can go. Where there are any stirrings of higher things, such desires, faint and flickering as they may be, seem to justify the admission of the individual to further opportunity when this earthly stage is ended.

REPLY OF THE REV. PROFESSOR WILLIAM ADAMS BROWN

The difficulty of which you speak in your full and interesting letter is the fundamental difficulty in connection with the subject of immortality. It is not difficult to make an argument for those whose lives show a spark of genius or even a germ of progress. The question concerns the great mass who seem to be without creative intelligence, neither good nor bad. As to them I do not know that one can go beyond the conclusion which you have reached in your letter.

Of these facts, however, I am very sure: that for all of us—the more or less advanced—there will be some period of further discipline and education in the life after death. The purgatory of the Roman Catholic is associated with so many superstitions that it is an impossible doctrine for the Protestant; but there must be some substitute on Protestant principles which meets the need that gives rise to the doctrine of purgatory. In the life which follows after death, it may well be that many of those who in this life have given no evidence of spiritual capacity will find the stimulus they need.

As to the argument from numbers to which you refer, that has been freshly dealt with by Professor William James in his Ingersoll Lecture on *Immortality*. The real question, however, is concerned with the fate of those who, whether sooner or later, do not realize the Christian ideal. Are we to think of them as forever tormented in a hell of endless suffering, or as passing out of existence? For myself, I have no hesitation in accepting the latter alternative. Nor do I think that it is difficult to reconcile it with the teaching of the Scripture. Indeed, there is much to be said for the fact that from the purely scriptural point of view the doctrine of conditional immortality is most consistent with the totality of Scripture teaching. If we are to believe, as the Universalists believe, in the final salvation of all, it can only be on the basis of a faith in the love of God so great as to overcome almost insuperable logical obstacles. For most of us, I suspect we shall rest on the point at which you have yourself come, a loyal acceptance of the conditions upon which immortality in the Christian sense depends, and resolve to do all that we can to multiply and extend them as widely as possible.

REPLY OF PROFESSOR EMERITUS A. SETH PRINGLE-PATTISON

I have read with much interest the letter in which you put so forcibly the main difficulty about immortality. It does not follow (from belief that man is an immortal spirit) that we are to think of personal immortality as an inherent possession of every human soul, or a talismanic gift conferred indiscriminately on every being born in human shape. We talk very loosely of "souls" and "persons," as if those were static entities, magically called into being, and complete from the outset. But it is manifestly a question of degree. A true self comes into being as the result of continuous effort, and the same effort is needed to hold it together and ensure its maintenance; for the danger of disintegration is always present. If a man is no more than a loosely associated group of appetites and habits, the self as a moral unity has either flickered out or has never yet come into existence. To the constitution of such a real self there must go some persistent purpose, or rather some coherent system of aims and ideals, and some glimpse at least, it would seem, of the eternal values. Eternal life, as a present experience, lends no support to the view that such experience is limited to the present life, nor to the view that it tends in any way to bring about its own cessation by dissolving the finite personality. It does, however, certainly suggest that the further life is to be regarded as the sequel and the harvest of what began here.

Dante is confronted by the problem of the characterless soul at the outset of his journey. Dante was obliged to find a place for them because of the Catholic dogma of the natural immortality of every soul. . . . . But why should the universe be permanently burdened by the continued existence of those who made no use of life while they had it? People talk as if the being of a soul were something which almost defied annihilation, which at any rate could be brought to an end only by a special fiat of the Deity. But surely it is quite the other way. It is but a relaxing of central control, and a process of dissociation at once begins. Nothing seems more fatally easy than the dissolution of this fashion of the coherent unity which we call a mind, if the process is allowed to continue and to spread. We can observe the phenomenon frequently in cases of disease, when it affects the practical activities of life; but the mere relaxation of moral effort may initiate the same process in the spiritual sphere. Without the unity implied in some continuous purpose, what prospect can there be of eternal life, or what meaning can it have? Man, if we look at him as entirely absorbed in his finite activities, is no fit subject for immortality; there is no more call to raise the question in his case than in the case of other animals.

Although immortality is not something that comes to us automatically but essentially something to be won and held, it would ill become us, in the phrase and spirit of a bygone theology, to seek to limit the number of the elect by making the destiny of any soul dependent on our finite and necessarily imperfect judgment of its character and possibilities. . . . . Our most peremptory judgments may often be the most fallacious. Are we not sometimes irritated by the unreasoning devotion of a woman—a wife or a mother—to a brute (as we say) whom everyone else has given up as hopeless and would think the world well rid of? And yet the dumb fidelity and ever repeated forgiveness of injuries depend on a faith in some spark of goodness in the wretch who appears to others so wholly vile. The faith and the love shame our impatience by the glimpse they seem to give us of the infinite long-suffering of a divine compassion. It is rash to imagine that patience exhausted in the short space of our earthly life. We know not what succession of experiences may be needed before the vision of love and goodness awakens a degraded soul to the hideousness of its own condition. And it may be that, in the end, no single soul shall be "cast as rubbish to the void, when God has made the pile complete." The idea of a final restoration seems to many minds the belief most consonant with our idea of the divine perfection and the ultimately constraining power of the good. To think otherwise is, for Browning, to confess a failure of the divine plan for the soul in question; "which must not be." It is the solution which commends itself to us as appropriate wherever a real self has come into being, were it only through rebellion and active sin. Spiritual energy may be shown in the pursuit of evil as well as of good.

But what of the "frustrate ghosts" who have taken no sides, who seem never to have achieved selfhood by an act of personal choice at all? If we insist that every such "soul" must go on forever, are we not allowing ourselves to be swayed by the conception of a soul-thing created once for all by God? But there is no soul (in any sense relevant to our present question) except the unified personality built up by our own acts. In the absence of such a personality, how can the question of an immortal destiny be properly said to arise? It is contrary to every principle of the spiritual life to conceive of immortality as a gift thrust upon a man without his active co-operation. Those who have not known "immortal longings" are not wronged if that is not granted which they have never sought. The ideal of universal restoration, if it is allowed to harden into a dogma, involves a danger and may easily lay itself open to the same criticism as the vaunted law of automatic progress in which the nineteenth century so profoundly believed. The operation of this natural law was to carry the race to ever higher heights, quite irrespective of the conscious co-operation of individuals, of their sluggish inertia or their open resistance. To proclaim universal restoration in similar fashion as a necessary law of the universe is to ignore the fact that, in the nature of the case, the destiny of a self-conscious spirit is committed to itself and depends upon a personal choice. To assure people that, whatever they do, all will come right in the end is not an effective method of awakening them to the gravity of decisions here and now, which bind upon the soul the fetters of habit and make it ever more difficult to find the way back. . . . .

You will gather from those passages that I do not believe in the unending existence of everything born in human shape. Where life is lived entirely on an animal level, there seems no reason whatever to suppose that the life does not come to an end with the death of the body. But where there are any stirrings of higher things, such desires, faint and flickering as they may be, seem to justify the admission of the individual to further opportunity when this earthly stage is ended.

THE GOOD AND EVIL IN SPIRITUALISM

Burnett H. Streeter

SPIRITUALISM AND PSYCHICAL RESEARCH

MOST OF US DISLIKE anything that may be called occult. The temperament of the average Anglo-Saxon is by nature unfortunately not characterised by scientific patience, and very many are too apt to think that a scientific temper consists in cutting the Gordian knot of some difficult question depending on evidence with the sword of pre-conceived, anti-superstitious opinion. . . .

It is important to distinguish clearly between scientific investigations such as those undertaken by the Society of Psychical Research (which as re-gards attempted communication with the dead, is carried on by mediumistic methods) and the religious or quasi-religious movement which goes by the name of Spiritualism in England and America and of Spiritism on the Continent. This distinction must be kept in mind, and with it one or two points which bear upon the literature of the subject. (a) It does not follow, because a man or woman has won a reputation in some department of science—say chemistry or electricity—that their investigation of occult matters will be scientific. Many people keep their science, just as many other keep their religion, in water-tight compartments. When this in-firmity of great minds is grasped we shall no longer be confused by the fact that Professor This, who has won real distinction in some special de-partment of science, disbelieves the possibility of communicating with the spirits of the dead, and Professor That, equally distinguished daily obtains such communications. (b) Another point to be remembered is that because a man, even a scientific man, belongs to the S. P. R. it does not follow that he works with the temper and caution which have characterized the official work of the Society. (c) Yet a further point is that, although certain prominent men who profess Spiritualism in the religious sense are also members of the S. P. R., that is no reason why we should confuse Spirit-ualism with the official work of this Society. . . .

What is our object in thus doggedly disbelieving that mind may act independently of the body? There is a purpose in it. Usually we want to preserve our friends and our families from contact with what appears to us an unhealthy interest. But if our friends and families sooner or later find that they are faced with inexplicable facts that they cannot disbelieve, they will set aside us and our judgments as valueless. If we show credulity in making negative assertions on insufficient evidence, they will show similar credulity in accepting deleterious superstitions. It is true that superstition inhibits the best activites of the soul by dwarfing the love of truth, but prejudice also dwarfs it. If any well-attested fact is subversive of our

From *Immortality*, New York, 1917, pp. 244-273. Reprinted by permission of the publishers, The Macmillan Company.

traditional beliefs, instead of getting angry or scornful, let us consider it patiently. If it be true we may be quite sure that it has been true from the foundation of the world. . . . .

Objections to the Spiritualist Hypothesis

We may now proceed to state the principal objections to the belief in detailed verbal communication from discarnate spirits which Spiritualism maintains.

(1) *Telepathy Usually an Adequate Explanation*

The first objection has been already indicated. It is that as yet we do not know the limits of the sub-conscious mind's power of access to other minds on earth, nor the length of time an impression thus made may persist before it is brought into consciousness. Because thought-transference or telepathy certainly accounts for so large a part of so-called "communications," we are forbidden by the Law of Parsimony to seek another cause till we are assured that this or some other known cause will not serve. While our knowledge of the limits and working of telepathy remains imperfect, this is not a final objection, but it has much greater weight than convinced spiritualists will commonly allow. They urge that the explanation of messages as obtained by telepathy from the living is often much more complex or roundabout than the spiritualist explanation, and this argument sounds plausible. But science has often found that what seems the simpler explanation is not the true one. Many people used to be indignant at the suggestion that the common cold is caused by an infectious microbe. They felt chill; they developed a cold; why drag in the more complex theory of the catarrhal microbe? Yet the more complex theory was the true one. And in every department of research science has had to replace simple and obvious explanations which were false by the more complex truth.

In our present problem we must remember that telepathy from the living is proved to be the source of part of the information imparted by mediums. No one who has studied the subject will deny this. I once had an interview with a fortune-telling gypsy whose ways were obviously mediumistic. She told me that I would receive a letter in the first week of the new year containing a hundred pounds. I was much impressed, because I expected this amount at exactly that time, believing the money was then due from my publisher. When the time came I discovered that the publisher did not pay till six months after the year's accounts were rendered, and that then ten pounds of it would go to the literary agent! The gypsy's information was obviously a reflection of my own mind at the time we met. . . . .

(2) *Automatic Writing*

The second objection concerns such "inspired" writing of the spiritualists, much of which is now published and has great currency. While it is impossible to assert of any one passage from published automatic writings that it certainly represents the earthly environment of the medium, and not the mind of any discarnate spirit, it is worthy of note that when we get whole books of automatic writing supposed to be inspired by some individual from the next life, we find that on the whole we have nothing that does not correspond with the intellectual, moral, and religious environment of the medium. Beside the automatic writings reported by the S. P. R. I may refer to three such books of whose origin I happen to know something. One was written in the house of a personal friend; one by a lady medium well known to some of my friends; the third by different members of one family all quite well known in a neighborhood where I often visit. I have reason to believe that each of these three books is an honest effort to give to the world what is honestly believed to be a revelation from another world, verbally inspired by a discarnate spirit. What is most striking about all these collections is that they reflect the general thought of the circles and households from which they emanate. What might be called the general telepathic environment of the medium is exactly reflected, and nothing more.

If "mediumship" means, as I believe it does, a greater awareness than the ordinary person possesses of telephathic environment, a greater quiescence of the individual judgment and the conscious reason, such faithful reflection of mental environment would be just what we should expect. I find no individual style or character in these books. They ripple on with serious but monotonous and insipid platitudes on a level with surrounding thought and belief.

Such physical and mental automatisms as writing or speaking or screaming or dancing are well known to medical science. They can be self-induced in various ways. A child, after its grief is appeased, will sometimes go on sobbing, unable to stop. The laughter of a hysteric is analogous. Public speakers, even of strong character, sometimes find themselves unable to bring a speech to a desired end: sentences which add nothing to the force of what they have said keep rising in their mind and rolling from their lips because mind and voice, habituated to the exercise, work automatically. Men who are forced to think on certain subjects by day often find that they cannot help thinking of them by night; their conscious thoughts go on and on, but produce no conclusion. Automatic speech or writing, so far as it is physical, may be precisely the same sort of affection in kind, although it is a further development of the power of mechanical habit. So far as it is mental it may be referred to the dream consciousness discussed later on. Responsible members of the S. P. R. are generally of the opinion that the fact that speech or writing is automatic is not in itself any evidence that it has any source beyond the subconscious mind of the medium. . . . .

(3) Dream-consciousness of the Medium

This brings us to the third objection to the claim of spiritualists to know the conditions of the next life: even if a discarnate spirit were striving to communicate through a medium's automatic speech or script, the medium's dream-consciousness would always, potentially at least, vitiate the message. Thus we must consider the working of the dream-consciousness of human beings. It has often been proved that dramatic dreams, which to the dreamer appear of long duration, have taken place in a few moments of time and have been suggested by some simple external circumstance, such as a knock at the door, a street cry, or the touch of something near the dreamer. This proves the facility with which the human imagination, when unbridled by conscious reason, groups scenes and narratives round some casual sensuous suggestion, a facility well known to every candid student of dreams. The scenes and narratives will depend upon the temperament, environment, and experience of the dreamer, but the imaginative power to produce them when in a dreaming state is common. The same sort of power is seen in those illusions which in mist or half light frequently startle waking people. Some half-seen object by its outline or colour suggests something else, and straightway the percipient sees the thing suggested in all its detail, although the detail can be proved afterwards not to be there. I once stood for a full minute with a friend gazing at a wonderful apparition of Mary Queen of Scots in the exact costume of her best-known portrait. She was kneeling by a chair in a darkened room, her hand and face uplifted apparently in prayer. We both saw the same person—the attitude, the costume—in the light from the door we had opened; but when we recovered from our astonishment and went forward to investigate, we found only a black velvet gown with lace frills, which a maid had thrown carelessly on the chair. The real outline suggested, but only suggested, what we saw. The imaginative element in all perception, heightened in such a case as this, is probably the same that runs riot in our dreams. . . . .

In the light of these considerations we may examine the conception of the "control" developed by mediums. Sir O. Lodge says: "The kind of medium chiefly dealt with in this book is one who, by waiting quietly, goes more or less into a trance, and is then subject to what is called 'control' . . . . which certainly *is* a secondary personality of the medium, whatever that phrase may really signify." It is to the dramatic imagination of the dream-consciousness that I should judge the apparent personality and communications of the "control" to be due. But Sir Oliver speaks of the "control" as receiving some, but only some, messages which he thinks are from "the next world," and "transmitting them through the speech or writing of the medium, and with mannerisms belonging either to the medium or to the 'control.' The amount of sophistication varies according to the quality of the medium and to the state of the medium at different times; it must be attributed in the best cases physiologically to the medium, intellectually to the control." It is when the dream padding is coherent that Sir Oliver apparently calls it "sophistication." When speaking of information given by Mrs. Leonard's control, "Feda," as to the nature of the next life, he says that some records are "of a very non-evidential and perhaps ridiculous kind, but I do not feel inclined to suppress them. . . . . I should think, myself, that they are of very varying degrees of value, and peculiarly liable to unintentional sophistication by the medium. They cannot be really satisfactory, as we have no means of bringing them to book. The difficulty is that Feda encounters many sitters, and though the majority are just enquirers, taking what comes and saying very little, one or two may be themselves full of theories, and may either intentionally or unconsciously convey them to the control; who may thereafter retail them as actual information, without perhaps being sure whence they are derived."

The passages in the sitting referred to are given by Feda dramatically as spoken by Raymond, or glibly, describing Raymond's experience. "He's been attending lectures at what they call 'halls of learning'; you can prepare yourself for the higher spheres while you are living in lower ones. He's on the third, but he's told that even now he could go on to the fourth if he chose; but he says he would rather be learning the laws ap-per-taining to each sphere while he's still living on the third. . . . . He went into a place on the fifth sphere—a place he takes to be made of alabaster. He's not sure that it really was, but it looked like that. It looked like a kind of temple—a large one. . . . . He went in, and he saw that though the building was white, there were many different lights; looked like certain places covered in red, and . . . . was blue, and the centre was orange. These were not the crude colours that go by those names, but a softened shade. And he looked to see what they came from. Then he saw that a lot of the windows were extremely large, and the panes in them had glass of these colours."

Before giving these and analogous passages, Sir O. Lodge says: "I am inclined myself to attribute a good deal of this to hypothetical information received by Feda from other sitters; but it seems unfair to suppress it. In accordance with my plan I propose to reproduce it for what it is worth." Sir Oliver does not himself pronounce a final decision as to whether these messages are from the discarnate spirit and therefore veridical, or not. He seems to admit the possibility of their genuineness without sufficiently emphasizing the grave dilemma involved. If these long, and—to us—certainly ridiculous accounts of the next life are genuine, it becomes impossible to defend their triviality, and the general triviality of spirit communications, on the ground that it is so difficult to get through coherent messages; yet that is the ground on which the scrappy or trivial nature of such communications is defended. On the other hand, if these long creeds of Feda's proceed from the medium's dream-consciousness, it must be observed that they come with just the same credentials as any other message from Raymond, or other discarnate spirit given by other mediums. If these are false there is no sufficient reason for accepting any spiritualistic description of the next life. . . . .

(5) Character of Messages

The fifth objection concerns the character of the messages put forward as coming from spirits of the dead. Moral and religious people are objecting that they are too trivial to be credible. But I do not conceive mere triviality or littleness to be a real objection. To the observant nothing is insignificant; and the characters of the greatest men may be read in their trifling, half-unconscious actions. On earth "God comes to us in the little things."

If the next life is continuous with this, we have no need to think of it as of huge, empty spaces in which a few magnificent realities loom dreadful to the naked soul. If God is Creator He is eternally Creator. To create means to manifest thought in form. There, as here, we must know Him in the beauty of His creation. If He is eternal Love, there, as here, life will be in the human family, social, hence interesting; there, as here, the reign of God will be within blessed souls, and their activities will make its outward manifestations, even in smallest words and actions. Therefore I think the objection of mere triviality cannot hold. . . . .

(6) Spiritualism Postulates Verbal Inspiration

The last and greatest objection which I have to urge concerns the whole question of the possibility of verbal inspiration from the unseen world.

If it be urged that communications from friends who have passed into the next world are not of the nature of a revelation or inspiration, but that they would naturally talk to us by words and signs just as they did upon earth, it may be answered, first, that we cannot possibly take communications from those who have passed into a discarnate state as though they were on the level of our earthly powers and experience. They have a great experience which we have not; presumably they have powers and opportunities of knowledge which we have not. We are therefore not in a position to judge what in their communications is probable and what is not, as we judge the communications of living people. Their words, if they reach us, have a new authority, or at least a new importance; and, unfortunately, today the air of large religious circles is rife with notions that are supposed to have been got in this way, notions which do not conduce to wisdom. If we receive from our dead communications concerning the next life, these communications, if true, are certainly revelations concerning that life, and therefore of vital import to us. Further, if we and they be religious we shall naturally believe that, while such revelations are given us through our friends, they are still given us by the grace of God. Thus we cannot blame people who receive even foolish notions as authoritative if they believe them to be communications from the dead. In the second place, the word "inspiration" implies some thought or message which a living person believes himself to receive, not through his senses, but within that sphere in which his supersensuous nature operates. Methods of mediumistic operation are thus described by Sir O. Lodge:

When the method of communication is purely mental or telepathic, we are assured that the communicator "on the other side" has to select from and utilise those ideas and channels which represent the customary mental scope of the medium. . . . . In many such telepathic communciations the physical form which the emergent message takes is that of automatic or semi-conscious writing or speech; the manner of the utterance being fairly normal, but the substance of it appearing not to emanate from the writer's or speaker's own mind: though but very seldom is either the subject-matter or the language of a kind quite beyond the writer's or speaker's normal capabilities. In other cases, when the medium becomes entranced, the demonstration of a communicator's separate intelligence may become stronger and the sophistication less. A still further stage is reached when by special effort what is called *telergy* is employed, i.e., when physiological mechanism is more directly utilised without telepathic operation on the mind. . . . .

If, then, we believe that by these methods we obtain messages verbally dictated by departed souls, we have returned to a belief in verbal inspiration, and I wish to submit that all the difficulties with which we are familiar in believing that our Scriptures were thus inspired are to be urged against any belief that our friends in the next world give verbally inspired messages to those who remain in the flesh. This may not be a final objection to all messages from another world, but it is a serious difficulty and must be faced.

ONE WORLD AT A TIME

Elmer George Homrighausen

THERE IS SOMETHING REALISTIC about the term, "one world at a time." And I think that Christians are entitled to use it rather than the humanists, who use it to puncture the bubble of interest in a religion of escape into some heavenly realm far removed from the normal relationships of life. Let it be granted that many think of religion in terms of immortality. As people grow old, and want the compensations of heaven, they are apt to go to church. After the novelty of the world wears off, after the cold realism of life has completely disillusioned them as to the possibilities of changing the world or their personal experience, then religion becomes for them a consolation to be sought in the world beyond.

One is hardly justified in taking exception to such a conception. It is true that, viewed from one aspect, religion is a refuge, as well as a strength, and that life carries within it the tragedy of the unfulfilled and the defeated. But it is not the whole truth. The idea of God, as well as of man, contained in the Christian tradition, refutes this notion.

No IMMORTALITY IN CHRISTIANITY

Bishop F. J. McConnell, in one of his recent books, calls attention to the fact that Christianity is the most materialistic of all world religions. It has little to say about heaven. The insistence of the historic church has been upon the humanity of its Savior. The New, as well as the Old, Testament has little to say about immortality. In fact I think that immortality, in the Greek sense, or in the modern idealistic understanding of that term, is not to be found in the true tradition of Christian faith at all. It is a far cry from the idea of the "immortality of the soul" to that of the "resurrection of the dead."

Immortality means that man by nature has a power in him to make himself immortal. This is naturalistic humanism, or pantheism. We needed no revelation to surmise "immortality." Resurrection means that only God gives and sustains man's life and hope. Immortality is related to a religion of self-salvation. It is man's doing. Resurrection is related to justification by faith and grace. Paul had little to say about the "resurrection" of the unrighteous. There is no such thing as "progress" from time to eternity, from corruption to incorruption. Christianity has nothing to do with transmigration, or with the idea of Nirvana.

In Jesus there is no sentimental hope for heaven. There is a desire to do the will of God in the human situation. Jesus has no interest in abstract words about immortality; he has a definite passion to do the works of God

Reprinted by permission from *The Christian Century*, November 11, 1936, with revisions by the author.

in the flesh, even to the point of dying a real death on the cross for men in this world. He accomplishes redemption by a real passion. He reveals God's eternity in the midst of time. His ministry was not to teach men about their worth in terms of Athenian wisdom, but to bring to light the power of divine action (resurrection) in human situations.

All of the stories of Jesus are set in human situations. He allowed himself to be baptized to show that he had actually entered the human lot. The early Christians seem not to have been so much surprised at the deity of Jesus, the man of Nazareth, as they were amazed at the condescension of so great a One to the human plane. They were amazed that religious reality should take on such human forms, for they habitually thought of religion in terms of temples, abstract words and weighty intellectual discussions, apart from the common life.

Perhaps that is why Jesus has little to do with the speculative side of life. He is concerned with active reality, with demonstrating the lordship of God in a sinful human world. He does not escape into a sentimental heaven-world; he assumes, as reality, a sinful human world. This is what accounts for his power to attract men to him, and his power to meditate God to them in all human situations. Jesus does not speculate about heaven. In the case of the heavenly husband of the poor widow who had seven husbands, he merely says that the questioner has no idea of the power of God, or what heaven is; for Jesus it is another dimension, a world where there is no marrying. Heaven is not to be interpreted in terms of a refined earth. We need a new understanding of the transcendence of God which the Bible teaches.

JESUS AND HEAVEN

Heaven, for Jesus, is not a glorified earth. Heaven is heaven, and earth is earth. Paul picks up the same idea and speaks of the other world in terms of a newly created body of corporeal existence. Paul likewise had no morbid interest in heaven. There is in his writings no intimation of an intermediary state of evolutionary progress in souldom, no hint of transmigration. All that belongs to the realm of speculation.

Christianity believes in the "resurrection of the dead" and not in a hazy and nebulous "immortality of the soul." It does not believe in the "infinite worth" of human life in its own right, and it does not think of spirtual life in terms of so much divine stuff in the soul. All this is paganism. It reckons life in terms of obedience in present life-situations. We do not live in heaven here. We live "in hope" on earth. Jesus believed in "one world at a time." Or, we may describe it as life in this real world lived in the realization of its eternal significance at every moment. Future eschatology is only one aspect of biblical eschatology. This world is the place where man lives as a creature, and man is not an angel but a mortal who needs to live his life filled with the transcendent purpose which God has for him *in this world*. One is amazed at the lack of sentimentality about Jesus in the garden of Gethsemane. He does not pray for heaven; he prays for strength to live life out *here*. Jesus was the humanest of humans. He brought God into life! He made "immortality" into "resurrection."

Time and Eternity

Jesus did not confuse, as many do today, time with eternity, transcendence with immanence. And there is no use trying to imagine what the future world will be like. People who want to possess the future do not care to live realistically by faith. The future is God's affair, and no man has a claim on it, nor does man know what it is. All man has is a hope based upon what God means to him now. The Holy Spirit is pledge of another life. Enough to live for God's purpose for and in this life. There is no heaven on earth, and there is no earth in heaven. Eternity is not endlessly prolonged time, and time is not diluted eternity.

It is no wonder that the early church was insistent upon the human reality of Jesus in the face of docetic doctrines, which involved the idea of Jesus' sham body. Docetism despised the world of human normality, in which Jesus lived, and it confused the nature of time and eternity by denying the one in favor of the other, which is the same as identifying them at the expense of time. To do this is to land in hopeless confusion and to become unrealistic about this life and unrealistic about transcendent life beyond. The doctrine of the incarnation is simple, and unaffected by abstractions. The same is true of the resurrection. The two belong together; they are two sides of the same reality.

Eternity Judges Life

No Christian can ignore the realities of this life. He must admit, with John Dewey, that man belongs to nature. Life must be lived with seriousness and divine concern in the light of the other world. Real life is not escape into unrealistic heaven-illusions. Eternal life is not endless life after death. It is present life in which one knows God is "for" him and that the limits of life have been "filled" with the eternal meaning of the Incarnation and "fulfilled" in the eternal dimension of the Resurrection. The Christian says "Yes" to life "in the Lord."

Nevertheless, no Christian dare exalt this life into the last word. This is making time into eternity. This is our modern danger. This is why Christians withstand totalitarian states—and totalitarian churches! To exalt created life to the ultimate is to fall into the pit of sentimental utopianism and, by a lack of realism regarding eternity, to "divinize" life so that it appears to create its own purposes. This is downright, self-sufficient paganism. Life has an eternal meaningfulness, but that does not make life something divine. Its purpose is beyond itself. It fills it with its true function.

The other world is not something we incorporate into life as we absorb food into the system. It is an eternal judgment upon life, like leaven in dough. It stands over and above us, it is in and through us, but it never can become a part of this created world with its sin. Our making of time into eternity is our sin and fault. And often it is a dilution of eternity to the plane of time that causes us the trouble. Honest, humble, agnostic humanism is far nearer the truth than Christian liberalism!

Leave Life as It Is!

This explains the "materialism" of Christianity, and why when Christ is proclaimed, social changes follow. This explains the intolerance with which Christianity has held to the historic nature of Jesus and the historic nature of Christianity. And it explains why Christianity is a realistic faith in God's resurrection of the dead, and not a sentimental belief in the human immortality of the soul. Resurrection of the dead is a gift of God's creative activity and not a reward for man's natural worth. The power of resurrection is present in all of life, not merely after this life. Christianity never mixes up transcendent realities with mundane life to become sentimentally utopian; it does not treat human life casually. It does not glibly glide over life's tragedy because of an absorption in heaven. That many people "talkin' 'bout heaven ain't goin' dere," may be quite true.

I must confess that in the three-cornered controversy carried on in the columns of *The Christian Century* a few years ago, my sympathies were often with Max Otto. I felt he was sincere in reading life as it is. He never made something out of nature and life that they were not. I became suspicious of Wieman and Macintosh because they were always looking for something "divine" in nature that did not seem to me to be there. Wieman was rebuked by Dewey for the same reason. I prefer to leave life as it is without trying to read anything of divine stuff into it whereby I can make myself believe this mortal existence is a little more "eternal" than it is, more than a "created" world. This truth makes me free from illusions.

Earth is earth, and heaven is heaven. The two interpenetrate but they are not identical. Christians believe that in Jesus Christ the eternal purpose of God was revealed, not through natural evolution, lest nature be made divine thereby, but through the special action of God and through strong personal faith. Revelation and faith are not natural. They are divine insights given of God through persons whereby man—who is realistically caught in the chain of nature, having lost his purpose and function through sin—might again see his life in terms of his creation. Salvation is partly a restoration. I cling to that as a faith, and in doing so, life opens up to me and I begin to see my life in terms of eternal meaningfulness. I live historically.

Suspended and Unproved

I live one world at a time, where I am, with what I have, in the light of God's promise. I admit my faith is foolish. But I am also convinced that without that faith I am lost, because nature by itself offers me no final refuge, no eternal strength and direction, no personal redemption, no adumbration of the "other side" of life which I feel is there, but which I cannot reveal to myself. But I am saved from sentimentalism, for I know I am a creature of earth. Yet I am saved from the agnostic despair of a Max Otto since, through the bars of the cage in which I find myself, there shines a light which tells of another world which I *cannot have here*, but which

I have in hope. It is "reserved" for me. But that world's inheritance cannot come to me except through obedience in this human world in which I live. Faithful obedience in little things keeps alive my hope.

I prefer to let the truth I get from Christ stand in its own right, suspended and unproved. Let those who need it come and receive, as those who need light come to the light. There is no coercion, there is no compulsion. The world beyond is offered those who through obedience have already tasted its meaning in this life.

Christians need to be redeemed from a lot of otherworldly quackery, and a lot of sentimental heavenism. Millennialists are right in their basic discoveries that this world is fragmentary and needs re-creation. They are right in their insistence that this is an "end" world; things here come to an end and have a limit. They are right in their insistence upon the other world, and in their emphasis upon the pull of God's power of resurrection. But their abnormal interest in the other world, their reading of eschatology in mathematical terms of time, their otherworldliness and consequent passivity as regards this world, is wrong.

But Christians need to be saved, too, from that modern dynamic materialism which romantically sentimentalizes this world into the ultimate. This identifies the time world with the eternal world. This paganism is a hybrid attempt on the part of man to make the creature into the creator. In Christian circles it makes the Kingdom of God a blue print for a world order. We admire this vehement realism, but we absolutely reject its presumptions that this world is a self-contained and a divine heaven. We live on earth! One world at a time! But our citizenship is not in this earth; it is in the heavenlies. Both are real, and while they interpenetrate, they are not identical. We live in a paradoxical situation, and so in the present and the future. The true Christian knows the Incarnation and the Resurrection in life now.

In some respects, John Dewey and Judge Rutherford have something!

THE FULFILMENT OF LIFE

Reinhold Niebuhr

I believe in the forgiveness of sins, the resurrection of the body and the life everlasting.

(The Apostles' Creed.)

THESE CLOSING WORDS of the Apostolic creed, in which the Christian hope of the fulfilment of life is expressed, were, as I remember it, an offense and a stumbling block to young theologians at the time when my generation graduated from theological seminaries. Those of us who were expected to express our Christian faith in terms of the Apostolic creed at the occasion of our ordination had long and searching discussions on the problem presented by the creed, particularly by this last phrase. We were not certain that we could honestly express our faith in such a formula. If we were finally prevailed upon to do so, it was usually with a patronizing air toward the Christian past, with which we desired to express a sense of unity even if the price was the suppression of our moral and theological scruples over its inadequate rendering of the Christian faith.

The twenty years which divide that time from this have brought great changes in theological thought, though I am not certain that many of my contemporaries are not still of the same mind in which they were then. Yet some of us have been persuaded to take the stone which we then rejected and make it the head of the corner. In other words, there is no part of the Apostolic creed which, in our present opinion, expresses the whole genius of the Christian faith more neatly than just this despised phrase: "I believe in the resurrection of the body."

The idea of the resurrection of the body can of course not be literally true. But neither is any other idea of fulfilment literally true. All of them use symbols of our present existence to express conceptions of a completion of life which transcends our present existence. The prejudice that the conception of the immortality of the soul is more believable than that of the resurrection of the body is merely an inheritance from Greek thought in the life of the church. One might perhaps go so far as to define it as one of the corruptions which Hellenistic thought introduced into biblical, that is, Hebraic thinking. It is, of course, not absent from the Bible itself. Hellenic and Hebraic conceptions of the after-life wrestled with each other in the mind and the soul of St. Paul; and his dictum, "Flesh and blood cannot inherit the Kingdom of God," belongs to the Greek side of the debate. Whatever may be the truth about the degree of Greek thought in either the Pauline Epistles or the Johannine literature, there can be no question that the dominant idea of the Bible in regard to the ultimate fulfilment of life is expressed

From *Beyond Tragedy*, New York, 1937, pp. 289-306. Reprinted by permission of the publishers, Charles Scribner's Sons.

in the conception of the resurrection. This is also true of the entire history
of the Christian Church until, at a recent date, it was thought that the
conception of immortality was more in accord with reason than the idea of
resurrection.

This latter prejudice is easily refuted. It is no more conceivable that the
soul should exist without the body than that a mortal body should be made
immortal. Neither notion is conceivable because reason can deal only with
the stuff of experience; and we have no experience of either a discarnate
soul or an immortal body. But we do have an experience of human existence which is involved in the processes of nature and yet transcends them.
It is conscious of them and possesses sufficient freedom from them to ana-
lyse, judge, modify and (at times) defy them. This human situation is a
paradoxical one and it is therefore not easy to do justice to it without falling
into the errors of either naturalism or dualism.

I

The idea of the resurrection of the body is a profound expression of an
essential element in the Christian world-view, first of all because it expresses and implies the unity of the body and the soul. Through all the
ages Christianity has been forced to combat, and has at time capitulated to,
the notion, that the significance of history lies in the banishment of the
good soul in an evil body and in the gradual emancipation of the soul from
the body. Involved in this conception, which is expressed most consistently
in Neo-Platonism, is the idea that finiteness and particularisation are of
themselves evil and that only the eternal is good. Pure spirit is thus conceived as an eternal principle, which is corrupted by its very individualisation
in time. Salvation is consequently thought of as release from physical life
and temporal existence. In these latter days such conceptions have been
related to modern individualism and made to yield the idea of personal
survival. But in its more classical and consistent forms this dualism involved the destruction of individuality, so that salvation meant the release
from all particularisation and individualisation and reabsorption into the oneness of God.

In contrast to such forms of dualism it must be recorded that the facts
of human experience point to the organic unity of soul and body, and do
not substantiate the conclusion, suggested by a superficial analysis, that the
evil in human life arises from the impulses of the flesh.

Soul and body are one. Man is in nature. He is, for that reason, not of
nature. It is important to emphasize both points. Man is the creature of
necessity and the child of freedom. His life is determined by natural
contingencies; yet his character develops by rising above nature's necessities
and accidents. With reference to the purposes of his life, it is significant
that the necessities of nature are accidents and contingencies. Sometimes
he is able to bend nature's necessities to his own will; sometimes he must
submit his destiny to them. But whether he dominates or submits to nature,
he is never merely an element in nature. The simple proof is that his life
is not wholly determined but is partly self-determining. This is a very ob-

vious fact of experience which is easily obscured by philosophies, which either lift man wholly out of nature or make him completely identical with it, usually for no better reason than to fit him into a completely consistent scheme of analysis.

The soul and body are one. This fact is more perfectly expressed in the more primitive psychology of the Hebrews than in the more advanced philosophy of the Greeks. The Hebrews conceived the soul, significantly, as residing in the blood. They did not even distinguish sharply between "soul" and "life" and expressed both connotations in several words, all of which had an original connotation of "breath." This unity of soul and body does not deny the human capacity for freedom. It does not reduce man to the processes of nature in which he stands, though yet he stands above them. It merely insists on the organic unity between the two. The mind of man never functions as if it were discarnate. That is, it is not only subject to the limitations of a finite perspective but also to the necessities of physical existence.

This very dependence of the soul upon the body might suggest that the finiteness of the body is the chief source of the corruption of the soul. It is because the mind looks out upon the world from two eyes, limited in their range, that it cannot see as far as it would like. And it is because rational processes are related to natural necessities that the mind is tempted to exchange its ideal of disinterested contemplation of existence for the task of special pleading in the interests of the body in which it is incarnate. But to explain human evil in these terms is to forget that there is no sin in nature. Animals live in the harmony assigned to them by nature. If this harmony is not perfect and sets species against species in the law of the jungle, no animal ever aggravates, but his own decision, the disharmonies which are, with restricted harmonies, the condition of its life.

The root of sin is in spirit and not in nature. The assertion of that fact distinguishes Christianity both from naturalism, which denies the reality of sin, and from various types of mysticism and dualism, which think that finiteness as such, or in other words the body, is the basis of evil. Even when sin is not selfishness but sensuality, man's devotion to his physical life and to sense enjoyments differs completely from animal normality. It is precisely because he is free to centre his life in certain physical processes and to lift them out of the harmonious relationships in which nature has them, that man falls into sin. In the first chapter of Paul's Epistle to the Romans he accurately defines sin, first, as the egotism by which man changes "the glory of the uncorruptible God into an image made like to corruptible man." But he continues by suggesting that sensuality is a further development in the nature of sin, "Wherefore God also gave them up to uncleanness through the lusts of their own hearts, to dishonour their own bodies between themselves." Whatever the relation of sensuality and selfishness in the realm of human evil, whether they are two types of sin or whether one is derived from the other, it is obvious that both are the fruits of the spirit and not of the flesh.

It is, of course, true that the peculiar situation in which man stands, of being a finite and physical creature and yet gifted to survey eternity, is a temptation to sin. The persistency of sin is probably derived from the perennial force of this temptation. When man looks at himself and makes himself an object of his own thought he finds himself to be merely one of many creatures in creation. But when he looks at the world he finds his own mind the focusing center of the whole. When man acts he confuses these two visions of himself. He knows that he ought to act so as to assume only his rightful place in the harmony of the whole. But his actual action is always informed by the ambition to make himself the centre of the whole. Thus he is betrayed into egotism. Quite rightly St. Paul suggests that, once he has destroyed his relation to the divine centre and source of life, man may go further and centre his life in some particular process of his own life rather than his own life in its totality. In fact, the second step is inevitable. Since the real self is related organically to the whole of life, it is disturbed in its own unity when it seeks to make itself the centre and disturbs the unity of life. Thus sin lies at the juncture of nature and spirit.

If it is untrue that the body is of itself evil while the soul or the spirit is good, it follows that the highest moral ideal is not one ascetic flagellation of the flesh but of a physical and spiritual existence in which mind and body serve each other. Browning was right in the anti-asceticism expressed in *Rabbi Ben Ezra*:

> "To man, propose this test—
> The body at its best,
> How far can that project thy soul on its lone way?
>
> . . . .
>
> Let us not always say,
> 'Spite of this flesh to-day
> I strove, made head, gained ground upon the whole!'
> As the bird wings and sings,
> Let us cry, 'All good things
> Are ours, nor soul helps flesh more, now, than flesh helps soul!'"

The possibilities of the fulfilment of this life transcend our experience not because the soul is immortal and the body is mortal but because this human life, soul and body, is both immersed in flux and above it, and because it involves itself in sin in this unique position from which there is no escape by its own powers. The fulfilment of life beyond the possibilities of this existence is a justified hope, because of our human situation, that is, because a life which knows the flux in which it stands cannot be completely a part of that flux. On the other hand this hope is not one which fulfils itself by man's own powers. God must complete what remains incomplete in human existence. This is true both because there is no simple division in human life between what is mortal and what is immortal so that the latter could slough off the former; and because the incompleteness of human life is not only finiteness but sin.

II

The hope of resurrection of the body is preferable to the idea of the immortality of the soul because it expresses at once a more individual and a more social idea of human existence. Human life has a paradoxical relation not only to nature but to human history. Each individual is a product of the social forces of human history and achieves his significance in relating himself to them. Most ideals of personal immortality are highly individualistic. They interpret the meaning of life in such a way that the individual is able to think of ultimate fulfilment without any reference to the social process of which he is a part. This process is interpreted in purely negative terms. It is merely a part of the whole world of mortality which the immortal soul sloughs off. In contrast to such an interpretation, it is significant that the biblical idea of the resurrection grew out of a social hope. The Messianic kingdom was conceived of as the fulfilment of a social process, first of all, of course, as the fulfilment of the life of Israel. The idea of individual resurrection arose first in relation to this hope. The righteous would be resurrected to participate in this ultimate triumph.

The idea of social fulfilment was consequently basic. Not only individual life, but the whole development of the human race was understood as standing under the curious paradox of pointing to goals which transcended the possibilities of finite existence. Social history, in other words, was a meaningful process to the prophets of Israel. Protestant Christianity has usually been too individualistic to understand this religious appreciation of the meaning of social processes. In consequence, the liberal idea of progress as the meaning of history and the Marxian idea of a revolution which will usher in a fulfilled history are justified protests against Protestant Christian individualism. They are both mistaken in not taking the idea of resurrection seriously enough. They think it is possible for a history, involved in the conditions and contingencies of nature, to overcome these by some final act of mind or will and establish a conditionless goodness in human history. Their Utopia is, in other words, the Kingdom of God minus the resurrection, that is minus the divine transformation of human existence. But whatever the defects in these social conceptions, they restore an important element to prophetic religion. Any religion which thinks only in terms of individual fulfilment also thinks purely in terms of the meaning of individual life. But man's body is the symbol of his organic relationship to the processes of history. Each life may have a significance which transcends the social process but not one which can be developed without reference to that process.

In the Cromwellian Revolution a great many sects sprang up, Levellers, Diggers and Anabaptists, who insisted on this old prophetic hope of the Kingdom of God in contrast to the individualism of the churches in which there was no appreciation of the meaning of history. These secretaries felt that the revolution in which they were involved had a religious significance and pointed toward a society in which the hopes of brotherhood and justice would be fulfilled. Significantly one of the best thinkers of this sectarian movement, a man named Overton, spent time and effort to refute the idea of immortality and establish the conception of the resurrection. It is not apparent from his writings that he consciously connected the idea of resurrection with his social hopes. But it is significant that he had this interest. The idea of resurrection is a rebuke and a correction of all too individualistic conceptions of religion. This individualism is always a luxury of the more privileged and comfortable classes who do not feel the frustrations of society sufficiently to be prompted to a social hope and who are not in such organic relation to their fellows as to understand the meaning of life in social terms.

It is true of course that modern men express their social hope in terms other than that of the idea of the resurrection. They are either liberals who believe in progress, or radicals who believe in a classless society on the other side of a revolution. But this secularisation is no advance. It is not, as assumed, a substitution of superior scientific ideas for outmoded religious myths. It is rather the proof of modern man's blindness to the paradoxes of human existence. He does not understand the hopes of an unconditioned perfection, both social and individual, which beckon the human conscience and which are involved in every concept of the relative and the historical good. He sees them in history but does not see that they point beyond history.

III

Strangely enough, and yet not strange to those who think profoundly upon the question, the body is the mark of individuality as well as of sociality. Pure nature does not, of course, produce individuals. It produces types, species and genera. The individuality of human life is the product of freedom; and freedom is the fruit of the spirit. Yet pure spirit is pure mind and pure mind is universal. Pure mind expresses itself in the universally valid concepts of mathematics and logic. These concepts are universal because they are forms without content. That is why "spiritual" religions, which may begin with a great degree of individualism than more earthy and social religions, end by losing the soul in some eternal and divine unity. All consistent mysticism (which does not include most Christian mysticism which is not consistent) regards individuality, egohood, as of itself evil. If Christian mysticism is not consistent upon this point that is due to the fact that Christianity, no matter how greatly influenced by more dualistic thought, never completely escapes the biblical ideas of the goodness of creation and the resurrection of the body.

The fact is that individuality and individualisation are the product of human history; and human history is a pattern which is woven upon a loom in which the necessities of nature and the freedom of the spirit are both required. Perhaps it would be more exact to describe one as the loom and the other as the shuttle. Whenever the significance of history is depreciated the ultimate consequence is also a depreciation of individuality.

To believe that the *body* is resurrected is to say, therefore, that eternity is not a cancellation of time and history but that history is fulfilled in eternity. But to insist that the body must be *resurrected* is to understand that time and history have meaning only as they are borne by an eternity which transcends them. They could in fact not be at all without that eternity. For history would be meaningless succession without the eternal purpose which bears it.

The idea of the fulfilment of life is very difficult, partly because of the dialectical relation of time and eternity and partly because of the dialectical relation of the individual to society. The old classical idealism resolved the difficulties by denying the significance of time and history; and modern naturalism seeks to resolve it by seeking to make time and history self-sufficing. The naturalists divide themselves into individualists and communists. The former destroy the dialetical and organic relation of the individual to his society and produce discrete individuals who have no interest in society or history. The communists on the other hand think it possible to offer the individual a satisfactory hope of fulfilment in terms of an ideal society. They do not understand that individual life always transcends the social process as well as being fulfilled in it. This will be true in the most ideal society. There are aspects of meaning in individual life which will escape the appreciation of even the most just society; and there are hopes of fulfilment which transcend the power of any society to realise.

The very genesis of the idea of resurrection lay in this dilemma. The great prophetic movement in Israel promised the fulfilment of Israel's hopes. But what would become of the individuals who perished before those hopes were realised? The question is put searchingly in one of the great apocalyptic books, Fourth Ezra: "Lo, Lord, thou art ready to meet with thy blessing those that survive to the end; but what shall our predecessors do, or we ourselves or our posterity? Couldst thou not have created them all at once, those that are, and those that shall be?" Or again in the same book: "What does it profit us that there is promised us an imperishable hope whereas we are so miserably brought to futility?"

Here is a very legitimate individualism. Social and political religions which do not understand it, stand on the level of Hebraic prophecy before the idea of the resurrection of the body answered those questions. It is an individualism which must emerge whenever human culture is profound enough to measure the full depth of human freedom. At such a time it becomes apparent that each individual transcends society too much to be able to regard it either as his judge or as his redeemer. He faces God rather than society and he may have to defy society in the name of God.

If an adequate prophetic religion expresses the real relation of the individual and society in terms of a hope of fulfilment in which the individual is resurrected to participate in the fulfilment of society, such a conception is rationally just as difficult as the idea of resurrection itself. The former seems to take no account of a society continually involved in flux just as the latter seems to defy the inevitability of mortality in nature. But that merely means that such a religion is expressing the idea that history is more than flux and that nature is not just mortality. Here, once more, religion is involved in myth as a necessary symbol of its faith.

It is important not to press the myth of the resurrection to yield us too detailed knowledge of the future. "It doth not yet appear what we shall be." Every effort to describe the details of fulfilment and to give plans and specifications of the heavenly city leads to absurdity. Such efforts have in fact encouraged the modern man to reject all conceptions either of individual fulfilment or of a Kingdom of God which fulfils the whole human enterprise. But it is instructive that these disavowals of mythical absurdities have tempted modern men to curious rational absurdities. Among the greatest of these is to revel in the relativities of historical flux and yet nourish a covert hope that history, as it is, will finally culminate by its own processes into something which is not history but a realm of unconditioned goodness. Every one who rejects the basic conceptions, implicit in the idea of the resurrection, is either a moral nihilist or an utopian, covert or overt. Since there are few moral nihilists, it follows that most moderns are utopians. Imagining themselvse highly sophisticated in their emancipation from religion, they give themselves to the most absurd hopes about the possibilities of man's natural history.

It is significant that there is no religion, or for that matter no philosophy of life, whether explicit or implicit, which does not hold out the hope of the fulfilment of life in some form or other. Since it is man's nature to be emancipated of the tyranny of the immediate present and to transcend the processes of nature in which he is involved, he cannot exist without having his eyes upon the future. The future is the symbol of his freedom.

The Christian view of the future is complicated by the realization of the fact that the very freedom which brings the future into view has been the occasion for the corruption of the present in the heart of man. Mere development of what he now is cannot save man, for development will heighten all the contradictions in which he stands. Nor will emancipation from the law of development and the march of time through entrance into a timeless and motionless eternity save him. That could only annihilate him. His hope consequently lies in a forgiveness which will overcome not his finiteness but his sin, and a divine omnipotence which will complete his life without destroying its essential nature. Hence the final expression of hope in the Apostolic Creed: "I believe in the forgiveness of sins, the resurrection of the body and life everlasting" is a much more sophisticated expression of hope in ultimate fulfilment than all of its modern substitutes. It grows out of a realization of the total human situation which the modern mind has not fathomed. The symbols by which this hope is expressed are, to be sure, difficult. The modern mind imagines that it has rejected the hope because of this difficulty. But the real cause of the rejection lies in its failure to understand the problem of human existence in all its complexity.

VALUATIONS OF LIFE

José Ortega y Gasset

WHAT WE ARE dealing with is a fresh manifestation of culture; a consecration of life, which has hitherto been a bare fact, and, so to speak, a cosmic accident; this consecration is converting it into a principle and a right. It may seem a matter for surprise when we come to think of it, but it is a fact, that while life has promoted the most various entities to the rank of principles it has never tried to make itself a principle. Life has proceeded under the guidance of religion, science, morality and economics; it has even proceeded under the capricious direction of art or pleasure; the one expedient that has never been essayed is that of living intentionally under the guidance of life. Fortunately, mankind has always more or less lived in this way, but such living has been unintentional; as soon as men saw what they were doing they repented, and experienced a mysterious remorse. . . . .

On identical grounds, every object enjoys a kind of dual existence. On the one hand it is a structure of real qualities, which we can perceive; on the other it is a structure of values, which are only apparent to our assessive capacity. And in the same way as there is a progressive experience of the properties of things—we discover, to-day, aspects and details which we did not see yesterday—there is also an experience of their values, a succession of discoveries of them, a greater subtlety in their assessment. These two experiences, the sensuous and the assessive, proceed independently of each other. Sometimes a thing is perfectly well known to us as regards its real elements, yet we are blind to its values. The paintings of El Greco hung for more than two centuries on the walls of the courts of justice, churches and galleries. Yet up to the second half of the last century their specific values had not been discovered. What had formerly seemed faulty in them was suddenly revealed as the repository of the highest aesthetic qualities. The assessive faculty, which makes us "see" values, is therefore completely distinct from sensuous or intellectual perspicacity. And there are men of genius in the domain of assessment as there are in that of thought. When Jesus, by enduring a blow without resentment, discovered humility, he enriched our assessive experience with a new value. In the same way, before Manet, no one had perceived the charm that lies in the trifling circumstance that the life of phenomena proceeds in the envelope of vague luminosity provided by the air. The beauty of "plein air" painting has made a definite contribution to the store of aesthetic values. . . . .

This mysterious mental activity which we call "preference" proves that values constitute a strict hierarchy of fixed and immutable ranks. We may be mistaken in our preference in any given case, and place the inferior above

---

From *The Modern Theme*, New York, 1933, pp. 60-70. Reprinted by permission of the publishers, W. W. Norton & Company.

the superior, just as we may make a mistake in calculations without that circumstance destroying the strict validity of arithmetical computation. When any error in preferential judgment becomes constitutional in a person, in age or in a nation, and the inferior comes to be placed habitually above the superior, thus disturbing the objective hierarchy of values, it is a perversion, an assessive malady, with which we have to deal. . . . .

Can it be that the specific vital values have not yet been discovered? And is there not some reason for the delay in such discovery?

It is extremely instructive to cast a glance, though a very summary one, at the different valuations that have been made of life. It will be sufficient for our most pressing needs to turn our attention to one or two of the outstanding peaks in the process of history.

Asiatic life culminates in Buddhism: this is the classical type, the ripe fruit, of the Oriental tree. In Buddhism the Asiatic soul expresses its radical tendencies with the clarity, simplicity and fullness characteristic of all classicism. And what is life according to Buddha?

The acute perception of Gautama hit upon the essence of the vital process and defined it as a thirst-*tanha*. Life is thirst, ardour, solicitude, desire. It is not attainment, for that which is attained is automatically converted into a starting point for some new desire. Existence regarded in this way, as an overwhelming and insatiable thirst, seems purely evil, and has no more than an absolutely negative value. The only reasonable attitude to it is to reject it. If Buddha had not believed in the traditional doctrine of reincarnation, his only dogma would have been that of suicide. But death does not annul life: the individual migrates in person through successive existences, a prisoner of the eternally and senselessly revolving wheel driven by cosmic thirst. How is one to escape life, how frustrate, the endless chain of rebirth? This is all that ought to occupy our attention, all that can have value in life: flight, the evasion of existence, annihilation. The *summun bonum*, the supreme value opposed by the East to the *summun malum* of life, is, precisely, not-life, the pure not-being of the individual.

It should be noted that Asiatic sensibility is, at bottom, of a type inverse to that of Europe. While the latter conceives happiness as fully developed life, as the life of life to its completest extent, the most vital solicitude of the Indian is to cease to live, to efface himself from life, to sink into an "infinite inane," to cease to be conscious of himself. The initiate says: "Just as the enormous seas of the world have but one savour, the savour of salt, so the whole of Law has but one savour, the saviour of Salvation." This salvation is simply extinction, *nirvana, parinirvana*. Buddhism furnishes a technique for the acquisition of such a state and he who practises its precepts is enabled to give life a sense that it does not naturally bear: he converts it into an instrument for the annulment of its own being. The life of a Buddhist is a "path," a road to the annihilation of life. Gautama was the "Master of the Path," the guide upon the highways to *Nihil*.

While the Buddhist starts with an analysis of life which results in a negative valuation of it, and then discovers his *summum bonum* in annihilation, the Christian does not assume, to begin with, an assessive attitude to earthly existence at all. I mean that Christianity does not start with meditations upon life itself, but that it commences at once with the revelation of a supreme reality, the divine essence, which is the meeting point of all types of perfection. The infinity of this *summum bonum* reduces all possible others to negligible quantities. Accordingly, "this life" is of no value, good or bad. The Christian is not, like Buddha, a pessimist, but neither is he, strictly speaking, an optimist as regards earthly things. The one value recognizable by man is the possession of God, the beatitude which is only attainable beyond this life in a future existence, the "other life" or the "blessed life."

The valuation of earthly existence begins, for the Christian, when such existence is brought into relation with beatitude. That which is in itself indifferent and devoid of all intrinsic or imminent value of its own can then be converted into a great good or a great evil. If we assess life on the basis of what it actually is, if we affirm it for its own sake, we desert God, who is the one true value. In that case life is an incalculable evil, absolute sin. For the essence of all sin consists, for the Christian, in the application of a worldly standard of judgment to our behaviour. Now, desire and pleasure imply a tacit and profound acquiescence in life. Pleasure, as Nietzsche said, "longs for eternity, longs for deep, deep eternity," its aspiration is to perpetuate the moment of delight and it cries "*da capo*" to the reality which charms it. Accordingly Christianity makes the desire of pleasure, *cupiditas*, its capital sin. If, on the contrary, we deny life all intrinsic value and maintain that it only acquires justification, sense and dignity when it is given an intermediate status and made a time of testing and practical training for the attainment of the "other life," then we invest it with a highly estimable character.

The value of experience lies, then, for the Christian, in something outside its own limits. Not in its own nature, but beyond its horizon; not in its own immanent qualities, but only in the transcendent and ultra-vital value that belongs to beatitude can life achieve any considerable dignity.

Temporal phenomena are mean and shallow streams of misfortune that acquire nobility only when they widen into the sea of eternity. This life is only good in so far as it is a medium for progress and adaptation to the other. Instead of living for its own sake man should transform it into a preparatory exercise and a continuous training for death, whose hour is the commencement for the only true life. Training is perhaps the contemporary word which best translates what Christianity calls asceticism.

In the arena of the Middle Ages was fought out, with gallantry on both sides, the battle between the vital enthusiasm of the Goth and the Christian disdain for life. Those feudal lords, in whose youthful organism the primitive instincts ramped like wild beasts in their cages, gradually surrendered their indomitable zoological violence to the ascetic discipline of the new religion. They were used to feeding on bears' meat and the flesh of deer and wild boar. As a consequence of this diet they had to be bled every month. The process of hygienic bleeding, which prevented the occurrence of a physiological explosion in the patient, was called "minutio." Well,

Christianity was the integrating "minutio" of the biological excess the Goth brought with him from his native forests. . . . .

The "Good, the Beautiful, the True" only achieve estimable importance in the service of culture. The doctrine of culture is a kind of Christianity without God. The attributes of the latter sovereign reality—Goodness, Truth and Beauty—have been amputated or dismantled from the divine person, and once they were separated they became deified. Scince, Law, Morality, Art, etc., are activities which were originally vital, magnificent and spirited emanations of life, which the culturalist only appreciates in so far as they have been antecedently disintegrated from the integral process of vitality which creates and sustains them. The life of culture is habitually called a life of the spirit. There is no great distinction between the latter and the "blessed life." Strictly speaking, the one cannot claim a larger share of imminence than the other in actual historical fact, which is always life. Upon investigation it is very soon apparent that culture is never a fact or an actuality. The movement in the direction of truth or the theoretical exercise of the intelligence is certainly a phenomenon whose existence can be verified in different forms to-day, just as it could be yesterday or at any other time, no less than the phenomena of respiration or digestion. But science, or the possession of truth, is, like the possession of God, an event that neither has happened nor can happen in "this life." Science is only an ideal. The science of to-day corrects that of yesterday, and that of to-morrow corrects that of to-day. Science is not a fact which is brought about in time: as Kant and his whole age thought, complete science or true justice are only produced in the infinite process of infinite history. Hence culturalism has always an extremely "progressive" character. The meaning and value of life, which is essentially present actuality, are forever awaking to a more enlightened dawn, and so it goes on. Real existence remains perpetually on the subordinate level of a mere transition towards an utopian future. The doctrines of culture, progress, futurism and utopianism are a single unique ism. Under one denomination or the other we invariably find the attitude of mind in which life for its own sake is a matter of indifference, and only acquires value if it is considered as an instrument or as a basis for the use of a culture operating in the "Beyond."

Is it not an alluring idea to reverse the present attitude completely and instead of looking outside life for its meaning to turn our attention to life itself? Is it not a theme worthy of a generation which stands at the most radical crisis of modern history, if an attempt be made to oppose the tradition and see what happens if instead of saying, "life for the sake of culture," we say, "culture for the sake of life"?

HUMAN IMMORTALITY

William James

ONE HEARS NOT only physiologists, but numbers of laymen who read the popular science books and magazines, saying all about us, How can we believe in life hereafter when Science has once for all attained to proving, beyond possibility of escape, that our inner life is a function of that famous material, the so-called 'gray matter' of our cerebral convolutions? How can the function possibly persist after its organ has undergone decay?

Thus physiological psychology is what is supposed to bar the way to the old faith. And it is now as a physiological psychologist that I ask you to look at the question with me a little more closely.

It is indeed true that physiological science has come to the conclusion cited; and we must confess that in so doing she has only carried out a little farther the common belief of mankind. Every one knows that arrests of brain development occasion imbecility, that blows on the head abolish memory or consciousness, and that brain-stimulants and poisons change the quality of our ideas. The anatomists, physiologists, and pathologists have only shown this generally admitted fact of a dependence to be detailed and minute. What the laboratories and hospitals have lately been teaching us is not only that thought in general is one of the brain's functions, but that the various special forms of thinking are functions of special portions of the brain. When we are thinking of things seen, it is our occipital convolutions that are active; when of things heard, it is a certain portion of our temporal lobes; when of things to be spoken, it is one of our frontal convolutions. . . . .

For the purposes of my argument, now, ... I beg you to agree with me to-day in subscribing to the great psycho-physiological formula: *Thought is a function of the brain.*

The question is, then, Does this doctrine logically compel us to disbelieve in immortality? Ought it to force every truly consistent thinker to sacrifice his hopes of an hereafter to what he takes to be his duty of accepting all the consequences of a scientific truth? . . . .

This, then, is the objection to immortality; and the next thing in order for me is to try to make plain to you why I believe that it has in strict logic no deterrent power. I must show you that the fatal consequence is not coercive, as is commonly imagined; and that, even though our soul's life (as here below it is revealed to us) may be in literal strictness the function of a brain that perishes, yet it is not at all impossible, but on the contrary quite possible, that the life may still continue when the brain itself is dead.

From *Human Immortality*, Cambridge, 1898, pp. 7-29. Reprinted by permission of the publishers, Houghton Mifflin Company.

The supposed impossibility of its continuing comes from too superficial a look at the admitted fact of functional dependence. The moment we inquire more closely into the notion of functional dependence, and ask ourselves, for example, how many kinds of functional dependence there may be, we immediately perceive that there is one kind at least that does not exclude a life hereafter at all. The fatal conclusion of the physiologist flows from his assuming offhand another kind of functional dependence, and treating it as the only imaginable kind.

When the physiologist who thinks that his science cuts off all hope of immortality pronounces the phrase, "Thought is a function of the brain," he thinks of the matter just as he thinks when he says, "Steam is a function of the tea-kettle," "Light is a function of the electric current," "Power is a function of the moving waterfall." In these latter cases the several material objects have the function of inwardly creating or engendering their effects, and their function must be called *productive* function. Just so, he thinks, it must be with the brain. Engendering consciousness in its interior, much as it engenders cholesterin and creatin and carbonic acid, its relation to our soul's life must also be called productive function. Of course, if such production be the function, then when the organ perishes, since the production can no longer continue, the soul must surely die. Such a conclusion as this is indeed inevitable from that particular conception of the facts.

But in the world of physical nature production function of this sort is not the only kind of function with which we are familiar. We have also releasing or permissive function; and we have transmissive function.

The trigger of a crossbow has a releasing function: it removes the obstacle that holds the string, and lets the bow fly back to its natural shape. So when the hammer falls upon a detonating compound. By knocking out the inner molecular obstructions, it lets the constituent gases resume their normal bulk, and so permits the explosion to take place.

In case of a colored glass, a prism, or a refracting lens, we have transmissive function. The energy of light, no matter how produced, is by the glass sifted and limited in color, and by the lens or prism determined to a certain path and shape. Similarly, the keys of an organ have only a transmissive function. They open successively the various pipes and let the wind in the air-chest escape in various ways. The voices of the various pipes are constituted by the columns of air trembling as they emerge. But the air is not engendered in the organ. The organ proper, as distinguished from its air-chest, is only an apparatus for letting portions of it loose upon the world in these peculiarly limited shapes.

My thesis now is this: that, when we think of the law that thought is a function of the brain, we are not required to think of productive function only; *we are entitled also to consider permissive or transmissive function.* And this the ordinary psycho-physiologist leaves out of his account.

Suppose, for example, that the whole universe of material things—the furniture of earth and choir of heaven—should turn out to be a mere surface-veil of phenomena, hiding and keeping back the world of genuine realities. Such a supposition is foreign neither to common sense nor to philosophy. . . . .

According to the state in which the brain finds itself, the barrier of its obstructiveness may also be supposed to rise or fall. It sinks so low, when the brain is in full activtiy, that a comparative flood of spiritual energy pours over. At other times, only such occasional waves of thought as heavy sleep permits get by. And when finally a brain stops acting altogether, or decays, that special stream of consciousness which it subserved will vanish entirely from this natural world. But the sphere of being that supplied the consciousness would still be intact; and in that more real world with which, even whilst here, it was continuous, the consciousness might, in ways unknown to us, continue still.

You see that, on all these suppositions, our soul's life, as we here know it, would none the less in literal strictness be the function of the brain. The brain would be the independent variable, the mind would vary dependently on it. But such dependence on the brain for this natural life would in no wise make immortal life impossible—it might be quite compatible with supernatural life behind the veil hereafter. . . . .

All abstract hypotheses sound unreal; and the abstract notion that our brains are colored lenses in the wall of nature, admitting light from the super-solar source, but at the same time tingeing and restricting it, has a thoroughly fantastic sound. What is it, you may ask, but a foolish metaphor? And how can such a function be imagined? Isn't the common materialistic notion vastly simpler? Is not consciousness really more comparable to a sort of steam, or perfume, or electricity, or nerve-glow, generated on the spot in its own peculiar vessel? Is it not more rigorously scientific to treat the brain's function as function of production?

The immediate reply is, that, if we are talking of science positively understood, function can mean nothing more than bare concomitant variation. When the brain-activities change in one way, consciousness changes in another; when the currents pour through the occipital lobes, consciousness *sees* things; when through the lower frontal region, consciousness *says* things to itself; when they stop, she goes to sleep, etc. . . . .

Just how the process of transmission may be carried on, is indeed unimaginable; but the outer relations, so to speak, of the process, encourage our belief. Consciousness in this process does not have to be generated *de novo* in a vast number of places. It exists already, behind the scenes, coeval with the world. The transmission-theory not only avoids in this way multiplying miracles, but it puts itself in touch with general idealistic philosophy better than the production-theory does. It should always be reckoned a good thing when science and philosophy thus meet. . . . .

The transmission-theory also puts itself in touch with a whole class of experiences that are with difficulty explained by the production-theory. I refer to those obscure and exceptional phenomena reported at all times throughout human history, which the "psychical-researchers," with Mr. Frederic Myers at their head, are doing so much to rehabilitate; such phenomena, namely as religious conversions, providential leadings in answer to prayer, instantaneous healings, premonitions, apparitions at time of death, clairvoyant visions or impressions, and the whole range of mediumistic capacities, to say nothing of still more exceptional and incomprehensible things. If all our human thought be a function of the brain, then of course, if any of these things are facts—and to my own mind some of them are facts—we may not suppose that they can occur without preliminary brain-action. But the ordinary production-theory of consciousness is knit up with a peculiar notion of how brain-action *can* occur—that notion being that all brain-action, without exception, is due to a prior action, immediate or remote, of the bodily sense-organs *on* the brain. Such action makes the brain produce sensations and mental images, and out of the sensations and images the higher forms of thought and knowledge in their turn are framed. As transmissionists, we also must admit this to be the condition of all our usual thought. Sense-action is what lowers the brain-barrier. My voice and aspect, for instance, strike upon your ears and eyes; your brain thereupon becomes more pervious and an awareness on your part of what I say and who I am slips into this world from the world behind the veil. But, in the mysterious phenomena to which I allude, it is often hard to see where the sense-organs can come in. A medium, for example, will show knowledge of his sitter's private affairs which it seems impossible he should have acquired through sight or hearing, or interference therefrom. Or you will have an apparition of some one who is now dying hundreds of miles away. On the production-theory one does not see from what sensations such odd bits of knowledge are produced. On the transmission-theory, they don't have to be "produced"—they exist ready-made in the transcendental world, and all that is needed is an abnormal lowering of the brain-threshold to let them through. In cases of conversion, in providential leadings, sudden mental healings, etc., it seems to the subjects themselves of the experience as if a power from without, quite different from the ordinary action of the senses or of the sense-led mind, came into their life, as if the latter suddenly opened into that greater life in which it has its source. The word 'influx,' used in Swedenborgian circles, well describes this impression of new insight, or new willingness, sweeping over us like a tide. All such experiences, quite paradoxical and meaningless on the production-theory, fall very naturally into place on the other theory. We need only suppose the continuity of our consciousness with a mother sea, to allow for exceptional waves occasionally pouring over the dam. Of course the causes of these odd lowerings of the brain's threshold still remain a mystery on any terms.

Add, then, this advantage to the transmission-theory—an advantage which I am well aware that some of you will not rate very high—and also add the advantage of not conflicting with a life hereafter, and I hope you will agree with me that it has many points of superiority to the more familiar theory. It is a theory which, in the history of opinion on such matters, has never been wholly left out of account, though never developed at any great length. In the great orthodox philosophic tradition, the body is treated as an essential condition to the soul's life in this world of sense; but after death, it is said, the soul is set free, and becomes a purely intellectual and non-appetitive being.   Kant expresses this idea in terms that come singularly close to those of our transmission-theory.   The death of the body, he says, may indeed be the end of the sensational use of our mind, but only the beginning of the intellectual use.   "The body," he continues, "would thus be, not the cause of our thinking, but merely a condition restrictive thereof, and, although essential to our sensuous and animal consciousness, it may be regarded as an impeder of our pure spiritual life."

INTELLIGIBLE IMMORTALITY

Francis J. McConnell

IF I HAD only one sermon to preach on immortality, I do not think I would trouble myself much with the formal scientific or logical considerations for or against the belief. Members of various psychical research societies have now and again told us of scientifically verifiable testimony as to the persistence of life after death, but the evidence is scanty at best—and even if it could be accepted at face value, would often leave us with the question as to whether such continued existence would be desirable. Some twenty-five years ago, when spiritualistic phenomena were attracting large attention in Boston, a medium declared that he was materializing Phillips Brooks. The great preacher's salutation to the audience was: "How are you fellows out there?" which would seem to indicate that the transformation in the Brooks style of speech had been quite complete. Most of the more credible and worthy evidence of survival advanced by the psychic research societies is of such nature as to be explicable on other suppositions than that of the survival of the persons who have passed from us. . . . .

And I certainly would not give much time to scientific disproofs—all for the simple reason that there are not any such disproofs worth the paper on which they are written. The most that can be said is that the mental activities are dependent on bodily activities, for it cannot be said that there is any way of explaining a thought-process in terms of body process. Everything material moves, or is, in space. A thought may not be possible till a particle of brain-tissue moves up or down, to the right or left, or forward or back, but thoughts themselves are not up or down, to the right or left, or forward or back. A thought has the power to hold things together in a logical fashion which has nothing to do with space terms. We say of one man's argument that it is more forceful than another, but the force we are thinking of is not to be measured in foot-pounds. We are thinking of another order of energy—that of ideas. No rearrangement of brain particles could ever necessarily give us thought. The arrangement might be the condition on which thought took place, but the arrangement moves according to its own laws and thought according to its laws. . . . , All I mean to say is that the connection between body and mind is not such as to make us believe that mind could not conceivably go on without bodies as we see them in this earthly existence. Science cannot prove that thought is necessarily caused by body. The door is open for us to believe in another life so far as anything science can say—not a wide door, but wide enough—and open.

From *If I Had Only One Sermon to Preach on Immortality*, edited by William L. Stidger, New York, 1929, pp. 161-175. Reprinted by permission of the publishers, Harper & Brothers.

The formal logician comes and tells us that the greatest argument for immortality is that souls are simple substances and therefore indestructible. All the materials that we see around us are combinations. Their destruction means pulling them to pieces. The child gets hold of the father's watch and destroys it by taking it apart. Even after we reach the chemical elements like gold we have not reached final simplicity, for an atom of gold is a little solar system, so to speak, with negatively charged electrons flying around a positively charged proton. If we could knock one of those negatively charged electrons out of the little solar system which we call an atom of gold, we could destroy that particle as gold—conceivably making it into something else. Now the soul, the logician tells us, is no such complexity. It shows itself in many ways, but it cannot be taken apart. It is indestructible.

But even though it is simple why might not its powers die down? Simple though it is, why might it not get tired and quit? If it had a beginning, it may conceivably have an ending. "Ah," says the apostle of logical exactness, "There's the rub! Or there isn't the rub—whichever you like. The soul will have no ending because it never had a beginning. It is simple, indestructible, eternal." Well! Well! Then what was I, a little over a half-century ago before I turned up on this bank and shoal of time? Our logical reasoner answers legitimately enough, that such a question is none of his business. I fear that it is none of mine either, for if I have been existing from all eternity without being aware of the fact what is the difference between such existence and none at all? Self-consciousness and memory are the heart of existence for me, and without those I don't see what advantage there is in my having a core of metaphysical indestructibility. . . . .

We may get an angle of approach to the sermon by asking what conditions would make immortality desirable. I heard a reputable thinker say recently that it is not necessary to believe in God in order to believe in immortality. I doubt if immortality apart from God would be attractive to many of us. Of course, if by some inescapable law of its own nature the universe is just moving on-and-up in an increasingly glorious evolution without the help of a God, and without the need of one, immortality might be worth while, but what reason have we to believe that such an impersonal evolution would be on-and-up? On-and-up is all right, but what about around-and-around? From what we see of the forces of the world which seem most to suggest the impersonal, they are more prone to go around-and-around. Now going around-and-around, even if it is free from positively disagreeable features such as pain of body or spirit, becomes an unspeakable bore. Who craves for an eternity of boredom?

Coming to close quarters with the problem, the only bases for belief in an immortality worth while is belief in a moral God—the God revealed in Christ. It is the glory of the Old Testament that the writers no sooner got hold of a new moral insight binding for man than they held to that insight as binding for God also—and thus they set forth through the centuries an increasingly moral conception of God—a conception in which prophets, lawmakers, poets, seers, and the corporate life of devoted groups, each played their part. On all this as a foundation was revealed the final glory in Jesus Christ.

Before we come to the climax in Jesus, however, suppose we look at some of the more elementary features of the moral in God's character wrought out in the Old Testament. We would not for an instant set moral qualities over against one another, or arrange them higher or lower in a scale. Nevertheless, the Scriptures make it plain that the love revealed in Christ, which God gives to men and seeks from men, is based upon moral fairness and justice. The pivotal question in the Old Testament is that of Abraham: "Shall not the Judge of all the earth do right?" The spirit of a ruler can never be proved in any formal sense. It has taken on trust. If the trusting mind finds that the total experience following such trust leads to fuller life— to mental peace and increased power of will—the trust will continue. Now the primary consideration in thinking of a moral God is justice. On that basis where does a denial of immortality for men leave God? . . . .

It may be alleged that I am chiefly concerned here with the character of God. I am. I freely admit that there are many persons who say that they are not interested in the question of eternal existence. They say that they have had enough of life at its best. "The fire sinks low and we are ready to depart." Judging by their own experience they avow that they cannot find any race-wide demand of humanity for immortality. Even the longing for loved ones, acute at the moment of separation, softens at last to a hallowed memory which the resumption of actual living contacts might disturb. Let us do the best we can, call it a day, and go to sleep.

The avowal of such an easy-going attitude, however, does not release the Almighty from the obligations of creatorship. An old-time Methodist theologian, who was preaching divine mercy, was once reproached with the remark that if he did not cease talking so much about the divine mercy, he would make hell tolerable; whereupon he replied that he was not especially concerned about making hell tolerable but that he was mightily concerned about making the idea of God tolerable. I assume that these sermons are being written for readers who believe in God. If that assumption is correct it becomes of vast importance to them as to what kind of God they believe in. Christianity believes in a moral God. That belief is the distinctive mark of Christianity. Morality, in Christian terms, demands that power be used under a sense of responsibility. Now if God brought men into this world without their consent—and obviously they could not be consulted beforehand—He is under obligation to give them every chance at the fullest and best life possible. That earthly conditions fall far short of giving such chance is apparent at a glance. If this earth is all God can do for me, then the question—not at all irreverent—becomes pertinent—why do anything at all? If God has the power which He is conceived of as having in Christian thinking, He can give men fuller and better life than this. If He does not have the power, He has to meet the Christian question as to how He should send the race forth into a gale like this earthly existence without enough power to carry men through to something better.

I know there is a type of believer to whom all this will seem very offensive. To such believers faith comes easily and naturally. Any questions of this order seem irreverent and even blasphemous. We are under obligations, however, if we are taking the idea of God seriously, to draw out the moral implications of the idea—and that is all I am trying to do. . . . .

Suppose we think now of the Christian scheme of values as holding good for God. What are the values which we on earth hold supreme? I suppose I shall not go far astray in listing them as goodness, truth and beauty. Probably few avowed atheists would today deny that these are the chief values, though they would insist on defining them concretely in their own terms. For the Christian the values are these virtues as made actual in the lives of men according to the life in Christ. The glory of men, according to the Christ-ideal, is that they are capable of being endlessly improved. It would seem to be a strange universe, to say nothing of a strange God, that would make it impossible for them to fulfill their possibilities of development.

It is a commonplace in Christianity that men are the ends-in-themselves, so far as earthly creatures are concerned. We have heard time and again that we can think meanly of man as science describes him, or as history records his deeds, but we can never think meanly of man as Christ looks at him. As a matter of fact a considerable volume of the thinking of the past hundred years or so concedes the value of man as an end-in-himself. . . . .

Present-day tendencies apart, however, Christianity unmistakably puts man at the center of all earthly values. This does not mean that the physical universe was made solely for man but it does mean that man is of more value than anything physical. . . . .

On the assumption that the earthly life ends all, what becomes of these human values? One man tells us that they have value to themselves—that life is supremely sweet. Which raises the question as to why it should stop just about the time when we have begun to appreciate its sweetness. Another man might say that the values are for others as well as for the living men themselves—but those others also pass away. It is true that the record of the achievements of successive generations becomes more impressive as we go along, but each generation has only time for a glimpse at these glories and then it too must fail. The last generation, before the curtain finally falls, will presumably get a chance to see the whole picture, but who knows but by the time that generation arrives earthly conditions may have become so severe as to leave no time for looking for pictures? If the human values are all treasured up in the vision of God and endure there as memories—well, all we can say is that such a God is not the Father of our Lord Jesus Christ. If men are the fairest fruit earth can produce, we can hardly think of the God of Christianity as allowing that fruit to fall to the ground and rot. This would argue an obliviousness to values which we cannot reconcile with the character of the God of Christ.

There is space for just a word more, but that word is the most important. I am convinced of the validity of what I have thus far said, but what I have said has not reached the highest Christian plane. We reach that plane when we think of Jesus' thought of God as father. Who of us that is a father would, if he had the power to keep his children living, allow them to sink into nothingness? The question answers itself. If this life is all, we may as well say that we cannot use the word "father" as implied to God in any intelligible sense. Of course, there are devout souls who avow that they are so consecrated to the will of God that if that will calls for the loss of their personal identity they are content. An old teacher of mine—a high authority in his line—used always to be saying that with moving unction. It is only fair to comment that his line was not one which called for close reasoning about moral principles and their implication. Such a remark may indicate a degree of grace on the part of the one uttering it, but where does it leave God? As for the remark itself—it is not over-intelligent. It declares in effect that one can love God so completely as not to care whether one has an opportunity to love him forever or not. Which is about as if I should say that I love my friend so deeply that I do not care whether I ever see him again or not. . . . .

I leave it all with the thought of the God revealed in Christ. Assuming such a God, it seems to me that we have to hold fast to human immortality to preserve the Christ-revelation of God. If we have not a God Christlike in moral qualities our reflections about immortality will not be worth much.

A few minor questions arise. One objector asks, if men mean so much to God, how could He have let ages upon ages pass before He created them. We do not know—but we do know that that is altogether a different matter from calling men into existence and then jerking the cup of life from their lips just as they have begun to sip its sweetness. Another protests that fatherhood may not be the highest characterization of God. Perhaps not, but what is higher? Remember that we are speaking of fatherhood at its best—not the fatherhood which gives children a start till they can go by themselves, and then lets them go, without diminishing interest in them. President Eliot once spoke a profound truth when he declared that in a true family sons and daughters grow more interesting to parents as the years pass. Still other critics will have it that we have not told what an eternal life would be like. Heaven itself forbid that we should make the attempt, for heaven would inevitably be caricatured by any of our imaginings. We do hazard one suggestion, however. Suppose we think of a state in which all human evils—selfishness, envy, insincerity—are done away. All manner of problems might remain to tax human resources to the utmost—but with every ground for suspicion removed, what human energies would be released! Suppose we could have a stage of existence in which every man's yea would be yea and his nay, nay. That would be enough for a start. The rest we could leave to the unfolding possibilities of the human spirit working with the Divine Spirit revealed in our Lord Jesus Christ.

DEATH, OR LIFE ETERNAL?

Arthur H. Compton

SCIENCE SPEAKS MUCH less clearly on the question of immortality than on the related one of the existence of an order and a supreme Intelligence in nature. A man trained in the school of science has a deep-seated reluctance to present evidence which can only be considered as suggestive. Yet many who profess to speak for science have drawn the definite conclusion that death is the end of all. It takes but little investigation to find that this faith in the completeness of physical death is usually based upon an uncritical acceptance of a common sense realism, similar to that which accepts a brick as the hard, heavy, red object that can be held in the hands. Just as a more careful examination shows the brick to consist of a group of molecules, atoms, and electrons—a complex system of electrical fields wholly different from the common sense picture—so the "obviousness" of death is found to disappear when more closely studied. Though it is true that science presents no weighty evidence for life eternal, it is only fair to point out also that science has found no cogent reason for supposing that what is of importance in a man can be buried in a grave. The truth is that science cannot supply a definite answer to this question. Immortality relates to an aspect of life which is not physical, that is, which cannot be detected and measured by any instrument, and to which the application of the laws of science can at best be only a well-considered guess.

If one is to have either a positive faith in a future life or a conviction that death is the end, such beliefs must, it seems to me, be based upon religious, moral, or philosophical grounds rather than upon scientific reasoning. It is primarily to clear the way for such metaphysical thinking that it seems desirable to consider certain scientific aspects of death. Few of us living in the present age would accept a doctrine which is demonstrably contrary to scientific fact or to the spirit of scientific thought. On the other hand our lives would be exceedingly narrow if we based our thoughts and actions solely upon facts that can be subjected to scientific tests. Science, that is, erects a foundation on which our emotional and religious life, if it is to be stable, must be built. The strength and form of the foundation, however, by no means determine the architectural merit of the structure that is to be erected. If a belief in immortality is found to be of value to man, it will not be because of any scientific basis on which the belief rests, but because certain important ideals toward which men are striving can be attained only by a more complete life than is possible in the flesh. . . . .

Immortality is a word with such a variety of connotations that it will be

From *The Freedom of Man*, New Haven, 1935, pp. 120-153. Reprinted by permission of the publishers, Yale University Press.

desirable to consider briefly some of its aspects regarding which there will be general agreement. No one doubts the influence of a great man's life after he has gone. The ideas of the discoverer of the use of fire are of permanent value. His "spirit" thus lives forever though his name may be all but forgotten in a legend of Promethus. The thoughts and actions of Washington and Lincoln intimately affect the present course of American life. Recognizing the persistence of such influence, we sometimes refer to the "immortals" as those great men of history who have permanently affected the direction of civilization. The hope of attaining such immortality is one of the most powerful driving motives of the world's leaders. We all, in fact, share with George Eliot the longing:

> "O, may I join the choir invisible
> Of those immortal dead who live again
> In minds made better by their presence: live
> In pulses stirred to generosity
> In deeds of daring rectitude, in scorn
> For miserable aims that end with self,
> In thoughts sublime that pierce the night like stars,
> And with their mild persistence urge man's search
> To vaster issues."

To a greater or less extent, for good or evil, all of us must have a certain degree of such continuous life.

Similarly, there is a very real biological sense in which life is eternal. Though each person, or to be more general each organism dies, the race or species lives on unless some world-wide catastrophe occurs which makes it extinct. In his recent book, *The Universe About Us*, Sir James Jeans assigns a million billion years as a reasonable life expectancy for the human race on earth. Though a million million years may not, strictly speaking, be life eternal, it is probably as long a life as most of us want.

The biological center of life is the germ cell, and this, with divisions and subdivisions, grows and lives forever. What the fruit of the apple is to the seed, the body of man is to his germ cell. The apple may decay, but the seed grows into a new tree, which flowers and begets new seeds. The fruit and the tree will die, but there is eternal continuity of life in the cells which develop from seed to tree to flower to seed, over and over again. It is thus because we concentrate our attention upon the tree or the fruit that we say the end of life is death. These are merely the outer wrappings, the hull which surrounds the living germ. Biologically speaking, life, whether it be of an apple seed or of the germs cells of man, is essentially continuous and eternal.

"But," you say, "that is not the kind of eternal life in which I am primarily interested. My body may be merely the hull that surrounds the living germ; but what will happen to me when the hull decays?"

Beyond this point we must cease to speak with assurance. For when you ask, "What will happen to me," you are concerned not with your body but with your consciousness, mind, or soul, however you choose to call it, which is not material, and regarding which science offers no objective data.

Direct observations can be made of the actions of the body, and for the body death is found to be the inevitable end. Our only knowledge of the state of consciousness of others is, however, that which can be inferred from their actions, as interpreted in terms of our own state of consciousness when we act in a similar manner. Since we have not experienced physical death, our idea of what happens to the consciousness associated with an organism at death can be only a reasoned guess, based upon some assumption about the relation between body and mind. In order to test whether such a guess is correct, it would be necessary to receive an authentic and reliable statement from one who has experienced physical death. Lacking such data, any affirmation regarding what happens to "me" cannot carry the assurance of the tested truths of science. At best such an affirmation is a kind of extrapolation far beyond the region of observational test. Even in such a relatively exact science as physics it is a rare theory whose predictions can thus be extrapolated with confidence.

THE CONFLICTING EVIDENCE OF SCIENCE

Let us examine, however, certain of the hypotheses regarding the relationship between body and mind which have been found useful, and follow out their consequences regarding consciousness after death. First there is the materialistic hypothesis used by certain psychologists, according to which thought is a function of the brain. Every sensation, every idea that we have, even every decision we make is a consequence of some action occurring in the brain. On this view it is obvious that destruction of the brain must carry with it the destruction of consciousness.

This hypothesis has been adopted primarily in order to simplify the problem of behavior by reducing it to a set of mechanical laws. If thought is a by-product of some molecular change in the brain, and if these molecular changes follow definite physical laws, there will be a straightforward sequence of molecular changes starting with the initial stimulus and ending with the final action of the organism. Thoughts may be associated with these various changes, but they cannot alter the end result, for this is determined by the physical laws which govern the molecular actions. The problem of man's behavior is thus simplified by reducing him to an automaton.

Chapter II gives in some detail my reasons for believing that this simplified behavior fails as a complete description of our actions. In some reflex actions and habitual acts we may behave as automata; but where deliberation occurs we feel that we choose our own counsel. In fact, a certain freedom of choice may, it seems to me, be considered as an experimental fact with which we must reconcile our theories. Because the mechanist's basic hypothesis leaves no room for such freedom, I see no alternative other than to reject the hypothesis as inadequate.

On the other hand, if freedom of choice is admitted, it follows by the same line of reasoning that one's thoughts are not wholly the result of molecular reactions determined by physical laws. For if they were, one's thoughts would be fixed by the physical conditions, and his choice would be made for him. Thus, if there is freedom, there must be at least some thinking possible independent of any corresponding physical change in the brain. On such a view it is no longer impossible that consciousness may persist after the brain is destroyed.

That there is a close correlation between the brain's activity and mental processes is, however, evident. Such phenomena as intoxication, anaesthesia, delirium, and so on, show an intimate connection between the condition of a man's brain and his state of mind. It is tempting likewise to interpolate the declining mental powers with advancing disease or old age to mean blank unconsciousness in death.

The problem of the connection between mind and matter is one regarding which all our efforts at solution have been baffled. Modern psychology dislikes the idea of a soul or spirit separable from the body. Certainly in a living organism, body and life cannot be separated. Similarly, if I understand my psychology aright, it is commonly supposed that consciousness is not a separable element, but an essential part of the organism. All throughout its evolution, increased complexity of function has been accompanied in some mysterious way by the development of consciousness. Following this view, Bishop Barnes contends "that concurrent psychical and physical phenomena are two aspects of a single process of change. . . . . Man's whole mental and spiritual nature is conditioned by his physical nature and its pathological states, no mental or spiritual movement taking place without a concomitant physical movement." [1] On the other hand, perhaps all psychologists would admit with William James that "it has not been proved, and it seems unprovable, that the actual body is the adequate cause and not a purely contingent condition of our spiritual life."

An examination of the evidence in fact shows that the correspondence between brain activity and consciousness is not as close as is frequently supposed. Thus my colleague Professor Lashley has pointed out that both in animals and man a large portion of the brain may be damaged, or even removed, without destroying consciousness or seriously disturbing the mental processes. On the other hand, such a relatively minor disturbance as a tap on the skull may, so far as we can tell, completely destroy consciousness for a considerable period of time. Moreover, Bergson has given what seems to be convincing evidence for his statement that "there is infinitely more in a human consciousness than in a corresponding brain," and that "the mind overflows the brain on all sides, and cerebral activity corresponds only to a very small part of mental activity."

It was in part from such considerations that William James was led to reject the view that thought is produced by the brain in favor of the hypothesis that the brain transmits the thought to the body, where the appropriate action occurs. On this view the brain would correspond to the detecting tube of a radio receiver, without which no music can be received. Stopping the sound by destroying the tube does not imply the destruction of the musician whose song is being carried by the ether waves. Such a

---

[1] E. W. Barnes, *Scientific Theory and Religion* (1934), p. 636.

view of the relation between thought and brain accounts satisfactorily for the observed parallelism between the two, and yet leaves room for the great diversity of the thought processes. James recognizes that during life thought needs brain for its organ of expression; but this does not exclude the possibility of a condition in which thought is independent of brain.

Can Conciousness Be of Value to a Dead Organism?

In view of this failure to get conclusive evidence of a direct character, let us consider some of the more important deductions that have been drawn from the theory of evolution. An argument against immortality which carries considerable weight is based upon the value of consciousness to the organism. From the biological point of view the appearance of consciousness in animals enables them to compete more successfully in the struggle of life. This suggests that consciousness is the servant of the biological organism. In the evolutionary process we should on this view expect consciousness to appear only where it can be of some value to the organism with which it is associated. For a babe at birth consciousness is of little value, and it seems to be only feebly developed. In youth and maturity, however, it is of vital importance that the organism be aware of what is going on, and consciousness is accordingly most highly developed. Clearly, consciousness can be of no value to a dead organism. From the biological point of view, therefore, we should expect an efficient evolutionary process to bring about the cessation of consciousness with death.

There is, however, an alternative position which is at least equally tenable, and which points toward the opposite conclusion. This is that the evolutionary process is working toward the development of conscious persons rather than toward the development of a physical organism. In the previous chapters we have indicated how evidence from both the physical and biological sciences makes it difficult to escape the conclusion that our world is controlled by a supreme Intelligence, which directs evolution according to some great plan. We could, in fact, see the whole great drama of evolution moving toward the making of persons with free intelligence capable of glimpsing God's purpose in nature and of sharing that purpose. In such a case we should not look upon consciousness as the mere servant of the biological organism, but as an end in itself. An intelligent mind would be its own reason for existence.

Our survey of the physical universe indicated that mankind is very possibly nature's best achievement in this direction. If in the world scheme conscious life is the thing of primary importance, what is happening on our earth is thus of great cosmic significance. The thoughts of man, which have come to control to so great an extent the development of life upon this planet, are conceivably to the Lord of Creation among the most important things in the world. From this point of view we might expect nature to preserve at all costs the living souls which it has evolved at such labor. This would mean the immortality of the individual consciousness.

Thus science finds itself incapable of giving a definite answer, at present at least, to the problem of immortality. While according to the mechanistic view the mind could not survive the brain, the evidence seems definitely against this view, and no cogent reason remains for supposing that the soul dies with the body. The evidence of revived persons brought back from Hades, though inconclusive, must be considered strongly against persistence of consciousness. If consciousness is merely the servant of the living organism, we should expect the two to die together; but if, as seems perhaps more plausible, intelligent consciousness is the objective of the evolutionary process, we might expect it to be preserved. . . . .

GOD AND IMMORTALITY

If we desire to reach a more definite result, we must go beyond science into ethics and religion. Such an excursion is outside of the proper scope of this book, and its author can serve only as an amateur guide. Yet for the sake of completeness the nature of these arguments should be indicated. It is recognized that they will not have the general appeal of well-tested scientific evidence; but for many of those who are prepared to accept the postulates on which they are based, these lines of thought carry such weight as to make a belief in immortality the basis for the planning of life.

One of the most effective of these arguments is that based on the belief that God is good. It is summarized by Barnes as follows:

We are forced to assume that the Universe is rational. The assumption is largely confirmed by our experience and, unless it were true, the Universe would be unknowable. In that case God's works and ways would be unintelligible and experience would not lead to any understanding of Him. Now if, on the contrary, the character of the ordering of all that happens is for our thought rational, we are forced to conclude that God would not have allowed the majority of human beings to have lives, so wretched and incomplete as we observe them to be, were it not that earthly existence is but the first part, a mere beginning of the complete life of the human spirit. . . . .

In brief, our plea for personal survival can be set out as follows. We have been led by the processes of reason to postulate that the world is the realm of Creative Spirit, of Mind which is purposive. Argument from the existence of the Moral Law, or, in other words, of man's feeling that he is compelled to believe that goodness is objectively valid—such argument leads us to the conclusion that the Creative Spirit, in and for Whom the Universe exists, is good. But our arguments must be pronounced unsatisfactory, and the conclusions derived from them must be rejected, unless personal immortality be a fact.[2]

We have found strong reasons for believing that, in spite of his physical insignificance, man as an intelligent person is of extraordinary importance in the cosmic scheme. If we were to use our own best judgment, what would we say is the most important thing about a noble man? Would it be the strength of his body, or the brilliance of his intellect? Would we not place first the beauty of his character? A man's body is at its prime before middle life, and his intellect probably somewhat after middle life. But it takes a whole lifetime to build the character of a noble man. The exercise and discipline of youth, the struggles and failures and successes, the pains and pleasures of maturity, the loneliness and tranquillity of age—these make

---

[2] *Loc. cit.,* pp. 645-646.

up the fire through which he must pass to bring out the pure gold of his soul. Having been thus perfected, what shall nature do with him? Annihilate him? What infinite waste!

> "Thou wilt not leave us in the dust:
>   Thou madest man, he knows not why,
>   He thinks he was not made to die;
>   And thou hast made him: thou art just."

Thus the poet cries, as he considers the impossibility that a God of justice and love should forget the men whom he has made to be his own companions.

APPENDIX

BIBLIOGRAPHY

PART I

THE NATURE OF RELIGION

AMES, E. S.: *Religion.* Henry Holt & Co.
AUBREY, E. E.: *Present Theological Tendencies.* Harper & Bros.
BIXLER, JULIUS SEELYE: *Religion for Free Minds.* Harper & Bros.
BRADEN, CHARLES S.: *Varieties of American Religion.* Willett, Clark & Co.
BRIGHTMAN, E. S.: *Religious Values.* Abingdon-Cokesbury Press.
BURTT, EDWIN A.: *Religion in an Age of Science.* Frederick A. Stokes & Co.
————: *Types of Religious Philosophy.* Harper & Bros.
DEWEY, JOHN: *A Common Faith.* Yale Univ. Press.
EDDY, S.: *New Challenges to Faith.* Doubleday, Doran & Co.
EDWARDS, D. M.: *The Philosophy of Religion.* Harper & Bros.
FADIMANN, CLIFTON (Editor): *I Believe.* Simon & Schuster.
FOSDICK, H. E.: *Adventurous Religion.* Harper & Bros.
————: *As I See Religion.* Harper & Bros.
HAYDON, A. E.: *The Quest of the Ages.* Harper & Bros.
HOPKINS, E. W.: *Origin and Evolution of Religion.* Yale Univ. Press.
JAMES, W.: *The Varieties of Religious Experience.* Longmans, Green & Co.
KNUDSON, A. C.: *Present Tendencies in Religious Thought.* Abingdon-Cokesbury Press.
LYMAN, EUGENE WILLIAM: *The Meaning and Truth of Religion.* Chas. Scribner's Sons.
MARITAIN, JACQUES, ET AL.: *Essays in Order.* The Macmillan Co.
MOORE, G. F.: *The Birth and Growth of Religion.* Chas. Scribner's Sons.
NIEBUHR, REINHOLD: *Does Civilization Need Religion?* The Macmillan Co.
————: *Moral Man and Immoral Society.* Chas. Scribner's Sons.
PRATT, J. B.: *The Religious Consciousness.* The Macmillan Co.
RANDALL, J. H., JR.: *Making of the Modern Mind.* Houghton Mifflin Co.
SELLARS, R. W.: *Religion Coming of Age.* The Macmillan Co.
WIEMAN, H. N.: *Religious Experience and Scientific Method.* The Macmillan Co.
————: *The Wrestle of Religion with Truth.* The Macmillan Co.
————: *The Issues of Life.* The Abingdon Press.
WIEMAN, H. N., and HORTON, W. M.: *The Growth of Religion.* Willett, Clark & Co.
WIEMAN, H. N., and MELAND, B. E.: *American Philosophies of Religion.* Willett, Clark & Co.
ZYBURA, J. S.: *Present-Day Thinkers and the New Scholasticism.* B. Herder Book Co.

PART II

THE FINDING OF RELIGIOUS TRUTH

ALEXANDER, H. B.: *Truth and Faith.* Henry Holt & Co.
BAILLIE, J. N.: *The Knowledge of God.* Chas. Scribner's Sons.
BARTH, K.: *The Word of God and the Word of Man.* Zondervan Pub. House.
BENNETT, C. A.: *The Dilemma of Religious Knowledge.* Yale Univ. Press.
BRIGHTMAN, E. S.: *A Philosophy of Religion.* Prentice-Hall.
BROWN, W. A.: *Pathways to Certainty.* Chas. Scribner's Sons.
DEWEY, JOHN: *The Quest for Certainty.* Minton Balch & Co.
FOSDICK, H. E.: *The Modern Use of the Bible.* The Macmillan Co.
HOLMES, J. H.: *Rethinking Religion.* The Macmillan Co.
HORTON, W. M.: *A Psychological Approach to Theology.* Harper & Bros.
JAMES, W.: *The Will to Believe.* Longmans, Green & Co.
————: *The Varieties of Religious Experience.* Longmans Green & Co.

JONES, R.: *Preface to Christian Faith in a New Age*. The Macmillan Co.
KNUDSON, C.: *The Validity of Religious Experience*. Abingdon Press.
LEWIS, EDWIN: *A Christian Manifesto*. Abingdon-Cokesbury Press.
———: *A Philosophy of the Christian Revelation*. Harper & Bros.
MACHEN, J. G.: *Christianity and Liberalism*. The Macmillan Co.
MACINTOSH, D. C.: *The Problem of Knowledge*. The Macmillan Co.
MONTAGUE, W. P.: *The Ways of Knowing*. The Macmillan Co.
MORRISON, C. C.: *What Is Christianity?* Willett, Clark & Co.
OTTO, M. C.: *The Human Enterprise*. F. S. Crofts & Co.
RALL, H. F.: *Christianity*. Chas. Scribner's Sons.
RANDALL, J. H.: *Religion and the Modern World*. Henry Holt & Co.
ROYCE, JOSIAH: *The Sources of Religious Insight*. Chas. Scribner's Sons.
SANTAYANA, GEORGE: *Reason in Religion*. Chas. Scribner's Sons.
THOMSON, J. A.: *Science and Religion*. Chas. Scribner's Sons.
TRUEBLOOD, O. E.: *The Trustworthiness of Religious Experience*. Geo. Allen & Unwin.
WIEMAN, H. N.: *Religious Experience and the Scientific Method*. The Macmillan Co.

PART III

THE IDEA OF GOD

AUER, J. A. F. C.: *Humanism States Its Case*. Beacon Press.
BALFOUR, A. J.: *Theism and Humanism*. Doubleday, Doran & Co.
BERGSON, HENRI: *The Two Sources of Morality and Religion*. Henry Holt & Co.
BOODIN, J. E.: *God*. The Macmillan Co.
BOWNE, B. P.: *Personalism*. Houghton Mifflin Co.
BRIGHTMAN, E. S.: *The Finding of God*. Abingdon-Cokesbury Press.
———: *The Problem of God*. Abingdon-Cokesbury Press.
BROWN, W. A.: *God at Work*. Chas. Scribner's Sons.
CALHOUN, R. L.: *God and the Common Life*. Chas. Scribner's Sons.
EDDINGTON, A. S.: *Science and the Unseen World*. The Macmillan Co.
GREY, R. M.: *Yahweh*. Willett, Clark & Co.
HOCKING, W. E.: *The Meaning of God in Human Experience*. Yale Univ. Press.
HORTON, W. M.: *Theism and the Modern Mood*. Harper & Bros.
JONES, R.: *Pathways to the Reality of God*. The Macmillan Co.
KNUDSON, A. C.: *The Philosophy of Personalism*. Abingdon-Cokesbury Press.
MATHEWS, S.: *Growth of the Idea of God*. The Macmillan Co.
MATHER, K. F.: *Science in Search of God*. Henry Holt & Co.
McCONNELL, F. C.: *Is God Limited?* Abingdon-Cokesbury Press.
MORGAN, C. L.: *Emergent Evolution*. Henry Holt & Co.
NEWTON, J. F. (Editor): *My Idea of God*. Little, Brown & Co.
OTTO, M. C.: *Things and Ideals*. Henry Holt & Co.
PAUCK, W.: *Karl Barth*. Harper & Bros.
PRINGLE-PATTISON, A. S.: *The Idea of God in the Light of Recent Philosophy*. Oxford Univ. Press.
RICHARDS, G. W.: *Beyond Fundamentalism and Modernism*. Chas. Scribner's Sons.
TILLICH, PAUL: *The Religious Situation*. Henry Holt & Co.
VAN DUSEN, H. P.: *The Plain Man Seeks for God*. Chas. Scribner's Sons.
———: *God in These Times*. Chas. Scribner's Sons.
WIEMAN, H. N., OTTO, M. C., and MACINTOSH, D. C.: *Is There a God?* Willett, Clark & Co.
WIEMAN, H. N. and R. W.: *Normative Psychology of Religion*. The Thomas Y. Crowell Co.

PART IV

THE PROBLEM OF EVIL

BENNETT, J. C.: *Social Salvation*. Chas. Scribner's Sons.
BRIGHTMAN, E. S.: *The Problem of God*. Abingdon-Cokesbury Press.

DURANT, W.: *On the Meaning of Life.* Julius Messner.
HORTON, W. M.: *Can Christianity Save Civilization?* Harper & Bros.
HINTON, J.: *The Mystery of Pain.* Kegan Paul, Trench, Trukner & Co.
JONES, E. S.: *Christ and Human Suffering.* Abingdon Press.
KNUDSON, A. C.: *The Doctrine of Redemption.* Abingdon Press.
KRUTCH, J. W.: *The Modern Temper.* Harcourt, Brace & Co.
McCONNELL, F. C.: *Is God Limited?* Abingdon-Cokesbury Press.
MONTAGUE, W. P.: *Belief Unbound.* Yale Univ. Press.
NIEBUHR, REINHOLD: *Beyond Tragedy.* Chas. Scribner's Sons.
———: *Moral Man and Immoral Society.* Chas. Scribner's Sons.
RASHDALL, H.: *The Theory of Good and Evil.* The Clarendon Press.
ROSS, F. H.: *Personalism and the Problem of Evil.* Yale Univ. Press.
ROYCE, J.: *Studies in Good and Evil.* The Appleton Press.
TALBOT, N. S.: *The Riddle of Life.* Longmans, Green & Co.
TILLICH, PAUL: *The Religious Situation.* Henry Holt & Co.
TITTLE, E. F.: *Christians in an Unchristian Society.* Association Press.
TSANOFF, R. A.: *The Nature of Evil.* The Macmillan Co.
WEATHERHEAD, L. D.: *Why Do Men Suffer?* Abingdon Press.
WELLS, H. G.: *The Undying Fire.* The Macmillan Co.

PART V

WORSHIP

BRIGHTMAN, E. S.: *Religious Values.* Abingdon-Cokesbury Press.
BROWN, W. A.: *The Life of Prayer in a World of Science.* Chas. Scribner's Sons.
BRINTON, H. H.: *Creative Worship.* Geo. Allen & Unwin.
BYINGTON, E. H.: *Quest for Experience in Worship.* Harper & Bros.
FOSDICK, H. E.: *The Meaning of Prayer.* Association Press.
HEILER, F.: *Prayer.* Oxford Univ. Press.
HERMAN, E.: *Creative Prayer.* Harper & Bros.
HUEGEL, F. VON: *The Life of Prayer.* E. P. Dutton & Co.
INGE, W. R.: *Personal Religion and the Life of Devotion.* Longmans, Green & Co.
JAMES, W.: *The Varieties of Religious Experience.* Longmans, Green & Co.
JONES, R.: *Studies in Mystical Religion.* The Macmillan Co.
———: *New Studies in Mystical Religion.* The Macmillan Co.
MAXWELL, W. D.: *An Outline of Christian Worship.* Oxford Univ. Press.
MELAND, B. E.: *Modern Man's Worship.* Harper & Bros.
OTTO, R.: *The Idea of the Holy.* Oxford Univ. Press.
———: *Mysticism, East and West.* The Macmillan Co.
PATERSON, W. P. (Editor): *The Power of Prayer.* The Macmillan Co.
SEIDENSPINNER, C.: *Form and Freedom in Worship.* Willett, Clark & Co.
SPERRY, W. L.: *Reality in Worship.* The Macmillan Co.
STEERE, D. V.: *Prayer and Worship.* Association Press.
STREETER, B. H., ET AL.: *Concerning Prayer.* The Macmillan Co.
UNDERHILL, E.: *The Life of the Spirit and the Life of Today.* E. P. Dutton & Co.
———: *Worship.* Harper & Bros.
VOGT, V. O.: *Art and Devotion.* Yale Univ. Press.
WIEMAN, H. N.: *Methods of Private Religious Living.* The Macmillan Co.

PART VI

IMMORTALITY

BAILLIE, J.: *And the Life Everlasting.* Chas. Scribner's Sons.
BEVAN, E.: *The Hope of a World to Come.* Geo. Allen & Unwin.
BIXLER, J. S.: *Immortality and the Present Mood.* Harvard Univ. Press.
BRIGHTMAN, E. S.: *Immortality in Post-Kantian Idealism.* Harvard Univ. Press.
BROWN, C. A.: *Living Again.* Harvard Univ. Press.
BROWN, W. A.: *The Christian Hope.* Chas. Scribner's Sons.

COMPTON, A. H.: *The Freedom of Man.* Yale Univ. Press.
FISKE, J.: *The Destiny of Man.* Houghton Mifflin Co.
——: *Life Everlasting.* Houghton Mifflin Co.
FOSDICK, H. E.: *The Assurance of Immortality.* The Macmillan Co.
GALLOWAY, S.: *The Idea of Immortality.* T. & T. Clark.
HICKS, G. D.: *Human Personality and Future Life.* Lindsey Press.
HOCKING, W. E.: *Thoughts on Death and Life.* Harper & Bros.
JAMES, W.: *Human Immortality.* Houghton Mifflin Co.
LAMONT, C.: *Issues of Immortality.* Henry Holt & Co.
——: *The Illusion of Immortality.* G. P. Putnam's Sons.
LEUBA, J. H.: *The Belief in God and Immortality.* Open Court Pub. Co.
LODGE, O.: *Immortality of the Soul.* Ball Pub. Co.
LYMAN, E. W.: *Meaning of Selfhood and Faith in Immortality.* Harvard Univ. Press.
MCTAGGART, J. M. E.: *Some Dogmas of Religion.* Edward Arnold & Co.
PRINGLE-PATTISON, A. S.: *The Idea of Immortality.* The Clarendon Press.
SIMPSON, J. Y.: *Man and the Attainment of Immortality.* Doubleday, Doran & Co.
STIDGER, W. L. (Editor): *If I Had Only One Sermon to Preach on Immortality.* Harper & Bros.
STREETER, B. H., ET. AL.: *Immortality.* The Macmillan Co.
TSANOFF, R. A.: *The Problem of Immortality.* The Macmillan Co.

BIOGRAPHICAL INDEX OF AUTHORS

AMES, EDWARD SCRIBNER: Born Eau Claire, Wis., 1870. Educated Drake Univ. (A.B. 1889, A.M. 1891), Yale Univ. (B.D. 1892), Univ. of Chicago (Ph.D. 1893). Prof. philosophy and pedagogy, Butler Univ., 1897-1900; since 1900 teacher philosophy, Univ. of Chicago, prof. 1926, prof. emeritus 1935; also pastor, University Church, Disciples, now pastor emeritus. He is author of *The Psychology of Religious Experience* (1910), *The Divinity of Christ* (1911), *The Higher Individualism* (1915), *The New Orthodoxy* (1918), *Religion* (1929), *Letters to God and the Devil* (1933). As a religious humanist, interpreting to both the classroom and the pew, he has been one of America's vital voices in that school of thought.

AUBREY, EDWIN EWART: Born Glasgow, Scotland, 1896; came to U. S. 1913, naturalized 1918. Educated Bucknell Univ. (Ph.B. 1919), Univ. of Chicago (A.M. 1921, B.D. 1922, Ph.D. 1926). Teacher Union Theol. Col. (Chicago), Carleton Col., Miami Univ., and Vassar Col.; prof. Christian theology and ethics, Univ. of Chicago, since 1929, dept. head since 1933, chairman of theological field since 1935. His writings include *Religion and the Next Generation* (1931), *Present Theological Tendencies* (1936), *Living the Christian Faith* (1939), and *Man's Search for Himself* (1940). As an American theist he has been an active figure in ecumenical Christianity.

BARTH, KARL: Born Basel, Switzerland, 1886. Educated universities in Bern, Berlin, Tübingen, and Marburg; holds degree D.Theol. Has been prof. theology, Göttingen, Münster, Bonn, and Basel; editor *Zwischen den Seiten*, 1922-1933. Writings translated into English are *The Church and the Churches, Credo, The Doctrine of the Word of God, The Epistle to the Romans, The Word of God and the Word of Man, God in Action, The Resurrection of the Dead, The Holy Ghost and the Christian Life, The Knowledge of God and the Service of God.* He has been evaluated by some as the most stimulating voice in Protestantism since Luther. He is an exponent of crisis theology, in which reason and feeling are ruled out as a means of knowing God, since God is known *only* in his revelation through Jesus Christ to men of faith. His thinking has been much affected by Kierkegaard and Calvin, and has in recent years been an interesting corrective of religious humanism's homocentric thought.

BEWER, JULIUS A.: Born Ratingen, Germany, 1877. Educated Union Theol. Sem. (B.D. 1898), Columbia Univ. (Ph.D.). Prof. Old Testament language and literature, Oberlin Theol. Sem. 1902-1904. Ordained Cong. minister 1906. Since 1904 teacher Union Theol. Sem., becoming prof. Old Testament history and theology 1914, Davenport prof. Hebrew and cognate languages 1927. Also lecturer biblical literature, Teachers Col., Columbia Univ., 1912-1928. His principal writings are *Commentary on Obadiah and Joel* (1911), *Commentary on Jonah* (1912)— both in "The International Critical Commentary"—*The Literature of the Old Testament* (1922), "Ezekiel" in Kittel's *Biblia Hebraica* (1932). *The Literature of the Old Testament* has proven to be one of the finest and clearest expositions of the Old Testament available for college classrooms and mature laity.

BREMOND, ANDRÉ: Born Aix-en-Provence, France, 1872. Entered Society of Jesus 1889, was trained in France and in England. Ordained 1905, making his tertianship at St. David's, Flintshire, Wales, 1906. Teacher philosophy, French Col., Cairo, Egypt, and Maison St. Louis, Jersey, Channel Islands. Since the present war he has resided at Marseilles. His books are *Le dilemme aristotelicien* (1933), *Rationalisme et religion* (1935), *La piété grecque* (1914), *Philosophy in the Making* (1939). With his brother Jean he wrote *Autor de l'humanisme* (1937). Americans made his acquaintance on his teaching at Fordham University summer school in 1937, where one person described him as "one of the most charming and intelligent personalities I have ever met."

BRIGHTMAN, EDGAR SHEFFIELD: Born Holbrook, Mass., 1884. Educated Brown Univ. (A.B. 1906, A.M. 1908), Berlin Univ. Marburg Univ., and Boston Univ. (S.T.B. 1910, Ph.D. 1912). Teacher philosophy and Greek, Brown Univ. 1906-1908; prof. philosophy and psychology, Nebraska Wesleyan Univ. 1912-1915; asso. prof. 1915-1917, prof. 1917-1919, ethics and religion, Wesleyan Univ., Conn.; since 1919, Borden P. Bowne prof. philosophy, Boston Univ. His chief writings are *Sources of the Hexateuch* (1918), *An Introduction to Philosophy* (1925), *Immortality in Post-Kantian Idealism* (1925), *Religious Values* (1925), *A Philosophy of Ideals* (1928), *The Problem of God* (1930), *The Finding of God* (1931), *Moral Laws* (1933), *Personality and Religion* (1934), *A Philosophy of Religion* (1940). He has been one of the most consistent interpreters of the school of thought known as "Personalism," in which personality is the key to the nature of reality, and coherent thinking is the test of truth.

BROWN, ARTHUR J.: Born Holliston, Mass., 1856. Educated Wabash Col. (A.B. 1880, A.M. 1884), Lane Theol. Sem. (graduate 1883). Recipient of several honorary doctorates. Ordained Presby. ministry 1883. Pastorates in Wisconsin, Illinois, Oregon; secretary, Presby. Board of Foreign Missions 1895-1929. He has been especially active on various boards relative to world Christian problems. Among his books are *The New Era in the Philippines* (1907), *The Foreign Missionary* (1907), *Russia in Transformation* (1917), *Japan in the World of Today*. He is a Christian figure whose broad experience has given him a comprehensive grasp of world cultures and their particular relation to the Christian influence.

BRUNNER, EMIL: Born 1889. For a number of years has been prof. systematic and practical theology, Univ. of Zurich, Switzerland. Holds degree D.Theol. Among his many books are *The Word and the World* (1931), *The Mediator* (1934), *The Theology of Crisis* (1935), *The Divine Imperative* (1937), *Philosophy of Religion* (1937), *Man in Revolt* (1939). As a member of the European neosupernaturalists, also allied with the crisis theological movement, his voice with that of Karl Barth has been very stimulating to American religious thinkers.

CALHOUN, ROBERT LOWRY: Born St. Cloud, Minn., 1896. Educated Carleton Col. (B.A. 1915), Yale Univ. (B.D. 1918, M.A. 1919, Ph.D. 1923). Teacher philosophy and education, Carleton Col. 1921-1923; teacher historical theology, Yale Divinity School, since 1923, prof. since 1936. He is author of *God and the Common Life* (1935), *What Is Man?* (1939); co-author of *Religious Realism* (1931), *The Nature of Religious Experience* (1937), *The Christian Understanding of Man* (1937), *Church and State in the Modern World* (1937), *The Meaning of the Humanities* (1938). He has constructed his thinking largely upon the data found in emergent evolution which point to a Cosmic Mind. He can be classified as a theist whose ideas arise from the honest, rugged facts of life. That "life is deeper than logic" he would agree in his proofs for God.

COFFIN, HENRY SLOANE: Born New York City, 1877. Educated Yale Univ. (A.B. 1897, M.A. 1900), Union Theol. Sem. (B.D. 1900). Holds numerous honorary doctorates from colleges and universities in France, Scotland, and U. S. Ordained Presby. minister 1900. Minister, Madison Ave. Presby. Church, New York City, 1905-1926; teacher practical theology, Union Theol. Sem. 1904-1926. Since 1926 president, Union Theol. Sem. Among his writings are *Social Aspects of the Cross* (1911), *The Ten Commandments* (1915), *Christian Convictions* (1915), *A More Christian Industrial Order* (1920), *What Is There in Religion?* (1922), *Portraits of Jesus Christ* (1926), *The Meaning of the Cross* (1931), *What Men Are Asking* (1933), *Religion Yesterday and Today* (1940). As a vital preacher and educator he has carefully balanced ethical-social values in his theistic thinking about God.

COMPTON, ARTHUR H.: Born Wooster, Ohio, 1892. Educated Col. of Wooster (B.S. 1913), Princeton Univ. (M.A. 1914, Ph. D. 1916). Recipient of numerous doctorates in America, and M.A. Oxford University. Several years research work in physics; prof. physics, Washington Univ. 1920-1923; prof. physics, Univ. of Chicago, since 1923. Charles H. Swift distinguished prof. since 1929. Among many honors awarded him was a Guggenheim fellowship, 1926-1927. Since 1926 consulting physicist, General Electric Co. He has written *Secondary Radiations Produced by X-rays* (1922), *X-rays and Electrons* (1926), *The Freedom of Man* (1935), *X-rays in Theory and Experiment* (with S. K. Allison) (1935), *Human Meanings of Science* (1940). In his Terry Lectures at Yale (*The Freedom of Man*) he portrays a type of theistic belief not uncommon among contemporary physicists.

DABBS, JAMES McBRIDE: Born Mayesville, S. C., 1896. Educated Univ. of S. C. (A.B. 1916), Clark Univ. (A.M. 1917), also Univ. of Edinburgh, Columbia Univ. Teacher English, Univ. of S.C., 1921-1924. Head of dept. of English, Cokes Col. 1925-1937; now part-time prof. English. He has written stimulating articles in *The Christian Century, Christendom,* and other magazines in which the Christian tradition has been evaluated with literary artistry.

DEWEY, JOHN: Born Burlington, Ver., 1859. Educated Univ. of Ver. (A.B. 1879), Johns Hopkins Univ. (Ph.D. 1884). Teacher philosophy, Univ. of Mich., Univ. of Minn., Univ. of Chicago; director of School of Education, Univ. of Chicago, 1902-1904. Since 1904 prof. philosophy, now prof. emeritus, Columbia Univ. Among his numerous writings are *Psychology* (1886), *Study of Ethics* (1894), *How We Think* (1910), *Democracy and Education* (1916), *Reconstruction in Philosophy* (1920), *Experience and Nature* (1925), *The Quest for Certainty* (1929), *Philosophy and Civilization* (1931), *Art as Experience* (1934), *A Common Faith* (1934), *Logic: The Theory of Inquiry* (1938). As a thinker who has touched education, art, logic, religion, and politics, he has been particularly effective as a pragmatist and scientific humanist.

DURANT, WILL: Born North Adams, Mass., 1885. Educated St. Peter's Col. (B.A. 1907, M.A. 1908), Columbia Univ. (Ph.D. 1917). Prof. Latin and French, Seton

Hall Col. 1907-1911; director, Labor Temple School, New York City, 1914-1927; instr. philosophy, Columbia Univ. 1917; prof. philosophy. Univ. of Calif. at Los Angeles, 1935. He is author of *Social Problems* (1917), *The Story of Philosophy* (1926), *Transition* (1927), *The Mansions of Philosophy* (1929), *A Program for America* (1931), *On the Meaning of Life* (1932), *The Tragedy of Russia* (1933), and *The Story of Civilization* (Part I, 1935; Part II, *The Life of Greece*, 1939). As a popular speaker and writer, he has particularly translated philosophic thought into an idiom which has widened its audience extensively.

EDWARDS, D. MIALL: Born Llemfyllin, Montgomery County, Wales, 1873. Educated Bangor Independent Col., University Col. of London Univ. (A.B.), Oxford Univ. (M.A. 1900). Minister, Salem Cong. Church, Brecon, 1900-1909. Since 1909 prof. religion and systematic theology, Memorial (Cong.) Col., Brecon, Wales. Among his writings are *Asboniad or Epistol Iago, Grefydd a Bywd*, and *the Philosophy of Religion* (1930). He has been particularly active in social service and associated church activities.

FOSDICK, HARRY EMERSON: Born Buffalo, N. Y., 1878. Educated Colgate Univ. (A.M. 1908), Union Theol. Sem. (B.D. 1904), Columbia Univ. (A.M. 1908). Many honorary doctorates have been conferred on him by American colleges and universities. Ordained Bapt. ministry 1903. Pastor, First Bapt. Church, Montclair, N. J., 1904-1915; instr. homilectics, 1908-1915, since 1915 prof. practical theology, Union Theol. Sem.; now minister, Riverside Church, New York City. He is author of many books, among which are *The Meaning of Prayer* (1915), *The Modern Use of the Bible* (1924), *Adventurous Religion* (1926), *As I See Religion* (1931), *A Guide to Understanding the Bible* (1938). Besides being one of America's foremost preachers, he has also been one of the most constructive Christian figures in creating a liberal intelligence within the contemporary Church.

HAYDON, A. EUSTACE: Born Brampton, Ont., Canada, 1880. Educated Univ. of Toronto (A.B. 1901, B.Th. 1903, M.A. 1907, B.D. 1906), Univ. of Chicago (B.D. 1911, Ph.D. 1918). Ordained ministry 1903. Pastor, Bapt. churches in Canada, 1903-1913; general secretary, Y.M.C.A., Saskatoon, Saskatchewan, 1911-1913; minister, First Unitarian Church, Madison, Wis., 1918-1924; teacher dept. comparative religions, Univ. of Chicago, since 1919, prof. since 1929. He is author of *The Quest of the Ages* (1929), *Man's Search for the Good Life* (1937), and *Biography of the Gods* (1941). As a religious humanist, he finds man's sense of cosmic "at-homeness" in both his environment and his biological heritage. Man has his bearings in nature in a sort of mystical manner, a type of nature which is large enough to include social environment. In fact, that social environment shows the only cosmic structure which man can grasp.

HEILER, FRIEDRICH: Born in Germany, 1892. Educated, Univ. of Munich (D. Theol. and D.Phil.). As a teacher of the history of religions and the philosophy of religion, he held positions at Munich, 1918-1920, until his call to Marburg in 1920. His German writings are many, his chief contribution, *Das Gebet*, being the only one translated into the English (as *Prayer*). Reared as a Roman Catholic, he has become an advocate of the Church Universal. For years in Marburg a. d. Lahn he conducted worship services Saturday evenings in an ancient chapel, where he put into effect his liturgical patterns.

HOLT, ARTHUR E.: Born Longmont, Calif., 1876. Educated Colorado Col. (A.B. 1898), Univ. of Chicago (Ph.D. 1904). Ordained Cong. ministry 1904. Minister, Pueblo, Colo., Manhattan, Kan., Fort Worth, Tex., 1904-1919; appointed social service secretary, Cong. Church, 1919. Now prof. social ethics, Chicago Theol. Sem., and Divinity School, Univ. of Chicago. His books are *The Bible as a Community Book* (1919), *Social Work in the Church* (1922), *Christian Fellowship and Modern Industry* (1923), *Christian Ideals and Industry* (with F. D. Johnson, 1938), *This Nation Under God* (1939). He has been especially constructive in his interpretation of Christianity as related to problems in the social-economic order.

Western Society at the Crossroads 33

HOMRIGHAUSEN, ELMER GEORGE: Born Wheatland, Iowa, 1900. Educated, Mission House Col. (A.B. 1921), Princeton Theol. Sem. (B.Th.), Univ. of Chicago, Dubuque Univ., Butler Univ., Rutgers Col., and Univ. of Iowa (M.Th., M.A., Ph.D.), Minister, First English Reformed Church, Freeport, Ill., 1924-1929; Carrollton Ave. Church, Indianapolis, Ind., 1929-1938. Lecturer church history and theology, Butler Univ., 1933-1938; since 1938 prof. Christian education, Princeton Theol. Sem. He is the co-translator of three volumes of Karl Barth and Ed. Thurneysen, and is the author of *Christianity in America—a Crisis* (1936), *Current Trends in Theology* (1937), and *Let the Church Be the Church* (1940), He is one of the most stimulating younger thinkers associated with neosupernaturalism in America. The article quoted from Dr. Homrighausen, a bit different from his present trend of thinking, offers an interesting and realistic portrait of the future life as seen through the eyes of supernaturalism.

One World at a Time 368

HOUGH, LYNN HAROLD: Born Cadiz, Ohio, 1877. Educated Scio Col. (A.B. 1898), Drew Theol. Sem. (B.D. 1905). Recipient of numerous doctorates from American colleges and universities. Ordained Meth. ministry 1898. Minister, Mount Vernon Place Meth. Church, Baltimore, Md.; Central Meth. Church, Detroit, Mich.; American Presby. Church, Montreal, Canada and others. Prof. historical theology, Garrett Biblical Inst., 1914-1919; president, Northwestern Univ., 1919-1920; prof. since 1930, dean since 1934, Drew Theol. Sem. He is the author of over thirty books, among which recent ones are *Adventures in the Minds of Men* (1927), *The University of Experience* (1932), *The Church and Civilization* (1934), *The Great Evangel* (1936), and *Free Men* (1939). As a Christian humanist he has evaluated the Christian tradition from the angle of the literary humanists.

The Heroic and Reconciling Word, from *Whither Christianity?*.................... 142

JAMES, WILLIAM: Born New York City, 1842; died, 1910. Educated private schools, Lawrence Scientific School, Harvard Univ. (M.D. 1869). Universities from five countries conferred doctorates upon him. Teacher anatomy and physiology, later psychology and philosophy, Harvard Univ., from 1872, prof. from 1881, prof. emeritus from 1907. Chief of his books are *Principles of Psychology* (1890), *Human Immortality* (1899, given as the Ingersoll lecture on immortality at Harvard), *The Varieties of Religious Experience* (1902, given as the Gifford lectures at Edinburgh), *A Pluralistic Universe* (1908), *Pragmatism* (1907), *The Meaning of Truth* (1909), *Some Problems of Philosophy* (1911). He stands as the chief exponent of American Pragmatism, popularized by him at the turn of the century.

Human Immortality, from *Human Immortality* 385

The Sick Soul, from *The Varieties of Religious Experience* 241

JONES, RUFUS M.: Born China, Maine, 1863. Educated Haverford Col. (A.B. 1885, A.M. 1886), Harvard Univ. (A.M. 1901). Doctorates have been conferred on him from numerous colleges and universities. Teacher philosophy, Haverford Col., since 1893, prof. since 1904, prof. emeritus since 1934. Chief among his books, which number more than forty, are *Studies in Mystical Religion* (1909), *The Inner Life* (1916), *The Story of George Fox* (1919), *Fundamental Ends of Life* (1924), *New Studies in Mystical Religion* (1930), *A Preface to Christian Faith in a New Age* (1932), and *The Flowering of Mysticism* (1939). He stands as the leading American exponent of Christian mysticism, viewed from the angle of a Quaker philosopher.

How Shall We Think of God?, from *Religious Foundations* 192

KEPLER, THOMAS S.: Born Mount Vernon, Iowa, 1897. Educated Cornell Col. (A.B. 1921), Marburg Univ., Cambridge Univ., Boston Univ. (S.T.B. 1927, Ph.D. 1931). Ordained Meth. ministry 1929. Prof. religion and philosophy, Mount Union Col., 1930-1934; since 1934 prof. religion, Lawrence Col. He has contributed a chapter to *New Testament Studies* (edited by E. P. Booth, 1941) and articles to various religious magazines on themes relative to religious philosophy and New Testament theology, viewing religion from the particular angle of ethical mysticism.

Modernism Seeks Depth 150

KRUTCH, JOSEPH WOOD: Born Knoxville, Tenn., 1893. Educated Univ. of Tenn. (A.B. 1915), Columbia Univ. (M.A. 1916, Ph.D. 1923). Teacher English since 1917, Columbia Univ., Polytechnic Inst. of Brooklyn, and Vassar Col.; prof. English, Columbia Univ., since 1937. Dramatic critic and associate editor, *The Nation*, 1924-1932. Guggenheim fellow 1930-1931. Books published are *Our Changing Morals* (1925), *Edgar Allen Poe—A Study in Genius* (1926), *The Modern Temper* (1929), *Five Masters* (1930), *Experience and Art* (1932), *Was Europe a Success?* (1934). His approach to life through scientific humanism savors of a pessimistic tone.

The Tragic Fallacy, from *The Modern Temper* 250

LAIRD, JOHN: Born Durris, Kincardineshire, Scotland, 1887. Educated Univ. of Edinburgh (M.A. 1908), Heidelberg Univ., Cambridge Univ. (B.A. 1911, M.A. 1920). Received LL.D. from Univ. of Edinburgh. Fellow of the British Academy. Prof. philosophy, Dalhousie Univ, Halifax, N. S., 1912; prof. logic and metaphysics, Queens Univ., Belfast, 1913-1924; since 1924, regius prof. moral philosophy, Univ. of Aberdeen. In 1939 he delivered the Gifford lectures at Glasgow Univ.; in 1923-1924 he gave the Mills lectures at the Univ. of California. Among his many writings are *Problems of the Self* (1917), *A Study in Realism* (1920), *A Study in Moral Theory* (1926), *The Idea of Value* (1929), *Morals and Western Religion* (1931), *An Enquiry into Moral Notions* (1935), *Theism and Cosmology* (1940). As a realistic theist he has concerned himself in evaluating religious values from the angle of their moral import.

The Problem of Evil, from *Morals and Western Religion* 235

LANDONE, BROWN: Born in England. Educated by private tutors and in European universities. Fellow of the Royal Economic Society of London. Lecturer, Sorbonne, 1915-1916. *Envoyé Spécial des Amitiés Françaises* to U. S. 1917, as appointed by President Poincaré of France. His view of religion allies itself to God as the All of reality, from which all are to find meaning for living.

My All-God 201

LEUBA, JAMES H.: Born Neuchatel, Switzerland, 1868; came to U. S. 1887. Educated Clark Univ. (Ph.D. 1895) and Leipzig, Halle, Heidelburg, and Paris. Prof. psychology, Bryn Mawr Col., 1889-1933, prof. emeritus since 1933. His books are *The Psychological Origin and the Nature of Religion* (1909), *A Psychological Study of Religion* (1912), *The Beliefs in God and Immortality* (1916),

The Psychology of Religious Mysticism (1925), *God or Man?—a Study of the Value of God to Man* (1933). As a religious humanist he has especially stressed the subjective aspect of religious values. His studies of mysticism have also brought interesting evaluations of man's subjective behavior.

LIPPMANN, WALTER: Born New York City, 1889. Educated Harvard Univ. (A.B. 1910). Asso. editor, *The New Republic;* editor, *New York World,* until 1931; now special writer, *New York Herald-Tribune* and other newspapers. Assistant to secretary of war, June-Oct., 1917. He is the author of *A Preface to Politics* (1913), *The Political Scene* (1919), *Public Opinion* (1922), *Men of Destiny* (1927), *A Preface to Morals* (1929), *The Good Society* (1937), *Some Notes on War and Peace* (1940), and other books of import. As a religious naturalist, he stresses the value of one's unselfish loyalty to a noble ideal as the means of adjusting oneself to the total problem of living. His humanistic tone is one of a melioristic nature.

LYMAN, EUGENE WILLIAM: Born Cummington, Mass., 1872. Educated Amherst Col. (A.B. 1894, A.M. 1903), Yale Univ. (B.D. 1899). Teacher in preparatory schools; prof. philosophy, Carleton Col. 1901-1904; prof. philosophy, Bangor Theol. Sem. 1905-1913; prof. religion and Christian Ethics, Oberlin School of Theology, 1913-1918; prof. philosophy of religion, Union Theol. Sem., 1918-1940. He is the author of *Theology and Human Problems* (1910), *Experience of God in Modern Life* (1918), *The Meaning of Selfhood* (1928), *Religious Idealism* (1931), *The Meaning and Truth of Religion* (1933); and joint author of *Contemporary American Theology* (1933), *The Kingdom of God and History* (1938). As a theist he views mystical intuition, validated by reason, as the approach to religious truths. Such truths, because they enhance living, prove their relationship to supreme value or Reality.

McCONNELL, FRANCIS J.: Born Trinway, Ohio, 1871. Educated Ohio Wesleyan Univ. (A.B. 1894), Boston Univ. (S.T.B. 1897, Ph.D. 1899). Ordained Meth. ministry 1894. Meth. pastorates 1894-1900; president, De Pauw Univ., 1909-1912; Meth. bishop since 1912. He has been president of the Federal Council of Churches, Lyman Beecher lecturer at Yale, and Barrows lecturer in India. Among his books are *The Divine Immanence* (1906), *Public Opinion and Theology* (1920), *Is God Limited?* (1924), *The Christlike God* (1927), *Borden Parker Bowne* (1929), *Christianity and Coercion* (1933), *John Wesley* (1939). He has been a leading exponent in focusing the philosophy of personalism toward a revamping of the social order into the kingdom ideal.

MATHER, KIRTLEY F.: Born Chicago, Ill., 1888. Educated Denison Univ. (B.S. 1909), Univ. of Chicago (Ph.D. 1915). Teacher geology, Univ. of Chicago, 1911-1915; Queensbury Univ., Kingston, Ont., 1915-1917; Denison Univ., 1918-1924; Harvard Univ., since 1924, prof. since 1927. Director, Harvard Summer School, since 1934. He is the author of *Fauna of the Morrow Foundation* (1915), *Old Mother Earth* (1928), *Science in Search of God* (1928), *Sons of the Earth* (1930), *Adult Education, a Dynamic for Democracy* (with Dorothy Hewitt, 1937), *A Source Book in Geology* (with S. L. Mason, 1939). In his religious viewpoint he holds that science supports a theistic conception of the universe.

MELAND, BERNARD EUGENE: Born Chicago, Ill., 1899. Educated Park Col. (A.B. 1923), Marburg Univ., Univ. of Chicago (B.D. 1928, Ph.D. 1929). Prof. religion and philosophy, Central Col. 1929-1936; asso. prof. religion, Pomona Col., since 1936. His books are *Modern Man's Worship* (1934), *American Philosophies of Religion* (1936, with H. N. Wieman), *Write Your Own Ten Commandments* (1938), *The Church and Adult Education* (1939). His religious position is that of a religious naturalism in which the poetic and aesthetic are linked to the religious appreciations.

MONTAGUE, MARGARET PRESCOTT: Born White Sulphur Springs, W. Va., 1878. Among her writings are *The Poet, Miss Kate and I* (1905), *Closed Doors* (1915), *Twenty Minutes of Reality* (1916), *England to America* (1920), *The Man from God's Country* (1923), *The Lucky Lady* (1934). She is best known to the realm of religious philosophy through her appreciation of aesthetic mysticism.

MORRISON, CHARLES CLAYTON: Born Harrison, Ohio, 1874. Educated Drake Univ. (A.B. 1898), Univ. of Chicago (1902-1905). Recipient of honorary doctorates. Ordained Disciples ministry 1902. Pastor in Iowa and Ill.; editor, *The Christian Century* since 1908; also since 1931 lecturer, Chicago Theol. Sem. Among his books are *The Daily Altar* (1918), *The Social Gospel and the Christian Cultus* (1933), *What Is Christianity?* (1939, the Lyman Beecher lectures at Yale). He founded the magazine *Christendom* and was its editor, 1934-1939, and has edited *The Christian Century Pulpit* since 1929. He has been particularly alert in ecumenical movements. Probably no religious editorials have been more constructively provocative than those which he has written for *The Christian Century*.

NIEBUHR, REINHOLD: Born Wright City, Mo., 1892. Educated Elmhurst Col., Eden Theol. Sem., Yale Univ. (B.D. 1914, A.M. 1915). Ordained minister, Evangelical Snyod of North America, 1915. Pastor, Detroit, Mich., 1915-1928; assoc. prof. philosophy of religion, Union Theol. Sem. 1928-1930; prof. applied Christianity since 1930. He is the author of *Does Civilization Need Religion?* (1927), *Leaves from the Notebook of a Tamed Cynic* (1929), *Moral Man and Immoral Society* (1932), *Reflections on the End of an Era* (1934), *An Interpretation of Christian Ethics* (1935), *Beyond Tragedy* (1937), *Christianity and Power Politics* (1940), *The Nature and Destiny of Man* (1941). He holds the stimulating position of being right wing in his theological position as a neosupernaturalist and left wing in his social ethics.

NIEBUHR, RICHARD: Born Wright City, Mo., 1894. Educated Elmhurst Col., Eden Theol. Sem., Washington Univ. (A.M. 1917), Yale Univ. (B.D. 1923, Ph.D. 1924). Ordained minister Evangelical Synod of North America, 1926. Pastor, St. Louis, Mo., 1916-1918; prof. Eden Theol. Sem., 1919-1922, 1927-1931; president, Elmhurst Col., 1924-1927; asso. prof. Christian ethics, Yale Divinity School, 1931-1938, prof. since 1938. He is author of *The Social Sources of Denominationalism* (1929), *The Kingdom of God in America* (1937), and *The Meaning of Revelation* (1941); editor of *The Church Against the World* (1935); and translator of Paul Tillich's *The Religious Situation*. He has made a contribution in relating a basic theological viewpoint to a social reconstruction in the world.

ORTEGA Y GASSET, JOSÉ: Born in Spain, 1883. Educated, Jesuit School in Magala (B.A.), universities in Berlin, Marburg, Leipzig, Univ. of Madrid (Ph.D.). Lecturer philosophy, Buenos Aires, 1916; has been editor, *Revista de Occidente*, one of Spain's leading literary magazines. His works in English translation are *The Revolt of the Masses* and *The Modern Theme*. His philosophic position has been particularly active in relating the life of the spirit to the realm of social-political culture, where the selected minorities have the responsibility of enlightened leadership.

OTTO, MAX C.: Born Zwickau, Germany, 1876; came to U. S. 1881. Educated Univ. of Wis. (A.B. 1906, A.M. 1908, Ph.D. 1911), Carroll Col., Heidelberg Univ., Univ. of Chicago. Teacher philosophy, Univ. of Chicago, since 1910, prof. since 1921. His books are *Things and Ideals* (1924), *Is There a God?* (with H. N. Wieman and D. C. McIntosh, 1932), and *The Human Enterprise* (1940). He is a stimulating teacher who has clarified religious ideas from the view of a scientific humanist.

OTTO, RUDOLF: Born Peine, Germany, 1869; died, 1938. Educated universities of Erlangen and Göttingen (D.Theol. and D.Phil.). Teacher systematic theology, Göttingen 1897-1911; Breslau 1915-1917; philosophy of religion, Marburg 1917-1929. His books, translated into English, are *The Idea of the Holy*, *The Kingdom of God and the Son of Man*, *India's Religion of Grace and Christianity Compared*, *Philosophy of Religion*, *Mysticism—East and West*. His stress upon the particular *numinous* as an aspect of the religious feeling has been basic in his interpretation of mysticism.

POTTER, CHARLES FRANCIS: Born Marlboro, Mass., 1885. Educated Bucknell Univ. (A.B. 1907, M.A. 1916), Newton Theol. Inst. (B.D. 1913, S.T.M. 1917). Ordained Bapt. ministry 1908, Unitarian ministry 1914. Pastor, Bapt. churches 1908-1914, Unitarian churches 1914-1925; prof. comparative religions, Antioch Col. 1925-1926; pastor, Church of the Divine Paternity, New York City, 1927-1929. Founder and organizer, First Humanist Society of New York, 1929. His books are *The Story of Religion*, *What Is Humanism?*, *Humanism: a New Religion*, *Humanizing Religion*, *Is That in the Bible?*, *Technique of Happiness*, *Beyond the Senses*. He belongs to the philosophic school of scientific humanism which bases religious values as valid when objectively observed.

SEIDENSPINNER, CLAERNCE: Born Kiel, Wis., 1904. Educated Northwestern Univ. (B.S. 1925), Garrett Biblical Inst. (B.D. 1928). Ordained Meth. ministry 1928. Minister, Meth. churches in Wis., now at First Meth. Church, Racine, Wis. He is the author of *Our Dwelling Place* (1940) and *Form and Freedom in Worship* (1941). He wrote the worship patterns for the first General Conference of the Methodist Church (1940). His particular interest is in relating the idiom of worship to the mood of contemporary life.

SPERRY, WILLARD L.: Born Peabody, Mass., 1882. Educated Olivet Col. (B.A. 1903), Oxford Univ. (A.B. 1907 as Rhodes scholar, M.A. 1912), Yale Univ. (M.A. 1909). Recipient of numerous honorary doctorates. Ordained Cong. ministry 1908. Pastor, Fall River, Mass., 1908-1913, Central Church, Boston, Mass., 1914-1922; prof. practical theology, Andover Theol. Sem., 1917-1925; dean, Harvard Divinity School, since 1922. Among his books are *Reality in Worship* (1925), *The Paradox of Religion* (1927), *Signs of These Times* (1929), *"Yes, But"* (1931), *We Prophesy in Part* (1937), *Strangers and Pilgrims* (1938). As a religious educator, he has widely touched the areas of life through literature, liturgy, and the prophetic voice.

STEERE, DOUGLAS V.: Born Harbor Beach, Mich., 1901. Educated Mich. State Col. (B.S. 1923), Oxford Univ. (B.A. 1927 as Rhodes Scholar), Harvard Univ. (M.A. 1925, Ph.D. 1931). Teacher philosophy Haverford Col., since 1928. His writings include *Prayer and Worship* (1938), a translation of Kierkegaard's *Purity of Heart* (1938), *Beyond Dilemmas* (1937, as co-author), *The Open Life* (1937, William Penn Lectures), and several essays. His religious position is that of a critical. realist, who apprehends an "Other" as of basic value in religious experience. His scholarship attempts to tie theology to devotion.

STREETER, BURNETT H.: Born Croydon, England, 1874; died, 1939. Educated Oxford Univ. (M.A.), King's College School, London. Recipient of the honorary D.D. from Edinburgh, Durham, and Manchester. Canon of Heresford, 1915-1934; fellow and dean, Pembroke Col., Oxford, 1899-1905; fellow and praelector, Queen's Col., Oxford, 1905-1933; Ireland prof. exegesis, Oxford Univ., 1932-1933. Among his many books are *Immortality* (1917), *The Spirit* (1919), *The Sadhu* (1921), *The Four Gospels* (1924), *Reality* (1926), *The Buddha and the Christ* (1932, Bampton lectures), *The God Who Speaks* (1936, Warburton lectures); he was contributor to the *Oxford Studies in the Synoptic Problem*, and editor and contributor to other volumes. He held a position of double dignity as New Testament scholar and philosopher of religion, whose writings savored of deep spiritual understanding from a Christian theistic viewpoint.

TALBOT, NEVILLE S.: Born in England. Educated Christ Church, Oxford (M.A.), Cuddeddon Col., Oxford, Haileybury Col.; recipient of honorary D.D. Chaplain and curate for a time; fellow, tutor, and chaplain, Balliol Col., Oxford, 1909-1914; chaplain in France 1914-1919; bishop of Pretoria, 1920-1933; dean of Nottingham since 1933; assistant bishop of Southwell since 1934. His books include *The Mind of the Disciples* (1914), *Thoughts on Religion at the Front* (1917), *Thoughts on Unity, The Riddle of Life, Great Issues*. As a churchman of broad, vital experience, his writings sound a depth of Christian interpretation.

TILLICH, PAUL: Born in Germany, 1886. Educated universities in Berlin, Tübingen, Halle (D.Phil.). Teacher philosophy of religion and social ethics, Berlin, Marburg, Dresden, and Frankfurt; prof. philosophical theology, Union Theol. Sem., since 1933. His books in English are *The Religious Situation* and *Interpretation of History*. His religious position is influenced by neosupernaturalism, in which he sees man's life taking on spiritual meaning only as he is loyal to God, the unconditioned. The present world finds its sense of tragedy in its loyalty to human values, for anything not done for God is a sin.

TITTLE, ERNEST FREMONT: Born Springfield, Ohio, 1885. Educated Ohio Wesleyan Univ. (A.B. 1906), Drew Theol. Sem. (B.D. 1908). Several schools have honored him with doctorates. Ordained Meth. ministry 1910. Pastor, Ohio, 1908-1918; First Meth. Church, Evanston, Ill., since 1918. He has given series of lectures at many colleges and universities, including the Lyman Beecher lectures at Yale and the Ayer lectures at Colgate-Rochester Divinity School. Among his books are *What Must the Church Do to Be Saved?* (1921), *The Religion of the Spirit* (1938), *The Foolishness of Preaching* (1930), *Jesus After Nineteen Centuries* (1932), *Christians in an Unchristian Society* (1939). Sounding a prophetic voice in regard to the social aspects of religion, he has been a clear interpretive voice to audiences in both the church and the college.

UNDERHILL, EVELYN (MRS. STUART MOORE): Born in England, 1875. Died 1941. Educated in King's Col. for Women, London, honorary fellow in 1913. D.D. from Aberdeen Col., 1939. Upton lecturer on religion, Manchester Col., Oxford, 1921-1922. Among her books are the following of major importance: *Mysticism, A Study in the Nature and Development of Man's Spiritual Consciousness* (13th edition, 1940), *The Mystic Way, Practical Mysticism, The Essentials of Mysticism, The Life of the Spirit and the Life of Today, Concerning the Inner Life, Worship.* Her contribution to religious thinking is particularly identified with that of Western mysticism, which correlates the good, ethical life with that of deep and meaningful devotion.

VOGT, VON OGDEN: Born Altamont, Ill., 1879. Educated Beloit Col. (A.B. 1901), Yale Univ. (M.A. 1909, B.D. 1911). Recipient of honorary doctorates. Ordained Cong. ministry 1912. Pastor, Cheshire and Chicago, 1911-1925. Since 1925 pastor, First Unitarian Church, Chicago; lecturer, Beloit Col., Chicago Theol. Sem. He is the author of *Art and Religion* (1921) and *Modern Worship* (1927), and co-editor of *Hymns of the Spirit and Services of Religion* (1937). His sensitive appreciation of worship in its total relationship to life, as especially found through the church, marks his prime contribution to religious thought.

WARD, HARRY F.: *Born London, England,* 1873; came to America, 1891. Educated Northwestern Univ. (A.B. 1897), Harvard Univ. (A.M. 1898). Ordained Meth. ministry 1899. Pastor, Chicago and Oak Park, Ill., 1899-1912; founder and general secretary, Meth. Federation of Social Service, 1911; prof. social service, Boston Univ. School of Theology, 1913-1918; chairman, American Civil Liberties Union, 1920-1940, American League for Peace and Democracy, 1934-1940; prof. Christian ethics, Union Theol. Sem. since 1918. Among his books are *The Social Creed of the Churches* (1913), *The Gospel for a Working World* (1918), *The Profit Motive* (1924), *Our Economic Morality* (1929), *Which Way Religion?* (1931), *In Place of Profit* (1933). He has been a forceful figure in allying the Christian religion to the eradicating of social evils.

WIEMAN, HENRY NELSON: Born Richhill, Mo., 1884. Educated Park Col. (A.B. 1907), Jena, Heidelberg, Harvard Univ. (Ph.D. 1917). Prof. philosophy, Occidental Col., 1917-1927; prof. philosophy of religion, Divinity School, Univ. of Chicago, since 1927. His books include *Religious Experience and the Scientific Method* (1926), *The Wrestle of Religion with Truth* (1927), *Methods of Private Religious Living* (1929), *The Issues of Life* (1931), *Normative Psychology of Religion* (with Regina Westcott Wieman, 1935), *American Philosophies of Religion* (with Bernard Meland, 1936), *The Growth of Religion* (with Walter Horton, 1938). He calls himself a naturalistic theist, who conceives God as a process or growth in the universe, immediately conceived and perceived. God works for good in every event to the degree that we co-operate with such a creative activity. Such a spirit of growth is superpersonal.

INDEX OF TITLES